2_{EDITION}

An Introduction to the

SOCIOLOGY
of WORK and
OCCUPATIONS

2
EDITION

An Introduction to the
SOCIOLOGY
of WORK and
OCCUPATIONS

Rudi Volti

Pitzer College

Los Angeles | London | New Delhi
Singapore | Washington DC

Los Angeles | London | New Delhi
Singapore | Washington DC

FOR INFORMATION:

SAGE Publications, Inc.
2455 Teller Road
Thousand Oaks, California 91320
E-mail: order@sagepub.com

SAGE Publications Ltd.
1 Oliver's Yard
55 City Road
London EC1Y 1SP
United Kingdom

SAGE Publications India Pvt. Ltd.
B 1/I 1 Mohan Cooperative Industrial Area
Mathura Road, New Delhi 110 044
India

SAGE Publications Asia-Pacific Pte. Ltd.
33 Pekin Street #02-01
Far East Square
Singapore 048763

Acquisitions Editor: David Repetto
Editorial Assistant: Lydia Balian
Associate Editor: Maggie Stanley
Production Editor: Eric Garner
Copy Editor: Megan Granger
Typesetter: C&M Digitals (P) Ltd.
Proofreader: Laura Webb
Cover Designer: Anupama Krishnan
Marketing Manager: Erica Deluca
Permissions Editor: Karen Ehrmann

Copyright © 2012 by SAGE Publications, Inc.

Printed in the United States of America

Library of Congress Cataloging-in-Publication Data

Volti, Rudi.

An introduction to the sociology of work and occupations/Rudi Volti. — 2nd ed.

p. cm.
Includes bibliographical references and index.

ISBN 978-1-4129-9285-5 (pbk.)

1. Work—History. 2. Occupations—Forecasting. 3. Globalization. I. Title.

HD6971.V64 2012
306.3'6—dc23   2011031310

This book is printed on acid-free paper.

14 15 10 9 8 7 6 5 4 3 2

Contents _____

INTRODUCTION   ix

ACKNOWLEDGMENTS   xix

ABOUT THE AUTHOR   xxi

1. Work Before Industrialization   1
   The Oldest and Longest Lasting Mode of Life and Work   1
   Gathering-and-Hunting Societies in the Modern World   2
   The Working Lives of Gatherer-Hunters   4
   The Agricultural Revolution   6
   Agricultural Labor and Cultural Change   8
   Artisan Work   10
   Time and Work   12
   Protestantism and the Rise of Capitalism   13

2. The Organization of Work in Preindustrial Times   19
   Traditional Societies and the Organization of Work   19
   The Family as a Basis of Work Organization   21
   Slavery   23
   Caste and Occupation   28
   The Guilds   29
   Apprenticeship   32
   An Assessment of Guild Organization   33

3. Industrialization and Its Consequences   39
   The Industrial Revolution   39
   Capitalism and Market Economies   41
   Wages and Working Conditions in
     the Industrial Revolution   43
   Women in the Industrial Revolution   45
   Industrialization and Social Protest   47
   Making Management "Scientific"   47
   The Assembly Line   51
   A Postindustrial Revolution?   54

4. **Bureaucratic Organization** — 59

   The Rise of Bureaucratic Organization — 59

   The Elements of Bureaucratic Organization — 61

   Where Bureaucracy Works and Where It Doesn't — 65

   Bureaucratic Organization, Work, and the Worker — 67

   Alternatives to Bureaucracy — 70

5. **Technology and Work** — 77

   Defining Technology — 77

   Technological Unemployment — 80

   Developing New Skills — 82

   Technology and Managerial Authority — 83

   Work, Skill, and Today's Technologies — 86

   Telework — 87

   Technology and Globalization — 90

6. **Globalization** — 95

   Governments and Globalization — 97

   Multinational Corporations and Globalized Production — 99

   The Economic Benefits of Foreign Trade — 100

   Workers Abroad — 102

   Workers at Home — 104

   Globalization and Job Creation — 105

   Immigration — 106

   Governmental Policies and Immigration — 107

7. **Getting a Job** — 113

   The Economics of the Job Market — 113

   Minimum-Wage Laws — 118

   Jobs, Human Capital, and Credentials — 120

   Networks and Their Significance — 126

8. **Workplace Culture and Socialization** — 133

   The Significance of Workplace Cultures — 133

   Socialization Into a Culture — 135

   Socialization as an Ongoing Process — 136

   Socialization and Identity — 137

   Occupational and Organizational Heroes — 139

   Socialization in Different Occupational Realms — 141

   Rites of Passage — 143

   Organizations and Subcultures — 145

   Supportive Workplace Subcultures — 147

   Deviant Subcultures — 148

   Socialization, Careers, and Strain — 149

9. **Professions and Professionalization** — 153

   The Checklist Approach to the Professions — 153

   The Professional Continuum — 156

Attaining Professional Status 158
Professionalization as a Means of Control 159
Professionals in Organizations 161
Today's Challenges to the Professions 163
Resource Control and Professional Autonomy:
    The Case of Medicine 166
Diversity and Professional Status 167

10. Who Gets What? **173**
The Determination of Wages and Salaries: Market
    Economics Once Again 173
The Widening Income Gap 175
Why Has Income Inequality Increased? 179
Unemployment and Income 180
Income Distribution in a Changing Economy 181
Computerization and Income Inequality 181
Globalization, Employment, and Income 182
Unions and Workers' Incomes 183
Immigration and Income 186
Occupational Prestige 188

11. Life on the Job I: Work and Its Rewards **195**
Employment and Unemployment 195
The Personal Consequences of Unemployment 197
Varieties of Employment 199
Work Without Pay 202
The Workplace as School 203
Job Training and Employment Opportunities 204
Work and Social Interaction 205
Social Relationships and Job Performance 208
The Intrinsic Satisfactions of Work 209

12. Life on the Job II: The Perils and Pressures of Work ... **215**
Work May Be Hazardous to Your Health 215
Stress at Work 217
Jobs, Secure and Insecure 219
Sexual Harassment at Work 220
Greedy Institutions 221
Alienated Labor 223
Manifestations of Discontent 225
Responses to On-the-Job Alienation 226
Job Satisfaction and Dissatisfaction Today 227
The Elusive Search for Job Satisfaction 228

13. Diversity in the Workplace **233**
Race, Ethnicity, and Hiring Practices 233
Women in the Workforce 237

Discrimination, Occupational Segregation, and Pay   240
Getting Ahead   244
Legal Remedies for Discrimination
     and Occupational Segregation   246
Comparable Worth Policies for the Workplace   248

14. Work Roles and Life Roles   **253**
The Separation of Work and Residence   253
Working Hours   254
Paid Work and Housework   260
Couples, Families, and Careers   263
Reconciling Work Roles and Life Roles   265

15. Conclusion: Work Today and Tomorrow   **273**
Technology, Work, and Occupations   273
Making Globalization and Technological
     Change More Equitable   274
Work and Demographic Change   275
Ethnicity, Gender, and Work   276
Women, Work, and Families   277
Closing the Income Gap   278
The Healthcare Morass   281
The Fate of the Professions   281
Organizations for the 21st Century   282
Workers and Jobs for the Future   283

GLOSSARY   **287**

CREDITS   **291**

INDEX   **292**

Introduction _____

Work is a central activity in the lives of most people. The jobs people hold and the work they do provide a sense of personal identity, a way of organizing the day, connection to a social network, a reason to get out of the house, a chance to use and develop skills, and of course a steady income. Because it is such an integral part of our lives, we tend to look at the work we do as an individualistic activity. It is up to us to prepare for a job or occupation, present ourselves to prospective employers, perform the required tasks to the best of our ability after we are hired, and receive rewards on the basis of our achievements. Yet, without denying the importance of our own efforts, we also have to recognize that work is a highly social activity. Success or failure at work reflects individual performance, but it also is influenced by the performance of coworkers. The formal and informal social interaction that takes place in the workplace imparts a set of skills, values, and attitudes that heavily influences how the work is done. On a larger scale, the way a society is structured will go a long way toward determining the kind of work that is done, who does it, how they go about doing it, and what they will get for their efforts. In sum, many aspects of working life are shaped by the structure of a society—its age composition; its racial, ethnic, gender, and class divisions; and its distribution of power and authority.

The occupations held, the jobs performed, and working life in general also are crucially affected by a society's degree of technological development. Here, too, social structure is highly relevant because technology is not something external to a society but is itself created and shaped in ways that reflect social arrangements. Individual technologies are not simply neutral tools and techniques; they may reflect, reinforce, or challenge social class divisions, gender roles, and power relationships. Nowhere is this more apparent than in the workplace.

Much of what follows in this book is an elaboration of these general topics and themes. Work is an important topic in its own right, but it takes on a particular salience when it is put into a sociological context. A large part of sociology consists of making connections, and this book represents an effort to connect work and occupations to some key subjects of sociological inquiry: race, ethnicity, gender, social class, education, social networks, and modes of organization.

Most discussions of work and occupations center on the here and now. This is understandable; we need to know what kinds of jobs are being done today, who is doing them, and what is happening in people's working lives. Yet it is also important to understand how we got to where we are today, and for this reason, some of the chapters to follow contain a fair amount of material drawn from economic and social history, as well as the history of technology. Studying the past helps us understand the present, and more than this, it gives us a broader perspective on where we are today. We all have a tendency to think of the lives we lead and the work we do as the normal state of human affairs, a kind of default option. In reality, life and work in early 21st-century industrial and postindustrial societies represent massive deviations from life as it was led and work as it was done for most of human existence. An understanding of historical change helps us realize that the society in which we live and the work we do represent mere blips in time. The working lives of most men and women were very different a century ago, and we can be sure that they will have undergone many changes a hundred years from now.

Many aspects of our working lives may be viewed as indications of social and economic progress, as few people in the economically developed world toil 12 hours a day for subsistence wages. But as we will see, a survey of the historical evolution of work shows that along with the gains, there have been losses, and these gains and losses have not been shared equally. From the emergence of sedentary agriculture onward, advances in technology and social organization have increased production and productivity. Yet these advances have been accompanied by social and economic changes that have left many people no better off and, in some cases, in a considerably worse position than before. No attempt has been made to present a precise tally of winners and losers here, but the reader should always remember that work and the social arrangements that support it are in a continuous state of flux and that not everyone benefits from the changes that are occurring.

Much of the material presented in this book, especially in the later chapters, centers on work and occupations in the United States. It is hoped, however, that this book will be of interest to readers in other parts of the world, as a considerable amount of material drawn from other places and times has been included. Although this book does not attempt a rigorous comparative analysis of work roles and activities, the material presented in its chapters can serve as the basis for reflecting on how working lives have been shaped by past history and current social arrangements.

The Plan of the Book

There is no ideal way to organize a complex subject. Each chapter of this book focuses on a particular aspect of work and occupations, but it has not always been possible to neatly contain each topic within a single chapter. The themes, topics, and issues covered in this book relate to one another in more than one context, making it necessary to occasionally refer to material presented in other chapters. I hope that the occasional use of the phrase "as we saw in Chapter . . ." and "as we shall see in Chapter . . ." will not disrupt the flow of the narrative excessively.

Chapter 1 demonstrates this book's commitment to a long-term historical perspective by beginning with a description of the oldest and longest lasting mode of work: gathering and hunting. Although humans were gatherers and hunters for far longer than they have been farmers, factory operatives, and office workers, the way they gained their livelihood is about as far from our way of work and life as can be imagined. Gathering and hunting differs profoundly from the work performed in more "advanced" societies; it can even be questioned whether gatherers and hunters envisaged the work they performed as an activity separate and distinct from other aspects of life.

In one way, however, the organization of work done in societies based on gathering and hunting represents a pattern that endured for a long time and still exists today: the assignment of work roles on the basis of ascribed characteristics. After discussing this mode of work organization, the narrative moves to one of the great dividing points in human history, the gradual yet revolutionary shift to sedentary agriculture. The chapter also introduces another topic that will re-emerge in a different guise in later chapters: small-scale craft work and the social and economic relationships in which it was embedded.

Agricultural and craft work reflected the technologies available at the time. In the late medieval era, a radically new technology, the mechanical clock, came to the fore and exerted a growing influence on the way work was scheduled and organized. While a change in material culture in the form of the clock was affecting work patterns, a religiously based cultural transformation, the rise of Protestantism, also influenced values and attitudes regarding work. As the last section of the chapter notes, the extent of that influence is still a matter of some debate. Still, the connection between religious and economic change has to be taken seriously, although the connection may be less direct than is sometimes assumed.

Chapter 2 continues the historical narrative through a discussion of the organization of work in times past, when ascribed statuses were the primary means of allocating jobs and occupations. The first section pays particular attention to the manner in which race, ethnicity, and gender determined the majority of past work roles. It also considers how family membership has been an important determinant of occupational choice. The narrative then shifts to the most despicable use of ascribed characteristics to determine the distribution of occupations: slavery. This section includes discussions of slavery in the ancient world and the even harsher form of involuntary servitude that was established in the New World and continued in the American South until the Civil War put an end to it. The chapter then covers caste, a less extreme but still confining way of determining occupational roles. The importance of ascribed social roles is further developed through a survey of medieval guilds and their significance for the organization of work. This is a topic of more than historical interest; some of the structures and processes introduced in this section bear similarities to how professions operate in today's world, the topic of a later chapter.

Chapter 3 resumes the discussion of technological, economic, and social change through an account of the Industrial Revolution and its many consequences for workers and the kind of work they did. The Industrial Revolution, as it first occurred in Great Britain, was a product of capitalism and a market-based economy, both of which are sometimes condemned as inherently exploitative of workers. This chapter attempts to assess some of the consequences of the Industrial Revolution on workers' lives, including its consequences for women. The narrative continues into the early 20th century with a discussion of two means of organizing and controlling an emerging industrial workforce: the assembly line and F. W. Taylor's attempt to make management "scientific." The chapter concludes with an introduction to a concept that will reappear in later chapters: what has been dubbed "postindustrial society."

In Chapter 4, we look into "modern" forms of organization through a consideration of that often berated mode of organization, bureaucracy. This chapter attempts to present a more balanced picture by laying out the basic elements of bureaucratic organization and their connection to the evolution of modern society. Although bureaucracies are thought to be inherently inefficient, this chapter argues that under the right circumstances, bureaucracies can work quite well. At the same time, however, it is noted that bureaucratic modes of organization are not appropriate for all occupations and modes of work. The chapter also introduces a theme that will be revisited in several later chapters: how the structuring of work organizations affects individual workers through the allocation of skills, responsibilities, and authority. The concluding sections of this chapter note how changes in the economy have created jobs and entire occupations that mesh poorly with bureaucracy and necessitate alternative modes of organization.

Chapter 5 discusses one of the major forces shaping work today: technological change. The chapter begins with a discussion of what technology is and what it isn't, followed by a consideration of what technology can and cannot do. The chapter then moves on to an analysis of how technological advances have affected overall levels of employment and, in so doing, attempts to provide a more nuanced account of the relationship between technological change and unemployment. It then returns to two earlier themes through an evaluation of the effects of technological change on workers' skills, as well as the use of certain technologies as instruments of control. On a more positive note, the chapter describes some technologies that have the potential to ease some of the tensions engendered by the competing demands of work and home.

Technological change is one of the major forces propelling the economic, social, and cultural changes that are subsumed under the term *globalization*. Although globalization is the topic of the next chapter, this chapter introduces the topic by presenting some of the key technologies that, coupled with economic, political, and cultural forces, have produced a more interdependent and integrated world.

Chapter 6 continues the topic introduced in the last part of the previous chapter with an identification of the key institutional actors that have promoted globalization. It notes some of the benefits of globalization but also tries to make it clear that these benefits are not evenly shared. The mixed effects of globalization on foreign and domestic workers are laid out, with particular attention paid to the growth and decline of particular occupations and communities. As with technological advance, globalization can bring substantial benefits, but it may produce a considerable amount of damage as well, as will be recounted in this chapter.

One of the most important aspects of globalization is immigration. As with the other topics discussed in this chapter, it is noted that the effects of immigration are complex and cannot be easily dismissed as totally beneficial or harmful. The chapter concludes by noting how demographic trends in the world's rich nations will change some of the terms of the immigration debate in the years to come.

With Chapter 7, the focus shifts from the large-scale forces that are affecting work and occupations and takes up an issue that may be of more immediate concern for many readers of this book: getting a job. This chapter describes how individuals find out about available jobs and the processes through which they are screened and hired by employers. The chapter analyzes how the forces of supply and demand affect the allocation of jobs, while at the same time taking into account the limitations of a purely market-oriented approach to hiring practices. The following section discusses minimum wage laws and notes the extent to which they have affected wages and employment.

Different levels of educational attainment are often invoked to explain why some individuals are more attractive job candidates than others. A section of this chapter stresses the importance of educational attainments, but it also explains what these really mean for prospective employers. In so doing, this chapter segment notes the importance of social background for educational attainment. Although individual characteristics have a sizable influence on the ability to land a job, the last section of this chapter emphasizes the importance of social networks in hiring processes as they affect both prospective employees and employers.

Organizations and workplaces can be seen as miniature societies imbued with their own values, norms, routines, and other cultural elements. Chapter 8 examines workplace cultures and how individuals assimilate them. Beginning with a discussion of culture in general, this chapter goes on to describe the major components of workplace cultures and how they are transmitted and absorbed. The chapter explains why socialization into a culture is not a once-and-for-all process but continues throughout a person's working life. The chapter also explores some key elements of an occupational culture such as dress, argot, and the general appearance of the workplace, as well as the long-term influence of occupational "patron saints." The strength and significance of occupational cultures vary, however, and the circumstances under which these cultures are likely to exert a substantial influence are discussed. The chapter goes on to describe an intense form of socialization known as a "rite of passage" and provides several examples drawn from the working world. The chapter then describes how occupational and workplace cultures can reinforce an organization's official goals or can work against them. It also notes how deviant subcultures can be the basis of workplace practices that actually support organizational goals. The final chapter segment describes how different agencies of workplace socialization shape workers' perceptions of their occupational careers.

Chapter 9 takes up a topic that has been of longstanding interest to sociologists: the professions. The status and role of professionals and would-be professionals has been and continues to be a matter of some contention. The chapter presents several different ways of defining what constitutes a profession. It notes the key attributes of a profession while at the same time indicating the limits to this approach. The chapter also explores the realm of what are sometimes called semiprofessions and paraprofessions, describing some of the obstacles they have encountered in their attempts to be recognized as full-fledged professions. Emphasis is placed on the ability of an occupational group to gain control over a particular line of work and why these efforts often come up short. Attention is also paid to deprofessionalization, the process through which members of an established profession lose their ability to control their work situations. Here, the particular economic and political pressures that threaten the established professions are presented. The chapter concludes with a discussion of the efforts of women and minorities to enter the established professions and the obstacles they have encountered along the way.

One of the perceived characteristics of professional occupations is that their practitioners are usually well paid. Chapter 10 takes up the general topic of remuneration by describing and analyzing the distribution of wages, salaries, and benefits. The economics of wage and salary determination is presented, but note is taken of how social and political factors also influence the remuneration of different categories of workers. The chapter then turns to a discussion of the wide income gap that separates different groups of workers, a pattern that is replicated in the provision of employer-sponsored benefits such as health insurance and pension funds. This chapter recounts the key reasons for the increase in income differentials in recent decades and then describes and assesses efforts to improve workers' incomes through unionization. This chapter segment examines the extent of unionization today, followed by a discussion of why union membership has declined in recent years.

Returning to an earlier topic, the chapter then analyzes the effects of technological change on the distribution of incomes in general, as well as the effects of computerization in particular. Extending a topic introduced in Chapter 6, the next chapter segment considers how globalization in general and immigration in particular have affected income distribution. The chapter's final segment looks into occupational prestige and explores why some occupations are held in higher regard than others.

The opportunity to earn a wage or salary is a prime motivation to be employed, but it is not the only one. Chapter 11 looks into the nonmonetary aspects of work. This chapter, for the most part, stresses positive aspects of work, beginning with the psychological benefits of being employed. This is followed by an analysis of what employment and unemployment statistics reveal and what they obscure. The next part of the chapter provides some data on the extent of labor force participation by different categories of workers, especially in regard to groupings of age and gender. Age and gender also influence the extent of participation in unpaid work, such as housework and volunteer activities, which are covered in the next section. This is followed by a discussion of some nonmonetary benefits of employment such as participation in training programs. The chapter then takes up the larger issue of the value of training programs for reducing unemployment and boosting wages. It concludes with a presentation of some other nonmonetary rewards of work, such as workplace friendships and the intrinsic satisfactions that work may bring.

Chapter 12 continues the discussion of life on the job but this time with an emphasis on some unfortunate aspects of working life, beginning with workplace deaths and injuries. Work also can be a source of psychological stress, the causes of which are outlined. The next chapter segment describes some potentially difficult conditions of employment, notably temporary work. As discussed in this segment, working as a "temp" need not be an unpleasant experience, and it may in fact be a preferred option for some workers, but for others, the drawbacks outweigh the advantages by a large margin. The next section takes up an all-too-common workplace problem, sexual harassment.

Some jobs are not dangerous or even a source of unusual degrees of stress, but they can be problematic because they are embedded in what have been called "greedy institutions," organizations that demand an excessive amount of involvement by workers. Following the exploration of this topic, the chapter goes on to note that while some employees may be absorbed in their work roles, other workers may feel a profound sense of detachment from their jobs, a condition that is often referred to as alienation. The discussion of on-the-job alienation begins with the seminal ideas of Karl Marx and Max Weber and then moves on to recent sociological approaches to worker alienation. The chapter presents workers' responses to on-the-job alienation and some efforts by management to reduce it. Also on a positive note, the next section points out that individual workers do not respond to the conditions that give rise to alienation in a uniform manner and that many workers have been able to find worthwhile aspects of their jobs even when working under thoroughly alienating circumstances.

Chapter 13 examines inequalities in the working world that are associated with race, ethnicity, and gender. It begins by recounting some of the research that has been done to determine the extent of discriminatory hiring practices. It then notes how social variables such as place of residence and educational attainment often accompany minority status and exert a considerable influence on hiring outcomes. The chapter then takes up the topic of women in the labor force, paying particular attention to gender-based occupational segregation and its consequences for women workers. Occupational segregation is an important cause of male–female pay differentials but not the only one, and some of the other sources of wage and salary inequalities are noted. This chapter also considers other differences in occupational careers of men and women—most notably, differential rates of promotion—and notes some of the reasons for these divergences. The last chapter segment reviews some current legal remedies for discrimination, as well as some that have been proposed but not enacted.

Important as it is to many men and women, work is not the sum total of human life. No matter how committed they are to their work, people have other matters to attend to, especially those that center on families and personal relationships. Chapter 14 notes some of the ways that the demands of a working life, including the time spent commuting to and from a job, have tended to crowd out other activities. The next chapter segment tackles the assertion that American workers are putting in more time on the job than they did a few decades ago. It describes and analyzes several studies of time spent at work, assesses their validity, and delineates which categories of workers are most likely to put in the longest hours.

Time pressures are most evident for workers with family responsibilities. The next segment of this chapter takes note of the disproportionate share of housework and child care done by women but also points out that the gap has been closing in recent years. The next section describes some of the difficulties encountered by husbands and wives when both pursue demanding careers and notes some of the ways they have addressed the challenge of reconciling work and family.

Although each family has to work out its own accommodation of work and other aspects of life, government and employer actions can make this accommodation less difficult. The next chapter segment notes how more flexible working arrangements can ease some of the difficulties of meeting the demands of work and family. It also takes note of some of the efforts of public and private agencies to provide child care but points out how the United States lags behind many other countries in the provision of this essential service.

Chapter 15 represents an effort to tie all the preceding chapters together by reviewing the forces that have shaped work and occupations in the past and are likely to do so in the future. This chapter also offers prescriptions for alleviating some of the problems presented in the previous chapters. The topics of technological change and globalization are taken up once again, this time in conjunction with a brief discussion of some ways to mitigate the inevitable problems they cause. The next section takes another look at demographic change and how it will affect future jobs and occupations. The consequences of two major trends are explored here: the aging of the population and the increased diversity of the workforce.

The next chapter segment describes some ongoing inequalities in the workplace that are associated with race, ethnicity, and gender, but it also takes note of recent successes, particularly in regard to women's occupational achievements. The following section goes on to note, however, that reconciling the demands of work and family continues to be a difficult task and will require the enactment of some creative policies by both employers and government agencies.

The next section addresses the earnings gap that has separated much of the workforce and reviews some ways of closing this gap. This is followed by a section that addresses similar inequalities in access to health care. Then comes an assessment of the prospects for the established professions, followed by a section that considers how organizations will have to change if they are to adequately address changing work environments.

The final chapter segment looks into the near future through a brief examination of the job market in the immediate years to come. It notes some of the key forces on both the supply and demand side that are shaping the distribution of future occupations. The chapter concludes with a listing of the occupations that are expected to add the greatest number of jobs in the next few years and what this list tells us about the workforce of the future.

Readers sometimes expect that a textbook will provide complete coverage of its subject matter and a clear resolution of the issues raised within. Such is not the case here. The complexities of work in today's world make generalization difficult, and many of the issues relating to the sociology of work and occupations remain subjects of controversy. Consequently, a tentative tone may occasionally be detected in some of the pages that follow. It can only be hoped that the presentation of these unresolved and often controversial issues will stimulate further thought and inquiry on the part of the reader. As a further stimulus to reflection on some of the key issues raised in this book, each chapter ends with several questions for discussion. These questions do not have a "right" answer, but the material presented in that chapter may allow responses to them to be better grounded in factual information and theoretical sophistication.

As a final point, this book is not intended to be a how-to-do-it book for men and women currently in the working world or about to join it. But it is my hope that it will not be dismissed as an irrelevant academic exercise and that the material presented here will occasionally be of use, perhaps when the reader least expects it.

Acknowledgments_____

All written works are collaborations to some extent. In writing this book, I was able to draw on a number of individuals for their helpful comments and provision of essential information: Jeffrey Douville, Crawford Judge, James Lehman, and Sheryl Miller, as well as reviewers Kwaku Twumasi-Ankrah, Dana Britton, Brendan Burchell, Elaine Draper, Betty Farrell, Alan Hudson, Thomas Ilgen, Richard Loder, Gerardo Marti, and Susan Seymour. Ben Penner, Camille Herrera, Nancy Scrofano, Astrid Virding, Gillian Dickens, Megan Granger, Maggie Stanley, and Eric Garner at SAGE Publications deserve a great deal of credit for converting numerous revised manuscripts into a final publication. I extend thanks to Joanne Zhang, one of our IT staff who helped in transmitting files to SAGE. I also would like to thank the students in my course on the sociology of work and occupations, who, through their questions and comments over the years, have kept me engaged with many of the topics and issues that appear in this book. In particular, I would like to thank three students in one of my recent classes—Cassandra Cona, Jesus Galaz-Duarte, and Daniel Chazin—for reading and commenting on several chapters of this book. Last but certainly not least, my gratitude extends to my wife, Ann Stromberg, and our daughter, Kate, for being unfailing sources of support and encouragement.

SAGE gratefully acknowledges the following reviewers:

Roy H. Fish, *Ohio State University*

Mindy Fried, *Massachusetts Institute of Technology*

Laurie L. Gordy, *Daniel Webster College*

Gerardo Marti, *Davidson College*

Sylvester Osagie, *Pennsylvania State University*

Catherine Richards Solomon, *Quinnipiac University*

About the Author_____

Rudi Volti is Emeritus Professor of Sociology at Pitzer College. His recent publications include *Cars and Culture: The Life Story of a Technology* (2005), *Society and Technological Change* (6th edition, 2008), *The Engineer in History* (2nd edition, 2001), *Technology Transfer and Economic Transformation in East Asia* (2002), and *The Facts on File Encyclopedia of Science, Technology, and Society* (1999). When not doing research or writing, he enjoys cycling and working on various hands-on projects, some of which are eventually completed.

1

Work Before Industrialization

The way we earn a living today is vastly different from what was done for most of human existence. Taking into account the full sweep of human history and prehistory, our working world of offices, factories, shops, and farms represents a radical departure from the ways our ancestors earned a living. For hundreds of thousands of years, humans were able to survive through the application of their skills and intelligence, and little else. Then, about ten thousand years ago, humanity took up a radically different mode of existence through the development of sedentary agriculture. Life, work, and the relationship between the two were dramatically altered, and not always for the better.

For centuries thereafter, the working lives of people throughout the world were broadly similar, as the labor required to bring in a crop took precedence over most other activities. But while life and work appeared to have settled into seemingly endless routines, technological and cultural changes were slowly creating the conditions for another revolution that would bring great changes to the working lives of men and women.

The Oldest and Longest Lasting Mode of Life and Work

The assignment of a date for the emergence of the first humans depends on the definition of *human*. The first hominids that occupy the genus *Homo* evolved from their ape-like predecessors more than two million years ago, but it was not until somewhere between 200,000 and 100,000 years ago that anatomically modern *Homo sapiens* appeared on the scene. However their emergence is reckoned, humans gained their livelihood through the same basic activities: gathering and hunting. Given the present state of archeological knowledge, not much can be said of how early humans went about gaining their livelihood, but the typical means of survival centered on some combination of gathering plants, fruits, insects, grubs, and reptiles; hunting animals large and small; and even scavenging animal carcasses.

Simple though these tasks may seem, they often required the development and use of tools and techniques not found anywhere else in the animal world. Human evolution proceeded in close conjunction with the invention and use of tools, which enhanced the survival prospects of individuals who were the most technically proficient. Throughout human evolution, tool use, manual dexterity, and brain development interacted in a mutually reinforcing manner.[1] Endowed with superior dexterity and brain power, early humans were able to make specialized stone tools, and by the late Paleolithic period, their manufactured artifacts included bows and arrows, spear throwers, scrapers, awls and needles, and even musical instruments.

These products may have been simple and crude, but producing them required considerable skill. The fashioning of a stone hand axe in Paleolithic times required proper procedures, beginning with the selection of stones from which flakes could be knocked off by percussion. Separating flakes from the selected stone was not simply a matter of randomly whacking it with another stone; production of a useful stone tool required well-aimed blows delivered with the right amount of force and at the proper angle.[2] Although the overall technological assemblage of early humans may not have been impressive, some of the techniques they used were of a high order. Many of us would be hard-pressed to duplicate the skills that our "primitive" ancestors demonstrated.

Important as stone tools and other artifacts were, the most important shaper of human life and work was the ability of people to communicate with one another. Collectively hunting down large animals must have called for a considerable amount of verbal and nonverbal communication, as did passing along essential knowledge about the physical environment and the techniques for making particular kinds of tools. Prehistoric but anatomically modern humans also were distinguished by their artistic creations, many of which may have related to the task of hunting large animals. Some cave paintings depict game animals pierced by spears or darts, which may represent the hope that portraying them in this way would contribute to a successful hunt. We know virtually nothing about religious beliefs of early humans and their ways of understanding the world, but it would be a mistake to arrogantly dismiss them as "primitive" and leave it at that. For tens of millennia, human life and work did not exhibit the material progress that we associate with the modern world, but prehistoric people were certainly not deficient in knowledge and skills, and in some ways, their capabilities exceeded ours.

Gathering-and-Hunting Societies in the Modern World

As recently as a century ago, societies based on gathering and hunting could be found in the Arctic, as well as in a few parts of Australia and Africa, the Amazon Basin, and New Guinea—although many of them had added horticulture to their working repertoires. Today, societies of this sort are close to extinct; well under 0.001 percent of the world's people are engaged in gathering and hunting as the primary basis of their subsistence.[3] These few remaining examples of societies based on gathering and hunting have been extensively studied by cultural anthropologists.[4] Their languages, technologies, religions, and kinship structures have their own distinctive features, but commonalities can be found in some aspects of their lives, giving us insights into what life and work might have been like for the vast bulk of human existence.

One group that has been extensively studied is the San of southern Africa's southwestern Kalahari Desert. Sometimes referred to as Bushmen, their ancestors have lived in this part of the world for an estimated 30,000 years. Research on one grouping, the !Kung San (the exclamation point indicates a clicking sound that is an integral part of their language), has provided some important clues regarding the activities pursued in gathering-and-hunting societies.

At first glance, the environment in which the !Kung San live seems harsh in the extreme. As the name implies, the Kalahari Desert is arid, but it is also home to a wide variety of plants and animals. The !Kung San take full advantage of what nature has provided; 85 species of plants are incorporated into their diet, of which 23 are regularly consumed.[5] Of particular importance is the mongongo nut, which provides an abundant source of plant protein. Animal protein is obtained by using poisoned arrows to bring down antelope and other game animals. This latter activity may be more exciting than gathering wild plants and trapping small animals, but it is not the major source of food for the !Kung San. Much more significant are the products of gathering; in terms of calories contributed to the diet, gathering is 2.4 times more productive than hunting. It is for this reason that the term *gathering and hunting*, instead of the more conventional *hunting and gathering*, has been used in this chapter.

The tendency of outside observers to emphasize hunting over gathering reflects a key feature of economic organization in !Kung San groups, as well as other gatherer-hunter societies. Hunting is largely done by men, whereas gathering is for the most part women's work. Here we see, as we shall see many more times in this book, a gender-based division of labor. Tasks are not apportioned in accordance with aptitude or interest but are determined by what sociologists call *ascribed characteristics*, attributes that cannot be acquired or changed but simply reflect an accident of birth, in this case whether one was born female or male. As we shall see, some key attributes of a job, such as pay and prestige, may have less to do with the intrinsic qualities of a job than with the gender of the majority of the people doing the work. Although gathering contributes the most to the group's survival, it tends to be downgraded in importance—at least in the outside world—because women do it.

Photo 1.1   !Kung San group

SOURCE: ©Peter Johnson/CORBIS.

A gender-based division of labor has little objective basis in today's economy and society, but in the case of gatherers and hunters, division of labor is strongly influenced by biological differences. For women, the demands of pregnancy and nursing, which may go on for 20 years or more, limit the mobility necessary for hunting far-ranging game. Moreover, women on average are not as strong as men, although their endurance is on par with or better than that of men. Still, one shouldn't generalize on the basis of this situation; biological differences are rarely a basis for gender-based divisions of labor in societies where gathering and hunting is not the dominant mode of survival. As we shall see in later chapters, gender-based occupational differences of the sort common in modern societies have little to do with innate biological differences and are better explained in terms of culture, prejudices, and power relationships.

The Working Lives of Gatherer-Hunters

Given the difficult environments and simple technologies of many gatherer-hunters, it seems reasonable to assume that they live on the thin edge of starvation and that they are engaged in an unremitting struggle for mere survival. In reality, people in many gatherer-hunter societies devote remarkably little time to meeting their subsistence needs. As the research of anthropologist Richard Lee has indicated, each week, the !Kung San devote an average of only 12 to 19 hours per person to gathering and hunting. Much more of their time is taken up by socializing with one another and engaging in dances that sometimes put them into a quasi-religious trance. After considering their daily lives, another anthropologist concluded that the !Kung San might best be described as members of "the original affluent society."[6]

People living in modern societies measure affluence in terms of money and possessions, but for the !Kung San, affluence lies in the ability to enjoy abundant leisure. And it is their limited interest in material possessions that allows them to devote more of their waking hours to socializing and dancing than to gathering and hunting. This lack of interest in material goods does not stem from a conscious choice to pursue an ascetic mode of life but is the natural result of the inability to stay in one place for an extended period of time. In most instances, a gathering-and-hunting mode of life is necessarily nomadic due to the periodic depletion of the local environment. Everything the !Kung San own has to be carried from one waterhole to another every few weeks, making material goods a burden rather than essential components of the good life.

Infants and young children are another "burden" that has to be carried from one place to another, usually by the women. Consequently, women have a strong personal interest in limiting their fertility by spacing births so that they usually have only one small child to carry as they go from place to place. Stretching out the times between pregnancies is accomplished by prolonged lactation, as women are much less likely to conceive when they are frequently nursing. Less benign means of limiting population size may also be employed; abortion and infanticide often occur in many gathering-and-hunting societies.[7] Natural attrition also keeps population in check. Among the Hadza of Tanzania for example, 25 percent of infants die before their first birthday, and about half are gone before reaching the age of 15.[8] Unpleasant or repugnant though these practices may be, they help prevent population growth from outstripping the carrying capacity of the !Kung San's territory, which might result in famines and other unfortunate consequences of overpopulation.

Although gatherer-hunters seem to have been generally successful at keeping their population in balance with their natural environments, individual members of gatherer-hunter groups may occasionally be unable to support themselves due to illness, infirmity, or misfortune. With no accumulated resources to fall back on, they are dependent on other members of the group to help them in times of need. Since everybody is potentially vulnerable, these societies are usually characterized by a social ethos that requires food and other vital commodities to be shared within the group. Sharing is not motivated by altruism; helping someone in a time of need is a kind of insurance policy that allows individuals to benefit from others' success should they find themselves in difficult circumstances at some future time.

Before ending this section on the !Kung San and other gatherer-hunters, it is appropriate to ask whether the gathering and hunting they do can even be called "work." In today's world, most of us distinguish the time when we work from other temporal spaces in our lives, some of which is labeled as "leisure." It is not so certain that gatherer-hunters make such a distinction. More likely is a frame of mind that looks on gathering-and-hunting activities as integral parts of life that are often done as a group activity, which itself can be a source of pleasurable interaction. People who gained their livelihood through gathering and hunting would probably be puzzled if you were to ask them if they liked or disliked the work they did.

Although the merger of life and work may be appealing, the lives of the !Kung San and other gatherer-hunters should not be romanticized. Most of us would find it very difficult to accept isolation from the outside world and the absence of the material goods and services we have come to depend on. And even in the homeland of the !Kung San, the mode of life based on gathering and hunting is disappearing as some of its few remaining practitioners are evicted from their ancestral lands and others are drawn into a world of cash wages and consumer purchases.[9] But, if nothing else, an examination of the lives of the !Kung San and other gatherer-hunters yields an important insight: if wants are kept in check, unremitting work is not essential to human existence.

The Agricultural Revolution

For millions of years, humans and their proximate ancestors were able to maintain themselves by gathering and hunting. Human life took a radically different turn around 12,000 to 10,000 years ago in several parts of the world when the deliberate cultivation of plants began to displace gathering and hunting as the prime means of subsistence. Although this transformation has been dubbed the Agricultural Revolution, change came gradually and incrementally as people combined rudimentary farming with traditional means of obtaining food. The causes of this transition are still being debated, but it seems reasonable to assume that some combination of population growth and environmental change motivated people to become sedentary agriculturalists.[10] In particular, in places where people depended on hunting for a major part of their food supply, the warming of the Earth's climate at the end of the Pleistocene era around 10,000 years ago may have affected the population size and migratory patterns of game animals, but it is possible that over-hunting by increasingly skillful humans also led to the demise of these animals. More positively, a warmer climate helped stimulate crop production and extended the area that could be brought under cultivation.

The initial stage in the cultivation of plants was horticulture, the form of agriculture that uses some kind of hoe to turn the soil, which aerates the soil, brings nutrients closer to the surface, and holds down the spread of weeds.

Horticulturalists often made use of a technique that has been given the graphic label "slash and burn." In this form of cultivation, trees are girdled or chopped down and then set on fire. This opens up land for cultivation, and at the same time, the ashes add useful nutrients to the soil. But this process can go on for only a few years before the soil is exhausted. Cultivated land then has to be abandoned for a number of years to allow the return of native plants and trees, at which point the process can be started anew.

Simple though its techniques are, horticulture provides much more food per unit of land than gathering and hunting does. This means that an agrarian economy can support far more people on a given area of land than a nomadic gathering-and-hunting economy can. According to one calculation, the maintenance of a single member of a gathering-and-hunting society requires about 10 square kilometers, an area that might support 20 or more horticultural-ists.[11] This disparity is reflected in the size of the respective societies; the average grouping of gatherer-hunters contained 40 people, while horticultural communities might have as many as 5,000 members.[12]

The ability to support much larger numbers of people might be reckoned as a major advantage of this form of productive activity, and at first, the transition to agriculture did not offset this advantage by exacting a greater demand for human labor. Slash-and-burn cultivation typically requires 500 to 1,000 person-hours per year of labor, about on par with the time put in by the !Kung San as they engaged in gathering and hunting.[13] But labor demands escalate when the same soil has to be tilled year after year. Lacking the long fallow periods made possible by slash-and-burn agriculture, the soil has to be systematically replenished through the application of fertilizers, weeds have to be controlled, and the soil requires some preparation prior to sowing.

Work requirements were further increased when farmers began to irrigate their crops instead of depending on the vagaries of rainfall. Preindustrial irrigated agriculture absorbed a great deal of labor needed for the construction and maintenance of dams, weirs, reservoirs, channels, and human-powered devices for moving the water to where it was needed. The payoff came in the form of much greater crop production per acre and the ability to feed significantly larger numbers of people. In extreme cases, such as that of China in the early 20th century, preindustrial irrigated agriculture could support as many as 6,000 people per square mile.[14] But the downside to higher production was much more work. The labor-intensive nature of preindustrial irrigated agriculture can be seen in contemporary Java, where in 1970, the operation of an average-sized farm required nearly 300 person-days of work per year.[15] Not coincidentally, Java is one of the most densely populated places on Earth, and in the absence of modern inputs such as chemical fertilizers and powered farm implements, the only way to feed large numbers of people has been through the application of a great deal of human labor.

Preindustrial agriculture reached a high level of development in terms of the ability to support large populations. It also made possible the development of more complex cultures. The greater productivity of agriculture released some members of the population from the daily task of securing food, allowing them to work as priests, artists, craftsmen, and government officials. But for the great majority of the population, a large portion of daily life was taken up by the demands of plowing, sowing, weeding, irrigating, fertilizing, and harvesting—all the while confirming the Biblical injunction that "in the sweat of thy face thou shall eat bread."[16]

Agricultural Labor and Cultural Change

While agriculture radically changed the size and density of populations, it retained the gender-based division of labor typical of gathering-and-hunting societies. Most forms of farming were characterized by a distinction between "men's work" and "women's work." In horticulture, the chief task for men was to clear the land. After this was done, women performed the more time-consuming tasks of planting, weeding, and harvesting.[17] As with economies based on gathering and hunting, economies that rested on horticulture were much more dependent on the labor of women than on the productive activities of men. Men, however, took on a larger role when horticulture gave way to agriculture. The primary distinction between horticulture and agriculture is found in the latter's use of a crucial piece of farm equipment: the plow. A plow turns the soil far more effectively than a hoe or digging stick can, and its effectiveness can be augmented by hitching it to a draft animal. Draft animals also have the added benefit of being sources of fertilizer. Why men are more involved in agricultural tasks than in horticultural ones is not altogether clear, although the increased physical requirements for maneuvering a heavy plow were certainly part of it.[18] In some societies, a gender-based division of farm tasks also was observed in paddy rice cultivation; the rice seedlings were often transplanted by women because it was believed that their fertility would transfer to the new crops.

The combination of the plow and the use of draft animals increased crop harvests substantially, while at the same time allowing humans to stay in one place for an indefinite period of time. This combination of higher crop yields and permanent residence served as the basis for a much higher level of occupational specialization. Freed from the need to be directly involved with raising their own food, men and women could be employed in a variety of occupational specialties. Food surpluses also provided the economic foundation for the emergence of towns and cities where these specialists had a permanent base for plying their trades. Sustained by the labors of peasant farmers, cities became the basis of what we call "civilization"—a word derived from *civitas*, the Latin word for city.

The availability of a surplus of food and other goods also stimulated another activity with far less beneficial consequences for humanity: warfare. Urbanization stimulated warfare because towns and cities offered greatly increased opportunities for plunder. At the same time, economic surpluses could be used to feed and equip large armies, either for defense or for conquests of their own. Further enhancing the capacity to pillage, destroy, and conquer was the development of new materials such as bronze and then iron, which skilled artisans formed into more effective arms and armor. Stoked by food surpluses and new weaponry, warfare expanded in scale and scope, and organized violence became much more common than it had been in gathering-and-hunting societies. Some wars were defensive in nature, but wars of conquest were often waged for the land and the slaves that they promised.

The expansion of warfare powerfully reinforced gender-based division of labor. It may be true that men have greater innate proclivities to aggression and warfare than women do, but as a practical matter, the demands of pregnancy, lactation, and the care of infants and children make women less suitable for prolonged combat. The transition from gathering and hunting to sedentary farming may also have made warfare a more attractive activity for large numbers of men. Raising crops was a tedious, routine activity when compared with hunting; for men who no longer pursued and killed game on a regular basis, combat may have provided an alternative source of excitement while giving them the opportunity to demonstrate their skill and valor. Women warriors were not unknown, but as with hunting, the greater physical strength of men, coupled with their freedom from the demands of pregnancy, lactation, and long-term child care, made warfare the ultimate kind of men's work.

Whatever its ultimate causes, warfare was a key concern of another product of the agricultural revolution: the state. Much larger and more complex than the forms of governance found in gathering-and-hunting bands, the agrarian state contained a multiplicity of roles and offices. Initially governing towns or small cities and their outlying environs, a few agrarian states evolved into vast empires exercising dominion over tens of millions of people, as was the case in ancient Rome and dynastic China.

The governance of these states required some kind of record keeping, if for no other reason than to ensure that subjects were paying their taxes. The rise of agricultural societies was, therefore, often accompanied by the invention and use of some form of writing, along with the appearance of a new occupational specialty: the scribe. Since governance was usually fused with religion, scribes were usually members of a priestly class, a conjunction that can be seen in the common origin and linguistic connection of the English words *clerk, cleric,* and *clergy.*

Writing was a key component of a new occupational role associated with the rise of powerful, expansionary states: the bureaucrat. Bureaucratic organization is a topic that will come up on numerous occasions in this book in a variety of contexts. In agrarian states, the duties and responsibilities of bureaucracies were limited, being largely confined to overseeing public works projects, maintaining order, and—inevitably—collecting taxes. Bureaucratic roles are far more diffuse today, but even long ago, the key characteristics typical of modern bureaucracies were evident: written records, specialized skills, established rules and procedures, and hierarchical authority.

Artisan Work

While a considerable amount of the economic surplus made possible by improved agricultural production was absorbed by military campaigns and the conspicuous consumption of the ruling elite, some of it was also used to support productive activities that benefited the population as a whole. On average, it can be reckoned that about 3 percent to 5 percent of the population of advanced preindustrial agricultural societies worked as potters, smiths, spinners and weavers, brewers, and other specialized artisans. Although they were employed in a diversity of tasks, artisans had several things in common; most important were the acquisition and development of specific skills, along with the possession of a fair amount of physical strength and endurance. Power was usually derived from human and animal muscles, although there are instances of the use of water and wind power. In regard to the former, the *Domesday Book* tallied more than 5,000 water wheels in 11th-century England.[19] Water power was used to run simple machinery for such processes as grinding grain, polishing metals, fulling cloth (i.e., increasing its density by pressing or beating it after it had been woven), sawing wood, making mash for beer, and operating forge hammers and bellows for blast furnaces.[20] Wind was more episodic and less commonly used, but in some places, notably the Low Countries (present-day Netherlands and Belgium), windmills made an essential contribution to agriculture by powering pumps that drained water from reclaimed land.

Whatever the source of power, the vast majority of craft enterprises were small in scale, typically containing no more than a dozen workers, and usually not even that many. Some specialization might be found in the larger enterprises; a few pottery workshops in ancient Rome employed one or more workers to mix clay, shape the bodies or the handles of urns, paint them, or operate the kilns.[21] More examples of specialization could be found in other crafts, but these were exceptions to the rule. Artisan work was by and large a small-scale activity involving family members and a few apprentices.

Although the independent artisan produced the bulk of manufactured items, during the Middle Ages, an alternate form of work organization known as the putting-out system emerged in the Flemish wool industry and then spread to England, Italy, and southern Germany. Entrepreneurial merchants bought unprocessed wool that was turned over to peasants and other small-time artisans who were responsible for the carding, spinning, and weaving that turned the wool into rough cloth. The merchant purchased the cloth, which was then dyed and finished by other workers. Cloth production often was incorporated into a well-developed pattern of international trade, where wool was supplied by English sheep, rough cloth was manufactured in Flanders, and the final finishing was done by Italian craftsmen.[22]

This system, which survived in parts of eastern Europe into early modern times, exhibited some elements of capitalism; that is, there was a clear separation between the individuals who supplied the materials, and sometimes the tools used to transform them, and the workers who had little more than their labor power to offer. The putting-out system did have advantages for both groups; it allowed farm families to earn an income at home at times when there wasn't much to do in the fields or any other work to be had, while at the same time providing cheap labor for nascent capitalists. All in all, it seems to have primarily benefited the merchants, who usually were in a position to sell wool at a high price and buy cloth at a low one. Moreover, many workers found it necessary to borrow money from the merchant, using their spinning wheels and looms as collateral. A default, which was not uncommon, resulted in loss of a key source of the worker's livelihood, and with it came further subordination to the merchant.[23] As one economic historian summed up the situation, the worker, "gradually deprived of all rights of ownership over the instruments of production, had in the end only his labor to sell and his wages to live on."[24]

This economic relationship did not always tilt in the merchants' favor. Workers sometimes could get the upper hand by selling the materials provided by the merchant, buying an inferior substitute, and pocketing the difference. In general, the lack of supervision allowed workers to cut corners whenever possible, and the seasonal nature of the work could result in imbalances between supply and demand. From our vantage point, the putting-out system can be seen as occupying an intermediary position between craft work done in the shops of independent artisans and factory-based industrial production. This latter phase came about as a key part of a revolution in production that will be explored in Chapter 3. Many things contributed to this revolution, not the least of which being the topic of the next section: new attitudes regarding time and its proper use.

Photo 1.2 A cabinetmaker and his family: French manuscript illumination, 15th century. The woman also is at work as she uses a distaff to spin thread.

SOURCE: The Granger Collection/New York.

Time and Work

Humans have always been aware of the passing of time, and many of life's activities have been geared to particular periods of time. Gatherers and hunters always have been attuned to seasonal cycles of plants and animals, just as agriculturalists have been keenly aware of the proper times for sowing, reaping, and other farm operations. But what is absent in these observances is division of time into artificial units such as months, weeks, hours, and minutes. This followed from the nature of their productive activities. For traditional gatherer-hunters, agriculturalists, and artisans, there was no need for precise scheduling. For the most part, attitudes regarding time and work were quite relaxed. There were episodes of maximum effort and long workdays, as when a harvest had to be brought in before it spoiled in the fields, but a leisurely approach toward getting the work done was also common. Agricultural work was characterized by slack periods where there wasn't much to do, and the working schedules of artisans and merchants usually had a considerable degree of flexibility. As Gideon Sjoberg has noted of work patterns in preindustrial cities,

> Merchants and handicraft workers generally do not adhere to any fixed schedule. Shopkeepers open and close their shops as they see fit. They may open one morning at nine, the next at ten, and so on. The lunch hour is likely to be longer on some days than on others. Ambulatory merchants likewise are apt to keep rather irregular schedules.[25]

Much less evident in the many centuries antedating industrialism and fully developed capitalism was a desire to improve one's material existence or social position through unremitting effort. Jacques LeGoff's summation of the medieval mentality can be taken as typical of many traditional cultures:

> On the whole, labor time was still the time of an economy dominated by agrarian rhythms, free of haste, careless of exactitude, unconcerned by productivity—and of a society created in the image of the economy, *sober and modest*, without enormous appetites, undemanding, and incapable of quantitative efforts.[26]

Why attitudes toward work and time began to change is still a matter of some debate. Part of the reason lies, not surprisingly, simply in the invention of artificial timepieces. People always have been able to perceive the passage of time by observing natural phenomena—sunrise and sunset, the changing of the seasons, and the migration of birds and other creatures. But there was little need for more precise measures because people did not need to coordinate their activities with individuals outside their family or small tribe.

Warfare was the great exception, but standing armies were not typical of most societies, and most of the armies that were mustered to wage war were temporary aggregations not noted for their cohesion and discipline.

In the civilian realm, the need to get everyone on the same time schedule became evident during the Middle Ages, when large numbers of men and women aggregated in monasteries and convents. Instead of pursuing salvation as a solitary activity, monks and nuns exercised their religious duties in a collective setting. This, in turn, required the scheduling of religious activities. For the monastic followers of St. Benedict, eight specific times of the day were set aside for prayer, beginning with *lauds* at dawn and ending with *the rosary* in the evening.[27] But not all of a monk's or nun's time was given over to prayer; collective physical labor also was an integral part of monastic life—in fact, *ora et labora* ("pray and work") was the motto of the Dominican order. As with prayers, work was performed according to a fixed schedule.

The passage of time was initially measured by means of sundials, hourglasses, candles, and devices that used a falling water level. Mechanical clocks first appeared in China toward the end of the 11th century, but it wasn't until the end of the 14th century that they made their appearance in Europe—although the custom of noting the passage of the hours by ringing bells had already been established in some towns.[28] Mechanical clocks were used to demarcate working hours soon after their invention and diffusion. One example could be found in the French city of Amiens, where Philip VI allowed the city to issue an ordinance

> concerning the time when the workers of said city and its suburbs should go each morning to work, when they should eat and when to return to work after eating; and also in the evening, when they should quit work for the day; and that by the issuance of said ordnance, they might ring a bell which has been installed in the belfry of said city, which differs from the other bells.[29]

The exact scheduling of work was also driven by the appearance of the new mechanical technologies that transformed work, the economy, and the people who worked in it. The introduction of machinery and mechanized operations required the close coordination of work activities, and this could be done only through exact, clock-driven schedules. In the end, time became a kind of commodity, something that was not to be "wasted" or "spent" unwisely. The unscheduled, unhurried pace that typified the lives of gathers and hunters, farmers, and preindustrial artisans gave way to a working environment governed by the relentless passage of hours, minutes, and seconds.

Protestantism and the Rise of Capitalism

Important as it was, the invention of the clock takes us only so far in explaining why Europeans took such an interest in the effective use of time.

Of equal or greater importance were the changes in values and behaviors brought on by the religious, political, and cultural upheavals collectively known as the Protestant Reformation. Beginning with Martin Luther's challenge to the Christian establishment in 1517, Protestantism rapidly fragmented into many sects and churches, each one energized by its own particular vision of proper Christian life and thought. One of the most important of these originated with Jean Calvin (1509–1564), a French-Swiss theologian who made belief in predestination the centerpiece of his theology. According to this doctrine, an omnipotent God had determined whether an individual was destined for an afterlife of eternal bliss in heaven or perpetual torment in hell. Given the stark prospect of heaven or hell and the belief that nothing could be done to change God's judgment, Calvin's followers must have experienced great anxiety concerning their personal fate. Fortunately, they had one important clue about their ultimate destination: their material success in this life, which indicated that they were a member of God's elect. This belief represented a sharp reversal of established doctrine, as amassing wealth had been viewed with great suspicion by traditional Christians, who were familiar with the condemnation of rich individuals in many New Testament passages, such as Jesus' admonition that "it is easier for a camel to pass through the eye of a needle than it is for a rich man to enter into the kingdom of God."[30] Even early Protestant reformers such as Luther himself remained deeply suspicious of wealth and its acquisition.[31]

Calvinist theology accepted and even glorified the accumulation of wealth, but it had to be acquired the right way, through hard work and frugality. Wealth was not to be expended in dissolute, luxurious living. An ascetic lifestyle was supposed to prevail, and profits were to be plowed back into productive enterprises. Inspired by the coupling of work with religious belief, the Calvinist businessman was more than a mere money-grubber; work took on the qualities of a religious "calling" or vocation. To work hard and prosper was to serve God, while material success provided an indication that death would not be followed by eternal damnation.

Calvinist Protestants also were distinguished by their attitudes regarding time. Like monetary wealth, time was not to be wasted in frivolous pursuits but to be "invested" in the sort of activities that contributed to one's material success. After all, as the old adage had it, "time is money." Many other sayings and phrases conveyed the idea of time as a commodity. Time was to be "saved" and not "wasted," while one could metaphorically "buy time" or "live on borrowed time."

This description of the historical connection between Protestantism and an ethos favorable to capitalist development was first articulated by Max Weber in *The Protestant Ethic and the Spirit of Capitalism*, which appeared in the early 20th century.[32] In the years that followed, Weber's formulation has been as controversial as it has been influential.[33] Evidence in support of the thesis can be found by looking at a map of Europe: the countries where capitalism first flourished and economic growth was most rapid were predominantly

Protestant—England and Scotland, the Netherlands, and the Protestant regions of France and Germany. Conversely, traditional economic organization and slow growth were evident in Italy, Spain, and other Catholic lands.

The geographical association of Protestantism with capitalism cannot be taken as proof of a direct connection between the two; important as theological differences were, Europe was divided by more than religious beliefs. Weber's thesis centers on the mental states of Catholics and Protestants, and for it to be convincing, we need strong evidence that ordinary members of the two religions had fundamentally different conceptions of the connection between economic life and religious belief. Specifically, what is needed is a deep insight into the minds of people in order to ascertain the sources of their economic behavior. This is difficult enough with people who are alive today, and it is obviously much more problematic in the case of individuals who have been dead for centuries. More than a hundred years after its publication, *The Protestant Ethic and the Spirit of Capitalism* continues to be a source of both inspiration and controversy.[34] It may very well be right about the connection between Protestant beliefs and the propensity to work hard, save money, and use time effectively, but in the end, its central thesis is difficult, perhaps impossible, to prove conclusively.

In explaining the connection between Protestantism and capitalism, it may be argued that less attention should be paid to religious doctrines and more emphasis placed on the medium through which these doctrines were disseminated. The Protestant Reformation began a few decades after the invention of printing with moveable type, a technological innovation that greatly lowered the cost of producing books and other printed materials. A great amount of early printed material involved religious subjects: Bibles, theological works, hymnbooks, prayer books, and tracts intended for mass distribution. The availability of inexpensive printed works gave a strong boost to literacy, a capability that in the past had been largely confined to the clergy. The combination of widespread literacy and inexpensive printed works gave a major impetus to the rise of Protestantism. Martin Luther was well aware of this when he characterized printing as "God's highest and extremist act of grace, whereby the business of the Gospel is driven forward."[35] A defining feature of Protestant religious practice was regular reading of the Bible, which often stimulated divergent interpretations of the word of God, and the resultant fission of Protestant Christianity into myriad churches and sects.

Although it may have been pursued out of religious motivations, literacy had great value for the conduct of business. A literate person had the ability to understand and enter into contracts, keep accurate financial accounts, and learn about new techniques and business practices, to name a few. All these contributed substantially to the success of Protestant businesses and helped propel the economic dominance of Protestant lands. In the final analysis, then, the greater economic success of Protestants probably owed more to higher rates of literacy than to religiously inspired attitudes regarding life, work, and salvation.

The 16th and 17th centuries in Europe were times of great social and cultural changes, and it is not surprising that work and economic life were profoundly affected by the conflicts, wars, and other upheavals that characterized the era. Meanwhile, momentum was slowly building for another massive set of changes that also profoundly affected life and work. This transformation came to be known as the Industrial Revolution, and as we shall see in Chapter 3, it marked as great a transformation as the one that replaced gathering and hunting with sedentary agriculture. A crucial part of this revolution was the introduction of new ways of organizing work. In order to get some perspective on this organizational revolution, it is useful to first consider the ways in which work was organized prior to industrialization, as will be done in the next chapter.

FOR DISCUSSION

1. How would you fare if you suddenly found yourself in the middle of the Kalahari Desert? Would any of your modern-era skills be of use? How would you develop the skills you need in order to survive in this environment?

2. The transition from gathering and hunting to sedentary agriculture made possible a significant increase in the human population and the development of settled communities. At the same time, the widespread adoption of agriculture resulted in more physical toil. Can this transition, therefore, be characterized as "progress"? What standards should be used when making this assessment?

3. This chapter invokes the physical differences of men and women as a prime cause of gender-based division of labor in preindustrial societies. Do you agree? To what extent are physical differences a significant source of gender-based occupational differentiation today?

4. Have you ever had a job that required you to record your hours on a time clock? Have you held a job where everything was rigidly scheduled? What was work like under these circumstances? Could less time-intensive modes of work have been possible for these kinds of jobs?

5. Although adherents to virtually all the world's religions can be found in the United States, the claim has been made that American culture has been influenced by Protestant Christianity more than by any other religious tradition. Do you agree? Are key elements of the Protestant Ethic still operational in the United States today?

Notes

1. Frank R. Wilson, *The Hand: How Its Use Shapes the Brain, Language, and Human Culture* (New York: Pantheon, 1998), 124–52.

2. Robert F. G. Spier, *From the Hand of Man: Primitive and Preindustrial Technologies* (Boston: Houghton Mifflin, 1970), 53–6.

3. Patrick Nolan and Gerhard Lenski, *Human Societies: An Introduction to Macrosociology* (Boulder, CO: Paradigm, 2004), 79.

4. Richard B. Lee and Richard Daly, eds., *The Cambridge Encyclopedia of Hunters and Gatherers* (Cambridge, UK: Cambridge University Press, 1999).

5. Richard B. Lee, "What Hunters Do for a Living, or How to Make Out on Scarce Resources," in *Man the Hunter*, eds. Richard B. Lee and Irven DeVore (Chicago: Aldine-Atherton, 1968), 30–48.

6. Marshall Sahlins, *Stone Age Economics* (New York: Aldine, 1972), 1–39.

7. Nolan and Lenski, *Human Societies*, 88.

8. Michael Finkel, "The Hadza," *National Geographic* (December 2009)

9. Robyn Dixon, "The Tug of Deep Roots," *Los Angeles Times*, January 3, 2005.

10. T. Douglas Price and Anne Birgitte Gebauer, eds., *Last Hunters, First Farmers: New Perspectives on the Prehistoric Transition to Agriculture* (Santa Fe, NM: School of American Research Press, 1995).

11. Nolan and Lenski, *Human Societies*, 116.

12. Ibid.

13. Robert McN. Netting, *Cultural Ecology* (Menlo Park, CA: Cummings, 1977), 62.

14. R. H. Tawney, *Land and Labor in China* (London: Allen & Unwin, 1932), 24.

15. Francesca Bray, *The Rice Economies: Technology and Development in Asian Societies* (Berkeley: University of California Press, 1986), 116, 149.

16. Genesis 3:19.

17. Lenski and Nolan, *Human Societies*, 112.

18. Murli M. Sinha, "Family," in *Encyclopedia of Science, Technology, and Ethics*, ed. Carl Mitcham (Detroit: Macmillan Reference, 2005), 248.

19. On the history of the water wheel, see Terry S. Reynolds, *Stronger Than a Hundred Men: A History of the Vertical Water Wheel* (Baltimore: Johns Hopkins University Press, 1983).

20. Frances and Joseph Gies, *Cathedral, Forge, and Waterwheel: Technology and Invention in the Middle Ages* (New York: HarperCollins, 1994), 113–5, 200–2.

21. Melvin Kranzberg and Joseph Gies, *By the Sweat of Thy Brow: Work in the Western World* (New York: Putnam, 1975), 43.

22. Ibid., 68–70.

23. Paul Mantoux, *The Industrial Revolution in the Eighteenth Century* (New York: Harper & Row, 1961), 64–5.

24. Ibid., 65.

25. Gideon Sjoberg, *The Preindustrial City: Past and Present* (New York: Free Press, 1960), 209.

26. Jacques LeGoff, *Time, Work, and Culture in the Middle Ages* (Chicago: University of Chicago Press, 1980), 44. Author's emphasis.

27. The Community of St. Benedict, "Liturgy and Prayer Hours," http://www.communityofsaintbenedict.com/liturgy-and-prayer-hours (accessed September 9, 2011).

28. On the history of timekeeping, see David S. Landes, *Revolution in Time: Clocks and the Making of the Modern World* (Cambridge, MA: Harvard University Press, 1983).

29. LeGoff, *Time*, 45–6.

30. Matthew 19:24.

31. R. H. Tawney, *Religion and the Rise of Capitalism* (1926; repr., New York: New American Library, 1954), 72–91.

32. Max Weber, *The Protestant Ethic and the Spirit of Capitalism*, trans. Stephen Kalberg (1905; repr. Los Angeles: Roxbury, 2002).

33. Gordon Marshall, *In Search of the Spirit of Capitalism: An Essay on Max Weber's Protestant Ethic Thesis* (London: Hutchinson, 1982).

34. See William H. Swatos Jr. and Lutz Kaelber, eds., *The Protestant Ethic Turns 100: Essays on the Centenary of the Weber Thesis* (Boulder, CO: Paradigm, 2005).

35. Quoted in Elizabeth Eisenstein, *The Printing Revolution in Early Modern Europe* (New York: Cambridge University Press, 1984), 147.

2

The Organization of Work in Preindustrial Times

All work has to be organized in some way. Even work performed by a solitary individual cannot be done in a random fashion; it is necessary to decide what needs to be done, the procedures to be adopted, the equipment to be used, the time to be allocated, and the sequence of activities to be followed. When several individuals are involved in a productive activity, things get a lot more complicated. Now it also is necessary to determine who does what, who will make decisions and exert authority over others, how individual tasks will be coordinated with the tasks performed by others, and how the workers will be motivated to do what they are supposed to do. Sometimes, all this can be done in an ad hoc manner as the need arises, but it is far more efficient to have structures and procedures already in place so it is not necessary to expend an undue amount of time and effort to get organized every time something has to get done.

The organization of work encompasses a great variety of structures and procedures. Some are based on traditional arrangements—"We've always done it this way"—that may or may not be effective. Others are the result of a great deal of prior thought and analysis. Most organizational modes fall somewhere in between, representing mixtures of longstanding precedents and new ways of doing things. In this chapter, we will concern ourselves with means of organizing work based on established social roles and statuses. In Chapter 4, we will bring the story into the modern era when we look into organizational structures and procedures deliberately designed according to principles that are supposedly "rational." In both cases, organizational forms will be put into a larger social context. While organizations have a large influence on the kinds of societies we live in, the converse is also true. In every society, the organization of work reflects existing social structures and processes, with all that entails—both good and bad.

_____ Traditional Societies and the Organization of Work

Hunters and gatherers do not need elaborate means of organizing their activities. When they go out to get some food, it is already quite clear what needs to be done and who is going to do it. The range of tasks is small, and there is not much day-to-day variation in these tasks. One of the key organizational issues, how tasks are to be allocated, is resolved by reliance on established social categories, which are limited in number. There isn't much specialization and division of labor, and work roles are allocated on the basis of what sociologists call *ascribed statuses*. An ascribed status is a position in society that is based on characteristics an individual cannot change, most notably age and sex, and very often race and ethnicity.

Unlike an *achieved status*, which is derived from ability, effort, training, or some combination of all these, an ascribed status is largely immutable. Barring a sex-change operation, there isn't anything we can do about being either male or female, and like it or not, aging is an inevitable process that carries us from infancy to old age. It must be said, however, that biology need not be destiny, as there is substantial variation from one society to another in regard to what is properly "men's work" and "women's work." In similar fashion, when viewed cross-culturally, age categories are quite flexible; the roles, responsibilities, rights, and privileges associated with a given chronological age vary a great deal from one place or historical period to another. In one society, a 14-year-old may be considered an adult who is expected to take on the tasks and responsibilities appropriate to adulthood, while in other societies, one may not step into a fully adult role until the mid-20s or even later. At the other end of the life span, in some societies, an elderly person may be considered a vital source of information regarding the best way to get things done, while in others, he or she may be deemed obsolete, irrelevant, and worn out.

Later chapters will explore how race, ethnicity, and gender continue to influence the jobs held and the work done in today's world. In regard to work roles in the oldest economic activity, gathering and hunting, ascribed attributes have had a substantial, and in some cases overwhelming, influence. As we saw in Chapter 1, gathering is socially defined as the work of women and children, while hunting is something that men do. A similar pattern can be seen in traditional farm work, where gender and age have been the primary influences on the allocation of work responsibilities, although there is quite a bit more variation in gender-based work roles. Tasks requiring considerable physical strength may be a male's domain, but there are many examples of women performing the most arduous farm chores. Farming is also a more complex activity than gathering and hunting in terms of the kinds of tasks that need to be performed, and many of these tasks can be, and have been, performed by women. As one tabulation of the allocation of work roles in a large number of different societies indicates, the cultivation of crops was largely a male activity in only 28% of the horticultural societies and 59% of the agrarian societies. In all the rest, cultivation was primarily the work of women or was equally shared by both women and men.[1] Specific farm tasks often reflect a sex-based division of labor, but the apportionment of these tasks may vary from society to society. In traditional China, picking cotton, tea, and mulberry leaves was considered "women's work," while rice cultivation was supposed to be exclusively a man's domain. By contrast, transplanting and harvesting rice in Japan and Southeast Asia was mostly done by women.[2]

Two other key sources of ascribed status are race and ethnicity. Race is often defined as a biological category manifested by certain physical attributes such as skin color, hair texture, and shape of facial features. In reality, race is at least as much a social category as a biological one. Although it is often assumed that people can be neatly sorted into specific races, in fact, racial identity is quite elusive. The movement of people through time and space has resulted in a great deal of genetic mixing, rendering the notion of "pure" races a fiction that has had many unfortunate consequences throughout history. That race is a social construct becomes evident when individuals are identified as belonging to a particular race even though their biological heritage may be mixed. On the societal level, official statistics such as census figures have sorted people into racial categories, but these categories have not remained constant over time—another indication of the arbitrariness of racial labels.[3] On the individual level, ideas about racial identities often overemphasize a single genetic component, as with the "one-drop rule," whereby a metaphorical one drop of "African" blood is deemed a sufficient basis for identifying a person as "black" or "African American."

Race is sometimes treated as interchangeable with ethnicity, notably with the use of "Hispanic" as a racial category in government statistics. But as a sociological category, ethnicity is not based on supposed biological differences; it centers on shared language, culture, and history. Yet as with race, the division of humanity into distinct ethnic groups is a hopeless endeavor. Unless a population remains confined to a small, isolated area for a long period of time, their ethnicity will reflect a wide variety of influences from other places. As with race, ethnic "purity" is rarely found among humans, who have always moved around, borrowed cultural elements from other people, intermarried with them, and in general formed ethnic identities that are amalgamations of indigenous and borrowed elements, all of which have evolved over time.

Although race and ethnicity have much less substance than is often assumed, they are anything but irrelevant to the apportioning of an individual's place in society. As the sociologist W. I. Thomas noted many years ago, if people define situations as real, they are real in their consequences.[4] If racial and ethnic identities are assumed to reflect actual differences, and if some groups and individuals find it advantageous to make these assumptions, race and ethnicity can be transcendent realities. And as we shall see, these imputed differences can affect many aspects of work organization.

The Family as a Basis of Work Organization

Along with gender, age, race, and ethnicity, the family one is born into is a significant ascribed status—after all, we can't choose our mother, father, siblings, and other blood relatives. Modern societies are inconsistent when it comes to delineating the connection between family-based status and an individual's economic opportunities. The inheritance of a family business is considered to be entirely proper, but in an organizational setting, it is seen as illegitimate to use family connections as a basis for hiring and promotions, a practice known as nepotism. Whether viewed as a legitimate influence or not, family ties often have been incorporated into the organization of work, and they continue to be important today.

Family membership was especially evident in preindustrial workplaces. Most of the work was done in family settings, so much so that there was scarcely any distinction between "family" and "work unit." One description of the French rural economy in the 17th and 18th centuries can be applied to many other times and places:

> The family and the enterprise coincide: the head of the family is at the same time the head of the enterprise. Indeed, he is the one because he is the other . . . he lives his professional and his family life as an indivisible entity. The members of his family are his fellow workers.[5]

Although this description of the linkage between work and family implies that the head of the operation was a man—presumably the husband and father—women, be they wives or daughters, also made essential contributions to family enterprises. On the farm, they were engaged in a variety of tasks, ranging from garden cultivation to the brewing of beer. In craft enterprises, women could often be found working alongside their husbands, and there are numerous instances of widows taking over the business upon the death of their husbands.

From the agricultural revolution until fairly recent times, the primary work activity for most people was farming. But rural work entailed considerably more than sowing, weeding, reaping, gleaning, and other agricultural tasks. Farm families had to supply many of the goods and services they needed, everything from making clothing and preserving food to treating illnesses and providing much of their own entertainment. Today's families, both rural and urban, generally do not exhibit this level of self-sufficiency, but a considerable amount of work continues to be done as a family-based activity. Necessities and luxuries are for the most part purchased rather than made at home, but the home continues to be the center of many work activities, even though they may not involve direct payments to those doing the work. In particular, the raising of children and the constant performance of household chores can surely be counted as work, even though it is not done for direct remuneration. Work of this sort is still disproportionately borne by the women members of a family. Their tasks have changed over time, but the total time spent on housework has not diminished as much as might be expected.[6]

A reliance on family ties and the ascriptive statuses inherent in them resolves a lot of organizational issues within an enterprise. For one, the assignment of particular tasks often parallels one's place in the family. This has been most evident in preindustrial societies, where fathers, mothers, children, and other members of the family all have certain kinds of tasks assigned to them. Family structure also provides a ready-made hierarchy that reflects age and gender, with fathers and older males usually exercising authority over women and younger members of the family. The fairness of this arrangement can certainly be questioned, but it does provide a basis for allocating and coordinating the work performed by individual family members, as well as a way of justifying who has authority over whom.

Families also offer something that is vital to the functioning of effective organizations: trust. To be sure, one may learn through bitter experience that not all family members are trustworthy, but because of their duration and intensity, family ties offer a better basis for relationships of trust than social connections that are more distant and ephemeral. This is especially true in societies where it can be presumed that extra-familial organizations such as the government, military, and even organized religious bodies are primarily out for themselves and that their relationships with individuals are likely to be exploitative. Under these circumstances, membership in a family unit constitutes a bulwark of protection and mutual support in a world full of dangers, uncertainties, and real and potential enemies.

Trust, of course, is a two-way street. In return for the physical and emotional benefits of family membership, individuals are usually expected to pull their own weight, and a great deal of pressure can be applied to those who don't. This aids considerably in addressing another issue confronting all organizations: motivation. An outside employer can punish or fire an employee for dishonesty or poor performance, but the loss of the respect of family members (and in extreme cases, expulsion from the family) is likely to be a far more severe sanction. More positively, the honor and respect that come from supporting one's family can be a powerful stimulus for hard work, as exemplified by the millions of immigrants from poor countries who send substantial portions of their incomes to their families back home.[7]

Slavery

Ascriptive statuses derived from family membership may result in the exploitation of some members of a family to the benefit of other members. But work roles based on other forms of ascription can be far more exploitative. The worst of these has used ascriptive statuses as the basis of involuntary servitude or, to put it more bluntly, slavery. In some slaveholding societies, the basis of ascription was ethnicity and often followed the conquest of one group of people by another—in fact, the word *slave* is directly derived from "Slav," the predominant ethnicity of Eastern Europe. A less common basis for the enslavement of a people was race, as was practiced in the American South prior to the Civil War. At the same time, racial and ethnic distinctions, both real and perceived, were reinforced by legal, social, cultural, and political power that maintained the boundary between the free and the enslaved.

Slavery has been widely practiced throughout much of human history; sad to say, it exists even today.[8] Slavery was a major source of labor in ancient Mesopotamian and Egyptian societies, although to a somewhat lesser extent in the latter. Slavery was tightly woven into the fabric of society throughout antiquity. Much of the work done in Greece and Rome was performed by slaves, and it is no exaggeration to say that slave labor was the foundation of a large portion of economic life in the ancient world. Under these circumstances, ideas about individual dignity and freedom were not universally applicable. In Athenian "democracy," for example, a sharp division between the rights of slaves and citizens was taken for granted.

Photo 2.1 Slave auction in the antebellum South

SOURCE: ©Leonard de Selva/CORBIS.

The number of slaves and their ratio to free citizens in ancient Athens and Greece as a whole have been matters of considerable debate among scholars. The number of slaves in Athens by the end of the 4th century B.C. has been estimated as ranging from 20,000 to 400,000, with a modal figure of about 100,000. This last number implies a ratio of one slave to every three free citizens, about the same proportion found in the American South on the eve of the Civil War—although slaveholding was probably more widely diffused through Greek society.[9]

Slave labor continued to be used in early medieval Europe, as there was nothing in contemporary Christian doctrine to discourage it, even when the slave and his or her owner were both Christians. At the same time, however, the spread of slavery was inhibited by the belief that Christians should not wage war against fellow Christians in order to enslave them. Even so, some substantial enterprises made abundant use of slave labor. For example, in the 13th century, Frederick II, emperor of the so-called Holy Roman Empire, had several textile workshops in Italy and Sicily in which the work was performed by female slaves.[10] Slavery continued to exist in urban settings, and some of the great merchant city-states such as Venice and Genoa gained a fair portion of their wealth by trafficking in slaves.[11] By the 13th century, the buying and selling of Christian slaves was forbidden by the Church, but people of other faiths, notably Muslims, continued to be fair game.

Slavery was less prominent in farming, and by the early Middle Ages, it had been replaced by serfdom as the primary form of unfree agricultural labor in western Europe. Under the conditions of serfdom, rural people were nominally free, but they were bound to the land they lived and worked on, which meant that when the land was sold to a new owner, they were included in the transaction. The freedom of serfs was further circumscribed by mandatory work on the landowners' properties, and they were required to hand over a portion of the crops they had grown. Serfs also had to use the landowners' facilities for milling grain (and pay for it), and they could be impressed as soldiers should the need arise. Although serfdom began to go into decline in England as early as the 14th century, it persisted on the European continent. Many French peasants had the legal status of serfs prior to the Revolution that began in 1789, and serfdom was not legally abolished in Russia until 1861.

Urban slavery also had considerable staying power in western Europe. After diminishing in the early Middle Ages, it became more common during the 14th century when the Black Death produced a substantial labor shortage.[12] Involuntary servitude was particularly prominent in the lands along the Mediterranean, where slaves were extensively used as domestic servants.[13] It wasn't until the late 15th century that slavery began to wane as the Turkish control of the Black Sea region cut off the supply of potential slaves, but even so, some vestiges of slavery could be found in Italy as late as the 18th century.

While slavery was slowly declining in Europe, it was gaining a new lease on life in the New World, where the plantation economies of the West Indies, the American South, and parts of Latin America created an enormous demand for slave labor. Unlike the situation in antiquity, military conquest was not the primary source of slave labor. Large numbers of slaves were supplied by profit-seeking enterprises that took advantage of the highly lucrative trade in humans from Africa to the New World. In another departure from ancient and medieval practices, slavery in the Americas was based solely on the ascribed characteristic of race. As noted above, "race" is a problematic, ambiguous characteristic only weakly grounded in biology, but owners of slaves were not troubled by such subtleties; any fraction of African ancestry rendered a person "black" and, hence, subject to enslavement. Early slavery in the New World had some of the flexibility found in other slaveholding societies in that some men and women of African ancestry could eventually attain their freedom. But as the plantation system became the foundation of the economies of the American South and islands of the Caribbean, slavery and racial differentiation powerfully reinforced each other.[14]

Slavery, in turn, had direct consequences for the way work was apportioned. In the antebellum South, slaves were forced to labor as field hands, or, if a bit more fortunate, they were put to work as domestic servants or workers in plantation-based industries such as sugar refining. Some slaves even worked as skilled craftsmen and as operatives in industrial enterprises. But whatever the tasks they performed, slaves in the New World worked under an economic and social order far more confining than many other examples of involuntary servitude. Slaves were defined as "chattel," and their legal status was no different from that of the inanimate property held by slave owners.

In contrast, slavery in ancient Rome and Greece was a looser system in some respects. For one, slavery was not always based on race or ethnicity, although the warfare that was the wellspring of slavery often pitted one ethnic group against another, as when Romans successfully took up arms against Germanic "barbarians" and brought them back as slaves. Slavery in the ancient world did have a strong hereditary component; no matter what talents they may have possessed, being born the child of a slave (especially when one's mother was a slave) usually destined a person to a slave's existence. At the same time, however, the working lives of some slaves might have entailed the exercise of considerable skills and responsibilities. Most slaves in the ancient world were agricultural workers, artisans, and household servants. The least fortunate worked under appalling conditions in underground mines, where free labor scarcely existed. But some slaves were employed in positions that required a fair amount of skill and responsibility, serving as artists and craftsmen, musicians, scribes, teachers, physicians, and even minor government officials.

Most important, to be a slave in the ancient world was not necessarily a permanent condition. Some slaves in the Roman empire were able to earn money through various means, such as taking on jobs outside their usual duties. In some cases, slaves even owned slaves of their own, who could be the source of a substantial income.[15] Over time, a few slaves amassed sufficient savings to buy freedom for themselves and their families. Other slaves were set free by their masters, an act known as *manumission*. Some slave owners ordered that their slaves be freed after their death, while others occasionally freed their slaves through humanitarian impulses or simply because they no longer could afford to keep them. A freed slave, however, did not immediately vault to the status of citizen; in Rome, full political status was not attained until two generations had followed the initial manumission.

Before leaving the topic of slavery, something should be said about slavery's effects on work and worker motivation. Unlike wage earners, slaves were a fixed cost for the owners; their food, clothing, and shelter were not directly linked to their output or general work performance. Moreover, slave labor usually was highly inefficient when compared with most forms of free labor. Work could be (and often was) coerced through a variety of punishments, but this necessitated a high level of supervision, and it was poorly suited to any kind of work that required initiative, innovation, or attention to detail. For the most part, slavery was an effective form of labor organization only when tasks were repetitious and relatively simple and when work could be closely monitored. Under these circumstances, slavery was hardly conducive to the development of a skilled labor force.

It frequently has been asserted that slavery also inhibited the development of labor-saving technologies. This is not altogether convincing; after all, if they were so inclined, slave owners could have increased their incomes by making their slaves more productive through the invention and use of newer and better ways of doing things. More likely, slavery inhibited technological advance in an indirect manner by causing work, especially physical labor, to be disparaged as an activity unworthy of free men. This attitude occasionally appears in statements by Greek philosophers, who of course were members of the privileged slaveholding class. When Aristotle claimed that "no man can practice virtue when he is living the life of a mechanic,"[16] his objection to manual work centered on the worker's need to sell his wares or serve as someone's employee. As Aristotle saw it, work done for another, even if it entailed selling items one had made, implied servitude, and this was not an appropriate role for citizens, whose chief concerns were supposed to be politics and pursuit of learning.[17] From this perspective, work done for an employer or a paying customer was bad enough, but slavery was the ultimate form of servitude. This belief may have been appropriate for an elite that had no qualms about being supported by slave labor, but it also constituted an obstacle to the development of productive technologies. Technological advance requires the mental capabilities prized by the Greek philosophers, but it also depends on the willingness of inventors and entrepreneurs to engage in the sort of hands-on activities that Aristotle found distasteful.

The ancient world's attitude toward work contrasts sharply with the Protestant Ethic described in Chapter 1. Neither perspective, that of Greek philosophers nor Protestant businessmen, was the decisive element in shaping the trajectory of economic change, but the denigration of work characteristic of the ancient world surely contributed to a slow pace of economic advance. In similar fashion, the perpetuation of slavery in the European Middle Ages and the enormous expansion of slavery that accompanied the settlement and colonization of many parts of the New World also inhibited the creation and development of workplace technologies that ultimately made slavery obsolete and unnecessary.

Caste and Occupation

Slavery based on race or ethnicity is the most extreme example of an ascribed status determining the conditions of one's working life, but ascribed statuses based on other group characteristics can also strongly affect the occupations people hold and the way they go about their work. The most striking of these is caste, the system of social differentiation that is usually associated with India, although some other societies have caste-like aspects.[18] A caste is a group that claims a common ancestry and practices endogamy, the choice of marriage partners from within the group to which one belongs. In India, caste[19] developed as a blend of indigenous cultural elements with practices brought by Aryan groups that migrated from central Asia into northern India from 1500 to 500 B.C.[20] As it became the dominant mode of social organization, society was divided into four major castes that were hierarchically arranged according to beliefs about purity and pollution. These qualities reflected karma, the actions in past lives that determine one's present life. Each of these four major castes corresponded to broad occupational categories: *Brahmins* (priests and scholars), *Ksyatriyas* (soldiers and rulers), *Vaisyas* (farmers and merchants), and *Shudras* (artisans and laborers). Below these four castes stood another grouping, whose work was deemed so defiling—activities such as removing the carcasses of dead animals—that they were given the name "untouchables" (the preferred term today is *Dalit*), because any contact with them was thought to pollute a higher-caste individual.

Within each of these broad castes were a large number of groupings, or *jati*, many of them associated with a particular occupation. In some cases, low occupational status corresponded to low status in the caste hierarchy. To take one example, tanners, shoemakers, and other leather workers were drawn from the ranks of the Dalit because this kind of work necessarily entailed working with the remains of dead animals. Other occupations, such as barbering and doing laundry, were a bit higher up the ladder but still would not be held by people who were born into jatis associated with less-polluting work.

Although traditional occupations reflected caste divisions, membership in a high-status caste did not necessarily entail holding a prestigious occupation. To take one noteworthy example, although Brahmins occupied the top position in the caste order, many of them worked as cooks, which is not a particularly high-status occupation. Brahmins were sought for this kind of work because, as members of the highest-ranked caste, they could cook for anybody, whereas cooks drawn from the ranks of a lower caste would pollute the food they prepared for members of higher castes. In similar fashion, caste and jati position did not always determine economic power. The value of a product or service in a particular locality often was the primary source of workers' ability to strike favorable bargains with their clients, no matter what jati they occupied.

In recent decades, a number of forces have weakened the caste system and its influence over the distribution of occupations. The government of India has discouraged caste organization and has even enacted a form of affirmative action for Dalits and other disadvantaged groups. At the same time, urbanization and geographic mobility have uprooted people from the traditional villages that preserved the fixed relationships between jatis. Expanded educational opportunities and the diffusion of ideas grounded in modern science have undermined the traditional ideas about purity and pollution that supported caste division. The establishment of a democratic political order, along with a host of socioeconomic changes, has resulted in political power and social class becoming more important bases of social differentiation. Finally, technological changes and the availability of industrially manufactured products have eliminated the need for many of the occupations that traditionally had been filled by particular jatis, such as carrying water and making pottery.[21]

The Guilds

In today's society, where individuals are at least nominally free to choose the kind of work they do, the traditional Indian coupling of caste and occupation seems a strange feature of a far-off, exotic society. In fact, many societies, our own included, reveal numerous examples of work and occupations embedded in particular social arrangements. In some places and times, these arrangements have been quite powerful; they determined who was allowed to practice a particular craft, how they went about it, and even the price that could be charged for their products. In medieval and early modern Europe, a particular kind of organization known as a *guild* (sometimes rendered as *gild*) was the predominant form of work organization in urban areas, and many aspects of working life reflected its importance.

A guild can be defined as a grouping of skilled workers performing a particular task or producing a particular product, usually within the confines of a single town or city. In medieval Europe, individual guilds encompassed weavers, stonemasons, metal smiths, shoemakers, and many other craft occupations. It has been said that in some parts of the world, there even have been guilds for beggars and thieves.[22] Guild membership centered on a particular craft, but it also entailed a number of noneconomic functions. Guilds served as charitable agencies and mutual aid societies that provided assistance for members in difficulties. They also had a strong religious component. The dominance of medieval Christianity meant that guild members all subscribed to the same religion, and celebration of a guild's patron saint would be an occasion for processions, feasting, and affirmation of guild membership.

Photo 2.2   The Doge of Venice receiving the bylaws of the weavers' guild

SOURCE: The Granger Collection, New York.

Guilds, by their nature, were restrictive; where guild power was strong, one could practice a particular craft only as a member of the relevant guild. These restrictions were enforced in a number of ways. Workshops were largely confined to specific neighborhoods, which made it easy for practitioners to monitor one another. Craftsmen also were required to put distinctive marks on their products so inferior goods could be traced back to their makers.[23] And social practices such as the ceremonies and festivals just mentioned contributed to a sense of guild solidarity that aided in the exclusion of nonmembers and the monopolization of a particular craft.

The cohesiveness of guild members also manifested itself in what we today would consider blatant discrimination. Women, for the most part, were not well served by guilds, although there are records of women belonging to guilds and of guilds composed exclusively of women in late 13th-century Paris.[24] Much later, that city contained all-women guilds populated by "dressmakers, combers of hemp and flax, embroiders, and hosiers."[25] Members of these guilds took in young women as apprentices, but in other places, there are a few instances of women taking in male apprentices.[26] A few occupations, notably silk weaving, employed large numbers of women workers,[27] and midwifery was an exclusively female occupation.[28] In general, however, women's occupational roles deteriorated over time, and by the latter part of the Middle Ages and the early modern period, women were largely excluded from guild-based artisan work. Women continued to work in craft industries, but in most cases, they were able to do so only because they were wives or daughters of guild members.[29] Membership in the appropriate guild was out of reach because women were usually denied the opportunity to serve a formal apprenticeship, a prerequisite for attaining the status of master. Even more restrictive measures applied to Jews, who were almost always excluded from craft occupations and their associated guilds.

Possessing monopoly power over a given trade, individual guilds were able to control many aspects of work within that trade. Guild regulations often specified the kinds of materials that could be used for particular products, as well as the times (such as the Sabbath and certain religious holidays) when work could not be done. Guild members also checked weighing scales, inspected workshops, and on occasion confiscated goods that were deemed to be of substandard quality.[30] In the name of maintaining quality, guilds limited the number of apprentices that could be employed, forbade working under artificial light (which in those times meant candlelight), and even set limits on the size of the windows in which wares could be displayed.

Self-regulation was fundamental to the structure and operation of guilds. To put it more blatantly, a primary purpose of a guild was to insulate the practitioners of a particular craft from the workings of the free market. By limiting membership, guilds were able to restrict the number of producers when demand for a product was high, thereby ensuring higher prices for their wares—although they may not have taken full advantage of this circumstance due to the medieval Christian stipulation that one should charge no more than the "just price" necessary for a decent level of subsistence.[31]

When demand dropped, artisans faced the prospect of abandoning what they were doing and confronting an uncertain economic future. But guild organization prevented this from happening by limiting what each guild member could produce. Under these circumstances, the incomes of individual members might decline, but nobody would have to go out of business. Guild regulations that enforced quality standards also can be seen as a way to circumvent the market by ensuring that products were not made in excessive numbers, which would result in depressed prices.

Efforts to limit competition reflected the belief of guild members that they lived and worked in a zero-sum economic environment. That is, they were embedded in an economy that grew at a very slow pace, if at all. Under these circumstances, any individuals' gains were assumed to be matched by the losses of others. Guild regulations and restrictions may have prevented some members from maximizing their incomes (if they were inclined to flout the "just price"), but at the same time, these rules preserved the livelihood of other guild members who may have been less endowed with skills, energy, and luck. This leveling of fortunes was well suited to an economy and culture that, as noted in Chapter 1, did not place economic success at the pinnacle of human values.

Guilds also reflected the surrounding society and culture in their replication of existing social institutions. In the first place, it was often the case that entry into a guild-regulated trade was open only to individuals who had family members already in the guild or who married into one.[32] No less important, the family also provided a model for many aspects of guild life. Guild members were craftsmen whose workplaces were also their places of residence. In most cases, a single structure housed a workshop, salesroom, and living quarters. This building also was the residence of one or more apprentices, who might be treated as junior members of the family. In addition to working alongside their employer and living in his house, apprentices took their meals with him, worshipped with him, and in general lived their lives under his tutelage and supervision.

Apprenticeship

The first stage of entering a guild was a period of apprenticeship, during which a novice developed essential skills. Until well into the 19th century, preparation for only a few occupations—primarily medicine, law, and the clergy—occurred in a university setting, and even these "learned professions" made considerable use of apprenticeships. For everything else, apprenticeship was the only structured educational route available. Apprenticeship was a formal status, often based on a sworn oath or a written contract guaranteed by the parents of the apprentice, who usually had not reached the age of majority and could even be a young child. The apprentice agreed to work for a stipulated period of time and not leave the master or get married unless allowed to do so. In return, the master promised to teach the apprentice and provide him (or, very occasionally, her) with room, board, and clothing. Violation of these stipulations by either side could result in the payment of a cash penalty to the aggrieved party.[33]

The exact terms of the agreements varied considerably, and it is likely that masters in lucrative crafts could drive a harder bargain, which might include a payment from the apprentice's family.[34] Apprentices learned their trade by working with the master, usually beginning with jobs that were easily mastered or unpleasant, or both. In time, an apprentice was given the opportunity to learn and practice the "mysteries" or skills of a particular craft. In addition to learning the technical aspects of a trade, apprenticeship was a time for occupational socialization—the assimilation of the values, norms, and attitudes characteristic of the people engaged in that trade.

The period of apprenticeship, which in some trades extended 10 years or more but much less in others, was often followed by elevation to an intermediate position known as journeyman. It is often said that this term reflects the practice of traveling from one place to another in the course of developing one's skills, and many journeymen did, in fact, ply their trades in a number of places. However, the word is actually derived from the French word for "day" (*journée*) because journeymen often were long-term employees who usually were paid on the basis of how many days they had worked.[35] Many of them remained stuck at this level, never attaining the rank of "master" and guild membership.

When apprentices or journeymen were in full possession of the necessary skills, they pursued guild membership through the creation of a "masterpiece" that bore witness to their capabilities. If it was deemed of sufficient quality, the masterpiece qualified its creator for admission to the guild, which also may have entailed paying a fee to government officials, securing sufficient capital to set up a shop, and taking an oath to uphold the guild's regulations.[36]

_____ An Assessment of Guild Organization

The guild has to be reckoned as a highly successful social and economic institution, if for no other reason than its survival for hundreds of years. But eventually, the power of guilds began to wane as they came under fire on two fronts, one political and the other economic. Political opposition came from the nation-state, which became the dominant form of government in many lands. Nation-states, even when they are democratic regimes, have low levels of tolerance for organizations that seek to regulate themselves and to remain insulated from state control, which is exactly what the guilds had been able to do for hundreds of years. But their autonomy, and even their very existence, came to an end when they were summarily abolished by legislative action in France (1791), England (1835), and Germany (1869).[37]

By this time, guilds were already under assault by forces that were transforming the world economy. First, the ability of guilds to maintain their control over their trades was undermined by alternative modes of production. We have seen how the putting-out system bypassed guild organization through the use of cheap, predominantly rural labor. At the same time, the growth of commerce expanded the size of markets, undercutting the local monopolies that guild members had enjoyed. Commercial growth and the parallel rise of capitalism also worked to the benefit of mercantile guilds, which exercised increasing control over the market for products made by the members of craft guilds, as well as the supply of raw materials used to make these products.[38] Finally, many of the technological changes that were an essential part of the Industrial Revolution resulted in machinery taking the place of skilled labor. Moreover, industrial production was oriented to the large-scale manufacture of inexpensive, low-quality goods, which was the antithesis of craft production under guild auspices.

The passing of the guilds and their influence over the economy was not universally mourned. Guilds came in for particular scorn on the part of free-market advocates such as Adam Smith, who looked askance at social institutions that dampened the operation of market forces. As Smith saw it, the free movement of labor was an essential part of an efficiently operating market system, but in Britain, it was stifled. The Elizabethan Statute of Apprenticeship stipulated that one could practice a craft only after being apprenticed for a minimum of 7 years. As a result, argued Smith, declining industries were stuck with a surplus of workers, while rising ones were hard-pressed to meet their labor needs. This, in turn, led to serious distortions in the wage rates: "while high wages are given to the workmen in one manufacture, those in another are obliged to content themselves with bare subsistence."[39]

Guilds also have been accused of retarding economic progress by suppressing technological innovation, both in regard to the kinds of products their members made and the procedures used to make them. This criticism contains more than a grain of truth. Guilds, by their very nature, were conservative institutions that aimed at maintaining a stable social and economic climate. Technological changes can destabilize economies and societies by bringing new products and processes to the fore while rendering obsolete many well-established ones. Consequently, it should not be surprising that guilds and their members often exhibited an indifference to, and even hostility toward, innovations of any sort.

But this isn't the whole story. In reality, the effects of guild organization on technological change were mixed and complex. Guild regulations and attitudes may have dampened the desire to innovate, but in contrast, the apprenticeship system embedded in guild organization was of considerable long-term importance for technological advance. Technological processes, be they old or new, have to be learned. Sometimes reading a book will be sufficient (assuming the ability to read, which was not usually the case in medieval and early modern times), but a great deal of learning, then as now, requires the acquisition of "tacit" skills that come only through observing these skills being practiced and then engaging in hands-on practice.[40] This is exactly what apprenticeship provided.

In return for receiving essential training in a particular craft, an apprentice provided low-cost labor.[41] The long periods of apprenticeship typical of guilds were hard to justify simply in terms of the time it took to learn a particular craft, but they made perfect sense as the key element of the bargain struck between apprentices and their masters. And if cheap labor was deemed an insufficient payment, a master could charge an apprentice fee, which might be likened to modern-day students taking out loans to finance their educations in the hope of boosting their future incomes. At the same time, the nonrefundable fee created a strong expectation that the apprentice would stay on the job during the stipulated period and would in general be a trustworthy member of the enterprise. Family members who entered into an apprentice position paid a low fee, or none at all, as it was assumed that family ties were a sufficient basis for a relationship of trust between master and apprentice.[42]

Guilds are usually associated with long-past times such as the European Middle Ages and with societies that are still enmeshed in traditional ways of doing things. It is certainly true that guilds, as they were constituted in medieval times, have passed from the scene, even though a few modern labor unions cling to the term—most notably, the Screen Actors Guild. Although traditional guild organization has been dissolved by a multitude of economic and political forces, some occupational settings maintain guild-like characteristics. Most important, today's professions resemble guilds in that their structures and processes eliminate or diminish market-based competition. Like the guild-based occupations of the medieval era, today's professions are able to resist competitive pressures through their control over recruitment and training procedures, government support, and their members' possession of specialized knowledge. Consequently, a certain sense of déjà vu may be expected when we take a close look at some key attributes of modern professions in Chapter 9.

Guilds and other traditional modes of organization are no longer as prevalent as they were in times past; the operation of a modern economy necessarily rests on more complex modes of organization. But what is meant by a "modern economy"? Social scientists have long argued about what demarcates a *modern* economy and society from a *traditional* one, but that peasant farmers and artisans are no longer at the center of economic life is indisputable. Beginning about 250 years ago, the nature of work has been transformed by a set of forces collectively known as industrialization. How this has happened is the topic of the next chapter.

FOR DISCUSSION

1. How important are circumstances beyond one's control, such as the family one was born into, for the choice of an occupation and the ability to prepare for it? How might research be conducted in order to determine the influence of social institutions such as the family on occupational choice?

2. Sociologists often look at race as a "social construction" rather than a biological reality. What do you suppose is meant by this phrase? Through what social processes is race constructed?

3. Are there particular kinds of enterprises where families are important units of production? What is it about these enterprises that makes them particularly well suited to be family-run operations? Do families necessarily provide benign work settings for their members?

4. Slave labor was extensively employed in most of the world's great preindustrial civilizations. These civilizations were the source of great achievements in philosophy, religion, the arts, astronomy, mathematics, and architecture. Would these achievements have been possible without the use of slave labor? If not, do these achievements justify slavery in the ancient world?

5. Are there any modern occupations that have some or all of the characteristics of medieval craft guilds? Why have they persisted? How have they been able to do so? Who has benefited from their persistence?

Notes

1. Gerhard Lenski and Patrick Nolan, *Human Societies: An Introduction to Macrosociology* (Boulder, CO: Paradigm, 2004), 118, Table 6.2.

2. Francesca Bray, *Technology and Gender: Fabrics of Power in Late Imperial China* (Berkeley: University of California Press, 1997), 5, 218–9.

3. Matthew Frye Jacobson, *Whiteness of a Different Color: European Immigrants and the Alchemy of Race* (Cambridge, MA: Harvard University Press, 1998).

4. William I. Thomas and Dorothy Thomas, *The Child in America,* 2nd ed. (New York: Knopf, 1929), 572.

5. Henri Mendras, *The Vanishing Peasant: Innovation and Change in French Agriculture,* trans. Jean Lerner (Cambridge: MIT Press, 1970), 76. Quoted in Louise A. Tilly and Joan Wallach Scott, *Women, Work, and Family* (New York: Holt, Rinehart, & Winston, 1978), 21.

6. Ruth Schwartz Cowan, *More Work for Mother: The Ironies of Household Technologies from the Open Hearth to the Microwave* (New York: Basic, 1983).

7. Krissah Williams, "Immigrants Sending $45 Billion Home," *Washington Post,* October 19, 2006, http://www.washingtonpost.com/wp-dyn/content/article/2006/10/18/AR2006101801756.html (accessed February 2, 2007).

8. According to the U.S. State Department, in 2001, as many as four million persons, most of them women and children, worked in slave-like conditions, many of them victims of the international sex trade. U.S. Department of State, "Trafficking in Persons Report," http://usgovinfo.about.com/gi/dynamic/offsite.htm?site=http://www.state.gov/g/tip/rls/tiprpt/2002/ (accessed May 11, 2007).

9. Yvon Garlan, *Slavery in Ancient Greece* (Ithaca, NY: Cornell University Press, 1988), 59–60.

10. David Herlihy, *Opera Muliebria: Women and Work in Medieval Europe* (New York: McGraw-Hill, 1990), 85.

11. Milton Meltzer, *Slavery: A World History* (New York: Da Capo, 1993), 221–2.

12. Melvin Kranzberg and Joseph Gies, *By the Sweat of Thy Brow: Work in the Western World* (New York: Putnam, 1975), 73.

13. Susan Mosher Stuard, "To Town to Serve: Urban Domestic Slavery in Medieval Ragusa," in *Women and Work in Preindustrial Europe,* ed. Barbara A. Hanawalt (Bloomington: Indiana University Press, 1986), 39–55.

14. Thomas Bender, *A Nation Among Nations: America's Place in World History* (New York: Hill & Wang, 2006), 45–60.

15. Meltzer, *Slavery,* 144.

16. *Politics* 1278, quoted in Alison Burford, *Craftsmen in Roman and Greek Society* (Ithaca, NY: Cornell University Press, 1972), 34.

17. Claude Mosse, *The Ancient World at Work* (New York: Norton, 1969), 45.

18. George De Vos, *Japan's Invisible Race: Caste in Culture and Personality* (Berkeley: University of California Press, 1966).

19. The word *caste* is not of Indian origin; it is derived from the Portuguese *casta,* which means "pure breed." The term generally used in India is *varna.*

20. Pauline Kolenda, *Caste in Contemporary India: Beyond Organic Solidarity* (Menlo Park, CA: Benjamin/Cummings, 1978), 29–32.

21. Ibid., 51–4.

22. Gideon Sjoberg, *The Preindustrial City: Past and Present* (New York: Free Press, 1960), 187.

23. Curt Tausky, *Work and Society: An Introduction to Industrial Sociology* (Itasca, IL: F. E. Peacock, 1984), 24.

24. Martha C. Howell, "Women, the Family Economy and Market Production," in Hanawalt, *Women and Work in Preindustrial Europe,* 200.

25. Tilly and Scott, *Women, Work, and Family,* 49.

26. Herlihy, *Opera Muliebria,* 96.

27. Ibid., 162.

28. Merry E. Wiesner, "Early Modern Midwifery: A Case Study," in Hanawalt, *Women and Work in Preindustrial Europe,* 94–113.

29. Daryl M. Hafter, "Women Who Wove in the Eighteenth-Century Silk Industry of Lyon," in *European Women and Preindustrial Craft,* ed. Daryl M. Hafter (Bloomington: Indiana University Press, 1995).

30. Kranzberg and Gies, *By the Sweat of Thy Brow,* 67.

31. Adriano Tilgher, *Homo Faber: Work Through the Ages* (1930; repr., Chicago: Henry Regnery, 1958), 39–41.

32. Mack Walker, "Hometowns and Guilds in Early Modern Germany," in *Work and Community in the West,* ed. Edward Shorter (New York: Harper & Row, 1973), 40–1.

33. Steven A. Epstein, *Wage Labor and Guilds in Medieval Europe* (Chapel Hill: University of North Carolina Press, 1991), 66–7.

34. Ibid., 76.

35. Ibid., 65.

36. Kranzberg and Gies, *By the Sweat of Thy Brow,* 69.

37. S. R. Epstein, "Craft Guilds, Apprenticeship, and Technological Change in Preindustrial Europe," *Journal of Economic History* 58, no. 3 (1998): 706.

38. Carlo M. Cipolla, *Before the Industrial Revolution: European Society and Economy,* 2nd ed. (New York: Norton, 1980), 295.

39. Adam Smith, *An Inquiry into the Nature and Causes of the Wealth of Nations,* ed. Edwin Cannan (1776; repr., London: Methuen, 1904), 136.

40. Pamela O. Long, "Invention, Secrecy, Theft: Meaning and Context in Late Medieval Technical Transmission," *History and Technology* 16 (2000): 223–41.

41. Epstein, "Craft Guilds," 690–1.

42. Ibid., 691.

3

Industrialization and Its Consequences

A s Chapter 1 noted, the Agricultural Revolution initiated massive changes in human life and work. In the centuries that followed, despite wars, religious upheavals, the rise and fall of ruling dynasties, and substantial population growth, the great majority of the world's population continued to earn a living in the same ways their ancestors had done for centuries, either by tilling the soil or engaging in small-scale handicrafts. Although technology advanced in fits and starts, a basic continuity in the way things were done prevailed. An 18th-century French peasant would find much that was familiar in the farm work performed during the early Middle Ages, and a contemporaneous shoemaker would feel right at home in a Roman workshop. Yet, within a relatively short space of time, many key aspects of work, technology, and economic organization were altered almost beyond recognition by another revolution.

The Industrial Revolution

The word *manufacture* literally means "production by hand," and it is an apt description of how things were made for thousands of years. Wielding simple tools and exercising considerable skill, artisans produced life's necessities and luxuries in small workshops, aided by family members and a few apprentices. This mode of work began to be radically transformed around the middle of the 18th century, first in Britain and then in many other parts of the world. The technological and organizational changes that were the basis of this transformation have been labeled the *Industrial Revolution*,[1] although the term is a bit misleading in that the word *revolution* implies a sudden, massive shift. The Industrial Revolution produced thoroughgoing economic and social changes, but these took many decades to unfold. Moreover, the Industrial Revolution did not represent a complete break with the past; radically new ways of doing things coexisted with traditional modes of production for a long time, and in fact, many preindustrial ways of doing things persist to this day. To note the most prominent example, despite many efforts to manufacture homes as though they were cars or washing machines, residential construction still largely proceeds through a series of craft operations.[2]

Although the Industrial Revolution was slow in unfolding and did not always mark a complete break with the past, it nonetheless embodied major changes in technology, work organization, labor processes, and economic relationships. In the technological realm, one of the signifying features of the Industrial Revolution was the large-scale use of external sources of energy. The Industrial Revolution is often identified with the development and use of steam power, but until the middle of the 19th century, the most common source of industrial power was flowing or falling water that acted on a wheel or turbine.[3] The steam engine, first used to pump water out of mines, was made substantially more efficient through the efforts of James Watt during the late 18th and early 19th centuries.[4] The development and utilization of new sources of power continued during the latter half of the 19th century, when what has been described as a Second Industrial Revolution was literally powered by electric motors and internal combustion engines.

These new sources of power were used to operate a host of mechanical devices that augmented or took the place of human labor. During the early phase of the Industrial Revolution, this occurred most prominently in the textile industry, where jennies for spinning thread and power looms for weaving displaced spinning and weaving by hand. Mechanization transformed many other industries; everything from pins to locomotives was made in large volumes through the use of innovative machinery.[5] At the same time, machine tools such as precision lathes and automatic milling machines made it possible to produce objects that would have been beyond the capability of the most skilled traditional craftsman.

These advanced modes of manufacture were located in a new kind of production locale, the factory. Before the Industrial Revolution, the largest productive enterprises were a small number of European shipyards that employed a few hundred workers at most. By the second half of the 19th century, the industrial landscape was dotted with textile mills, meatpacking plants, steel mills, shoe factories, and other productive enterprises that put large numbers of workers under one roof. By the end of the century, factory complexes employing thousands of workers had spread over large tracts of real estate in Britain, continental Europe, the United States, and other parts of the world.

In part, this shift to large-scale production was a consequence of the use of power sources such as water turbines and steam engines. According to standard accounts of industrialization, new sources of power influenced the scale of factory-based manufacture because large, capital-intensive pieces of equipment such as steam engines and water turbines were not well suited for supplying power to a multiplicity of small, independent enterprises. But this is not the whole story, as the linkage between the adoption of advanced power technologies and large-scale factory organization is not as solid as often has been assumed. The typical factory was a large structure where a complex of shafts and belts transmitted power from a central power source to dozens of individual machines, but there are intriguing instances of large steam engines powering clusters of decentralized, small-scale manufacturing enterprises. One such example was the Coventry ribbon-weaving industry, a collection of enterprises lined up in a row so that their looms could be powered by a single steam engine.[6] Similar examples could be found in the prototypical Industrial Revolution cities of Sheffield and Birmingham, where a multiplicity of small workshops made use of a single power source, and "Power to Let" signs notified artisans of the availability of steam power that was conveyed by transmission belts to each shop.[7]

At best, the technical requirements of new sources of power provide only one reason for the rise of the large factory. At least as important was the need to organize and supervise large numbers of workers who had no personal stake in effective and efficient factory production. One important consequence of the Industrial Revolution was the emergence of large numbers of wage workers, or proletarians, to use the term favored by Marxists. Unlike independent artisans of the preindustrial era, factory workers did not own the tools they worked with, the materials they transformed into finished products, or the buildings where the work was done. What they brought to the job was their ability to put in a day's work using whatever skills they might have, along with at least a grudging willingness to submit to supervision. For this, they received a wage that might not meet much more than their subsistence needs. Put simply, the majority of workers were treated as commodities with no personal stake in the enterprise that employed them. Further diminishing their motivation was the rural background of many workers, which made them disinclined to accept the rigid work schedules that were prominent features of these enterprises. In the factory, the clock ruled, enforcing a working day of 10 to 12 hours, six days a week.[8] Under these circumstances, close supervision was essential if workers were to perform their tasks adequately and at a sustained pace. Factories provided settings in which workers could be confined to clearly delimited spaces and kept under the watchful eyes of foremen and other managerial representatives of the owners of these enterprises.[9]

Capitalism and Market Economies

Gatherers and hunters, with their limited stock of personal possessions and their ethos of sharing, live in societies with little in the way of social differentiation other than age and gender. In contrast, agricultural societies usually contain definite class divisions that center on the possession of land or the lack of it. In preindustrial Europe, large landowners (including institutional bodies such as the Church) were at the summit of economic and political power, where they were able to strongly influence "high culture"—the literature, paintings, music, and architecture we associate with particular times and places. Land was not the only basis of wealth, of course; many agrarian societies had wealthy merchants who, in addition to profiting from trade, might acquire more wealth through their control of small-scale manufacturing enterprises. In this sense, they could be considered early capitalists, but in its purest form, capitalism is an economic system in which some individuals derive the bulk of their income through their ownership of productive assets such as mines, railroads, banks, and factories. Lacking ownership of these assets (which Marxists and others call "the means of production"), the great majority of the population have had to earn their livelihood by selling their labor to capitalists and receiving a wage or salary in return.

Industrialization greatly expanded this form of economic differentiation. Factories and other industrial enterprises supplanted land as the primary source of wealth and income, while large numbers of people earned their livelihood as employees of capitalist enterprises. Some individuals became members of the capitalist class through their own entrepreneurial efforts, while others did so by investing funds in a firm as a partner or stockholder. In both cases, a fair amount of risk was usually involved; enterprises could fail for many reasons, leaving entrepreneurs and investors in severe financial difficulties. But whether it was through skill, luck, or some combination of both, some industrial capitalists were able to amass wealth that rivaled or exceeded the holdings of the old, landed aristocracy.

Closely associated with the rise of capitalism, but distinct from it, was the extension and development of market economies. In considering the significance of market economies, it is well to begin by noting that there are only three fundamental ways of distributing goods and services. The first is through sharing relationships of the sort found in the !Kung San economy and society. Reciprocal sharing arrangements can be practical and effective forms of distribution in small communities with close and recurrent person-to-person interactions guided by well-accepted social norms. Economies encompassing thousands or even millions of individuals lack these attributes, and for much of human history, the distribution of goods and services was controlled by those who held positions of power; in other words, a "command economy" prevailed. Command over portions of the economy can be exercised by many different kinds of political actors—tribal chiefs, clan heads, tax collectors, or officials of modern planned economies.

The third mode of distribution, one based on market exchanges, is markedly different because it has no external sources of control or guidance. It is entirely self-regulating, guided by Adam Smith's famous "invisible hand."[10] All that a market requires is one set of individuals who supply goods or services and another set who wants these goods or services and has the ability to exchange something in return for them. In most cases, these transactions involve the transfer of money, but it is also possible to directly trade goods and services, a process known as barter.

Although we tend to think of market exchanges as involving the buying and selling of physical commodities, as we have just seen, there also can be markets for labor, and in fact, one of the key social and economic changes brought on by the Industrial Revolution entailed the expansion of labor markets. With the spread of industrial capitalism, relatively fewer workers earned their livelihood as independent artisans or peasant farmers locked into traditional economic arrangements with the owners of the land they tilled. In the place of these ancient arrangements, an increasing number of workers received a wage in return for the tasks they performed for their employers.

Wages and Working Conditions in the Industrial Revolution

Any discussion of labor markets and wage labor leads us to the inevitable question: did workers as a whole benefit from the spread of industrial capitalism? One important part of this question centers on workers' wages, an issue that has drawn opposing responses that often reflect particular political stances. Scholars influenced by Karl Marx have seen capitalism as an inherently exploitative system, one in which capitalist profits are extracted from the productive efforts of workers, whose low wages do not fairly compensate them for the work they perform. Others have taken the opposite position, arguing that capitalist industrialization, although uneven in its consequences, brought about a rise in incomes and living standards for the bulk of the working population.

Resolving this debate through a precise reckoning of industrialization's effects on its workers is a difficult task, one that has been marked by considerable controversy from the 19th century onward.[11] Regional variations, substantial differences between industrial sectors and between different categories of workers, varying levels of employment and unemployment, fluctuating prices for consumer goods, and a lack of comprehensive statistics on employment and prices all affect the ability of economic historians to precisely determine how the Industrial Revolution affected the industrial workforce's material standards of living.

As a starting point in evaluating the overall effects of the Industrial Revolution on workers' lives, it is important to remember that preindustrial life and labor were marked by poverty, periodic unemployment, physically exhausting work, and short life spans. The great majority of the population earned a living through agriculture, and rural life was anything but a bucolic idyll. Work had to be done in all kinds of weather for meager rewards. Many European countries experienced periodic crop failures, and widespread hunger and malnutrition were common even in places not marked by chronic famines. Unemployment also was endemic; according to one estimate, half the population of the English countryside prior to the Industrial Revolution were paupers with limited opportunities for full-time employment.[12]

Under these circumstances, industrialization created at least the potential for higher incomes and elevated living standards. Although per capita income in Britain grew at a slow pace during the early phase of industrialization, it still doubled over a 50-year span.[13] To be sure, not all this gain was shared equally. Workers on average benefited from higher wages after about 1820, but income inequality also increased until the late 1860s.[14] Not only did the income gap separating members of the working class from the middle and upper classes widen, the same thing happened with the remuneration of workers at the higher and lower reaches of the income scale.[15]

Although the benefits of industrialization were spread unevenly, for many workers, factory labor was the preferred alternative to traditional ways of making a living. Wages were appallingly low by today's standards, but industrialization also resulted in falling prices for manufactured goods, which meant an increase in real wages and higher levels of consumption. In addition to acquiring a few manufactured items, the typical industrial worker enjoyed a better diet. Higher nutritional standards and other improvements in material existence were reflected in demographic trends. Between the years 1780 and 1860, the British population "increased to an astonishing and unprecedented degree."[16] Much of that growth was the result of longer life spans and increases in fertility, a fair portion of which may be attributed to higher material standards of living. Despite crowding, poor sanitation, and excellent conditions for the spread of epidemic diseases, mortality rates even improved in the cities.[17]

While monetary incomes generally trended upward, industrial working conditions often were barely tolerable. Many writers have invoked William Blake's "dark, satanic mills" when describing factory life during the early phases of the Industrial Revolution, and in some ways, it is an apt description. Long working days and weeks were the norm, and operatives usually had to remain at their workstations at all times, except for brief meal breaks. Work was, for the most part, monotonous and physically demanding in the extreme, and industrial accidents were a frequent occurrence. Work and the people who performed it were strictly governed by foremen, who had direct responsibility for hiring and firing workers, as well as determining their rate of pay. Management practices were anything but subtle, as foremen made abundant use of profanity, threats, and physical abuse.[18] It also was a time when children were an important part of the labor force in many industries. Children as young as 6 were put to work oiling machines, replacing bobbins on spinning machines, and, in some extreme cases, pulling mine carts hundreds of feet below ground.

The abuses associated with the Industrial Revolution are undeniable, but not all of them can be attributed to industrialization or capitalist exploitation. Life was also being transformed by rapid urbanization. To take one important example, from 1760 to 1830, Manchester, a center of early industrialized textile production, grew more than tenfold, from 17,000 to 180,000 people.[19] Many of the hardships of the era were the result of severely overcrowded living conditions and an appalling lack of sanitation. Laissez-faire theories of governance prevailed, resulting in an unwillingness to address the strains brought on by rapid urbanization. Municipal governments were slow to deal with smoke and other sources of air pollution, unpaved streets, and massive quantities of sewage and refuse. Polluted water supplies were sources of epidemic diseases, and parks and open spaces were rare. Making matters worse were antiquated laws in some municipalities that assessed property taxes based on the number of windows in a building, adding interior gloom to skies polluted by smoke and soot.

Assessing the mixture of material progress and misery brought on by the Industrial Revolution is a difficult task; equally problematic is the effort to determine the effects of early industrialization on the working lives of early factory operatives. Factory work entailed a more regimented pace than farm work or traditional artisanal activities, and for some critics of the early industrialization, this along with rapid urbanization and other far-reaching social changes may have caused more distress than long hours and low wages.[20] But much of this is necessarily speculation, tinged with our tendency to project our own expectations onto people living in a different era. Not only is there a lack of solid evidence regarding how people felt about their working lives, even if there were, it would have to be compared with similar assessments of rural laborers and artisans, which are almost completely nonexistent. Even so, our inability to precisely assess the psychological consequences for workers during the Industrial Revolution does not mean that the topic should be abandoned altogether, and we will return to the issue of worker alienation, morale, and job satisfaction in subsequent chapters.

Women in the Industrial Revolution

One of the striking social changes that accompanied the Industrial Revolution was a significant movement of women into paid employment. This was not the same thing as an increase in the number of "working women." Women have always worked, but much of their work was performed in a household setting and was not done for a cash wage or salary. The Industrial Revolution gave women new wage-earning opportunities, especially in the textile industry. In some enterprises, as was the case with the early New England textile industry, the majority of the workforce was made up of young, unmarried women. The owners of many of these enterprises exhibited a paternalistic attitude regarding their employees. Young women workers were housed in company dormitories, where they were closely supervised but also provided with company-sponsored cultural activities such as lectures, plays, and musical performances.[21] Whether or not the women benefited from this early example of factory work is a debatable point. On one hand, they can be viewed as prototypical exploited workers; they typically worked 10 to 12 hours each day, six days a week, for low wages. On the other hand, most of them worked only a few years prior to getting married, and saving up for a dowry was often a prime motivation for taking on mill work. It also can be noted that their prior life had plenty of hardships; for many, putting in long hours in a textile mill might have been preferable to milking the cows before dawn in the middle of a New England winter.

The mill owners certainly profited from women workers, as their employment drove down the cost of labor.[22] In general, the low wages of women factory workers were often justified on the grounds that these workers were members of families headed by higher-earning men, so they did not have to depend on these wages for their subsistence.[23] Lower wages paid to women also reflected a gender-based division of labor that confined women to tasks that required less skill than the work done by men. Occupational segregation of this sort had much less to do with the inherent abilities of men and women than it did with male workers appropriating jobs that involved working with advanced equipment, leaving women to work with older, less productive technologies.[24]

Industrialization created new opportunities for women, but it also reflected and even reinforced gender-based divisions of labor. Paid employment gave women the potential for greater independence, a situation that was not always welcomed by the heads of their families or by contemporary social commentators.[25] And in most cases, whatever freedom women workers gained was short-lived; it has been estimated that half of them had married and left factory work by their mid-20s.[26]

In assessing the effects of the Industrial Revolution on women's work, it also has to be kept in mind that early industrialization did not create large

Photo 3.1   Power loom weaving of cotton cloth in a textile mill, 1834

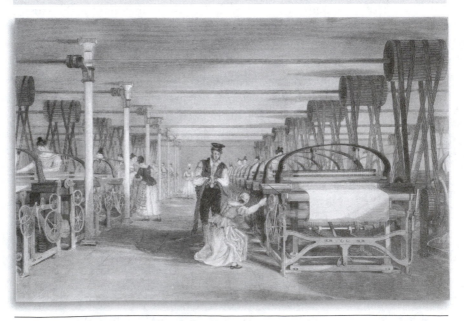

SOURCE: The Granger Collection, New York.

numbers of jobs for women. Household-based manufacture remained an important part of the national economy, where it continued to employ many women for the production of textiles and clothing.[27] And despite the growth of the mechanized textile industry and other industrial enterprises, far more women continued to be employed as domestic servants than worked as factory operatives. This, in fact, is an important clue regarding the willingness of women factory workers to put up with long hours and low wages: difficult and poorly paying though it was, many women preferred factory work to working as servants, which usually entailed subservience, submission to the whims of capricious masters, forced politeness, and even longer working hours.

Industrialization and Social Protest

One important consequence of the Industrial Revolution was the emergence of a distinct industrial working class.[28] Forged amid the hardships and dislocations of the era, working-class consciousness at times was manifested in organized social protest. One of the most prominent examples of worker militancy was the wave of machine smashing that took place in the early 1800s. This action was given the name "Luddism," which, according to one interpretation, took the name of Ned Ludlum, an apprentice who answered a foreman's reprimand by smashing the machine he operated.[29] Luddite attacks are often portrayed as attempts to prevent the spread of labor-replacing machines, but machine breaking also was an extreme example of collective protest against low wages and poor working conditions.

The Luddite movement was eventually put down through the deployment of large numbers of soldiers and the execution, imprisonment, and exile to Australian penal colonies of the movement's members and their leaders. Luddite protests were also dampened by the emergence of large industrial enterprises, which made it easier to unionize workers who could pursue their goals through less violent means. In some ways, however, the Luddite spirit was never completely extinguished, and as later chapters will indicate, concerns over deleterious consequences of technological advance are still very much with us.

Making Management "Scientific"

The Luddite movement and other militant actions by workers underscored the fact that the Industrial Revolution had created two new socioeconomic classes, factory workers and their employers. This division was at the core of Karl Marx's conceptualization of modern society, but one did not have to be a Marxist to recognize that conflicts between workers and their bosses seemed to be an inherent part of the social order. In today's terminology, the industrial economy and society was seen by many as a zero-sum game. That is, the gains of some individuals or groups were matched by the losses of other individuals or groups. This idea is an integral part of Marxist economics because profit comes from the extraction of "surplus value." As Marx saw it, workers' wages represented only a portion of the economic value that their labors had created; the rest was appropriated as profits by the capitalists who owned the factories they worked in.

Photo 3.2   English workers and Luddites smash looms in a factory during the riots of 1811–1816

SOURCE: The Granger Collection, New York.

Later chapters will cover worker remuneration today. For now, we will shift our attention to Frederick W. Taylor, whose ideas and practices stood in sharp contrast to Marx and others who viewed the industrial economy in zero-sum terms. Taylor was the scion of a well-to-do Philadelphia Quaker family who, after undergoing a health crisis while he was in college, went to work in a steel mill. Through a combination of work experience and self-study, he became a renowned engineer. He did pioneering work in the development of high-speed tools for cutting and shaping metal, and he created detailed charts to help machinists select procedures aimed at maximizing efficiency as they went about their tasks.

The industrial environment of the late 1800s and early 1900s was a turbulent one. Hostility between labor and management was often intense, as reflected in strikes that sometimes turned violent, industrial sabotage, or simply the tendency of workers to do as little as possible while on the job—a behavior that Taylor called "systematic soldiering." All of this could be avoided, thought Taylor, if both workers and employers adopted production methods that substantially improved productivity. In that way, both groups could each get a big slice of a large pie instead of endlessly arguing about how to cut up a small one.

Taylor had already shown how the application of scientific principles had increased production and productivity in machine shops. It seemed reasonable, then, that the use of these principles could effect improvements in worker output in general. The key research method employed by Taylor and his associates centered on "time-and-motion studies." These consisted of carefully observing the actions of workers, breaking them down into their basic constituents, and using a stopwatch to precisely time each action. Through these observations and measurements, Taylor determined that workers went about their jobs in a highly inefficient manner, which limited their output and, ultimately, the wages they received. It was, therefore, necessary for Taylor's experts, many of whom had a background in engineering, to determine the optimal way for them to go about their work. Every action was strictly programmed, even the timing and duration of rest breaks.

Some of the flavor of Taylor's approach can be sampled in his influential book, *The Principles of Scientific Management*. In it, Taylor presents a dialogue in which he first asks "Schmidt," an unskilled worker, if he is a "high-priced man"—that is, if he is worth $1.85 a day instead of the $1.15 he is currently earning. When Schmidt answers in the affirmative, Taylor responds,

"Of course you want $1.85 a day—everyone wants it. You know perfectly well that that has very little to do with your being a high-priced man. For goodness' sake answer my questions, and don't waste any more of my time. Now come over here. You see that pile of pig iron?"

"Yes"

"You see that car?"

"Yes."

"Well, if you are a high-priced man, you will load that pig iron on that car tomorrow for $1.85. Now do wake up and answer my question. Tell me whether you are a high-priced man or not."

"Vell—did I got $1.85 for loading dot pig iron on dot car tomorrow?"

"Yes, of course you do, and you get $1.85 for loading a pile like that every day right through the year. That is what a high-priced man does, and you know it just as well as I do."

"Vell, dot's all right. I could load dot pig iron on the car tomorrow for $1.85, and I get it every day, don't I?"

"Certainly you do—certainly you do."

"Vell, den, I vas a high-priced man."

"Now, hold on, hold on. You know just as well as I do that a high-priced man has to do exactly as he's told from morning to night. You have seen this man before, haven't you?"

"No, I never saw him."

"Well, if you are a high-priced man, you will do exactly as this man tells you tomorrow, from morning till night. When he tells you to pick up a pig and walk, you pick it up, and you walk, and when he tells you to sit down and rest, you sit down. You do that right straight through the day. And what's more, no back talk. Do you understand that? When this man tells you to walk, you walk; when he tells you to sit down, you sit down, and you don't talk back at him. Now you come on to work here to-morrow and I'll know whether you are really a high-priced man or not."[30]

According to Taylor, this condescending conversation had its intended effect. Expertly guided by one of Taylor's associates, Schmidt went from carrying 12½ tons of pig iron a day to 47½ tons, and he received his promised $1.85 daily wage. Accomplishments such as these, Taylor claimed, could be used to increase productivity and output in many other industries. Even more generally, the principles of Scientific Management could be

applied with equal force to all social activities: to the management of our homes; the management of our farms; the management of the business of our tradesmen large and small; of our churches; of our philanthropic organizations, our universities; and our governmental departments.[31]

Scientific Management was a potent intellectual force during the late 19th and early 20th centuries. Even in the newly founded Soviet Union, no less a personage than Vladimir Lenin expressed the belief that

the possibility of building Socialism will be determined precisely by our success in combining Soviet government and the Soviet organization of administration with the modern achievements of capitalism. We must organize in Russia the study and teaching of the Taylor System and systematically try it out and adopt it to our purposes.[32]

As things turned out, Scientific Management did not meet expectations in the Soviet Union, the United States, or anywhere else. Part of the problem lay in the nature of the work to be done. Time-and-motion studies were reasonably easy to conduct for simple operations such as loading pig iron into a railroad car, but much more difficult when the tasks were more complex and variable. Even more important was the resistance Scientific Management engendered in the workplace. Most workers were understandably hostile to a managerial practice that strictly controlled all their activities. The promise of higher wages did not mitigate their hostility, for they feared—often with considerable justification—that improved productivity would cause management to adjust piece rates downward, leaving them no better off financially than before. Traditional managers were no less hostile to Scientific Management, because they were unwilling to share or even give up their authority to Taylor's expert minions.[33] Most foremen and other lower-level managers had come up from the ranks, and they were not eager to cede their territory to college-educated 20-somethings armed with stopwatches and clipboards.

The Assembly Line

Opposition from both workers and management resulted in Scientific Management being of more theoretical than practical significance. Far more important in changing the nature of industrial work were advances in manufacturing technologies. Whereas Taylor was concerned with getting workers to perform their tasks at peak levels of efficiency, others wanted to eliminate human labor altogether or, when that was not possible, to use technology to keep it under tight control.

The most significant of these new manufacturing technologies was the assembly line. Assembly lines are based on the idea that industrial operations can be performed more efficiently when workers stay in one place while the work comes to them. During the second half of the 19th century, several industries, such as biscuit making and food canning, began to use this technique. Perhaps the most notable example was found in an industry that employed a kind of "disassembly line": meatpacking in the American Midwest. A carcass was hung from an overhead conveyor, and as it moved down the line, workers would perform all the operations necessary for converting a recently slaughtered animal into particular cuts of meat and other products. Some workers removed sections of the hide, other workers cut off various body parts, and others extracted the internal organs, so not much was left by the time the carcass literally reached the end of the line.

One industrialist who said he took his inspiration from this procedure was Henry Ford. A pioneer manufacturer of automobiles, Ford was determined to cut production costs to the point where automobiles would be in the financial reach of what he called "the great multitude." In part, he was able to achieve this goal by engineering a car, the legendary Model T, to be light and simple yet durable, reliable, and capable of carrying four passengers at a reasonable rate of speed (35 mph) over the miserable roads of the time. But he also was determined to make manufacturing more efficient. In part, this was realized by making components to precise standards so that they could be immediately put in place with no need for filing, scraping, or reaming. The Model T's basic design also remained largely unchanged from year to year so that the costs of retooling could be kept low. But Ford's key cost-cutting innovation was the assembly line. In 1913, Ford and his associates laid out a line for the assembly of a part of the magneto, the electrical component that energizes the spark that ignites the air-fuel mixture in the engine's combustion chamber. The first assembly line did not use a moving conveyor; the magneto part was simply slid along rails from one workstation to another. Even so, the improvement was substantial; under the old procedure, one worker could do the complete operation in 18 minutes. After the process had been subdivided into a number of simple operations, only 13 man-minutes were required, and after a moving line was installed, the figure fell to 5 minutes.[34] So successful was this experiment that within a year, the whole car was being put together on an assembly line. The time required to produce an engine was cut in two, from 12 hours to 6, while the time to assemble a chassis went from 12½ hours to 1 hour and 33 minutes.[35] Many refinements of assembly-line production ensued, and by the early 1920s, productivity gains had pushed the price of a new Model T runabout down to $290, and half the cars on America's roads were Ford "Flivvers."

Photo 3.3   Postcard of Ford Motor Company's River Rouge plant

An Assembly Line
of the
Ford Motor Company

SOURCE: ©Rykoff Collection/CORBIS.

While it promoted economical and efficient manufacturing, the assembly line extracted a severe toll on the workers who manned it. The pace of work was relentless, the monotony of doing the same operation over and over was deadening, and noise was pervasive. It was all too much for most workers, as was reflected in a turnover rate of 370 percent in 1913. So bad were working conditions at Ford that 71 percent of new hires quit after fewer than five days on the job. Employee turnover of this magnitude took its toll on the bottom line; although much of the work had low skill requirements, Ford still incurred substantial costs in hiring, deploying, and training new workers.

Ford's response was not to make assembly operations less physically and psychologically taxing but to make the work sufficiently rewarding financially that the workers would put up with just about anything. In 1914, Ford announced his intention to pay his workers at the rate of $5 a day, a stupendous sum at the time, about double the going rate for unskilled manufacturing labor. The $5 a day wage had its intended results; prospective workers poured into the Ford manufacturing complex, and once hired, the majority stayed on the job. As an added bonus, Henry Ford was hailed as a great benefactor of American workers. As subsequent events would show, however, this reputation would fall wide of the mark as wages fell relative to the cost of living and as Ford showed himself to be an implacable foe of unionization.

In some respects, the productive innovations that culminated with the assembly line represented a continuation of a long historical process. From the 18th century onward, industrial operations had been accompanied by the modes of work that were faster paced, more rigidly controlled, and more divorced from other aspects of life than had been the case with traditional farming and artisan work. Yet for many contemporary observers, oppressive working conditions in industry were the inevitable consequence of mechanized production. Even Friedrich Engels, a staunch supporter of working men and women and the coauthor with Karl Marx of *The Communist Manifesto*, argued that tight discipline and strict managerial authority were essential elements of industrial production, no matter who the owners might be:

> If man, by dint of his knowledge and inventive genius has subdued the forces of nature, the latter avenge themselves upon him by subjecting him, in so far as he employs them, to a veritable despotism independent of all social organization. Wanting to abolish authority in large-scale industry is tantamount to wanting to abolish industry itself, to destroy the power loom in order to return to the spinning wheel.[36]

Engels's views can be characterized as a version of technological determinism, the belief that technology acts as an independent source of social change and resultant economic structures. It is a belief that has fallen out of favor with historians and sociologists, but there can be no denying that the kinds of technologies used on the job will have a significant influence on the way work is done, how it is organized, and the working lives of the people who use it. The Industrial Revolution was the scene of fundamental changes in technology, work organization, remuneration, and working conditions. We will return to these interrelated topics in some of the pages to come.

A Postindustrial Revolution?

The key technologies in the opening phase of the Industrial Revolution were water and steam power; machinery for carding, spinning, and weaving; rail and canal transportation; and innovative processes for the large-scale production of iron and steel. Toward the end of the 19th century, a new set of technologies began to propel what has been described as the Second Industrial Revolution. Again, the ability to make use of new sources of energy was crucial. The internal combustion engine invented in Germany by Nicolaus Otto in 1876 began to compete with the steam engine as a more compact and efficient source of industrial power before it became the standard automotive power plant.

Of even greater importance to industry was the use of electricity to power a variety of industrial processes. In addition to serving as a new source of power, electricity allowed the layout of factories to be more flexible and efficient because individual machines could be run by their own electric motors, obviating the need for complex power transmission systems that were difficult to change once they were in place. When complemented by new ways of organizing and scheduling work, such as the assembly line, the result was a massive increase in productivity, whether reckoned in terms of output per worker or output per unit of capital. By the early 20th century, the first and second industrial revolutions had transformed the economies of many nations and fundamentally changed the nature of employment and work. At the same time, advancing productivity provided the underpinnings for levels of material prosperity that would have been inconceivable a century ago.

But nothing in modern economic life stands still for long. While industrialization was changing the economic and social landscape during the 19th and 20th centuries, another revolution was under way, one that continues to this day. To understand the nature of this revolution, we need to go back to preindustrial times, when agriculture was the dominant means of making a living, typically employing the great majority of the workforce. The primacy of agriculture as a source of employment began to diminish as industrialization created large numbers of new jobs outside the farm sector. In addition to shrinking in relative terms, the agricultural workforce also declined in absolute terms as mechanization and other technological advances eliminated the need for a great amount of human labor. All these changes took place amid population increases that, had it not been for industrialization, would have produced even more unemployment than is usually found in agrarian societies.

During the early years of the Industrial Revolution in Britain, rising farm output kept up with population growth, although food supplies were squeezed as a result of the war with France that occupied the early years of the 19th century.[37] Over the long run, industrialization pushed agricultural production to much greater heights as chemical fertilizers, pesticides, herbicides, irrigation pumps, and farm machinery greatly expanded crop yields on existing acreage. These technologies also eliminated the need for a great deal of farm labor so that, by the middle of the 20th century, many developed countries were able to feed large and growing populations and export substantial surpluses, even as the number of farmers and other agricultural workers had dropped to fewer than 5 percent of the total workforce.

The same pattern eventually emerged in the industrial sector. Improved manufacturing processes, along with the new sources of energy to power them, steadily boosted worker productivity. Where a single preindustrial artisan may have been able to produce a few shoes, ceramic pots, or bolts of cloth a week, the technological and organizational changes associated with industrialization increased output per worker many times over. Higher levels of productivity allowed people to obtain vast quantities of material possessions, but consumer spending didn't stop there. In addition to acquiring cars, domestic appliances, clothing, sporting goods, and all the other products of industry, people were devoting increasing shares of their incomes to services.

Sometimes referred to as the "tertiary sector" (agriculture and raw materials extraction compose the "primary" sector, and manufacturing occupies the "secondary" sector), the service sector encompasses an enormous variety of activities and occupations. Service sector outputs have been facetiously referred to as "anything that you can't drop on your toe" because they are not tangible products like a bushel of wheat or a DVD player. Included within the service sector are medical care, education, transportation, entertainment, government, and a lot more. A service sector "product" can be something as simple and inexpensive as a haircut or as complex and costly as a medical school education.

The relative decline of manufacturing and the growth of the service sector in a modern economy can be seen in changing employment statistics. In 1950, manufacturing, construction, agriculture, and raw materials extraction employed 20,512,000 workers in the United States, while 28,215,000 men and women were employed in transportation, trade, finance, education, healthcare, and other services. By 2008, after the addition of more than 102,000,000 workers, the figures were 23,461,000 and 116,452,000, respectively.[38] In 1950, the United States had the world's most productive manufacturing sector, yet its importance as a source of jobs was eroding. In that year, it employed 15,241,000 workers. By 2008, the number of manufacturing workers had dropped to 13,431,200; during the same span of time, the service sector added nearly 90 million positions.[39] Even these figures underestimate the importance of the service sector because many workers included in the manufacturing sector are actually supplying a service of some sort. For example, an attorney or an accountant employed by General Motors is counted as a manufacturing employee, even though he or she has nothing to do with the actual manufacture of cars.

The reasons for the relative decline of employment in the primary and secondary sectors can be largely attributed to two factors: productivity improvements and the economic changes that fall under the term *globalization*. Technological advance has been the main force propelling productivity improvements, but also contributing have been higher worker skills, more effective organization and management, and a better-educated workforce. The roles of technology and globalization in altering the structure of the economy and the jobs it provides are complex and will be covered in Chapters 5 and 6.

In aggregate, the erosion of jobs in the manufacturing sector has been more than offset by increased numbers of jobs in the service sector. But aggregate changes are not always reflected in the fates of individual workers, and while many displaced manufacturing workers have found work in one of the service occupations, limitations of training and skills have prevented many of them from moving into well-paying segments of this sector. Today, matching workers to the needs of a changing economy is a serious economic and social problem, one that will be revisited on several occasions in the chapters to come.

As we have seen in this and in the first chapter, working lives have undergone enormous changes from Paleolithic times to today's postindustrial society. Still, some basic themes remain. Gender and other ascribed statuses continue to be strong influences on the occupations that people assume. Technological change remains a major force shaping the evolution of work and occupations, but it does not occur in an economic and political vacuum. Economic divisions, along with conflicts between workers and management, are intertwined with the choice and application of technologies and many other aspects of work as well. On a personal level, we still find ourselves wondering how our work fits into the totality of our lives. These and many other topics will be explored in the following chapters, but first we need to take a closer look at the organizational structures and processes that emerged during the Industrial Revolution and how they are changing today.

FOR DISCUSSION

1. One of the key features of industrialization has been the increasing size of productive enterprises. Could a multitude of small enterprises have produced the same results? Would such a pattern of industrialization have resulted in better working environments with no loss of efficiency?

2. Many poor countries have embraced industrialization as the primary way to elevate living standards. Are they correct in this belief? Are there any other ways to pursue economic development other than through industrialization?

3. Karl Marx believed there was an inherent and irreconcilable conflict between capital and labor, whereas Frederick W. Taylor held to the opposite belief. With which side are you inclined to agree? Has contemporary capitalism changed to such a degree that the perspectives of both Marx and Taylor are no longer relevant?

4. Does there seem to be anything "unnatural" about an economy where the great majority of workers are not directly engaged in the making of a tangible product? Is an economy strongly oriented to the provision of services sustainable over a long period of time?

5. According to critics, industrialization has brought many benefits to humanity, but an industrial economy's enormous appetite for energy and raw materials makes it unsustainable in the long run. Do you agree? What sort of changes need to be made so that industrial production can be maintained in the future?

Notes

1. The term *Industrial Revolution* was coined by the revolutionary activist Louis Aguste Blanqui in 1837 and popularized by Arnold Toynbee in the late 19th century. See his *Lectures on the Industrial Revolution in England* (London: Rivingtons, 1884).

2. Arthur L. Stinchcombe, "Social Structure and Organization," in *Handbook of Organizations*, ed. James G. March (Chicago: Rand McNally, 1965), 153–4.

3. Richard L. Hills, *Power in the Industrial Revolution* (Manchester, England: Manchester University Press, 1970).

4. D. S. L. Cardwell, *Steam Power in the Eighteenth Century: A Case Study in the Application of Science* (London: Sheed & Ward, 1963).

5. Brooke Hindle and Steven Lubar, *Engines of Change: The American Industrial Revolution 1790–1860* (Washington, DC: Smithsonian Institution Press, 1986).

6. Malcolm I. Thomis, *The Town Laborer and the Industrial Revolution* (New York: Harper & Row, 1974), 108–9.

7. Charles F. Sabel, *Work and Politics: The Division of Labor in Industry* (Cambridge, UK: Cambridge University Press, 1985), 46–7.

8. N. L. Trantner, "The Labor Supply 1780–1860," in *The Economic History of Britain Since 1700: Vol. 1. 1700–1860*, eds. Roderick Floud and Donald McCloskey (Cambridge, UK: Cambridge University Press, 1981), 218–22.

9. Lindy Biggs, *The Rational Factory: Architecture, Technology, and Work in America's Age of Mass Production* (Baltimore: Johns Hopkins University Press, 1996).

10. Adam Smith, *An Inquiry Into the Nature and Causes of the Wealth of Nations* (1776; repr., Oxford, UK: Clarendon, 1976).

11. R. M. Hartwell, *The Industrial Revolution and Economic Growth* (London: Methuen, 1971), 81–105.

12. Thomis, *Town Laborer*, 147.

13. Hartwell, *Industrial Revolution*, 165.

14. Jeffrey Williamson, *Did British Industrialization Breed Inequality?* (Boston: Allen & Unwin, 1985), 64–9.

15. Ibid., 15.

16. D. N. McCloskey, "The Industrial Revolution 1780–1860: A Survey," in Floud and McCloskey, *The Economic History of Britain Since 1700*, 105.

17. Pat Hudson, *The Industrial Revolution* (London: Edward Arnold, 1992), 149–50.

18. Sanford M. Jacoby, "The Way It Was: Factory Labor Before 1915," in *Working in America: Continuity, Conflict, and Change,* ed. Amy S. Wharton (Boston: McGraw-Hill, 2002), 16–20.

19. Thomis, *Town Laborer,* 48.

20. P. K. O'Brien and S. L. Engerman, "Changes in Income and Its Distribution During the Industrial Revolution," in Floud and McCloskey, *The Economic History of Britain Since 1700,* 180–1.

21. Thomas Dublin, *Women at Work: The Transformation of Work and Community in Lowell, Massachusetts 1826–1860* (New York: Columbia University Press, 1979).

22. Hudson, *Industrial Revolution,* 161–2.

23. Deborah Valenze, *The First Industrial Woman* (New York: Oxford University Press, 1995), 89.

24. Hudson, *Industrial Revolution,* 228–9.

25. Ivy Pinchbeck, *Women Workers and the Industrial Revolution 1750–1850* (London: Routledge, 1930), 313–4.

26. M. E. Rose, "Social Change and the Industrial Revolution," in Floud and McCloskey, *The Economic History of Britain Since 1700,* 265–6.

27. Louise A. Tilly and Joan W. Scott, *Women, Work, and Family* (New York: Holt, Rinehart & Winston, 1978), 104–5.

28. E. P. Thompson, *The Making of the English Working Class* (New York: Random House, 1963).

29. Malcolm I. Thomis, *The Luddites: Machinery Breaking in Regency England* (New York: Schocken, 1972).

30. Frederick Winslow Taylor, *The Principles of Scientific Management* (1911; repr., New York: Norton, 1967), 44–6.

31. Quoted in Samuel Florman, *The Existential Pleasures of Engineering* (New York: St. Martin's, 1976), 8.

32. V. I. Lenin, "The Immediate Tasks of the Soviet Government," *Izvestia,* April 28, 1918. Translated in V. I. Lenin, *Selected Works,* vol. 2 (Moscow: Foreign Languages Publishing House, 1947), 327.

33. Daniel Nelson, *Managers and Workers: Origins of the New Factory System in the United States, 1880–1920* (Madison: University of Wisconsin Press, 1975), 75–6.

34. James R. Bright, "The Development of Automation," in *Technology in Western Civilization,* vol. 2, eds. Melvin Kranzberg and Carroll W. Purcell Jr. (New York: Oxford University Press, 1967), 648; David A. Hounshell, *From the American System to Mass Production: The Development of Manufacturing Technology in the United States* (Baltimore: Johns Hopkins University Press, 1984), 247–8.

35. John B. Rae, "The Rationalization of Production," in Kranzberg and Purcell *Technology in Western Civilization,* 45–6.

36. Friedrich Engels, "On Authority," in *Selected Works,* Karl Marx and Friedrich Engels (Moscow: Foreign Languages Publishing House, 1962), 637.

37. Hartwell, *Industrial Revolution,* 356–60.

38. Bureau of Labor Statistics, "Employment by Major Industry Sector," http://www.bls.gov/emp/ep_table_201.htm (accessed July 26, 2010).

39. U.S. Bureau of the Census, "Nonfarm Establishments: Employees, Hours, and Earnings by Industry: 1919 to 2002," http://www.census.gov/statab/hist/02HS0031.xls (accessed August 20, 2010).

4   Bureaucratic Organization

Although modern societies are for the most part lacking in castes, guilds, and other socially embedded ways of recruiting, training, and organizing workers, it is still the case that personal connections and social networks are highly relevant to many aspects of working life. In a parallel fashion, the rules and procedures governing the way particular kinds of work are done may simply reflect longstanding customs, even when they may not be effective or efficient. In today's world, however, a great many aspects of work organization are governed by a markedly different approach, one that is encompassed by the term *bureaucracy*. At first glance, this hardly seems like a progressive step, as bureaucracies are often thought to be collections of semicompetent plodders hopelessly ensnarled in red tape. As we shall see, there is some truth to this stereotype, but bureaucracies have a number of positive features, and for many kinds of work, their virtues far outweigh their vices.

The Rise of Bureaucratic Organization

Bureaucracies have been around for a long time. They were an essential feature of preindustrial empires such as Rome and dynastic China. In both cases, much of the extension and endurance of these empires can be attributed to the development and use of effective bureaucracies.[1] These administrative bodies were staffed by functionaries charged with the governance of territories hundreds or even thousands of miles distant from the empire's capital. In these far-flung realms, bureaucratic tasks and responsibilities were limited in number. Above all, preindustrial governments had to defend their territories from external enemies (often disparaged as "barbarians") seeking land and plunder. The control of their own populations was another priority, as domestic rebellions were regular features of imperial domains. Then, as now, defense was expensive business, and the maintenance of an empire rested to a considerable degree on the ability of the bureaucracy to collect taxes from the empire's subjects. Taxes also provided much of the financial support for the art, architecture, literature, and philosophy that remain as enduring cultural legacies of long-gone civilizations. Taxes were no more popular then than they are today, and they were a major source of tension between the government's bureaucrats and its subjects. Still, they were and are a necessary evil; as former Justice of the United States Supreme Court Oliver Wendell Holmes Jr. (1841–1935) has admonished us, "Taxes are the price we pay for civilization."

Along with maintaining order and collecting taxes, preindustrial bureaucracies occasionally involved themselves in economic activities. Their efforts were generally not oriented to the economic development of the realm. The chief incentive was the opportunity to reap monopoly profits through government control of important industries such as salt production and distribution. But direct government involvement in the economy was limited, and most of an empire's work was done on farms and in workshops staffed by family members and slaves, using traditional modes of organization. As noted in Chapter 2, these organizations were small in scale and were staffed on the basis of ascribed roles or apprenticeships that mimicked family relationships.

In addition to imperial governments, complex bureaucratic structures could be found in the realm of religion. Some of the success of the early Christian church can be attributed to its effective adaptation of Roman organizational principles. At the same time, however, many of the world's great and enduring religions—notably Hinduism, Buddhism, and Islam—have thrived for centuries with much looser organizational structures. Today, many religions struggle to achieve a balance between spontaneous spirituality and the routinization and formalization typical of bureaucratic administration.

Bureaucratic organization began to spread from a few political and religious domains into private enterprise as economies became larger and more complex. By the second half of the 19th century, the scope of management had been significantly enlarged, as some industrial enterprises employed hundreds or even thousands of workers. At the same time, advancing technologies were creating a host of new occupational specialists. Coordinating the activities of large numbers of specialized workers posed new organizational challenges. While the size and complexity of enterprises were increasing, improvements in transportation expanded the territory served by many of these enterprises, creating more administrative difficulties.[2]

These changes in enterprise scale and scope necessitated heavy infusions of bureaucratic organization. Businesses ranging from steel mills to department stores needed new ways to coordinate the actions of hundreds of workers, to precisely schedule their work activities, and in general to keep things moving along in a smooth and predictable manner. Firms also were faced with the need to train and supervise a multitude of new workers, many of them from rural areas or foreign lands, who had been thrust into the new industrial environment.

While economic and social change was creating new challenges, it also was supplying a set of tools to address them. First railroads and then automobiles allowed administrators and managers to travel to widely diffused organizational units with relative ease, while new communications technologies—everything from telephones and typewriters to lowly carbon paper—made it possible to supervise and coordinate the activities of large numbers of employees.[3] These technologies complemented new ways of organizing enterprises and their constituent workplaces. By the beginning of the 20th century, an organizational revolution was well under way, and bureaucratization was transforming the organization of work.

The Elements of Bureaucratic Organization

In delineating the key features of bureaucracy, it is useful to begin with what the German sociologist Max Weber (1864–1920) referred to as "an ideal type." This is a mental construct that delineates the key features of a social phenomenon that may not entirely correspond to real-world situations. One such phenomenon is bureaucracy. In analyzing bureaucratic organization, Weber delineated the essential elements of bureaucratic organization while being fully aware that actual, functioning bureaucracies only partially conformed to his ideal-typical schema.[4]

In addition to presenting the major components of bureaucratic organization, Weber devoted considerable attention to the cultural values and modes of thought that gave rise to modern bureaucracies. Bureaucratic structures and processes reflected what Weber took to be the dominant cognitive orientation of modern societies: rationality. *Rationality*, of course, is a loaded word with a multiplicity of meanings, so it is important to be clear on what Weber meant by it and how it related to bureaucratic organization. At the most general level, Weber saw rational thought patterns as a prime element of a historical process that he called "the disenchantment of the world." By this, he meant the ability and willingness to explain the causes of events without invoking supernatural agents. When imbued with a rational approach to the world, people no longer conjured up devils, ghosts, and goblins in order to explain worldly phenomena. Instead, logic and empiricism were the primary sources of understanding why things happened as they did. For example, a rational approach to the avoidance of famines would not attribute crop failures to the actions of malevolent spirits but would look for the presence of plant diseases and other material causes of these problems.

Weber saw rationality as crucial to the design and operation of modern organizations because this mode of thought provided the most effective and efficient way of attaining particular goals. At this point, however, it is important to note that the goals pursued by a person or an organization may not themselves be the result of rational thought. Rationally designed structures and processes can be used to achieve goals that defy rational comprehension; as Captain Ahab in *Moby Dick* said of his pursuit of the great white whale, "All my means are sane, my motive and my object mad."[5] Equally important, rationality can serve goals that are not just irrational but are unethical, immoral, and criminal as well. History has provided us with plenty of examples of rationality being used for barbaric ends, Nazi Germany being a particularly repellent case.

Weber recognized the difference between the application of rationality to means and to ends with his distinction between "formal" and "substantive" rationality. The latter referred to the rational use of means to achieve goals that were in accordance with a society's ethical values, whereas the former was more restricted, being concerned with quantitative calculation and accounting in the service of the economy and its individual components.[6] What was missing in Weber's distinction, however, was the recognition that the ethical standards of some societies may not be in accordance with humane values. Again, the case of Nazi Germany, which emerged a little more than a decade after Weber's death, provides a ghastly example.

When applied to the description and analysis of bureaucratic organizations, rationality is embodied in the way an organization has been put together and the manner in which its members go about their work. From this perspective, modern bureaucracies are best conceived not as "rational organizations" but as organizations with structures and procedures that reflect an effort to use appropriate means for the achievement of specific ends.[7] Of all the types of organizations, Weber viewed bureaucracies as the most efficient, effective, and predictable; as he put it, "The fully bureaucratic mechanism compares with other organizations exactly as does the machine with nonmechanical modes of production."[8]

Photo 4.1   Organization charts indicate the hierarchical nature of bureaucracies.

SOURCE: ©Stefan Klein/iStockphoto.

Modern bureaucracies exhibit specific structural and procedural features that contribute to effective and efficient goal attainment. In the first place, bureaucracies are characterized by *impersonality*. This, of course, is a quality that often infuriates people when they deal with bureaucracies—"they treat you like a number, not a person." But this unpleasant reality is only part of a larger picture. Bureaucratic impersonality also means that everyone is supposed to be treated equally. Race, gender, ethnicity, and other ascribed characteristics should have no bearing on one's interaction with a bureaucracy and the outcomes it produces. Ascribed characteristics are also irrelevant when it comes to filling positions within the bureaucracy. In direct opposition to working arrangements based on ascribed statuses, bureaucracies are staffed by workers who are chosen according to their ability to perform the tasks assigned to them, or at least their capacity to learn to do these tasks. Another common feature of bureaucracies, therefore, is a formal recruiting process. In traditional China, officials (often referred to in the West as "mandarins") were selected on the basis of their performance in official examinations that tested their knowledge of the Confucian classics.[9] Absorption of Confucian ideals gave these officials a common cultural mooring, but it had limited practical application to the actual performance of their duties. In modern societies, government bureaucracies generally employ civil service examinations to recruit new employees, and many private organizations use job-specific tests for the same purpose. In similar fashion, promotion is supposed to be based on objective assessments of performance and not on attributes that have nothing to do with getting the work done. In short, bureaucratic impersonality, coupled with the use of rationally derived procedures, produces a "meritocracy" in which positions are staffed and jobs are done in accordance with the employees' capabilities.

An emphasis on merit and expertise of some sort also ties in with another key characteristic of bureaucratic organization, an elaborate division of labor. Unlike societies based on gathering and hunting or traditional farming, industrial societies have a great variety of occupational specialties. The *Dictionary of Occupational Titles*, compiled by the U.S. Bureau of the Census, lists 842 occupational categories, encompassing 30,000 distinct job titles such as "emulsification operator," "welt trimmer," and "pickling grader."[10] A single organization may have dozens or even hundreds of specialized job titles. At the organizational level, these specialized tasks are often incorporated into formal roles that define an employee's area of responsibility. These roles are in turn governed by specific rules that set out what should and should not be done by the person holding down that role.

Beginning with Adam Smith in the 18th century, many observers have noted that the division of labor into a number of specialized tasks has been a major source of economic and technological dynamism. In a famous passage, Adam Smith wrote about the benefits of the division of labor in the manufacture of a simple product, pins. Instead of a single worker performing all the necessary operations, one worker cut wire into segments, another sharpened a point on them, another soldered a head to the shaft, and so on, for a total of 18 separate operations. Dividing up the tasks allowed workers to develop specialized skills and to work at a regular, uninterrupted pace, while at the same time inspiring the invention of specialized machinery "which facilitate and abridge labor, and allow one man to do the work of many."[11]

The benefits of the division of labor also were highlighted by a 20th-century economist, John Kenneth Galbraith, who took the analysis well beyond the manufacture of pins. According to Galbraith, much of the dynamism of the modern world could be attributed to the advance of science and technology, which in turn resulted from "taking ordinary men, informing them narrowly and deeply and then, through appropriate organization, arranging to have their knowledge combined with that of other specialized but equally ordinary men."[12]

As Galbraith implied, specialization creates the need for coordination. Bureaucracies bring order out of potential chaos in two ways. The first of these is what people tend to think of when they hear the word *bureaucracy*: rules, regulations, and strict procedures. All bureaucracies make abundant use of explicit and implicit Standard Operating Procedures to guide and control the activities of their employees. This, of course, can be another source of frustration when dealing with a bureaucracy because there may be situations not covered by existing rules, or the rules may be of dubious appropriateness. But even more frustrations, as well as endless opportunities for corruption and abuse, would ensue if the members of an organization simply made decisions on the basis of personal connections or individual whims.

Along with the use of formal roles and rules, bureaucratic organizations coordinate the work of their members through another property that is distasteful to many: hierarchical authority. The structures of most bureaucratic organizations can be (and usually are) depicted in an organization chart that puts every position at a hierarchical level that clearly indicates who is subordinate or superordinate to whom. In addition to aiding in the coordination of work, organizational hierarchies serve a number of other functions, such as delineating responsibilities and motivating workers by holding out the prospect of promotion. Organizational hierarchies are especially prominent in military and paramilitary organizations such as police forces, where observing rules and obeying orders issued by superiors are of paramount importance. Other kinds of organizations can get by with more egalitarian structures, but some degree of hierarchical ranking will be found in all bureaucratic organizations.

A final characteristic of bureaucratic organizations is their extensive use of, and reliance on, written records. It is no coincidence that the first extensive government bureaucracies emerged in Egypt, Babylonia, and China, places where written languages were first created and developed. As a practical matter, written records are essential for the preservation and dissemination of rules, regulations, and operating procedures, along with essential documents such as contracts, tax records, and voter registrations. What began thousands of years ago with the first scratchings on clay tablets continues to a greatly magnified degree today, as modern information and communications technologies such as computerized databases and e-mail have extended the reach and potency of the written word.

At this point, many readers are probably thinking that this discussion of bureaucracy is seriously divorced from reality as they have experienced it. And they are right—not only do bureaucracies in the real world often depart from the above principles, but the imputation that they are the embodiment of rationality seems quite a stretch. Here we will again simply note that an ideal-type presentation of bureaucracy is only a starting point for further analysis, just as a mathematical description of the acceleration of a falling body has to first set aside the effects of air resistance in order to derive the formula for determining the rate at which the body gains speed. There are several places in this book where real-world organizational structures and procedures and their consequences for the way work is done will be presented, along with the reasons for their departure from ideal-type bureaucracies. As a starting point, we need to consider which kinds of work environments are well suited to bureaucratic modes of organization and which are not.

Where Bureaucracy Works and Where It Doesn't

By now it should be apparent that *bureaucracy* and *bureaucrat* are not simply terms of abuse. Bureaucratic organization has some real strengths, but these are evident only under certain circumstances; when situations are different, bureaucracy's virtues can become its vices. Above all, bureaucracies are most effective when the tasks performed by their members can be reduced to routines. In turn, routines and the application of unambiguous rules allow the employment of workers who are not expected to demonstrate much in the way of creativity, innovation, or the ability to solve unique problems. All that is necessary is to efficiently and honestly follow formal procedures and see to it that established rules are applied.

We can see bureaucratic principles effectively operating in organizations such as a state department of motor vehicles. One of the primary tasks of the DMV is processing hundreds of thousands of vehicle registration applications every year. In quantitative terms, this is a daunting task, but it is greatly facilitated by reducing the process to a set of procedures governed by specific rules. For example, the cost of registering a car or truck is not negotiated for each vehicle, nor is the social and economic status of the vehicle's owner taken into consideration. Instead, a set fee is assessed on the basis of unambiguous criteria such as the weight or purchase price of a car or truck. Since the rules that govern the registration process have been established, all that is necessary is to figuratively—and in many cases literally—check the boxes in order to note if the owner's address has changed, proof of insurance has been submitted, and the required fee has been paid.

At the same time, however, many kinds of work are poorly suited to bureaucratic organization. For example, scientists engaged in cutting-edge research are exploring unknown intellectual territory, and with all such endeavors, the outcomes are unpredictable. A scientist may achieve a break-through next week, next month, or maybe never. He or she may even have a moment of serendipity—searching for one thing but coming across something of value that was quite unexpected. As the history of science reveals, some important discoveries have occurred in the course of looking for something quite different. The unpredictability of research, along with the vagaries of the creative process, makes bureaucracy an unsuitable mode of organization. Unlike the situation with routine activities, there are no clear-cut structures, procedures, and rules to ensure a scientific breakthrough.

Many, if not most, work activities are located somewhere in the broad middle between motor vehicle registration and basic research. Within a single organization, some activities can be reduced to set routines, while other efforts at routinization make it more difficult to get things done. The education of children and teenagers provides good examples of the uses, misuses, and abuses of bureaucratic organization. In the first place, public education is a large business at both the national and the local levels. Public K–12 education absorbed an estimated $611,800,000,000 in 2009.[13] During that period, American elementary, middle, and high schools employed 3,612,000 teachers who were responsible for the education of 49,470,000 students.[14]

Making at least an effort to educate such a large number of young people requires the efforts of bureaucratic organizations ranging from the federal government's Department of Education to the departments of education of individual states to local school districts and, finally, to the administrators of individual schools. The advantages of bureaucracy are evident when we consider the operation of a single school district and its constituent schools. They have many routine duties that mesh easily with bureaucratic organization: ordering and stocking supplies, issuing paychecks, maintaining buildings and grounds, scheduling extracurricular activities, and so on. But what about the core task: educating young people? On one hand, a fair amount of learning can be—and usually is—highly routinized. Children acquire essential information such as multiplication tables and grammatical rules through drills, exercises, and other rote activities, and through it all, their progress is monitored through the use of standardized tests. These educational experiences usually do not conjure up pleasant memories of school days, but it cannot be denied that they provide an essential foundation for further learning.

On the other hand, many educational researchers and practitioners believe that formal rules and procedures are not particularly well suited to a school's educational mission because, despite decades of research, the process of learning is still only dimly understood. It is, therefore, difficult to construct effective routines when there are no clear-cut principles on which they can be grounded. Further complicating matters is the simple fact of human diversity: what enhances the learning process for one individual may not work for another. In sum, an effective educational process cannot be reduced to routinized procedures that can be enacted for any group of students in any school setting.

The questionable value of using bureaucratic procedures in the educational realm is thrown into sharp relief when we look at recent efforts to more precisely evaluate educational outcomes. Evaluation is a basic requirement for effective bureaucratic organization; a goal-oriented organization has to periodically determine if its efforts are having their intended effects. Sometimes, this can be a straightforward exercise: is the team winning games, is the hospital curing sick people, is the business making a profit? But schools, like many other organizations, lack straightforward standards of success or failure. In the first place, it isn't reasonable to apply the same set of standards to every school. Schools differ dramatically from one another in regard to how well incoming students are prepared for the next phase of their education, the extent to which their families are able to offer their support, the adequacy of their educational budgets, and so on. Second, and even more difficult to resolve, what exactly is the "learning" that is to be measured? Is it the simple absorption of facts, or is it a subtler, more diffuse kind of knowledge? Is it sufficient that high school students are able to solve linear equations and note the date of the Battle of Gettysburg, or should they also be able to evaluate abstract ideas and apply them to real-world situations?

One thing is certain: it is far easier to measure the first kind of learning than the second. Consequently, standardized tests that focus on specifics, often through the use of multiple-choice or true–false questions, are favored tools for determining how well students are being educated. But this is the bureaucratic tail wagging the educational dog. Tests of this sort are routinized procedures that allow certain tasks to be accomplished quickly and efficiently, but their validity and utility are far from certain. To repeat, bureaucratic procedures work best when the goals are unambiguous and when the organizational structures and procedures employed are well suited to the attainment of these goals. Neither of these stipulations is likely to be met when it comes to teaching and learning, and effective schools have to use bureaucratic structures and procedures when they are appropriate and avoid them when they are not.

Bureaucratic Organization, Work, and the Worker

The previous section stressed that the extent of bureaucratization should reflect the nature of tasks being performed along with the skills that employees need to bring to their jobs. In short, routine tasks should be bureaucratically administered, while others should not. But this is not the whole story. Bureaucracy is a powerful tool because it allows the mobilization and control of large numbers of people. Consequently, a lot depends on who controls the tool and the purposes for which they use it. This brings us to the next issue, the exercise of power in bureaucratic organizations and its consequences for individual workers.

Although the extent of bureaucratization should reflect the kind of work being done, the decision to organize things along bureaucratic lines may also reflect existing economic and social cleavages. As several critics have argued, a key element of bureaucratic organization, the division of labor, may represent an effort by management to simplify workers' tasks to the point where no skill is required to get the job done. From the perspective of management, this has two advantages. First, it lowers labor costs by allowing the use of unskilled, low-paid workers. Second, "de-skilling" removes an important source of potential power within the workforce. Employees with special skills are hard to replace, and this significantly improves their bargaining power when it comes to wages, benefits, and working conditions.[15] In similar fashion, bureaucratic hierarchies may be established and maintained not because they contribute to the effective functioning of an organization but because they confer authority and prestige to some of its members at the expense of others. These points have been emphasized by Marxist critics of capitalist organizations, who have argued that both division of labor and hierarchy are organizational devices used to control workers and accumulate profits.[16]

Marxists have not been the only ones to take a critical stance toward bureaucracy. Other critics have been particularly concerned with the effects of bureaucratic organization on employees and the world in which they live. One of the most trenchant criticisms of the effects of bureaucracy came from Max Weber himself. For Weber, the formal rationality embodied in bureaucratic structures and procedures was itself problematic. After all, what Weber saw as the cultural basis of rationality, the "disenchantment of the world," carries a double meaning. Especially in everyday use, *disenchantment* connotes a sense of disillusionment to the point of cynicism. As Weber fully realized, a totally disenchanted world is flat and gray, containing little to elevate the spirits of men and women. As Weber noted in a famous passage in *The Protestant Ethic and the Spirit of Capitalism,* a totally disenchanted culture produced "narrow specialists without mind, pleasure seekers without heart; in its conceit this nothingness imagines it has climbed to a level of humanity never before attained."[17]

A more sharply focused insight into the effects of bureaucratic organization on individual workers has been provided by Robert Merton through his description of the "bureaucratic personality" and the circumstances that give rise to it.[18] For Merton, bureaucratic structures and procedures are established to get certain things done, but sometimes they become ends in themselves. When this happens, we may see the emergence of the "bureaucratic virtuoso," a functionary who closely adheres to all the rules and procedures but hardly accomplishes anything of significance. Organizations and their personnel can succumb to this malady for both organizational and personal reasons. In the case of the former, "bureaucratic ritualism" may be used by organizations as a defense mechanism in a hostile political climate. For the individual bureaucrat, job insecurity may provoke a need to do everything "by the books" so no blame can be assigned when things go badly.

A more recent description and analysis of contemporary bureaucracy and its consequences for working life comes from George Ritzer, who has invoked the McDonald's chain of fast-food restaurants as the archetypical early 21st-century organization.[19] Echoing Weber, Ritzer describes four key features of McDonald's operations: efficiency, calculability, predictability, and the control of people through the use of nonhuman technologies. There is nothing dramatically new here; "McDonaldization" has a lot in common with Taylor's Scientific Management and Ford's assembly line. But while Taylor's ideas were never fully implemented and the use of assembly lines was largely confined to the manufacturing sector, McDonaldization has gone well beyond the fast-food industry. The procedures, technologies, and managerial values that have made McDonald's the world's largest hamburger chain are now being applied to a great variety of organizational settings: retail establishments, schools, and even the commercial sex industry.[20]

Although critics have assumed that McDonaldization necessarily results in a thoroughly unpleasant and alienating work environment, careful research into the actual experiences and feelings of McDonald's workers has presented a more complex picture. The most intensive effort at assaying the effects on employees of McDonald's organizational structure and operating procedures was conducted in the mid-1990s by Robin Leidner.[21] In some ways, her research supports the conception of McDonald's as a stereotypical, impersonal bureaucratic organization. Although dealing with individual customers, one of the central activities in any fast-food establishment, is difficult to routinize, this is accomplished through the use of numerous formal rules and procedures, as well as prepared scripts that workers use when interacting with customers. Food preparation is highly routinized through the technologies that require little or no judgment on the part of the cooks, such as dispensers that always supply an exact quantity of ketchup and cash registers that tell cashiers how much change to give customers. For managers and owners of individual restaurants, McDonald's provides "the Bible," an exhaustive manual covering all the procedures and standards to be employed.[22] In addition, the firm requires that prospective owners of franchises attend "Hamburger University" in Oak Brook, Illinois, where they are taught operational procedures and, more generally, are imbued with McDonald's corporate philosophy.[23]

These key elements of McDonaldization have served the firm well, although they have been criticized for making work at McDonald's a routinized, poorly paid job that requires little in the way of worker skills. At the same time, however, these organizational rules and routines can work to the advantage of McDonald's employees. The well-defined routines reduce uncertainty and conflict over who is supposed to do what. Routinization also shields employees from clashes with customers because the workers can defend and justify their actions by noting that they are simply doing what they were required to do. In Leidner's summation,

> Depending on the context, service routines can help workers do their job, can boost their confidence, can limit the demands made upon them, can give them leverage over service-recipients, and can offer psychic protection from demeaning aspects of the job.[24]

Of course, it is precisely this ability to invoke bureaucratically established rules that has allowed some individuals to justify unethical or even criminal behavior by claiming "I was just following orders." Several classic experiments in social psychology have demonstrated the willingness of people to inflict harm when they are ordered to do so.[25] We, therefore, also have to take into account the moral dimension when assessing the advantages and disadvantages of bureaucratic organization. Rules and regulations are an essential part of bureaucratic administration, but they also may allow, and even encourage, actions that individuals would not do on their own volition.

Alternatives to Bureaucracy

Up to now, it has been argued that, in direct opposition to everyday perceptions, bureaucracies actually provide an effective and efficient way to get things done. Bureaucracies at least have the potential to work very well when the tasks performed by their members can be reduced to routines without violating the goals of an organization. But in today's world, a great deal of work does not lend itself to routinization. As was noted in Chapter 3, the majority of workers in the developed economies are employed in the various branches of the service sector. Many service sector jobs are quite routine and, therefore, easy to fit into a bureaucratic mold; think, for example, of cashiers, fast-food workers, and custodians. But many other jobs in this sector lie at the other end of the spectrum. A physician's practice, to take one example, includes a fair amount of routine, but at any moment, a patient can walk into the office with a malady that is hard to diagnose and even harder to treat. And even if treatment can be reduced to a routine with a predictable outcome, patients are notably reluctant to be treated impersonally. The same can be said of students and other recipients of services. In many sectors of the economy, people seem to be willing to spend considerable sums of money in order to avoid being treated as just another bureaucratically administered case. In parallel fashion, many aspects of bureaucratic organization—especially division of labor and hierarchical authority—have been implicated as major sources of job dissatisfaction, as will be noted in Chapter 12.

Changing expectations of customers and workers, along with economic and technological advances, have rendered many of the features of classic bureaucratic organization irrelevant and even harmful. Consequently, a variety of different organizational arrangements have emerged in both the private and public sectors as alternatives to bureaucracy. One of these is *matrix organization*. Instead of straight-line hierarchical authority extending from the top down, a matrix organization has both a vertical and a horizontal dimension, which puts the exercise of authority in a state of flux. The vertical dimension is composed of functional departments such as sales, manufacturing, and personnel. The horizontal dimension encompasses working teams centered on particular projects or geographical areas. To take an example of the latter, employees in the sales department report to both the sales manager in the firm's home office and the chief executive for a particular geographical region. In a manufacturing firm, a matrix organization has traditional departments such as engineering, purchasing, and marketing, but personnel from these departments are organized into teams to work on the creation of a new product. This allows a cross-fertilization of ideas so, for example, the engineers will be more inclined to design products that are easy to manufacture at a reasonable cost, and the manufacturing staff will use production methods that result in high-quality products that appeal to customers and make life easier for the sales staff. Matrix organizations are often set up on a temporary basis, bringing together personnel from different parts of an organization to work on a new project. They have the advantage of flexibility and the potential to make the best use of personnel, but their ambiguous lines of command and competing claims to authority have to be sorted out in the course of working on a project.[26]

One noteworthy example of matrix organization was Chrysler's use of "platform teams" in the late 1980s for the development of three new vehicles: a midsize family sedan, a sport utility vehicle, and a pickup truck.[27] In addition to involving all the relevant departments, such as engineering, finance, and styling, the team also included line workers and foremen to provide shop-floor experience in manufacturing realities. Not everyone accepted this organizational innovation; some engineers and managers quit because they (correctly) saw an erosion of the authority they once wielded. Others were reassigned to lesser duties or forced to take early retirement. Chrysler's top executives also had to accept diminished control. They could not simply issue orders; they had to convince team members that the changes they wanted had merit. Their willingness to delegate authority eventually paid off, and the validity of platform teams was vindicated when all three vehicles emerged on time and within budget and then went on to be strong sellers in a competitive market.

An even looser form of organization may emerge when the environment is so unsettled that although there may be an agreement on general goals, there is no consensus on how to translate these goals into specific actions. Under these circumstances, the most appropriate organizational form may be what has been labeled an "adhocracy." Participants in an adhocracy have to make it up as they go, continually determining what to do, who will do it, and even how to define success or failure. The members of an adhocracy are necessarily in a perpetual learning mode where feedback from the environment continuously influences their actions.[28]

Two recent examples of adhocracy are the Linux open-source computer operating system and the Wikipedia online encyclopedia. It is even open to question whether these ongoing projects can be described as organizations. Both are fluid operations that allow inputs from a large number of contributors with little in the way of specialization and hierarchical control. But they both work. Linux is widely used as an alternative to commercial operating systems,[29] and although questions have been raised about the accuracy of some of its entries, Wikipedia contains a large and constantly growing number of articles that are consulted by millions of people every day.[30]

Other, less radical organizational arrangements have retained some features of classic bureaucracy while diminishing or even eliminating others. One popular target is hierarchical authority. A "flatter" organizational structure with few hierarchical levels, it is claimed, makes better use of the people it employs, facilitates communication, and increases employee motivation. Similarly, the empowerment of workers can increase organizational effectiveness. As one organizational analyst, Thomas W. Malone, has summarized in a number of studies, "When people make their own decisions about how to do their work and allocate their time, they often put more energy, effort, and creativity into their jobs."[31]

Similar challenges have been mounted against another key attribute of bureaucratic organization, the division of labor. The division of work into a set of narrow tasks performed by workers with limited skill repertoires may be well suited to the efficient production of standardized goods and services, but it is manifestly unsuited to work activities that demand innovation, creative problem solving, and flexibility. Excessive division of labor, it has been argued, results in "trained incapacity," the inability to depart from well-established routines, even when they are obviously inappropriate and counterproductive. It also can be harmful to the psychic well-being of workers. Adam Smith, whose description of pin manufacture was presented earlier, noted what may happen to workers when their jobs are reduced to narrowly specialized routines:

> The man whose whole life is spent performing a few simple operations, of which the effects are perhaps always the same, or very nearly the same, has no occasion to exert his understanding or to exercise his invention in finding out expedients for removing difficulties which never occur. He naturally loses, therefore, the habit of such exertion, and generally becomes as stupid and ignorant as it is possible for a human creature to become.[32]

While cultural, economic, and social changes have made bureaucratic modes of organization unsuitable for many kinds of jobs, advances in technology have deepened this trend. Recent years have seen great strides in the development of technologies for gathering, distributing, and analyzing information, and for many observers of organizational life, these technologies are profoundly challenging longstanding assumptions about organizational structures and processes. In Frank Levy and Richard Murnane's summation, "Because information and work are inseparable, any technology that changes how we use information has the potential to reorganize how work is done."[33]

Whether or not this potential will be realized on a large scale remains to be seen. Although computers have a great ability to store, manipulate, and communicate large quantities of information at high rates of speed, there is no consensus on their long-term consequences for the structure of organizations and the way work is done in them. For some observers, computers and other information technologies have simply reinforced organizational hierarchies and the division of labor. From this perspective, computerized information-processing technologies have augmented the tendency of capitalism to lower skill requirements by simplifying tasks and converting more and more operations to preprogrammed routines.[34] Other observers have been more sanguine about the effects of computers on work organization because, as they see it, computers have empowered many workers by taking over routine procedures and increasing the need for higher-level work activities. While many office tasks such as taking sales orders, billing, and keeping financial accounts are easily handled by computers, others require human involvement of a nonroutine sort. To take one important example, one human quality that cannot inhere in a computer is the ability to build trust. Many transactions, ranging from ordering a blouse costing $30 to the purchase of shares in a mutual fund worth tens of thousands of dollars, often require more than interaction with an impersonal, computer-based information system. A purchase often entails some discussion and even negotiation regarding price, delivery time, warrantees, and so on. Even when buyers have decided to buy one of the organization's products or services, they still may need advice and guidance in order to decide exactly what to get. A computerized system can aid in the decision-making process, but customers need more than advice; they need to have a reason for trusting the advice they get. This requires employees who are knowledgeable about their organization's products and services, are able to communicate this knowledge, and are able to gain the confidence of customers and clients that they are competent and ethical.[35]

By now, it should be apparent that the shortcomings of bureaucratic organization are mirror images of its advantages. Bureaucracy is an indispensable part of modern life, but a world run solely according to bureaucratic principles would not work very well—and it certainly would be an unpleasant place in which to live. The dilemmas and paradoxes engendered by the bureaucratic organization of our working lives will be a theme to which we will return on several occasions.

In the previous chapters, we have noted how work has been shaped by fundamental changes in the ways things are produced, from gathering and hunting to our present industrial, and even postindustrial, era. An inherent element of these changes in production has been technological advance, which up to now has been presented indirectly. In the next chapter, we will take a head-on approach to the topic.

FOR DISCUSSION

1. In addition to the registration of motor vehicles, what other sorts of activities are well suited to bureaucratic modes of organization? Is anything lost when these activities are bureaucratically organized?

2. In the course of your education, what has been the mix of routine and nonroutine learning activities? Which have predominated? Do you think you might have learned more if different teaching strategies had been used?

3. Have you ever worked in a fast-food restaurant or some other enterprise that exhibited some aspects of "McDonaldization"? What were they? On the whole, did they make your job easier or harder? How so?

4. A Nazi official, Adolf Eichmann, infamously defended his role in the slaughter of millions of Jews during the Holocaust by arguing that he was "just following orders." Is this ever an adequate defense for acts done in an organizational setting? Under what circumstances should the exercise of individual responsibility take precedence over doing what the rules, procedures, and hierarchical authorities require?

Notes

1. Henry Jacoby, *The Bureaucratization of the World* (Berkeley: University of California Press, 1973).

2. Alfred D. Chandler Jr., *The Visible Hand: The Managerial Revolution in American Business* (Cambridge, MA: Harvard University Press, 1977).

3. Joanne Yates, *Control Through Communication: The Rise of System in American Management* (Baltimore: Johns Hopkins University Press, 1989).

4. Max Weber, "Bureaucracy," in *From Max Weber: Essays in Sociology,* eds. H. H. Gerth and C. Wright Mills (New York: Oxford University Press, 1958), 196–244.

5. Herman Melville, *Moby Dick,* eds. Hershel Parker and Harrison Hayford (New York: Norton, 2002), 157.

6. Max Weber, *The Theory of Social and Economic Organization,* trans. A. M. Henderson and Talcott Parsons (New York: Free Press, 1964), 184–91.

7. Martin Albrow, *Bureaucracy* (London: Macmillan, 1970).

8. Max Weber, *Economy and Society,* vol. III, trans. Gunther Roth and Claus Wittich (New York: Bedminster Press, 1968), 973.

9. Ho Ping-ti, *The Ladder of Success in Imperial China: Aspects of Social Mobility, 1368–1911* (1962; repr., New York: Da Capo, 1976).

10. U.S. Department of Labor, *Dictionary of Occupational Titles,* http://www.oalj.dol.gov/libdot.htm (accessed June 6, 2006).

11. Adam Smith, *An Inquiry into the Nature and Causes of the Wealth of Nations,* vol. 1 (1776; repr., London: George Bell & Sons, 1896), 9.

12. John Kenneth Galbraith, *The New Industrial State* (New York: New American Library, 1967), 73.

13. U.S. Census Bureau, "Table 216, School Expenditures by Type of Control and Level of Instruction in Constant (2005 to 2009) Dollars: 1980 to 2009," http://www.census.gov/statab/2011/tables/11s0215.pdf (accessed September 9, 2011).

14. U.S. Census Bureau, "Table 217, School Enrollments, Faculty, Graduates, and Finances—Projections: 2009 to 2015," http://www.census.gov/statab/2011/tables/11s0217.pdf (accessed September 9, 2011).

15. Harry Braverman, *Labor and Monopoly Capital: The Degradation of Work in the Twentieth Century* (New York: Monthly Review Press, 1974), 75–83.

16. Ibid.; Richard Edwards, *Contested Terrain: The Transformation of the Workplace in the Twentieth Century* (New York: Basic, 1979); Stephen Marglin, "What the Bosses Do: The Origins and Functions of Hierarchy in Capitalist Production," *Review of Radical Political Economics* 6 (Summer 1974): 60–112.

17. Max Weber, *The Protestant Ethic and the Spirit of Capitalism,* trans. Stephen Kalberg (Los Angeles: Roxbury, 2002), 124.

18. Robert K. Merton, *Social Theory and Social Structure* (New York: Free Press, 1968), 249–60.

19. George Ritzer, *The McDonaldization of Society,* rev. ed. (Thousand Oaks, CA: Sage, 2004).

20. George Ritzer, ed., *McDonaldization: The Reader* (Thousand Oaks, CA: Sage, 2002).

21. Robin Leidner, *Fast Food, Fast Talk: Service Work and the Routinization of Everyday Life* (Berkeley: University of California Press, 1993).

22. Ibid., 49.

23. Ibid., 54–60.

24. Ibid., 220.

25. The best-known example is Stanley Milgram, "Behavioral Studies in Obedience," *Journal of Abnormal Psychology* 67 (1963): 371–8.

26. W. Richard Scott, *Organizations: Rational, Natural, and Open Systems,* 2nd ed. (Englewood Cliffs, NJ: Prentice Hall, 1987), 223.

27. Charles K. Hyde, *Riding the Roller Coaster: A History of the Chrysler Corporation* (Detroit, MI: Wayne State University Press, 2003), 280–4. For a top Chrysler manager's perspective on these teams, see Robert A. Lutz, *Guts: Eight Laws of Business from One of the Most Innovative Business Leaders of Our Time* (Hoboken, NJ: John Wiley, 2003).

28. Scott, *Organizations,* 281–2.

29. Ragib Hasan, "History of Linux," https://netfiles.uiuc.edu/rhasan/linux/ (accessed September 9, 2011).

30. "Wikipedia," http://en.wikipedia.org/wiki/Wikipedia (accessed June 8, 2006).

31. Thomas W. Malone, *The Future of Work: How the New Order of Business Will Shape Your Organization, Your Management Style, and Your Life* (Boston: Harvard Business School Press, 2004), 34.

32. Smith, *The Wealth of Nations*, 178.

33. Frank Levy and Richard J. Murnane, *The New Division of Labor: How Computers Are Creating the Next Job Market* (Princeton, NJ: Princeton University Press, 2004), 15.

34. Joan Greenbaum, *Windows in the Workplace: Technology, Jobs, and the Organization of Office Work*, 2nd ed. (New York: Monthly Review Press, 2004).

35. Levy and Murnane, *The New Division of Labor*, 83–92.

5

Technology and Work

Throughout history, many things have shaped the occupations people have held and the work they have done. Today, as in the past, one of the most important of these is technological change. The technologies used in the workplace exert a powerful influence on the kinds of tasks performed, how they are organized, and the kinds of skills needed to perform them. Technological advance also has helped propel another major change in work patterns by expanding the boundaries of economic, social, and cultural relationships. One common term for this expansion is *globalization*. We will take on globalization in the next chapter, but first, we will consider the interaction of technological change with employment and unemployment, the occupational structure, and the distribution of power and authority in the workplace.

Defining Technology

In the preceding chapters, we saw how first the Agricultural Revolution and then the Industrial Revolution profoundly altered work and life. In both cases, technological change was one of the major driving forces of these transformations. In the case of the Agricultural Revolution, the adoption of plant cultivation transformed humans from nomadic gatherers and hunters into sedentary farmers. Thousands of years later, the Industrial Revolution fundamentally altered the economy and society through the intertwined development of new machines, power sources, production processes, and methods of work organization.

It is often said that we are currently undergoing a third, technologically driven revolution that has given rise to a "postindustrial" economy and society.[1] To a certain extent, this is indisputable. As we saw in previous chapters, the primary and secondary sectors have been eclipsed by the service sector, numerically, as the most important source of jobs in the American economy. As with the two earlier revolutions, this one did not happen overnight, but its long-term effects have been profound. Less than a century ago, the majority of the workforce was employed in farming, the extractive industries, and manufacturing, leaving only 36.4 percent of workers in the service sector.[2] In the decades that followed, millions of these jobs were lost as a result of technological change, yet widespread unemployment did not occur because these losses were offset, and then some, by the emergence of a great number of new service-sector occupations. The rise of the service sector as the dominant source of employment represents one of the most important transformations of life and work in human history, and we will trace its consequences many times in the pages to come.

There is no need to belabor the point that technological change has been a crucial source of these economic and social transformations, but what exactly is meant by *technology?* Technology is more than machinery and other artifacts, and it goes well beyond the electronic devices that are sometimes equated with it, as in the Wall Street term *technology stocks.* To begin, technology can be defined in the most general way as the use of knowledge and organization to produce objects and techniques for the attainment of specific goals.[3] Such a schematic definition necessitates the elaboration of several of the words contained in it. In the first place, what sort of "knowledge" serves as a foundation for technological applications? Scientific knowledge is often thought to be paramount, as when technology is commonly defined as "applied science." But this is at best a partial truth. Many technologies, both past and current, have been created and developed without any help from science. To take a few examples, early mechanisms such as water wheels and textile looms were developed through trial and error—empirical, but not exactly scientific processes. More complex technologies also were developed with no scientific inputs, as when ironworkers were able to make high-quality steel for centuries without possessing what today would be considered the most basic metallurgical knowledge.[4] And long before steel was produced, makers of beer and wine had no idea of how the ingredients they used were converted into alcoholic beverages. Even today, many technologies are created and developed through cut-and-try processes that owe little to science. This practice-based source of technological advance is particularly relevant to a discussion of the relationship between work and technology because many new products and new ways of doing things have been created by engineers, technicians, and shop-floor workers who have made little or no use of scientific knowledge.[5]

Another important issue in the above definition of technology is embedded in the phrase "for the attainment of specific goals." Here, we need to ask *whose* goals are being pursued and how these goals have been chosen. For more than a generation, economists have understood that technological advance has been one of the most—if not *the* most—important sources of aggregate economic growth.[6] But, while improvements in productive technologies have propelled economic expansion, not everyone has benefited equally from them. As we shall see, some technologies have caused considerable injury, economic and otherwise, to particular groups and individuals.

Many times, the damage is unintentional, but in some cases, particular technologies have been used as weapons wielded in conflicts between contending parties.

A lot, therefore, depends on who has the power to shape the course of technological innovation. If nothing else, recognizing that technological change often has a political dimension serves to undermine the notion that technology is an independent force in human affairs. Belief in the autonomy of technology in effecting social change is known as *technological determinism*. Its rejection doesn't mean, of course, that technology and technological change have been of no consequence; the most cursory glance at the modern world demonstrates technology's influence on our daily lives through everything from antibiotics to zippers. What matters for gaining a deeper understanding of technology's significance is the willingness and ability to understand how specific technologies came into being; who promoted them; who resisted them; and how they affected the distribution of wealth, status, and power.

A focus on the social and political dimensions of technology also helps us recognize the merits and limitations of "technological fixes." A technological fix is the use of a technology to solve a problem that is not purely technological in nature. For example, billions of dollars are spent annually on devices and dietary supplements aimed at helping people lose weight. But an individual's weight is governed by a host of factors—body type, metabolism, lifestyle, eating habits, and general attitudes about food. Under these circumstances, there is no technological "silver bullet" that can guarantee a slim figure, no matter what miracles are promised by marketers of such products.

Equally important, even a technological fix that does rectify a problem is likely to yield some negative consequences. To take one example, from the 1920s onward, American railroads took a financial beating as cars, buses, and trucks took away a substantial portion of the market for the movement of goods and people. But in the mid-1930s, the diesel-electric locomotive began to replace the venerable steam locomotive, and the ensuing cost savings did much to restore the financial health of the railroads. At the same time, however, the new locomotives made the work of the traditional fireman unnecessary. Their displacement was temporarily averted by the requirement that a fireman ride along in the locomotive, even though there was little or nothing for him to do—a practice that railroad management derided as "featherbedding." The ability of locomotive firemen to resist the negative consequences of technological change was hardly typical of the relative power held by workers and management, however. As we shall see later in this chapter, workplace technologies have at times been developed and applied by enterprise managers not simply because they were more efficient but because they strengthened management's hand. But before we take up this issue, we need to explore another fundamental issue of work and technology: the fear that technological advances will result in long-term, permanent unemployment.

Technological Unemployment

For centuries, workers have worried about the destruction of their jobs by machines and other technological innovations. Sometimes, they did more than just worry. As we saw in Chapter 3, textile workers in early 19th-century England—collectively known as "Luddites"—rose in rebellion, smashing machines and destroying the homes of the factory owners who had installed them.[7] Many more recent incidents of job losses caused by technological advance can be cited. In the music industry, for example, the use of electronic synthesizers has drastically reduced the number of studio musicians because one operator can take the place of a large ensemble of musicians.[8] Throughout the manufacturing sector, advanced production technologies have allowed employers to maintain or even increase production while reducing the number of workers. To note just two examples, the Ford Motor Company was able to make as many vehicles in 1988 as it did in 1978 while employing half as many workers.[9] No less dramatic was the case of the steel industry, which from 1955 to 1960 increased production by 20 percent even as it was eliminating 17,000 jobs.[10]

Concerns about the replacement of human workers by machines occasionally have motivated governments to try to put the brakes on technological innovation, as happened in 1638 when the government of England banned "engines for working of tape, lace, ribbon, and such, wherein one man doth more amongst them than seven English men can do."[11] Fears about the job-destroying potential of labor-saving technologies were not confined to the preindustrial past; they forcefully reemerged in the 1930s when a severe economic depression seemed to portend an era of permanent unemployment on a massive scale.[12] Although few blamed technological advances as the sole cause of the depression, some government officials seriously considered implementation of a "technotax" to be levied on firms that replaced employees with new equipment.[13] The issue of unemployment induced by technological change did not disappear with the return of prosperity after World War II. During the 1950s, the newly coined term *automation* was associated with the spectre of permanent unemployment. Advances in computers, sensors, materials handling, and automatic machine tools appeared to be ushering in a new era of industrial production that required little or no input from human workers.

As we have just seen with the example of "featherbedding" on the railroads, organized labor has at times been able to avert or at least delay the loss of jobs caused by technological change. Today, technological changes even more far-reaching than the introduction of new kinds of locomotives can be found in many industries, carrying the threat of job losses along with them. But do new, labor-saving technologies necessarily result in unemployment? In fact, there is some basis for optimism. In the first place, new technologies open up new employment possibilities. After all, there were no jobs for X-ray technicians before the development of X-ray technologies or for webpage designers before the creation of the Internet. Second, technological advances within an existing industry can increase employment through productivity improvements that lower the price of its products, which may in turn induce people to buy more of them. Increased sales may not result in the retention or stepped-up hiring of production-line workers, but it may expand employment opportunities in sales, shipping, administration, bookkeeping, and so on.

Even in the digital age, hands-on factory work is still needed. For a number of decades now, engineers, managers, and economists have foreseen a new era of fully automated industrial plants where machines would run themselves in factories, with scant need for human workers. To some extent, this prophecy has come true, as computer-controlled machinery has taken over many of the jobs that previously had been done by flesh-and-blood workers. But glib portrayals of the "lights-out factory" have proven to be overblown. Although robots are now doing many of the jobs previously performed by welders, spray painters, and other factory operatives, plenty of industrial operations remain the province of working men and women. Even when automated processes have become well entrenched, a substantial need for human operators remains. Problems inevitably arise that need human intervention, often by workers who stand rather low in the official hierarchy.[14] Meanwhile, a large number of industrial operations remain stubbornly resistant to automation. Manufacturing processes involving the assembly of components of varying size and shape are especially hard to automate, and some firms have even scrapped computer-controlled machinery in favor of human workers, who have proven to be faster, more accurate, and even less expensive than the robots they replaced.[15]

At a more fundamental level, an optimistic perspective on technology and employment hinges on making a clear distinction between *work* and *jobs*. It is undeniable that some technologies have rendered certain jobs obsolete and will continue to do so. Employment in the buggy-whip industry plunged as mass automobile ownership took hold, and there was not much hope for assemblers of vacuum-tube–based radios after the commercial diffusion of the transistor and other solid-state electronic devices. But the loss of particular jobs, either through the obsolescence of an entire industry or the replacement of workers by labor-saving technologies need not result in increased unemployment. In the case of one industry giving way to another, the economic resources tied up in dying firms or industries can be transferred to more dynamic ones, creating new jobs in the process. In the vivid phrase of the Austrian economist Joseph Schumpeter, economic advance is often the product of "creative destruction," the process whereby obsolete industries, materials, processes, and jobs are replaced by new and better ones.[16]

One of the costs of a growing economy is, therefore, the loss of particular jobs. But the loss of these jobs, individual tragedies though they often are, is not the same thing as the loss of work as a whole. Technological change, in addition to giving rise to new industries, also can create new employment opportunities indirectly. Labor-saving technologies are used because they diminish production costs. These lower costs can result in lower prices for consumers, greater profits for owners, higher wages for the remaining workers, or a combination of some or all of these. All these situations improve the financial situations of the parties who have benefited from the reduced costs. A considerable portion of their increased incomes will likely be spent on other goods and services, and these expenditures will pay the wages and salaries of the people who produce the goods and services that are purchased. Alternatively, the extra income may be invested in capital equipment, but this also translates into jobs in the industries that receive the investment funds.

The erroneous equation of technological change with widespread unemployment is in part based on what economists have labeled "the lump of labor fallacy." Here, the underlying idea is that within any particular economy, there is only so much work to be done and, hence, a fixed number of jobs. Accordingly, if labor-saving technologies take over some of that work, the result must be more unemployment. In recent years, a few governments bought into this idea by mandating shorter workweeks in order to create more work opportunities for the unemployed. There are several good reasons for moving to shorter workweeks, but stimulating employment isn't one of them. The idea that there is only so much work to be done is properly labeled a fallacy because there will never be a shortage of essential tasks. Today, for example, many jobs could be filled in the course of rectifying environmental damage, rebuilding crumbling transportation infrastructures, and providing healthcare for underserved groups. The absence of these employment opportunities can be attributed both to the lack of appropriate skills among the unemployed and the inability or unwillingness of a society to pay for the work that needs to be done. But the idea that there is an unchanging amount of work to be done doesn't stand up to scrutiny, and there is no inherent reason why new work opportunities cannot be expanded in order to alleviate unemployment caused by technological change.

Developing New Skills

As just noted, a major obstacle to putting unemployed workers in new jobs may be the lack of needed skills. Although there may be an abundance of new jobs, there is no guarantee that workers displaced by labor-saving technologies will be able to fill those jobs; the "creative destruction" wrought by technological change necessitates the development of new skills as it renders obsolete the relevance of other skills, a particularly difficult situation for older workers. While this mismatch between existing and needed skills is problematic for individual workers, especially those over the age of 50, it also threatens future economic growth for the nation as a whole. In 2002, there were about 62 million people aged 55 or older. By 2025, there will be an estimated 103 million of them, and many in this cohort will need to develop new skills to match the requirements of new technologies and a changing economy.[17]

Developing new skills for veteran workers is a difficult but not insur-
mountable task. An abundance of psychological research has shown that
the ability to learn new things declines from early adulthood onward. It
would, therefore, seem to be a quixotic hope that older workers will be
able to develop the skills needed to successfully work with new technologies. But relative differences in learning need not be fatal impediments;
old dogs can learn new tricks, although it may take them longer to do so.
When older workers fail to develop new skills, it may be the result of a
self-fulfilling prophecy whereby employers offer few retraining opportunities because they believe that their older employees would not benefit
from them. Yet it seems evident that most older workers do not have an
inherent resistance to learning, as shown in a study of a number of state
agencies in Pennsylvania where older workers demonstrated a greater
willingness to learn new office technologies than their younger counterparts did.[18] Another study focused on facility with the use of computers,
often thought to be the special domain of young workers. In fact, this
study found no significant differences in computer use between younger
workers and workers who were in their 50s. Computer use did drop off
for workers in their 60s, but this apparent lack of interest may be an indication of a significant obstacle to the retraining of older employees: if a
worker anticipates being excluded from new workplace opportunities or
is close to retirement, he or she is not likely to devote time and energy to
the acquisition of new skills.[19]

Technology and Managerial Authority

Although technological change may be acquitted as a source of across-the-
board unemployment, it is not an unqualifiedly benign force. For one thing,
it has been indicted as a major source of widening income inequalities, an
issue that will be taken up in Chapter 10. It also may be the case, as some
have argued, that the trajectory of technological change has reflected and
reinforced differences in economic power and that specific technologies
have been used to advance the interests of one group over another. In regard
to the organization of work, critics have pointed out that on numerous
occasions, new technologies have been developed and applied in order to
consolidate or increase managerial control over workers. This process was
particularly evident in the early 20th century with the rise of mass-produced
industrial products. One of the key elements of mass production was the
use of specialized machine tools that allowed the production of standardized, interchangeable components by workers with minimal skills. This
made for cheaper consumer products, but it also strengthened the hand of
management by reducing the need for skilled workers, whose difficult-to-
replace skills helped insulate them from the exercise of managerial power.
In sharp contrast, unskilled workers could be treated as though they themselves were interchangeable parts. As one Ford engineer who was involved

in the early development of mass-production technologies put it, his firm had "no use for experience." Rather,

> it desires and prefers machine-tool operators who have nothing to unlearn, who have no theories of correct surface speeds for metal finishing, and will simply do what they are told, over and over again, from bell-time to bell-time.[20]

According to Marxist-oriented scholars, this ability to employ an unskilled and easily controlled workforce made mass-production technologies especially appealing to enterprise owners and managers. This has been reflected, say the critics, in ongoing efforts to develop and deploy industrial technologies that "deskill" their employees.[21] One of the ways to accomplish this has been through the division of manufacturing work into a series of small, repetitive tasks that demand little more than regular attendance at a workstation and the willingness to do the same thing over and over again. Once again, a prime example of this approach can be found in the early years of the Ford Motor Company, where

> the assembling of the motor, formerly done by one man, is now divided into eighty-four operations . . . in the chassis assembling [room] are forty-five separate operations or stations. The first men fasten four mudguard brackets to the chassis frame; the motor arrives on the tenth operation and so on in detail. Some men do only one or two small operations, others do more. The man who places a part does not fasten it. . . . The man who puts in a bolt does not put on the nut; the man who puts on the nut does not tighten it.[22]

Ford did not invent the division of labor, even in this extreme form, but he did pioneer another revolutionary productive technology: the assembly line. As noted in Chapter 3, Ford and his associates transformed automobile production by having the work come to the worker instead of the other way around.[23] The result was dramatically lower production costs that put the purchase of a Ford Model T within the financial means of a large segment of the American population. Some of the purchasers of these cars were the workers who built them. The cars were reasonably priced, and Ford employees earned a wage that was well above the earnings of the average manufacturing employee. But assembly line work exacted a toll. The line moved relentlessly, the work was monotonous and physically taxing, and the noise level could be deafening. Even young, able-bodied workers were physically exhausted at the end of the day. As the wife of one worker complained in a letter to Henry Ford,

> The chain system that you have is a *slave driver. My God!*, Mr. Ford. My husband has come home & thrown himself down & won't eat his supper—so done out! Can't it be remedied? That $5 a day is a blessing— a bigger one than you know, but *oh* they earn it.[24]

While mass production technologies based on unskilled labor brought material benefits at the cost of exhausting work performed in an oppressive work environment, other innovative technologies were being developed to increase productivity while at the same time enhancing managerial control. As David Noble has argued, numerically controlled (NC) machine tools allowed faster and more accurate shaping of metal components, but their key appeal to management lay in reducing the influence and autonomy of skilled machinists. Although the automatic operation of machine tools could have been effected by recording the actions of human machinists, managers preferred to reserve the task for engineers who were part of the managerial team. As one manager asserted, "With NC, control over the process is placed firmly in the hands of management—and why shouldn't we have it?"[25]

Electronic technologies also may enhance managerial power when they are used to monitor workers and keep track of the work they do. For example, many commercial word-processing programs include a function that counts key strokes in order to determine a typist's productivity. Monitoring technologies are also widely used outside the clerical realm, as when GPS-based technology is used to continuously track the location of long-distance truck drivers. To some observers, then, "computers are the electronic equivalent of an assembly line to mechanically pace and control workers rather than a tool to enhance a job."[26]

Although some employers and managers continue with their attempts to control their workers through close monitoring or deskilling or both, many industries still need a cadre of skilled workers who enjoy a fair amount of autonomy as they go about their work. For all its use of mass-production technologies and routinized work, the automobile industry still finds it necessary to employ significant numbers of millwrights, machinists, tool and die makers, and other skilled workers, whose skills continue to confer a fair degree of independence. According to the recollections of one industry executive,

> These fine old tool makers worked hard and were very proud of their craft. They kept their big tool boxes right underneath their work benches. If you looked at them the wrong way or dealt with them in any manner other than a man-to-man, professional fashion, they would simply reach under their work benches without saying a word, throw their tools into the big box, lock it up and leave. That was it. Each guy figured, "What the hell. I don't have to take this from anybody. I'm a pro. I know this business and I am not depending on you or anyone else.[27]

Today, the autonomy enjoyed by skilled manual workers has been replicated in some occupations through the widespread use of computers. Although computerization has facilitated both deskilling and monitoring, it also has increased the capabilities of many rank-and-file workers and has undercut managerial authority in the process. The crucial element has been the facility with which computers can gather, sort, analyze, and distribute information. By making information inexpensive and readily available, computers have threatened a key source of managerial authority. As one manager mused in an interview with Shoshana Zuboff,

> The classic managerial role has been that of the handler, manipulator, dealer, and withholder of information. An issue that the technology is forcing us to face involves the loss of managerial control. . . . Suddenly you are vesting in folks at the control station, folks who are interfacing with a tremendous technology power—power to see all the functions of the operation. That is kind of scary to some managers.[28]

The loss of some of their powers may be a disturbing prospect for some managers, but it can be argued that deskilling employees and keeping them on a short leash are poor business practices that hinder the effective operation of a firm. As noted above, no productive process runs itself; breakdowns, unforeseen disruptions and opportunities, and novel situations always crop up, and these require the intervention of a skilled, well-motivated cadre of employees.[29] Moreover, many of today's businesses are primarily service providers, and a firm is not likely to prosper if its employees are incapable of responding to the needs of clients and customers in an intelligent and creative fashion.

The ongoing need for interventions by skilled workers even in highly mechanized operations presents something of a conundrum for the managers of these facilities. On the one hand, they need a cadre of effective workers to keep everything on an even keel, but at the same time, it is evident that hard-to-replace skills and freedom of action can invest workers with a potential source of power in the workplace. Although some critics may have overstated the extent to which deskilling has been a deliberate managerial ploy, conflicts over the possession and control of skills will inevitably accompany the course of technological change in the workplace.

Work, Skill, and Today's Technologies

As we have seen, only a relatively small portion of the labor force works in the manufacturing sector today. Once again, technological change has contributed to a radically new work environment, as a large number of productive tasks are now done by robots and other automated processes. As has happened in the past, the introduction of new technologies has had mixed consequences as far as skill requirements are concerned. In some cases, the introduction of computers into the workplace has done little to stimulate the development of new skills. Sitting in front of a computer monitor while doing data entry is not as physically taxing as working on an assembly line, and the work environment is likely to be more pleasant, but the skill requirements are still minimal. Under these circumstances, workers are not likely to have much more control over their jobs than assembly line workers do. At the same time, however, many recent technological developments have required the ministrations of workers with advanced levels of technical skill.

Given these conflicting tendencies, do 21st-century jobs require more or less in the way of skill than required in times past? The issue is hard to resolve because "skill" is an elusive concept with a multiplicity of meanings, and the widely different skill requirements of different industries further complicate things. Although it cannot be taken as the last word on the subject, one study found that workers' skills in recent years have increased in some occupations while they decreased in others and that the two trends have largely cancelled each other out, leaving no net change either way.[30] Another study was more optimistic, concluding that from 1960 to 1985, the jobs done by American workers had moved in the direction of greater cognitive and interactive skills.[31] Finally, to return to the automobile industry, another research project concluded that advances in mechanization and automation had eliminated many low-skill jobs and increased the number of workers in skilled occupations.[32]

The above discussion should help reinforce the point that technological change may influence the distribution of workers' skills, but it does not operate as an independent agent. As ever, it is important to avoid falling into the trap of technological determinism. In the realm of work, the power dimension always has to be taken into account when assessing technological trajectories. In any industry or individual firm, the distribution of power will strongly affect the choice of technologies, as will the attitudes and beliefs of those in positions of power. When managers believe they should call the shots in a work environment where the employees are viewed as hostile and unreliable, they will be attracted to production technologies based on the use of unskilled, easily replaced employees who can be controlled by the use of routinized procedures and electronic monitoring. When, on the other hand, workers are seen as essential resources to be valued and cultivated, there is a much greater likelihood that the technologies chosen will require a fair amount of skill and initiative on the part of the workforce.

Telework

In recent years, significant numbers of workers have made use of new technologies that have the potential to confer greater control over their work environments while at the same time partially alleviating the conflicting demands of work and home. All this has become possible because, as already noted, many of today's employees do not work with or produce anything with a physical substance. Their primary tasks center on the production, reception, interpretation, and analysis of information and then acting on the basis of that information. To put it more concretely, what writers, accountants, journalists, computer programmers, diagnosticians, book-keepers, teachers, and researchers all have in common is that they work with information of some sort.[33] Today, relatively new communications technologies such as fax machines and e-mail, together with the long-established telephone system (which has benefited from greatly reduced charges for long-distance calls), allow the transmission of information rapidly and inexpensively from one place to another. This means that an employee may not have to show up at a central office day after day but can work at home instead.

Dubbed *telecommuting* or *telework*, this mode of employment has grown in recent years. In 2010, more than 34 million workers—24.4 percent of employed adult Americans—worked at home at least occasionally.[34] The actual time spent working at home is limited, however; most teleworkers do it only 5 or 6 days a month.[35] These figures should be taken as only a rough approximation, as definitions and survey procedures can affect the tally, but they do give a general idea of the extent of telework.

An obvious advantage of telework is that it allows workers with young children to take care of them while working at home, and in fact, working parents are more likely to engage in telework than workers without children are.[36] As with many other aspects of work, the extent of telework reflects gender divisions in society and the differential responsibilities of parenting. On average, mothers spend more time on parenting than fathers do, and it is, therefore, not surprising that women are more likely to be teleworkers than men are.[37]

Although it is based on modern electronic technologies, telework represents a return to typical patterns of work and residential life that existed before industrialization, urbanization and suburbanization, population growth, and new transportation technologies combined to separate the workplace and the home, making commuting a way of life for the majority of workers. Although in times past, the home served as the workplace of skilled craftsmen working at their own pace, it also was the scene of sweated labor, where miserably paid workers put in 12-hour days in cramped cottages and noisome tenements. Memories of the exploitative nature of this variety of homework initially caused telework to be greeted with scepticism and even hostility by organized labor. As a practical matter, unions also had a long history of opposition to work done in the home because dispersed and easily replaced workers have been difficult to organize and recruit as members of unions. This is not necessarily the case today, as seen in the comments of the president of the National Treasury Employees Union, who in 2010 noted at a White House forum on workplace flexibility that telework "allows employees to avoid long, expensive, and tiresome commutes, enables them to better balance work and family life, and increases job satisfaction."[38]

Although some contemporary teleworkers remain poorly paid and have little opportunity for advancement, the majority of these workers appreciate that telework can reduce some of the stresses of trying to reconcile the demands of work and family. At the same time, however, telework can produce new stresses by creating an environment in which work and family responsibilities may frequently collide, and worker-parents may not be able to pay full attention to either role. Many telecommuters report that they are more productive when working at home because they have fewer distractions and interruptions,[39] but offsetting these advantages are a number of drawbacks. The home environment can be just as distracting as the workplace—sometimes even more so—with consequent deleterious effects on worker productivity. Under these circumstances, the demands of working at home can be the source of considerable family tensions over the allocation of time between work and family responsibilities.

Telework may also inhibit career advancement. For many workers, extended periods of absence from the workplace, even when they do not result in diminished output, put them at a disadvantage in regard to promotions, pay raises, and assignments to new projects. Working exclusively at home makes it difficult to gather information, to form working relationships with other employees, and to participate in job-related networks. In many kinds of jobs, being physically present is essential for effectively working with others. As Joel Mokyr notes of conventional working relationships,

> Proximity in a plant or office created personal familiarity and thus conditions of trust and believability. There is always a role of body language, intonation, and general demeanor in human communications.[40]

In short, modern communication technologies allow the effective implementation of many tasks, but they cannot completely obviate the need for "face time" at work.

Although telework has both advantages and disadvantages for individual workers, its contribution to reducing the individual and collective costs of daily commuting should also be taken into account when assessing its overall value. One economist has reckoned that the time spent commuting comes to 25.4 billion person-hours. If that time had been spent on gainful employment at $14/hour, it would have amounted to $356 billion.[41] Commuting also entails psychic costs in the form of stress, but it confers some benefits as well. For some, commuting offers a time to be by oneself and a reminder that the home and the workplace are separate spheres of existence. For many others, however, it may mean a crowded bus or gridlocked traffic, so the stresses of commuting are piled onto the ones endured at work.

Frustrating traffic, along with higher energy prices, may motivate more workers to work at home whenever possible. At the same time, the ongoing development of communication technologies will surely improve the effectiveness of teleworkers. These forces will likely propel an expansion in the extent and scope of telework. Even so, a large-scale merger of home and workplace is not likely to happen anytime soon.

Technology and Globalization

The next chapter will address one of the most powerful forces affecting work today: globalization. Globalization has many dimensions, but in the final section of this chapter, we will confine ourselves to the interplay between globalization and technological change.

Advancing technological capabilities have been essential to globalization, past and present. An earlier phase of globalization, the European "discovery" of the New World, owed much to the development of oceangoing vessels and improved navigational techniques, while its subsequent colonization was secured by firearms, the destructive power of which was complemented by diseases against which indigenous peoples had no natural defenses.[42] Today's globalization also owes much to radically improved transportation technologies. Where trips from one country to another may have taken days or even weeks a century ago, superhighways and high-speed trains allow them to be completed in a few hours today—while air travel puts entire continents less than a day's journey apart.

Although they are the fastest means of getting from one place to another, commercial air carriers transport their passengers at the rather leisurely speed of around 500 miles per hour. In contrast, digitized information travels at the speed of light. The rapid movement of information through electronic media is a key component of globalization, and it, too, represents the latest phase of a process that started long ago. The first great breakthrough came in the middle of the 19th century, when the telegraph made communication almost instantaneous.[43] Once the wires were strung up, a message could be sent and received as fast as telegraph operators could convert texts to dots and dashes, and vice versa.

Today, digital technologies make long-distance communication faster, cheaper, and more accurate than could have been imagined a generation ago. Computers and their associated networks greatly expand the ability to communicate because anything that can be digitized—numbers, letters, and sound and light frequencies—can be transmitted electronically and then reconstituted as music, texts, images, and much else.[44] Electronic communication technologies propel globalization when investors buy and sell shares in foreign firms and government-issued bonds, fans of Afropop tune in to the latest releases, and scientists share experimental data with colleagues on other continents.

Not all the technologies that have moved globalization forward are based on digitization and electronics, or even embody state-of-the-art technologies. One of the most significant commercial technologies of recent decades has been a plain metal box: the shipping container. A common sight at ports and on railroads and highways, standard-sized containers are the building blocks of intermodal transportation. *Intermodal* simply means that containers can be transported on many different types of carriers, including ships, railroad flatcars, and flatbed trucks. The use of containers has made global transportation cheaper, safer, and much more efficient. Before the widespread use of containers, the long-distance haulage of cargo usually entailed several episodes of "breaking bulk," as when crates of merchandise were loaded into trucks, taken out of the trucks and stowed in a ship's hold, unloaded after a sea voyage and transferred to railroad boxcars, and then finally moved from the boxcars to delivery trucks. Each of these transfers required gangs of workers to unload and load cargo every time it was transferred to a new mode of transportation, incurring substantial labor costs and likelihood of damage during each phase. Further increasing costs, cargo spent a lot of time just sitting around in a holding area, where it was vulnerable to more damage, the effects of the weather, and pilferage. These problems are avoided through the use of containers, as the merchandise stays securely in the same container from when it leaves the factory to the time it is unloaded at a warehouse or retail establishment. Due to all its advantages, containerized intermodal transportation now accounts for the vast majority of international transportation, and in 2008, the world's intermodal facilities handled the equivalent of 152 million standard, 20-foot-long containers.[45]

The shipping container, along with all the other technologies that make globalization possible, has contributed to an interconnected world. To some extent, globalization represents a new stage in human affairs, but it also has many historical precedents. For its supporters, globalization has increased incomes and improved workplace conditions. For its critics, it has had the opposite effect. Most serious students of globalization would agree, however, that it has been a multidimensional process containing many contradictions. The next chapter will take a look at this complex phenomenon and its consequences for work in the 21st century.

Photo 5.1   Shipping containers

SOURCE: ©Olivier Lantzendorffer/iStockphoto.

FOR DISCUSSION

1. Why are technological fixes so appealing? To what extent can new technologies substitute for other changes? Can you think of some examples of effective technological fixes, as well as some that have not lived up to expectations? What accounts for the differences between the two?

2. Technological change has produced many benefits, but it also has done a fair amount of damage to particular regions, industries, occupations, and individuals. Should governments develop policies and programs to alleviate problems caused by technological change? What might these be?

3. Do you agree that the owners and managers of business firms have deliberately tried to deskill their employees? What sort of evidence can be used to support or reject this idea?

4. Can you think of any jobs that have required increased levels of skill as a result of technological change? Have some jobs required *less* skill due to technological change?

5. Would you like to be a teleworker? How would telecommuting ease some problems of combining work with other roles? What sorts of new problems might it create for you?

Notes

1. One early statement of this thesis is Daniel Bell, *The Coming of Post-Industrial Society: A Venture in Social Forecasting* (New York: Basic, 1973).

2. Calculated from *Statistical Abstract of the United States 1920*, "Table 192: Population 10 Years and Upward Engaged in Gainful Occupations, Census Year 1910," http://www2.census.gov/prod2/statcomp/documents/1920–01.pdf (accessed July 19, 2006).

3. This is the definition I use in *Society and Technological Change*, 6th ed. (New York: Worth, 2008), 6.

4. John D. Verhoeven, "The Mystery of Damascus Blades," *Scientific American* 284, no. 1 (January 2001): 74–9.

5. See, for example, Walter Vincenti, "Technological Knowledge Without Science: The Innovation of Flush Riveting in American Airplanes, ca. 1930–ca. 1950," *Technology and Culture* 25 (July 1984): 540–76.

6. F. M. Scherer, *New Perspectives on Economic Growth and Technological Innovation* (Washington, DC: Brookings Institution Press, 1999), 25–48.

7. Malcolm I. Thomis, *The Luddites: Machine-Smashing in Regency England* (New York: Schocken, 1972), 14–5.

8. Allan Jalon, "Synthesizers: Sour Sound to Musicians," *Los Angeles Times*, December 6, 1985.

9. Neal Templin, "A Decisive Response to Crisis Brought Ford Enhanced Productivity," *Wall Street Journal*, December 15, 1992.

10. Melvin Kranzberg and Joseph Gies, *By the Sweat of Thy Brow: Work in the Western World* (New York: G. P. Putnam's Sons, 1975), 177.

11. Thomis, *The Luddites*, 14–5.

12. Amy Sue Bix, *Inventing Ourselves Out of Jobs? America's Debate Over Technological Unemployment, 1929–1981* (Baltimore: Johns Hopkins University Press, 2000).

13. Ibid., 76–8.

14. Marietta L. Baba, "Work and Technology in Modern Industry: The Creative Frontier," in *Meanings of Work: Considerations for the Twenty-First Century*, ed. Frederick C. Gamst (Albany: State University of New York Press, 1995), 139.

15. Emily Thornton, "Japan Lays Off Its Robots," *World Press Review* 43, no. 7 (July 1996): 31–2.

16. Joseph A. Schumpeter, *Capitalism, Socialism, and Democracy* (1942; repr., New York: Harper, 1975), 82–5.

17. Sara J. Czaja and Joseph Sharit, *Aging and Work: Issues and Implications* (Baltimore: Johns Hopkins University Press, 2009), 259.

18. T. E. Rizzuto and S. Mohammed, *Workplace Technology and the Myth About Older Workers*. Paper presented at the Annual Conference of the Society for Industrial and Organizational Psychology, Los Angeles, CA, 2005. Cited in Ron P. Githens, "Older Adults and E-learning: Opportunities and Barriers," http://www.rodgithens.com/papers/older_adults_elearning_2007.pdf (accessed August 26, 2010).

19. Leora Friedberg, "The Impact of Technological Change on Older Workers: Evidence From Data on Computers," (Department of Economics, University of California, San Diego, 1999), http://www.escholarship.org/uc/item/1s97n77x#page-2 (accessed August 26, 2010).

20. Horace L. Arnold and Fay M. Faurote, *Ford Methods and Ford Shops* (New York, 1915), 41–2. Quoted in David Montgomery, *Workers Control in America: Studies in the History of Work, Technology, and Labor Struggles* (Cambridge, UK: Cambridge University Press, 1979), 119.

21. Harry Braverman, *Labor and Monopoly Capital: The Degradation of Work in the Twentieth Century* (New York: Monthly Review Press, 1974).

22. Quoted in Alfred D. Chandler, *Giant Enterprise: Ford, General Motors, and the Automobile Industry* (New York: Harcourt, Brace, & World, 1964), 39–40.

23. David Hounshell, *From the American System to Mass Production, 1800–1932: The Development of Manufacturing Technology in the United States* (Baltimore: Johns Hopkins University Press, 1984), 216–301. For a more recent account of life as an assembly line worker, see Ben Hamper, *Rivethead: Tales From the Assembly Line* (New York: Warner, 1991).

24. Quoted in Hounshell, *From the American System*, 259.

25. David F. Noble, "Social Choice in Machine Design: The Case of Automatically Controlled Machine Tools," in *Case Studies in the Labor Process*, ed. Andrew Zimbalist (New York: Monthly Review Press, 1979), 34.

26. Cathy Trost, "The Price of Progress," *Wall Street Journal*, September 16, 1985.

27. J. Patrick Wright, *On a Clear Day You Can See General Motors* (New York: Avon, 1979), 94.

28. Shoshana Zuboff, *In The Age of the Smart Machine: The Future of Work and Power* (New York: Basic, 1988), 250.

29. Larry Hirschhorn, *Beyond Mechanization: Work and Technology in a Post-Industrial Age* (Cambridge: MIT Press, 1984), 62–86.

30. Kenneth I. Spenner, "Deciphering Prometheus: Temporal Change in the Skill Level of Work," *American Sociological Review* 48, no. 6 (December 1983): 824–37.

31. David R. Howell and Edward N. Wolff, "Trends in the Growth and Distribution of Skills in the U.S. Workplace, 1960–1985," *Industrial and Labor Relations Review* 44 (1991): 486–502. Cited in Chris Tilly and Charles Tilly, *Work Under Capitalism* (Boulder, CO: Westview, 1998), 159.

32. Ruth Milkman and Cydney Pullman, "Technological Change in an Automobile Assembly Plant: The Impact on Workers' Tasks and Skills," *Work and Occupations* 18, no. 2 (May 1991): 123–47.

33. Robert Reich has labeled information workers as "symbolic analysts," and he has viewed the growth of their activities as one of the fundamental forces reshaping the workplace. See *The Next American Frontier* (New York: Times Books, 1983).

34. Cindy Krischer Goodman, "Balancing Act: Telecommuting Is On The Rise," *Pittsburgh Post-Gazette*, June 7, 2010, http://www.post-gazette.com/pg/10158/1063247–407.stm (accessed January 7, 2011).

35. Diane E. Bailey and Nancy B. Kurland, "A Review of Telework Research: Findings, New Directions, and Lessons for the Study of Modern Work," *Journal of Organizational Behavior* 23 (2002): 384.

36. Phyllis Moen and Patricia Roehling, *The Career Mystique: Cracks in the American Dream* (Lanham, MD: Rowman & Littlefield, 2005), 179.

37. Ibid.

38. *Federal Daily*, "Telework Unlocks Workplace Flexibility, Union Leader Says," April 6, 2010, http://fcw.com/articles/2010/04/06/telework-key-to-workplace-flexibility.aspx (accessed August 31, 2010).

39. Bailey and Kurland, "A Review of Telework Research," 383–400.

40. Joel Mokyr, *The Gifts of Athena: Historical Origins of the Knowledge Economy* (Princeton, NJ: Princeton University Press, 2002), 160.

41. Ibid., 155.

42. Carlo M. Cipolla, *Guns, Sails, and Empire: Technological Innovation and the Early Phases of European Expansion* (New York: Pantheon, 1966); William H. McNeill, *Plagues and People* (New York: Anchor Books, 1976).

43. Tom Standage, *The Victorian Internet: The Remarkable Story of the Telegraph and the Nineteenth Century's On-Line Pioneers* (New York: Walker, 1998).

44. Darin Barney, *Prometheus Wired: The Hope for Democracy in the Age of Network Technology* (Chicago: University of Chicago Press, 2000), 62–4.

45. Jean-Paul Rodrigue, Claude Comtois, and Brian Slack, *The Geography of Transport Systems*, 2nd ed. (New York: Routledge, 2009), http://people.hofstra.edu/geotrans/eng/ch3en/conc3en/worldcontainertraffic.html (accessed January 10, 2011). For a discussion of intermodal transportation and its implications for labor, see Edna Bonacich and Jake B. Wilson, *Getting the Goods: Ports, Labor, and the Logistics Revolution* (Ithaca, NY: Cornell University Press, 2008).

6

Globalization

As noted in the previous chapter, technological change has been a major force in propelling the manifold changes collectively known as globalization. But globalization is not simply a response to technological advance in communications and transportation; it also reflects decisions and actions by governments, business firms, and other organizational actors. In this chapter, we will look into forces propelling globalization and assess its consequences, both positive and negative. The last segment of this chapter will take up one of the most controversial aspects of globalization: the movement of people across national borders.

Many definitions of globalization have been offered, but in the most general terms, it can be characterized as a large and expanding process of economic, political, and cultural interaction among the nations of the world and the people who inhabit them. The extent and importance of these transnational linkages can be seen in the growing volume of cross-border trade; foreign investment; and international flows of capital, cultural elements, and technology.[1] Globalization is one of the key trends in the world today. Individual countries and regions have differed in the extent to which they participate in globalization, but few places have escaped it completely.

Many institutional actors have been driving globalization. Private enterprises of every description have been heavily involved in the enlargement and interconnection of the international economy. Especially prominent are multinational corporations, such as Microsoft, Hyundai, Royal Dutch Shell, and Toshiba. But smaller, little-known firms—many of them suppliers to big multinational corporations—are also important players in the globalized economy. National governments are deeply involved in global issues as they seek to protect their interests and extend their influence. Globalization also has been actively promoted and guided by quasi-governmental international bodies—most notably the World Bank, the International Monetary Fund, and the World Trade Organization, along with the many agencies of the United Nations. Finally, numerous nongovernmental organizations, such as Planned Parenthood, Doctors Without Borders, and the World Wildlife Fund, are heavily involved in global issues.

Aside from the work of myriad private, governmental, quasi-governmental, and nongovernmental organizations, globalization has been propelled by diffuse processes through which cultural elements travel from one place to another—something that is apparent to anyone who has traveled abroad only to encounter music, food, and artistic styles common in his or her home country. Although globalization is often identified with Westernization, not all the transported cultural elements have come from Europe and North America, as we now see everything from Sufism to sushi being embraced far from their places of origin.

Although the term *globalization* is a recent coinage, the processes encompassed by it have been around for a long time. Writing in the middle of the 19th century, Karl Marx and Friedrich Engels could have been describing the current scene with their narration of capitalism's relentless efforts to bring all parts of the world into its economic orbit:

> The need of a constantly expanding market for its products chases the bourgeoisie over the whole surface of the globe. It must nestle everywhere, establish connections everywhere. The bourgeoisie has through its exploitation of the world market given a cosmopolitan character to production and consumption in every country.[2]

Although the reality of globalization cannot be denied, its extent and speed have been matters of considerable debate. If trends in world trade can be taken as key indicators of the magnitude of international economic relationships, then globalization, in some ways, was more evident in the years prior to World War I than it is today. Backed by the international gold standard for currency, capital flowed freely between nations, travelers could journey to foreign countries without a passport, and immigration was virtually unchecked. Today, however, globalization is more evident in the realm of international trade. In 1890, exports from the United States constituted about 5 percent of the nation's gross domestic product (GDP). In 2008, exports accounted for 12.7 percent of the country's GDP.[3]

Economic globalization looks even more pervasive when the spotlight is put on tradable goods, products that lend themselves to transportation across national boundaries. As we have seen in previous chapters, a great amount of economic activity takes place in the service sector. Although some services, notably banking and finance, have been an essential part of globalization, other services such as hairstyling and the preparation of meals are largely limited to a local market. In contrast, goods such as raw materials, agricultural products, and manufactured items are well suited to cross-border trade. It is in these sectors that the acceleration of economic globalization has been particularly evident. At the end of the 19th century, 20 percent of the tradable goods produced in the United States were exported; a hundred years later, the percentage had doubled.[4]

While economists, sociologists, and politicians may debate the extent to which globalization has affected human affairs, there can be little question that it has exerted a powerful influence on economic relationships in general, and on jobs and employment in particular. The essence of economic globalization is the large-scale integration and interdependence of individuals and organizations residing in separate nation-states. To put it succinctly, as the title of the best-selling book by Thomas Friedman has it, "the world is flat."[5] What this means is that 21st-century transportation and communication technologies have eliminated or greatly diminished the importance of geographic barriers and have tied many disparate parts of the world into a single, interconnected system. It is important to repeat, however, that these technologies have made globalization possible, but they have not done so in a deterministic manner. As we have seen in the previous chapter, large-scale changes cannot be attributed solely to technological advances; human agency is always the most important force. New technologies create possibilities, but it is people and the organizations through which they operate that determine how a technology is implemented, or if it is to be used at all. Throughout the process of globalization, as with all other important long-term trends, the aggregated decisions of individuals and organizations are much more important than the latest developments in air travel or digital communications. This means that globalization is not an impersonal, inexorable force. Like technology, it is a human creation, with at least the potential to be shaped and guided in accordance with human needs.

Governments and Globalization

Much of the advance of globalization can be attributed to decisions made by actors in the realms of government and politics, most importantly through actions that have eroded trade barriers and promoted economic integration. The most extensive of these have been the steps taken toward European economic integration during the post-World War II era. Although this is properly termed *regionalization* rather than *globalization,* it does demonstrate how individual countries have been able to transcend differences in languages, cultures, and governmental systems in the course of developing an integrated economic order. In 1951, Germany, France, Italy, the Netherlands, Belgium, and Luxemburg took the first steps toward economic integration when they agreed to jointly manage their coal, iron, and steel industries. In the years that followed, many more countries agreed to eliminate trade barriers and work toward economic integration under the aegis of an organization known as the European Community. By 2007, the European Community had become the European Union, a confederation of 27 nations committed—with varying degrees of enthusiasm—to social as well as economic integration and to the pursuit of common goals. One of the major products of that integration has been the emergence of the euro, which in 2002 became legal tender in 16 of the European Union's member nations. The modest steps initiated in 1951 have culminated in an economic colossus. As an aggregate, the nations of the European Union had a GDP of nearly $16.5 trillion in 2009, making the European Union the world's largest economic entity.

Other regions of the world have been brought into closer economic relationships through various trade agreements, treaties, and the operation of global organizations. In regard to the latter, the World Trade Organization (formerly the General Agreement on Tariffs and Trade, or GATT) has fostered wider and deeper international economic relationships through the establishment of rules governing trade, along with the adjudication of disputes among its members that have involved everything from Europe's prohibition of imports of American beef (due to the use of hormones) to the setting of emission standards for gasoline imported into the United States.[6]

The most significant—and contentious—trade treaty affecting jobs and employment in the United States has been the North American Free Trade Agreement (NAFTA). Enacted in 1994, NAFTA eliminated or began to phase out most of the tariffs and other trade barriers that had inhibited the flow of goods between Canada, the United States, and Mexico. The enactment of NAFTA threw a spotlight on the factories, known as *maquiladoras*, located on the U.S.–Mexico border—although NAFTA's role in their expansion is still a matter of scholarly debate. These enterprises, about 3,000 in number, produce a large variety of manufactured goods bearing the brand names of multinational companies. Their major advantage is low labor costs; maquiladoras offer daily wages about equal to what an average American worker makes per hour.

The cost advantages offered by the use of cheap labor have understandably led to deep concerns that this aspect of globalization imperils the jobs of many workers in the United States and other developed countries. NAFTA in particular has been excoriated in the United States as a major cause of unemployment and diminished wages. NAFTA's potential to affect jobs and wages is a valid concern, but it needs to be put in perspective. In 2007, total trade between Canada, Mexico, and the United States came to $903 billion—a hefty sum to be sure but one that represented less than 6 percent of the three nations' aggregate gross national product of $15.3 trillion. Moreover, much of that trade volume centered on oil, minerals, and services, further shrinking the relative importance of cross-border trade in manufactured items for the economies of the three nations.

In regard to employment, there is no question that some American workers lost their jobs when their firms moved manufacturing operations to Mexico. This has resulted in NAFTA being widely blamed for the decline in manufacturing employment that has occurred in recent years, but as noted in the previous chapter, technological changes were also taking a toll. It is also undeniable that the wages of some workers were frozen or even cut because their employers could hold out the threat of closing their workplaces and moving operations to Mexico.

Although NAFTA in general and maquiladoras in particular have been widely blamed for unemployment and stagnant wages in the United States, their influence has not been as simple as it is often made out to be. Without downplaying the real pain suffered by workers as a result of their places of employment moving to Mexico, it is important to credit NAFTA with the creation of new jobs based on the export of goods and services to Canada and Mexico. Also, as mentioned previously, other forces—notably technological change—were altering the structure of work and remuneration. Sorting out the consequences of these different forces is a complicated business, one best left for Chapter 10, which will more comprehensively take up the causes and consequences of recent changes in employment and remuneration.

Photo 6.1   Maquiladora workers

SOURCE: ©Bob Daemmrich/CORBIS.

Multinational Corporations and Globalized Production

The establishment of maquiladoras in Mexico has been one aspect of a larger trend, the increased presence of multinational (or transnational) corporations (MNCs). An MNC can be succinctly defined as a firm that wholly or partially owns and operates enterprises in more than one country. A great variety of firms meet this simple criterion, making it difficult, if not impossible, to make general statements about their impact.

Some of the earliest MNCs were involved in mining or other extractive industries. Others established and operated large plantations for the production of crops such as bananas or rubber. Many of them earned deservedly horrible reputations for their treatment of workers, the ruination of local environments, and their propensity to meddle in the political affairs of their host nations, sometimes to the point of engineering military coups. MNCs of this ilk are sometimes taken as being typical, but in recent years, it is much more common for MNCs to be involved in manufacturing, retailing, and the provision of services. Their presence has not necessarily been benign, but today's MNCs rarely have approached the depredations of the United Fruit Company in Central America or Belgian mining interests in the Congo.

Much of the apparent homogeneity of today's world is due to the highly visible presence of consumer-oriented MNCs such as Wal-Mart, McDonald's, and the Hard Rock Cafe. As with MNCs in general, the presence of consumer-oriented MNCs has had mixed consequences. Wal-Mart and other huge retailers have used systematization, advanced technologies, and sheer size to lower costs and bring inexpensive goods to an expanding customer base, while at the same time driving many small retailers out of business. Global fast-food chains have attracted a large following, but they also have been at least partially responsible for lowered nutritional standards and growing numbers of overweight men, women, and especially children. They also have threatened to marginalize local cuisines, thereby giving rise to an oppositional "slow-food movement" in Italy and other countries.

MNCs have become prominent players in other services such as banking, accounting, insurance, and advertising. Much of their growth in these sectors has been made possible by the ability to render information into digital codes that can be rapidly and inexpensively sent from one place to another, often over great distances. With the transmission infrastructure in place, it hardly matters if the information is sent 50 miles or 5,000 miles.

At the lower end of the globalized service economy, billing and bookkeeping services are provided by workers in some low-wage countries, and consumers are no longer surprised when telephone inquiries to technical support personnel are answered by call-center workers in India. At the upper end of the service economy, foreign doctors read and interpret medical diagnostic tests such as X-rays and EKGs, programmers a dozen time zones away from the home office write sophisticated computer codes; and professionals offshore complete a growing number of engineering and accounting tasks.[7]

Service-providing MNCs now account for more foreign investment funds than do MNCs in the extractive and manufacturing sectors.[8] MNCs in the service sector typically pay wages and salaries that are relatively low when compared with the home country but high for the host country. Up to now, at least, their operations have not displaced many workers in the MNCs' home countries.

The Economic Benefits of Foreign Trade _____

The increased influence of MNCs is part of the larger phenomenon of expanded trade between nations and regions. Before dealing with some of the consequences of MNC activity, it is useful to consider some fundamental justifications for foreign trade in general. Throughout most of the history of their discipline, economists have generally been staunch supporters of free trade and international economic relationships. Some of this support rests on the obvious fact that no modern nation can be completely self-sufficient; for example, it would defy economic logic for Norway to attempt to produce bananas or for Saudi Arabia to try to develop a timber industry. But there is a subtler, less obvious basis for international trade: the theory of *comparative advantage*. First formulated by the British economist David Ricardo during the second decade of the 19th century, this important idea is closely tied to another basic concept of economics, the *opportunity costs* that underlie all economic actions. Whenever an individual or organization spends time, money, or any other resource to accomplish something, they are giving up the opportunity to do something else. For example, as I write these sentences, I am missing out on the opportunity to earn more money on a per-hour basis by mowing my neighbor's lawn.

According to the theory of comparative advantage, individual businesses and nations as a whole should seek to minimize their opportunity costs. Consequently, the Republic of Freedonia may have the capability of doing everything better than the Kingdom of Sylvania can, but it still should buy certain goods and services from the latter country, even though it has an absolute advantage in producing the same goods and services. What matters is comparative advantage; by buying certain goods and services from Sylvania, Freedonia is able to use its labor, capital, and resource endowments for the production of the particular goods and services in which it has an even greater advantage. Decisions regarding what to produce and what not to produce are not, of course, made by countries as a whole but by individual firms. Comparative advantage comes into play for these firms because it results in lower input costs than would be the case if their home country tried to produce everything in which it has an absolute advantage.

Trading relations based on comparative advantage should also guide decisions about overseas investments. It makes good economic sense for individual firms to set up offshore subsidiaries in accordance with the comparative advantages of the home country vis-à-vis the country in which the subsidiary firm is to be located. But important as it may be, comparative advantage is not the only basis for setting up subsidiaries in foreign lands, and it can even be argued that the growing influence of MNCs has resulted in investment patterns that do not fit neatly into established trade theory.[9]

Without delving too deeply into this issue, a number of reasons for MNC investments in overseas subsidiaries can be noted. First, efforts to liberalize trade are incomplete at best, and many potential exporters remain thwarted by tariffs and other barriers to the sale of their products abroad. Under these circumstances, setting up an overseas subsidiary may be necessary in order to circumvent these restrictions. Second, even in an era of sharply reduced shipping costs due to containerization and other technological innovations, transportation costs are not negligible, so the production of goods in closer proximity to one's customers may produce substantial savings. Third, being close to the places in which a firm's goods and services are marketed may lead to a better understanding of the needs, desires, and tastes of local customers. Fourth, the fluctuating exchange rates at which currencies are traded can be a major barrier to overseas sales, especially when one's currency appreciates in relation to the currencies of present and potential trading partners. The establishment of a local subsidiary can, therefore, mitigate uncertainties about the direction of exchange rates. Last, but certainly not least, it has to be recognized that the decisions and activities of MNCs, as with business firms in general, are not always governed by pure economic logic. Some firms may pursue expansion for the sake of expansion ("We're number one!"). Not infrequently, this goal is driven by the ambitions of top executives who seek the power, prestige, and income associated with the leadership of a large and growing MNC.

Workers Abroad

The many motivations for offshore expansion by MNCs do not necessarily negate a common critique of MNCs: that for quite a few of them, the real appeal of establishing subsidiaries abroad, especially in poor countries (sometimes referred to collectively as the Third World), lies in the availability of cheap labor. At the same time, however, it must be recognized that the attractiveness of setting up shop in a poor, low-wage country may be offset by a host of disadvantages. After all, if the availability of low-cost labor were the only thing that mattered, most of the world's manufacturing would take place in sub-Saharan Africa. Labor costs are only one part of the recipe for successful manufacturing. Firms also have to take into account the availability and competence of suppliers; transportation costs; worker skills; financial, communication, and energy infrastructures; and the effectiveness and relative honesty of host governments and their officials.

That being said, it is still the case that many poor countries have large numbers of unemployed and underemployed workers, which makes them attractive to MNCs seeking low-cost labor. They also may have certain industries and sectors that confer some comparative advantages over those in more developed countries. Therefore, it may be financially advantageous for foreign firms with significant labor requirements to establish factories in countries where workers will put up with low wages and long hours. But economic rationality does not always mesh with social justice. Critics of globalization as it has been promoted by MNCs claim that it has resulted in the exploitation of workers in Third World countries by taking advantage of the limited bargaining power of these workers. In response, supporters of MNC-sponsored globalization point to the rising standards of living that have occurred in places such as China, Taiwan, South Korea, and Brazil; a significant share of their impressive rates of economic growth has been propelled by production for export markets, although not all of it has been based on the efforts of MNCs. Proponents of globalization under the aegis of MNCs also can note that sub-Saharan Africa, the least globalized region in the inhabited world, is also the poorest.[10]

A definitive evaluation of the benefits and drawbacks of MNCs in Third World countries remains elusive, but even the most stalwart supporters of globalization, whether led by MNCs or by indigenous firms, generally agree that its economic benefits have been spread unevenly. This pattern of lopsided growth is exemplified by China, the most dramatic example of economic transformation through globalization. Through three decades of communist rule, beginning in 1949, China remained largely insulated from the international economy. As might be expected of a communist nation, it had a relatively egalitarian distribution of income, but also an equality of shared poverty. The situation began to change a few years after the death of Mao Zedong in 1976, when China initiated large-scale participation in the world economy. The success of this policy can be seen in an economy that, for the past two decades, has grown by about 10 percent per year—a phenomenal rate that results in a doubling of national income every 7 years or so. Despite having more potential consumers than any other place on Earth, much of this growth has been based on aggressive export-promotion policies; in 2005, for example, about half the goods manufactured in China were sold abroad.[11] Export-led growth has been responsible for much of the dramatic reduction in poverty that has occurred in China in recent years. Yet poverty has hardly been banished; although hundreds of millions of people have emerged from poverty as a result of China's rapid economic growth, a vast number of rural inhabitants—about half the country's total population—are still desperately poor. Not only has absolute poverty stubbornly endured, the rural-urban income gap has actually widened. In the late 1980s, when China's far-reaching economic reforms were about a decade old, the per-household ratio of urban incomes to rural incomes was 2.2 to 1; by 2004, that ratio had widened to 3.2 to 1.[12]

Many Chinese workers have tried to escape the dire poverty of the countryside by pursuing job opportunities in China's cities. An estimated 211 million internal immigrants, commonly referred to as the "floating population," now live in China's cities.[13] Although migration to urban areas has improved the economic circumstances of many of these migrants, their status has been likened to that of undocumented workers in the United States and Europe. They differ from the latter in that they have the legal right to reside in the city, but they do not enjoy the benefits of healthcare, housing, education, and other perquisites available to urban residents who possess an internal passport, known as a *hukou*. And although their jobs generally provide higher incomes than they had earned in the countryside, the work they do is often difficult, hazardous, and poorly remunerated. Although internal migration has boosted their incomes, the situation of this floating population is hardly enviable.

Supporters of economic globalization do not deny that an abundance of workers in China and other developing nations receive low wages and work in unpleasant circumstances, but as they might ask rhetorically, what is the alternative? Workers in low-wage countries are paid poorly because employment opportunities have not kept up with population growth, and, perhaps more importantly, the social and governmental structures of many of these countries have impeded economic development. As with China, much of the population of the Third World still resides in the countryside amidst conditions of extreme poverty and with little hope that life will get much better if they stay where they are. Working long hours at a monotonous and sometimes dangerous job for the equivalent of a few dollars a day is not an attractive prospect for the inhabitant of an economically advanced country, but for the children of impoverished farmers, manufacturing jobs that supply a global market hold out at least the promise of improved economic circumstances.

As we saw in Chapter 2, during the early decades of the 19th century, a cadre of young women was employed—some would say "exploited"—in New England textile mills. Similar situations can be found in the economic history of Europe and Japan.[14] These young women workers put in long hours for wages that were not much above subsistence levels, and they were subjected to restrictions that would be deemed intolerable by today's standards. Yet, by leaving the farm and achieving a measure of economic self-sufficiency, they were in the vanguard of the women's liberation movement. As Pietra Rivoli has noted,

> The irony . . . is that the suffocating labor practices in textile and apparel production, the curfews and locked dormitories, the timed bathroom visits and production quotas, the forced church attendance and the high fences—all of the factors throughout industrial history designed to control young women—were at the same time part of the women's economic liberation and autonomy.[15]

Workers at Home

In the developed world, globalization has been beneficial to consumers seeking low-priced goods, but as with the Third World, globalization's benefits have not been distributed equally. Although it is certainly not the only cause, globalization has eliminated jobs and caused the virtual disappearance in the United States of entire industries, such as footwear manufacture and the assembly of inexpensive electronic devices. The loss of these industries and the jobs they supported has devastated communities and even entire regions. The textile industry in North Carolina is a particularly striking example. From 1996 to 2006, more than 870 textile mills and apparel factories closed. As a result, during those 10 years, the region suffered a loss of 150,000 jobs in textile production and 48,000 in the apparel industry. Most of these laid-off workers have met great difficulties trying to find new jobs. Only 62 percent were able to find work within 2 years of losing their jobs, and these new jobs paid on average only 88 percent of what they had previously earned. Workers over the age of 55 were hit particularly hard, earning an average of only 78 percent of their pre-layoff wages—if they found work at all.[16]

Globalization and Job Creation

Many other examples of globalization's baleful effects on individuals, firms, industries, and regions could be cited. But it is important to keep in mind that the effects of globalization and the replacement of American and European workers by cheap Third World labor is a more complicated issue than is often presented. For one thing, there is far more to globalization than investments in and exports from Third World countries. A large portion of international trade takes place between the industrially developed countries, not between the rich and poor countries; trade within Europe and between Europe and the United States accounts for 35 percent of all the world's trade.[17] The same is true of direct foreign investment; through the past two decades, an average of 58 percent of it went to countries that are already developed, even though these countries hold only 17 percent of the world's population.[18] In similar fashion, exports from Third World countries still compose a small portion of total sales in the United States, Europe, and Japan. Consumers may have the impression that just about everything sold at Target or Wal-Mart is made in China, yet manufactured items imported from developing countries still equaled only 6.2 percent of the U.S. GDP in 2006.[19]

Globalization, moreover, is a two-way street, and there are many instances of jobs being created through increased exports of goods and services in the United States and other developed countries. In 2008, American exports accounted for nearly 7 percent of total employment, and even in the beleaguered manufacturing sector, one-third of the jobs were tied to exports.[20] Globalization also has brought jobs and capital to a variety of industries and individual firms in the U.S. through the actions of foreign MNCs. Although the relocation of American manufacturing plants to foreign countries has received more publicity, a parallel trend of "onshoring" has supported a lot of jobs in the United States. Direct investment by foreign MNCs is a sizeable part of the American economy, accounting for 15 percent of the nation's GDP. More to the point of the present discussion, foreign corporations directly employ 5.3 million American workers and indirectly account for another 4.6 million jobs.[21]

In sum, the overall effects of economic globalization have many similarities to those brought on by advances in production technologies. Although particular jobs, firms, and industries will be injured or vanish altogether, they are not the whole story. As with technological advances, the lower production costs made possible by globalization will translate into some combination of lower prices, higher wages and salaries, and greater profits. As a result, spendable income will increase (at least for some segments of the society), which in turn will expand the demand for goods and services—at least some of which will be supplied by workers in the home country. This is the good news, but the uncomfortable fact remains that both technological advance and globalization create winners and losers, sometimes in spectacular fashion. As will be elaborated in Chapter 10, these two powerful forces have been implicated in the widening disparities of wealth and income that have been all too evident in recent years.

Immigration

Globalization isn't just about the international movement of goods, capital, and information; it also encompasses the large-scale migration of people across national borders. Immigration is a major source of economic, social, and cultural change today, as indicated by the estimated 125 million people currently living in countries other than those in which they were born.[22] There are many reasons for people to leave their homeland for other places, but the draw of improved economic prospects is usually high on the list.

As with globalization in general, immigration is not a new phenomenon. Large waves of immigrants, primarily from southern and eastern Europe, arrived in the United States from the 1880s to the early 1920s, accounting for nearly a quarter of the increase in the American labor force during this period.[23] In the years that followed, immigration dramatically subsided as a result of changed laws, wars, and economic stagnation. It revived after 1965, when new immigration laws abolished country-by-country quotas that had set sharp limits on the number of people, especially non-Europeans, who could legally enter the United States. Since that time, the number of immigrants has increased substantially, to the point that by the 1990s, 40 percent of U.S. population growth was the result of immigration, about the same as during the earlier high tide of immigration.[24]

Immigrant labor has been particularly evident in certain parts of the United States. California, New York, Texas, Florida, and New Jersey received the largest numbers of legal immigrants in 2003, collectively accounting for 47 percent of the U.S. total.[25] Large portions of the American South and Midwest also have substantial immigrant populations who have been attracted by the availability of jobs in meatpacking, construction, farming, and manufacturing. All in all, in 2008, more than 37 million noncitizens and naturalized citizens resided in the United States, about 12.5 percent of the nation's total population.[26]

Although the distinction between legal and illegal entrants is sometimes lost in discussions of immigration, the majority of recent immigrants have entered the United States with the proper documentation. The number of illegal immigrants residing in the United States is difficult to ascertain, but 12 million is a commonly accepted tally. Of these, an estimated 59 percent have come from Mexico, which is understandable, given that country's proximity to the United States.[27]

Immigration, legal and otherwise, has been stimulated by one of the key forces propelling globalization: the rapid advance of the electronic media. Movies, television programs, CDs, DVDs, and the Internet have exposed people in the Third World to the (often romanticized) high-consumption lifestyles of the developed world, underscoring the material poverty of their own countries. Advances in media technology also have smoothed some of the dislocations caused by immigration by allowing immigrants to stay in close touch with their native land through movies, radio and television broadcasts, international telephone services, the Internet, e-mail, and social networking sites. Electronic money transfers also have facilitated an important motivation for immigration, supporting families back home through cash remittances.

Governmental Policies and Immigration

One of the basic principles of the European Union has been the free flow of people within its borders. In North America, the free flow of goods and services mandated by NAFTA has not been accompanied by the free movement of people. Quite the opposite—in recent years, the United States has spent billions of dollars in an attempt to seal the U.S.–Mexico border. According to some students of current immigration patterns, these efforts have had the ironic consequence of increasing the number of illegal immigrants in the United States. As they see it, a border that is less easily crossed has upset the previous immigration patterns by preventing the cyclical movement of Mexican workers between the United States and their home country. Consequently, tighter border controls have motivated illegal immigrants to stay in the United States, and to encourage their family members to join them.[28]

One of the hopes underlying the enactment of NAFTA was that it would reduce illegal immigration by improving economic opportunities in Mexico. This hope has not been realized, and it has even been argued that NAFTA increased illegal immigration by undermining Mexico's agricultural sector. According to the critics, NAFTA's promotion of free trade in agricultural commodities has put Mexican farmers in a losing competition against more productive American farmers. The availability of inexpensive food from the United States has lowered the incomes of Mexican farmers, motivating many of them to abandon their farms and seek work in the United States. This critique is logically consistent, but it lacks empirical support. It is true that the price of corn in Mexico has fallen and, as a result, has depressed the income of many indigenous farmers, but this trend was evident long before the passage of

NAFTA.[29] Making matters worse are the policies of the Mexican government, which have subsidized large-scale farming operations but done little for poor farmers.[30]

Whatever the reasons for leaving the countries of their birth, the great majority of illegal immigrants from Mexico and elsewhere have come to the United States seeking employment. In 2006, immigrant workers constituted an estimated 4.9 percent of the U.S. labor force, accounting for 29 percent of agricultural workers, an equal percentage of roofers and drywall installers, 25 percent of construction laborers, 21 percent of private household workers, and 14 percent of workers in food production.[31] Current figures are likely to be lower, as the Great Recession has significantly reduced employment opportunities for undocumented immigrants. According to one study, the size of this group dropped by 12 percent between the first quarter of 2007 and the first quarter of 2009.[32]

This reduction notwithstanding, there remains a large number of illegal immigrant workers in certain industries, which poses a key question about the role of immigrant labor in the American economy: could these industries survive without these workers? It is often asserted that immigrants, especially illegal ones, "do the work that native-born Americans are unwilling to do." There is no question that many of the jobs held by immigrant workers are dangerous, physically taxing, and poorly paid. There is evidence, however, that at least some of these jobs would be taken by American workers if they were paid better and if their working conditions were improved.[33]

The effects of immigration on wages and salaries will be taken up in Chapter 10. Yet, important though it may be, immigration's influence on wages and salaries has not been the only source of concern. Even if immigration has had generally positive consequences for the economy, large-scale immigration—especially the flow of undocumented workers—may in some places create cultural conflicts, while increasing the burdens borne by schools, hospitals, and other public services. Illegal immigrants defray at least some of these costs when they pay sales, income, property, and payroll taxes. Whether or not these payments are greater or less than the cost of the services received by these workers has been the source of considerable debate, but the issue has been difficult to resolve due to a lack of adequate empirical data.

One possible way of damping illegal immigration while accommodating the need for temporary workers in particular industries is through "guest worker" programs. Guest workers are men and women from other lands who have been given the legal right to work but only for fixed amounts of time. Several European countries made extensive use of guest workers during the economic boom years of the 1950s and 1960s, drawing on the populations of poor regions of the continent, such as Spain, Yugoslavia, and southern Italy. The United States also made substantial use of guest workers in the 1940s and 1950s through the *bracero* program, which allowed farmworkers from Mexico to work legally in the United States during busy times in the farming season.

Guest worker programs, however, usually fail in their goal of employing foreign workers for only limited periods of time. Even when they originally intend to work only for a few months or years, many guest workers end up being disinclined to leave the host country, and they may make every effort to remain there, legally or illegally. At the same time, their employers often are unwilling to part with well-trained and effective workers. Together, these pressures make it difficult to allow the employment of immigrant workers for fixed periods of time with the expectation that they will return to their places of origin. Further issues arise when the children of guest workers are born in the host country. Children born within the borders of the United States are automatically U.S. citizens, whereas those born in most European nations are not assumed to be citizens of those countries. But in both cases, a significant population of children and adults has little connection to the countries from which their parents came. Some may eventually immigrate to the lands of their parents and grandparents, but the great majority are likely to remain in the countries of their birth. Efforts to encourage them to abandon the lives to which they have been accustomed are not likely to be successful.

Immigration, as with globalization in general, is often viewed in a negative light, but its positive contributions to the American economy and society should be underscored. A cursory examination of American history provides many examples of immigrants who made major contributions to their adopted land, individuals such as Charles Steinmetz and Nicola Tesla in electrical engineering, Jacob Riis in social reform, Carl Schurz in government, and Andrew Carnegie in industry. Today, a significant number of immigrants have founded start-up firms, resulting in the creation of many new jobs for both native and foreign-born workers. Immigrants have been particularly prominent in high-tech enterprises; according to one study, between 1995 and 2005, 25.3 percent of new technology and engineering firms, which accounted for 450,000 jobs, had foreign-born founders, chief executives, presidents, or chief technology officers.[34]

A more positive light is also cast on immigration when long-term demographic trends are taken into account. The populations of the United States and many of the countries of Europe are growing slowly, and in some countries—notably Spain, Italy, Russia, and Japan—the birth rate is too low even to maintain the present size of the population. At the same time, life expectancies in the developed world have been moving upward. The result is a steady increase in the average age of the native-born populations of these countries and a growing ratio of retirees to workers. In the United States, there are now about 65 million members of the baby-boomer cohort born between 1946 and 1964, the oldest of which are now well into their 60s. At the end of the first decade of the 21st century, even the youngest members of the cohort reached middle age. At the same time, succeeding demographic cohorts, sometimes labeled Generation X and Generation Y, are much smaller than the boomer generation. Under these circumstances, a continuing influx of immigrant workers may be essential to the economic well-being of the rich nations of the world by making up for the expected shortfall of workers. Moreover, as the baby-boomer generation moves inexorably into the ranks of the elderly, its members will require more health and personal care services. Many of the jobs in these sectors are low-paying and, in general, not very appealing. These jobs are already disproportionately staffed by immigrants, and this pattern is likely to be even more pronounced in the years to come.

Many of the themes and topics introduced in this and the previous chapter will reappear in later chapters. But before considering how, for example, technological change and globalization have affected the distribution of wages and salaries, we will shift the focus from these large issues and turn our attention to more individualized concerns. More specifically, we will consider the initial stage of employment: getting a job.

FOR DISCUSSION

1. In what ways has economic globalization been apparent to you? In what ways has it benefited you, your family, and your community? Have you witnessed any negative consequences of globalization?

2. When faced with high levels of unemployment, some politicians, labor unions, and others call for tariffs and other restrictions on imports in order to preserve jobs in the home country. Is this a wise course of action? Who is likely to benefit from efforts to thwart this aspect of globalization? Who will be hurt by them?

3. On balance, have multinational corporations been a force for good or a force for evil? What are the criteria you would use when making this assessment?

4. To what extent do you take globalization into account when thinking about your present or future career? What sort of skills could be particularly useful for a job in a globalized environment?

5. Although immigration, even when it is illegal, may produce economic benefits overall, it does bring certain problems. What are they? On balance, do the benefits of immigration outweigh its costs? Do legal and illegal immigration differ in this regard?

Notes

1. Jagdish Bhagwati, *In Defense of Globalization* (New York: Oxford University Press, 2004).

2. Karl Marx and Friedrich Engels, "Manifesto of the Communist Party," in *Selected Works* (Moscow: Foreign Languages Publishing House, 1962), 37.

3. John Tschetter, "Exports Support American Jobs" (Washington, DC: United States Department of Commerce, International Trade Administration), http://trade.gov/publications/pdfs/exports-support-american-jobs.pdf (accessed November 30, 2010).

4. Michael D. Bordo, Barry Eichengreen, and Douglas A. Irwin, "Is Globalization Today Really Different Than Globalization a Hundred Years Ago?" Paper prepared for the Brookings Trade Policy Forum on Governing in a Global Economy, Washington, DC, April 15–16, 1999, http://www.econ.berkeley.edu/~eichengr/research/brooking.pdf (accessed November 30, 2010), 7.

5. Thomas L. Friedman, *The World Is Flat: A Brief History of the Twenty-First Century* (New York: Farrar, Straus, & Giroux, 2006).

6. Michael Paulson, "Examples of Disputes Resolved by the WTO," *Seattle Post-Intelligencer,* November 22, 1999, http://www.seattlepi.com/national/case1.shtml (accessed September 7, 2010).

7. Martyn Day, "Offshore Outsourcing: Engineering Goes Overseas," http://www.caddigest.com/subjects/industry/select/011204_day_outsourcing.htm (accessed May 11, 2007); Outsourcing Institute, "Finance and Accounting Outsourcing to Reach $48 Billion," http://www.outsourcing.com/content.asp?page=01b/other/oe/q204/finance/html (accessed May 11, 2007).

8. Stephen D. Cohen, *Multinational Corporations and Direct Foreign Investment: Avoiding Simplicity, Embracing Complexity* (Oxford, UK: Oxford University Press, 2007), 81.

9. Ibid., 222–9.

10. Although in relative terms sub-Saharan Africa currently lags in regard to direct foreign investment and MNC involvement, it historically has been the scene of some of the worst exploitation of resources and people by foreign countries and firms. Even today, oil production and the extraction of minerals have produced, directly or indirectly, a great deal of human suffering. See, for example, Tume Abenba, "Nigerian People Seeing Little Benefit From Record Oil Revenues," *New York Times,* July 21, 2008, http://www.nytimes.com/2008/07/21/business/worldbusiness/21iht-oil.1.14650030.html (accessed September 17, 2009).

11. W. Michael Cox and Richard Alm, "China and India: Two Paths to Economic Power," *Economic Letter* 3, no. 8 (August 2008), http://www.dallasfed.org/research/eclett/2008/el0808.html (accessed September 8, 2010).

12. Xubei Luo and Nong Zhu, "Rising Income Inequality in China: A Race to the Top," working paper (World Bank, East Asia and Pacific Region, August 2008), http://library1.nida.ac.th/worldbankf/fulltext/wps04700.pdf (accessed September 8, 2010).

13. "China's 'Floating Population' Exceeds 210 million," *China Daily,* June 27, 2010, http://www.chinadaily.com.cn/china/2010–06/27/content_10024861.htm (accessed September 8, 2010).

14. For a history of women textile workers during Japan's early industrialization, see E. Patricia Tsurumi, *Factory Girls: Women in the Thread Mills of Meiji Japan* (Princeton: Princeton University Press, 1990).

15. Pietra Rivoli, *The Travels of a T-Shirt in the Global Economy: An Economist Examines the Markets, Power, and Politics of World Trade* (Hoboken, NJ: John Wiley, 2005), 94.

16. "North Carolina in the Global Economy: Textiles and Apparel," http://www.soc.duke.edu/NC_GlobalEconomy/textiles/workers.shtml (accessed September 8, 2010).

17. Robert C. Feenstra and Alan M. Taylor, *International Economics* (New York: Worth, 2008), 7.

18. Cohen, *Multinational Corporations,* 149.

19. Lawrence Mishel, Jared Bernstein, and Heidi Shierholz, *The State of Working America 2008/2009* (Ithaca, NY: Cornell University Press, 2009), 187.

20. U.S. Department of Commerce, "Secretary Locke Speaks at the Virginia Summit on Export Opportunities," http://www.commerce.gov/ (accessed September 14, 2010).

21. Micheline Maynard, *The Selling of the American Economy: How Foreign Companies Are Remaking the American Dream* (New York: Random House, 2009), 22.

22. Anthony Giddens, Mitchell Duneier, and Richard Appelbaum, *Introduction to Sociology,* 5th ed. (New York: Norton, 2005), 600.

23. Jeffrey Williamson, *Globalization and Inequality Then and Now: The Late 19th and Late 20th Centuries Compared* (NBER Working Paper No. 5491, Cambridge, MA: National Bureau of Economic Research, 1996). Cited in Dani Rodrik, *Has Globalization Gone Too Far?* (Washington, DC: Institute for International Economics, 1997), 8.

24. Robert Cherry, *Who Gets the Good Jobs? Combating Race and Gender Disparities* (New Brunswick, NJ: Rutgers University Press, 2001), 115.

25. U.S. Department of Homeland Security, Office of Immigration Statistics, *2003 Yearbook of Immigration Statistics,* http://www.uscis.gov/graphics/shared/aboutus/statistics/2003Yearbook.pdf (accessed July 14, 2006), 9.

26. Calculated from U.S. Census Bureau, "Population by Sex, Age, Nativity, and U.S. Citizenship: 2008," http://www.census.gov/population/socdemo/foreign/cps2008/tab1–1.xls (accessed September 14, 2010).

27. Pew Hispanic Center, "Mexican Immigrants in the United States, 2008," April 15, 2009, http://pewhispanic.org/files/factsheets/47.pdf (accessed October 8, 2009).

28. Patricia Fernandez-Kelly and Douglas S. Massey, "Borders for Whom? The Role of NAFTA in Mexico–U.S. Migration," in *NAFTA and Beyond: Alternative Perspectives in the Study of Global Trade and Development,* eds. Patricia Fernandez-Kelly and Jon Shefner (Los Angeles: Sage, 2007), 98–118.

29. Antonio Yunez-Naude, "Liberalization of Staple Crops: Lessons From the Mexican Experience in Maize." Paper presented at the International Association of Agricultural Economists Conference, Beijing, China, August 16–22, 2009, http://ageconsearch.umn.edu/bitstream/50827/2/Paper%20%23%20586.pdf (accessed October 7, 2010).

30. Ibid.

31. Jonathan Peterson and Richard Simon, "Affected Industries Clamor for Consideration," *Los Angeles Times,* April 6, 2006.

32. Jeffrey S. Passel and D'Vera Cohn, "U.S. Unauthorized Immigration Flows Are Down Sharply Since Mid-Decade" (Pew Hispanic Center, September 1, 2010), http://pewhispanic.org/files/reports/126.pdf (accessed May 3, 2011).

33. Ivan Light, *Deflecting Immigration: Networks, Markets, and Regulation in Los Angeles* (New York: Russell Sage Foundation, 2006).

34. "Immigrants Lead Many Tech Start-Ups, Study Says," *Los Angeles Times,* January 4, 2007.

7

Getting a Job

Just about everybody has had the experience of being hired to do a particular job at some time in his or her life. Sometimes, it is as simple as answering an advertisement in a newspaper or responding to a "help wanted" sign in a store window. At the other extreme, a job may be filled only after an extensive search on the part of both a prospective employer and the person who ends up being hired. The way jobs are allocated reflects many of the essential features of an economy and society—racial, ethnic, and gender divisions; the distribution of power; social networks; and laws and regulations. In this chapter, we will look at the process of getting a job, paying special attention to the interplay of the structural features of a society and the abilities, motivations, and social connections that individuals bring to the process of looking for and finding work.

The Economics of the Job Market

In assessing the employment situation today or in the past, economists, politicians, and members of the public frequently refer to the "labor market." But underlying this commonplace term is a massive historical shift in the way people have found and held jobs. In Chapters 1 and 2, we saw how jobs were apportioned largely on the basis of ascribed characteristics for the bulk of human history and prehistory. For most people, the work they did reflected their gender, ethnicity, and age, along with the family and social position they were born into. In modern societies, by contrast, it is assumed that the operation of an impersonal market sorts people into particular jobs at appropriate rates of pay. Just as there are markets for goods such as soybeans, petroleum, cars, and shoes, labor can be described as a kind of commodity allocated by market forces. Although we will soon see that the way jobs are filled entails considerably more than the workings of an impersonal labor market, it is still an important force in determining who does what in a modern economy.

Markets operate through the interaction of supply and demand. In the case of labor markets, employers are the source of demand, while individuals seeking work provide the supply. Markets bring supply and demand into equilibrium through the price mechanism. When the price of something is high, suppliers will be motivated to offer a lot of it, and when the price is low, less will be offered. In parallel fashion, a low price will lead buyers to acquire more of an item, while a high price will turn them away from it. In regard to labor markets, the price that drives the market is the wage or salary paid to workers.[1] A high wage or salary will bring out many job seekers, while a comparatively low one will result in many potential workers electing to look for better-paying work, if there is any to be had. Similarly, a high rate of remuneration will motivate workers to put in more hours on the job if they are being paid by the hour. On the employers' side, low wages and salaries make it worth their while to hire more workers and/or offer more hours of work than would be the case if these wages and salaries were at a relatively higher level.

Similar reasoning can be applied to the matching of individuals to particular occupations. Occupations that require a lot of innate talent and specialized training, so the argument goes, bring in large salaries because these are what motivate talented individuals to devote themselves to a lengthy period of arduous study. Without the lure of high future earnings, individuals might be unwilling to forgo income lost while preparing for a career that requires years of education and deferred gratification. On the flip side, a large number of occupations offer low wages because the pool of prospective workers is large, with little required in terms of innate ability and educational achievement. The tasks performed by low-wage workers may be of great importance—think of what life would be like if no one picked up the garbage—but remuneration for these jobs is poor because so many people are able to perform them.

The level of remuneration that motivates workers to seek particular jobs and employers to offer them is not fixed. On the demand side, an upturn in economic activity may induce employers to offer higher wages to attract more workers when this will result in more production, greater revenues, and higher profits. At the same time, a period of economic expansion is likely to result in a "tighter" labor market and consequent higher wages and salaries. It also may be the case that increasing productivity in terms of output per worker will be accompanied by higher wages and salaries because increased remuneration will be matched or exceeded by higher production levels. Conversely, a fall in worker productivity may cause employers to reduce wages and salaries.

One of the assumptions underlying this description of labor markets is that work is what economists call a "disutility," something that diminishes the quality of life. From this perspective, work takes the place of other, more enjoyable, activities. Consequently, the main or perhaps only reason for working is to get a wage or salary. A job that pays poorly will not be attractive, even if the work itself is a source of personal satisfaction. On the other side of the coin, a good-paying but unpleasant job will be hard to resist. High wages and salaries will lure workers to firms that pay their workers well, and they will motivate workers already on the payroll to put in longer hours even though they find the work inherently distasteful.

Employers pay wages and salaries that are sufficient to recruit and retain their workforces, but levels of remuneration do not always reflect the idea that work is a disutility and that high wages and salaries have to be paid in order to motivate workers to take jobs they dislike. On the contrary, some of the most interesting and satisfying occupations are among the best paid, while some of the dullest and most degrading ones pay very little; compare professional athletes and musicians with dishwashers and farmworkers. The apparent paradox is easily resolved when we note that the least attractive jobs tend to be ones with low skill requirements. As a result, large numbers of potential workers are likely to be competing for these jobs, driving down the rate of remuneration. In contrast, jobs that are interesting and enjoyable usually entail specific abilities and skills not widely distributed among the workforce as a whole.

Up to now, the discussion has contained the implicit assumption that monetary concerns are paramount for both workers and employers. From this perspective, the wages and salaries paid to workers by their employers are the primary determinants of the number of workers employed and how much time these workers devote to their jobs. More generally, both workers and employers are assumed to be "rational maximizers." They know what they want, they can directly connect their actions with the attainment of particular goals, and they have all the information necessary to make optimal decisions when pursuing these goals. This, of course, is a caricature of how men and women think and behave, and no economist believes that we are uncomplicated rational maximizers. Assumptions about economic rationality are a useful starting point for understanding the behavior of workers and employers, but many qualifications have to be attached to economically-based explanations of how individual actions govern the supply of labor and the demand for it.

Although wages and salaries are rarely irrelevant, not all human behavior, even in the economic realm, can be explained solely on the basis of economic motivation. In Chapter 11, we will consider a number of nonmonetary reasons for going to work. But problems arise even when the discussion is confined to the relationship between levels of remuneration and the number of hours worked. If the supply of labor is plotted as a graph where one axis represents wages per hour and the other axis represents the number of hours worked, it seems reasonable to expect that the line would look like Figure 7.1.

Figure 7.1   Supply of Labor

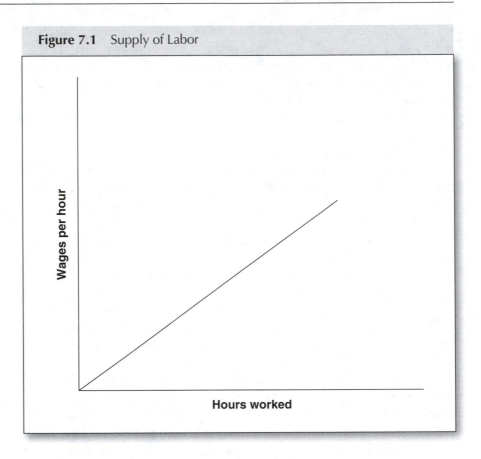

What this means is that the more a worker is paid per hour, the more hours he or she will work. Time spent not working is income lost, and the higher the per-hour wage, the more money forgone. In economic parlance, a worker is faced with a high "opportunity cost" (i.e., time spent pursuing leisure activities represents a greater financial sacrifice at higher rates of pay).

It is also possible, however, that the graph for an individual worker may look like Figure 7.2. This is called a "backward-bending supply curve" for obvious reasons. The curve begins to bend backward at a point where a worker decides that he or she has a sufficiency of income for the lifestyle he or she has chosen; so when hourly wages go up, the same income can be obtained for fewer hours of work. This phenomenon was noted by Max Weber many decades ago when he described the performance of agricultural workers who earned a set sum for a particular task, such as harvesting an acre of grain. According to Weber, an increase in the rate of pay motivated the workers to do *less* work because their customary needs were met by higher wages, so they could enjoy shorter working days and have more time to devote to other activities.[2]

Figure 7.2   Backward-Bending Supply Curve for an Individual Worker

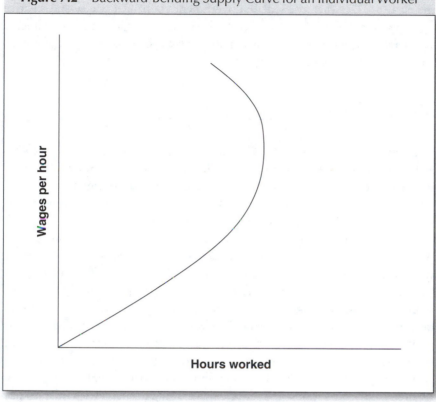

Whether or not a backward-bending curve typifies the supply of labor, along with the conditions under which it occurs, is a matter for empirical research. It does seem likely, however, that it is less common today than it was in Weber's time. The decision of German farmworkers to work fewer hours when they received higher wages might have been a frequent occurrence a hundred years ago, when Weber recorded his observations, but it is almost certainly less evident in today's economy and society, where a proliferation of consumer goods and services stimulates a spirit of endless acquisition and the consequent need to continually boost one's income, even if this requires more hours at work than most people prefer.

Finally, the simple supply-and-demand model fails to give a complete picture of labor markets as they actually operate because it assumes that both employers and employees are independent actors and that rates of remuneration for individual jobs are the result of autonomous decisions made by millions of individuals. This is hardly in accordance with the workings of real-world labor markets. Wages and salaries certainly reflect market conditions, but they also are strongly influenced by the presence of institutional actors such as licensing boards, as will be discussed in Chapter 9. There also have been times when levels of remuneration have been determined by government actions, most notably during World War II, the Korean War, and the early 1970s, when the federal government controlled wages and salaries in response to inflationary pressures. Today, federal and state governments still play a role, albeit a minor one, in affecting wage levels through minimum-wage laws, the topic of the next section.

Minimum-Wage Laws

The first effort by the federal government to establish minimum-wage standards came in the 1930s as part of the Roosevelt administration's National Recovery Act. These standards had to be abandoned when the Act was ruled unconstitutional by the Supreme Court, but the minimum wage returned as part of the Fair Labor Standards Act of 1938. Initially set at 25 cents per hour, the federal minimum wage has been increased many times since then. A few workers—notably waiters, waitresses, and others service employees who receive tips—are not covered by minimum-wage laws. Fifteen states have a minimum wage that exceeds the federal minimum wage of $7.25 per hour, with Washington having the highest at $8.67 in 2011. State legislatures occasionally enact minimum-wage increases, as well as exceptions to these minimums, making it necessary to periodically review these figures.[3] Some cities and counties have their own minimum-wage laws that exceed the federal or state standards. Finally, a few municipal governments have enacted "living wage" regulations that require firms doing business with them to pay a wage deemed sufficient for living above the poverty line.

Unlike Social Security payments, the federal minimum wage is not automatically adjusted for inflation, causing its real value to drop over time unless Congress votes to increase it. In recent years, Congress has not been much inclined to do so. In terms of purchasing power, the minimum wage was at its peak in 1968, and since then, it often has fallen relative to average wage levels, as can be seen in Figure 7.3. In 2007, the Democratic Party gained control of Congress, leading to the first increase in the minimum wage in many years. Even so, the new federal minimum-wage standard leaves many workers receiving the federal minimum wage in difficult financial circumstances; an hourly wage of $7.25 keeps most families well under the poverty line if only one member is working.

The effect of minimum-wage regulations on employment has long been a subject for debate. Even low minimum-wage standards, it has been argued, make some workers too expensive for many employers.[4] Following the logic of market economics, unemployment will necessarily ensue if workers' pay exceeds the revenues they generate. The logic of this argument is inescapable, but more may be involved than a simple calculus of wages, revenues, and employment. Some supporters of a high minimum wage claim that it actually may improve a firm's bottom line by motivating workers to stay on the job and develop the skills that make them more productive employees. In the

Figure 7.3   Purchasing Power of the Minimum Wage Over Time

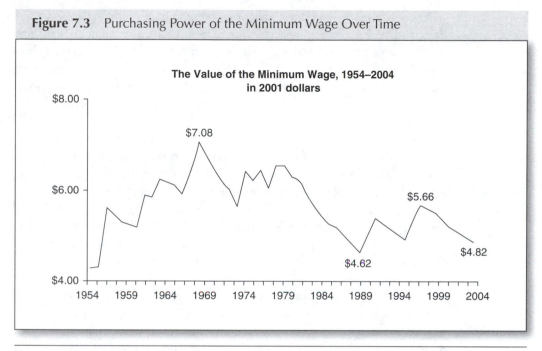

SOURCE: ©The Economic Policy Institute.

(Updated graph from The State of Working America 2008–2009, p. 208)

terminology of economics, this is known as an "efficiency wage." It was most famously demonstrated in 1914 when Henry Ford began to pay his workers $5 per day. As we have seen, although it was almost double the average wage paid to manufacturing workers in those times, Ford claimed that a higher wage rate more than paid for itself by reducing employee turnover and training expenses.[5] Similarly, a high minimum wage may also boost productivity by motivating employers to make more of an effort to develop the skills of their relatively expensive workers, purchase equipment that makes them more productive, or some combination of the two.

Theoretically based arguments for and against minimum-wage standards take us only so far, yet we still lack the kind of factual material that would allow us to decisively determine whether or not minimum-wage regulations cause job losses. Minimum-wage regulations are only one of many fluctuating influences that affect employers' propensity to take on workers, making it difficult to determine their effect on employment. Several research projects on the effects of minimum-wage provisions have been conducted in recent years, but their results have not been universally accepted. Research projects done in a number of states concluded that minimum-wage laws did not result in higher levels of unemployment.[6] These studies have been criticized on methodological grounds, but no compelling evidence has led to the opposite conclusion, that the minimum wage has substantially reduced job prospects for workers at the bottom end of the wage scale.

There is no denying that if it went high enough, a minimum wage would dampen the demand for workers, but current and future standards do not seem to come anywhere close to reaching that point in the United States. It is possible that minimum-wage standards may cause some unemployment in the few metropolitan areas that set them at relatively high levels for firms doing business with these cities, but if they do so, it is to a slight degree because few workers are covered by these regulations.

The other major objection to minimum-wage standards is that their primary beneficiaries are not the working poor. This is true in a statistical sense. Typical minimum-wage earners live in middle-income families where their wages serve as supplements to total family income. Many of them are teenagers working at part-time jobs. Only about one-fifth of minimum-wage earners are members of poor families.[7] But it is important to keep in mind that for these individuals, an increase in the minimum wage can substantially improve their financial situation. As will be discussed in greater detail in Chapter 10, the distribution of income in the United States is highly skewed, with households occupying the bottom quintile receiving only 5 percent of the nation's total income. This means that workers occupying the lowest rungs of the income ladder gain disproportionately from increases in the minimum wage; 35.4 percent of the last minimum-wage increment prior to 2007 went to this lowest quintile of the income distribution scale.[8] The minimum wage also has been particularly beneficial for minority women workers. In the late 1990s, when 13.7 percent of white women earned $5.78 per hour or less, 19.4 percent of Latinas and 27.5 percent of African American women earned the same wage.[9] It is fair to state that as a means of addressing poverty, the minimum wage is a blunt instrument—but without it, poor people would be even worse off.

Minimum-wage regulations also tend to elevate the wages of other workers by reducing or eliminating competition from workers earning very low wages. For example, while an employer might be inclined to hire a worker who will earn $3.00 per hour instead of a better-skilled worker who wants $8 per hour, the skill premium may prevail when the low-wage worker is required to receive an hourly wage of $5.50. For this reason, minimum-wage regulations have been strongly supported by labor unions even though members of these unions usually earn considerably more than the minimum wage.

Jobs, Human Capital, and Credentials

From the vantage point of employers, the workers they employ constitute a cost of doing business, but these employees also are productive assets that make a major contribution to the revenues and profits of their firms. How much these employees contribute to the bottom line is affected by the quantity and quality of the physical capital they work with—such as computers, checkout scanners, and machine tools. Of equal or perhaps greater importance are the aptitudes, skills, abilities, and personal qualities the workers themselves bring to a job. These attributes are analogous to the physical capital that increases productivity and revenues. For this reason, they are labeled—perhaps somewhat crassly—as *human capital*.[10]

For individual workers, the likelihood of getting a job and earning a good income on that job is strongly affected by the amount of human capital amassed. The most common source of human capital is educational attainment. This can be seen in the relationship between education and various aspects of work. At the most basic level, whether or not one is counted as being in the labor force (i.e., presently employed or actively looking for work) is strongly affected by educational attainment. In 2009, 64.0 percent of Americans 25 years of age or older were in the workforce, but only 46.5 percent of men and women without a high school diploma were in that category—a sharp contrast to the 77.5 percent of college graduates counted as members of the labor force. Intermediate levels of education were accompanied by intermediate levels of labor force participation: 62.1 percent of high school graduates and 71.2 percent of men and women who had attended college but did not receive a degree were counted as members of the labor force.[11]

Photo 7.1 An interview gives a prospective employer the opportunity to discover virtues and shortcomings that may not appear on a job application.

SOURCE: ©CORBIS.

Educational attainments matter a great deal when one is in the job market. They also strongly affect the wages and salaries received after being hired. In 2008, U.S. households had a median annual income of $50,303. Households headed by someone who had attended high school but did not graduate had a median annual income of only $25,321. Households headed by an individual with a high school diploma did considerably better, with a median annual income of $39,962, while the median annual income for households headed by men and women with some college but no degree was $50,323. At the upper reaches of income distribution, households headed by holders of bachelor's degrees brought in a median of $78,290, and households headed by men and women with doctoral or professional degrees topped the list at an even $100,000.[12]

If years of education can stand as a proxy for human capital, schooling is an investment that pays abundant rewards. This perception surely has been a major motivating force in the historical expansion of school enrollments at ever higher levels. In 1970, only 52.3 percent of Americans 25 years and older had completed 4 years of high school, and a mere 10.7 percent were college graduates. Twenty years later, the figures had jumped to 77.6 and 21.3 percent, respectively, and by 2009, they stood at 86.2 and 30.1 percent, respectively.[13] Thus, in a period of less than four decades, high school graduation rates went up by a significant margin, while the number of men and women who had college diplomas increased nearly threefold.

The statistical correlation between formal education and subsequent earnings is evident, but the causal connection between the two is not as straightforward. In the first place, in recent years, the "education gap" in earnings has reflected a precipitous drop in the wages of high school graduates and dropouts rather than a surge in wages and salaries of college graduates.[14] Second, education has affected the distribution of earnings in ways that may have little to do with intellectual attainments. Education plays a variety of roles in a nation's economy and society, not all of them directly tied to the transmission of knowledge and the development of intellectual capabilities and job-relevant skills.

It already has been noted that throughout most of human history, the great majority of jobs were filled on the basis of ascribed characteristics. Race, gender, and ethnicity usually were the most important classifications that determined if one was to be a hunter or gatherer, shoemaker or stonemason, slave or free citizen. As we shall see in Chapter 13, ascribed characteristics are by no means irrelevant to job placements today, but neither are they completely decisive. Individual achievements count for a lot when applying for a job, and the attractiveness of a job candidate is closely tied to the capabilities he or she brings to the job. But to what extent are achieved characteristics such as the possession of academic degrees and the number of years spent in school accurate indications of these capabilities?

Consider how an employer might view two prospective candidates of the same age, gender, race, and ethnicity—one with a college degree, the other with only a high school diploma. According to a strict interpretation of human capital theory, when compared with a high school graduate, the holder of a college degree may be presumed to be more knowledgeable and possibly even more intelligent. But these may not be the most essential qualities many employers are looking for. As some observers of the contemporary occupational structure have noted, it is by no means certain that jobs today require higher levels of skill and expertise than they did a generation or two ago.[15] Some occupations are more knowledge-intensive than they were in the past, but this is probably not the case for the majority of the occupations people hold today. Although educational achievements powerfully affect many aspects of occupational life, such as hiring decisions, levels of remuneration, and prospects for promotion, in many cases, their primary significance does not lie in the job-related abilities they bestow.

To put a more positive spin on the role of education, it can be argued that—the acquisition of knowledge aside—a college degree indicates that a job candidate has shown some degree of self-discipline, has been able to meet deadlines (think of all those papers that have to be handed in by the due date!), demonstrated the perseverance needed to stick things out for 4 years or more, has indicated an ability and willingness to follow orders, and has been able to defer gratification to some extent. Note, however, that none of these has much to do with the actual content of one's education or with direct preparation for the work most graduates end up doing.

But more may be operating here than presumed differences in the accumulation of human capital in the form of knowledge and a general ability to work effectively. Enrollment and eventual graduation from college are, for the most part, governed by two variables: academic ability and socioeconomic status. Of the two, academic ability may be the more important, but class background is undeniably influential. According to a survey conducted by the U.S. Department of Education in the early 1990s, 81 percent of high-income students went straight from high school to college, compared with 57 percent of middle-income students and 41 percent of low-income students.[16]

A similar pattern could be found for graduation rates of those who went to college: 80 percent of students in the upper-income quartile finished college in 6 years or less, double the percentage of those from the lowest quartile.[17] It can be argued, of course, that children from upper-income families have more innate ability than do the children of lower-income families. This is challenged by another study, which looked at college completion rates of students who had achieved the highest test scores when they were in the eighth grade. Of this group, 74 percent of the students from the wealthiest families graduated from college, whereas only 29 percent of the students from low-income families did so. In fact, this percentage is almost the same as the graduation rates for the lowest-scoring students who came from high-income families (30 percent).[18]

A major reason for these different educational outcomes is that postsecondary education is expensive. Even public colleges and universities require the expenditure of thousands of dollars for tuition, books, and living expenses. Students also pay a price in opportunity costs, the income forgone while attending 4 or more years of college. Taken together, these costs can constitute a formidable barrier to attaining a postsecondary education. Access to college may be further stymied by family obligations; attendance at a poor-quality high school; and numerous other economic, social, and cultural obstacles.

It should come as no surprise, then, that educational attainment is strongly correlated with family background or, to put it more directly, social class. It is, therefore, fair to ask if occupational success or failure reflects the extent and quality of one's education or if both are directly linked to something over which individuals have little control: the family and social class into which they were born and raised. From this standpoint, the class standing of one's family affects occupational attainment in some obvious ways as well as some that are not so obvious. A middle-class or better standing means that more financial resources can be devoted to the pursuit of education. Somewhat less obviously, it also provides *cultural capital*, the package of class-based attributes such as values, tastes, leisure pursuits, and speech patterns that can be of great value, first at school and then on the job.[19] Alternatively, college attendance can itself be an important source of cultural capital for students coming from more modest socioeconomic backgrounds.

According to some critics, increased educational opportunities have not changed the distribution of income or improved access to desirable occupations to any significant degree. Far from being a vehicle of upward mobility, education provides essential credentials for the children of families that already occupy the upper echelons of the occupational structure in American society. Employment opportunities are necessarily more limited for the remainder of the population, the majority of whom lack these credentials.[20]

Others who have studied the connection between education and occupational achievement have paid less attention to the ways in which education serves to replicate existing inequalities. Instead, they have focused directly on the credentialing process itself. From this standpoint, the real significance of formal education in general and higher education in particular is that they act as filters, screens, or signals that favor some job candidates for hiring and promotion while others are blocked.

It may be conceded that a formal education enhances people's skills and may make them more productive on the job (although it occasionally happens that applicants are turned down for a job because they are thought to be "overqualified"), but the presumed greater store of knowledge and skill imbued by formal schooling is not the whole story. Requiring college degrees for job applicants simplifies an employer's search process. What matters here is not that potential employees have acquired specific, job-related skills but that they have passed through an educational "filter." From this perspective, a diploma is an important source of information in an impersonal labor market where not much is known about the applicants for a particular job. A diploma is a credential that attests to the supposedly superior qualities of the applicant, but what has gone into the attainment of the credential is not a matter of much concern. It is the rare prospective employer who asks for an applicant's academic transcript or even inquires about his or her grade point average.

According to critics, two unfortunate consequences follow from an emphasis on education as a mechanism of credentialing. First, it is likely to reinforce existing patterns of inequality because, as just noted, not everyone has an equal opportunity to acquire the necessary credentials. Second, the fixation of students on obtaining the necessary credentials subverts the essential goal of all educational institutions: advancing the knowledge and intellectual abilities of their students. Instead of pursuing learning for its own sake, students end up with a highly instrumental view of their education, doing whatever it takes to get into a prestigious institution and, once there, doing only what is necessary to get the essential credential in the form of a diploma.[21]

The credentialing role of education has been especially notable in Japan, where high school students spend much of their time cramming for the entrance examinations that largely determine who is accepted and who is rejected for positions at the nation's most prestigious universities. If they successfully navigate "examination hell," they can look forward to a prestigious, high-paying career with a top-tier company or government agency, provided they do the minimal amount of work necessary to graduate from that university. For prospective employers, that these individuals got into a top-ranked university carries more weight than the actual content of their education.[22]

Whatever the underlying reasons for tying job opportunities to educational achievements, young people and their parents clearly understand that failure to get a college degree or more results in a significant handicap in today's job market. The response, as noted above, has been a large increase in college and university enrollments. But at the aggregate level, these individual decisions have been self-defeating to some extent. With more job applicants bearing college degrees, employers have demanded higher educational achievements. A half-century ago, possession of a high school diploma was adequate certification for most jobs. After all, as mentioned above, only a minority of adult workers had completed high school, and a small minority had college degrees. But as greater numbers of men and women completed high school and had at least a few semesters of college, a process of "certification escalation" began to set in. A high school diploma no longer serves as an adequate qualification for many jobs, and a college degree is a minimal requirement for many positions, even though the jobs themselves may not require the presumed talents of a college graduate. Some new occupations that have emerged in recent years require a high level of educational preparation, and some long-established occupations now demand more prior training. But when the entire workforce is taken into account, it is likely that the number of overqualified workers has grown in recent decades.[23]

An overemphasis on educational qualifications reflects the eagerness of many employers to make use of diplomas as filtering devices and of students and their families to accede to this reality, but there are other reasons for the coupling of formal education and occupational attainment. As will be elaborated in Chapter 9, many occupations have been, and continue to be, engaged in a continual effort to upgrade the status of their members and to elevate the work they do. The most crucial source of occupational prestige, it is widely believed, is the educational qualification of its practitioners. Consequently, preparation for a large number of occupations is now embedded in college and university programs. Some of these courses of study are universal, such as accountancy, which is available in thousands of colleges and universities. Others are more idiosyncratic, as with "farrier science" (shoeing horses), offered at a few agriculturally-oriented institutions. Both reflect the prevalent notion that the perceived value of an occupation and its practitioners is directly tied to the existence of a program of formal education for that occupation.

In considering the escalation of formal education requirements, it can of course be argued that an ongoing "knowledge explosion" has made formalized training an essential preparation for a successful occupational career. There is no denying that, as a general statement, it is true: there is much more relevant information for practitioners of engineering or medicine than there was 100 or even 10 years ago. But several objections can be leveled against the argument that more education makes for more capable (and, hence, higher-paid) workers. First, most of the formal education that occurs as preparation for professional occupations is concentrated in a period of time that precedes, often by many years, the bulk of a practitioner's career. Many professions require a few days or weeks of continuing education every year as a requirement for recertification, but this pales in comparison with years of undergraduate education, professional training, and internships that have preceded actual practice. A great deal is certainly learned during these years of preparation, but questions can be raised about the long-term value of a substantial portion of it. At a time when knowledge in many fields is advancing rapidly, much of the content of formal education may have a short shelf life. Even when a student has had an opportunity to learn things of enduring value, one can reasonably wonder how much of this knowledge is actually remembered and then applied to current professional practice. As critics of current educational practices have argued, if formal education is essential to effective on-the-job performance, it might be better achieved in conjunction with the actual work being done. This would not eliminate the need for formal education; learning could be pursued for other purposes, such as intellectual development and being a responsible citizen in a democracy, and not because it provides a credential.[24]

Networks and Their Significance

Up to this point, a fair number of readers are probably thinking, "All this may be interesting from a theoretical standpoint, but what does this chapter have to offer individuals who are looking for a job, or will do so in the near future?" This is a fair question; it is important to understand how large-scale economic and social forces have shaped the labor market, but they are not of much immediate significance when one needs to find a job in order to support oneself and one's family. Fortunately, there is a body of research that not only makes an important contribution to sociological knowledge but also is of direct relevance to anyone who is or will be a participant in the labor market.

One of the great intellectual pleasures of being a sociologist is that it occasionally confers the opportunity to refute ideas and facts commonly taken to be true—"debunking," in other words. But occasionally, it is necessary to concede that some folk wisdom is essentially true. One such example is the adage "it's not *what* you know, it's *who* you know" that matters when you're looking for work. But this is not the end of the matter. As we shall see, personal relationships are of considerable importance in finding a job, but we need to go well beyond folk wisdom in order to understand how labor markets at all levels actually operate. In this section, personal relationships will be put into a larger social context in order to explain why they are important, how they operate, and who is advantaged and disadvantaged when these relationships play out.

An important contribution to the subject has been provided by Mark Granovetter, who studied how a sample of male managerial, professional, and technical workers in Newton, Massachusetts, found jobs.[25] According to Granovetter's study, "formal means" of finding a job (i.e., newspaper advertisements, employment agencies, the placement services provided by universities and professional associations, and cold calls to prospective employers) yielded only 44 percent of job leads. The rest came through direct personal contacts, often once removed (e.g., "a friend of a friend") and occasionally more remotely.

Granovetter's study demonstrated that an economic analysis of labor markets takes us only so far and that a sociological approach is an essential complement to it. As has been noted, market-based theories of employment such as the one presented at the beginning of this chapter are built on the assumption that job seekers have access to essential information about job openings, the working conditions found in these jobs, and the wages and salaries they pay. Some of this information can be gained through newspaper ads, and in recent years, hundreds of Internet sites have offered job postings. Information of this sort can be useful, but it is necessarily limited, and its relevance to someone looking for work cannot be assumed.[26] In contrast, men and women who combine knowledge of available jobs with some understanding of the abilities of individual job seekers are likely to be much more useful sources of information.

Networks also make employers' recruitment of new workers easier because they provide a means of screening applicants. In the place of setting up and using elaborate procedures for determining the suitability of various job candidates, employers can simply assume that a person's social connection to one of their employees (or even a friend or relative of that employee) at least qualifies them for further consideration. And when that employee or employee's friend is known to be competent and trustworthy, an employer may be more inclined to hire an applicant who has a connection, even a tenuous one, to one or the other.

Tapping into a social network can be beneficial for both job seekers and prospective employers. This was evident in a study that centered on the hiring practices of a large regional bank, where referrals by current employees were a major source of new employees.[27] The bank was able to use preexisting social ties to increase the applicant pool and, equally important, increase the number of applicants who were likely to be suitable employees. At the same time, social connections with present employees also were beneficial for the men and women seeking employment at the bank. As the research demonstrated, these job-seekers were more likely to be invited to interviews and to receive job offers than other applicants were, even after controlling for other variables that could affect the hiring process.

Networks also have been shown to be of major significance for landing jobs at lower levels of the income and status scale. One study of hiring practices by employers in four large metropolitan regions found that referrals from current employees and other personal contacts accounted for 35 to 40 percent of the employees who had been hired for positions not requiring college degrees. This practice was especially evident for jobs that demanded little in the way of cognitive and social skills.[28]

Personal connections are particularly useful when an employment opportunity is in an area a job seeker may never even have considered. Granovetter's research showed that many of the employees in his sample had obtained jobs that were quite different from the ones they had been actively seeking. He also found that many people left their current employer for a new one even though they had not been actively seeking to change jobs prior to making the change. What happened in both cases was that someone in their social network had alerted them to an attractive employment prospect they had not known about because they were looking for work in another field or had not even been actively engaged in finding a new job. But presented with the prospect of a job that met their needs or improved their position, they successfully applied for it.

Granovetter also discovered something about the process of finding a job that at first seems counterintuitive. It might be assumed that strong interpersonal ties—the sort found among kinfolk, friends, and neighbors living in close proximity—would be the prime foundations of the social networks that lead to successful job placements. In fact, the opposite prevailed: *weak* ties were much more important. "Weak ties" are the ones that connect acquaintances rather than close friends; customers and merchants; and second-order relationships, such as "a friend of my uncle Mel." This follows from the likelihood that one's close personal relationships involve people who travel in similar economic and social circles. As a result, their information regarding available job opportunities is not much better than one's own. In contrast, connecting with a less intimate social network considerably expands the sources of information about where work can be found. And, as subsequent research found, weak ties are more likely than strong ties to connect a low-status job seeker with higher-status individuals.[29]

The job a person is currently holding also is a major source of potentially useful weak ties. A job tenure of 2 to 5 years seems to be optimal in this regard because a shorter period does not allow for the accumulation of a large number of network members, while a longer-term job may produce strong interpersonal ties rather than the weak ones that are particularly valuable for learning about new job opportunities.[30] In any event, the presence of work-related networks helps explain why many people change jobs even though they seemed content with the jobs they already had. A connection to one of these networks also is a key reason why an employed worker is likely to have fewer difficulties finding a new job than someone who is unemployed. Once again, folk wisdom seems to be correct: "It's a lot easier to get a job when you already have one."

Studies of the significance of social networks for employment indicate that quite a lot of historical continuity can be seen in the workings of labor markets. As we have seen, for most of human history, jobs were primarily filled on the basis of ascribed statuses. Early industrialization did not change this situation fundamentally. Long before there were specialized personnel offices, educational requirements, aptitude tests, and written applications, the task of filling rank-and-file industrial jobs was handled informally. Lower-level managers such as foremen did much of the hiring, and they usually made their hiring decisions on the basis of existing personal connections.[31] It also often happened that families, rather than individuals, were hired and that child labor was a taken-for-granted accompaniment of this policy until progressive labor legislation put an end to it. Today, personal connections continue to be important for successful job searches. Weak ties often provide job seekers with essential information about employment prospects, and strong ties can be used to convey trustworthy information about a candidate to a prospective employer.[32]

Filling jobs on the basis of ascription is more indirect today, and ascriptive statuses often center on connections to social networks rather than traditional sources of ascription such as race, gender, and ethnicity. At the same time, however, these latter three sources of ascription have a great influence on the kind of social networks to which a person belongs. As we have just seen, for individual job seekers, exclusion from the right sort of social networks can seriously reduce the chances of finding employment or moving to a better job. In particular, many members of minority groups may be especially disadvantaged by the limitations of their social networks.[33] This situation at least partially contradicts the widespread belief that in modern societies, achievement is far more important than ascription for sorting people into specific occupations and other positions. It is also the case that, even ignoring the influence of social networks, a person's race, gender, and ethnicity are anything but irrelevant to the kinds of jobs they get and the experiences they have on the job, as we shall see in Chapter 13.

Being hired is the first stage of holding down a job. As we have seen, this process is likely to be strongly influenced by ethnicity, place of residence, network membership, and other social factors. But this is only the beginning. From his or her first day on a job, an employee will be at the center of all the processes subsumed under the term *workplace socialization*. Some aspects of socialization mold people into employees who follow rules and help their organizations effectively pursue goals. But as we shall see, some aspects of workplace socialization may have the opposite effect.

FOR DISCUSSION

1. In considering an occupation or a particular job, how important is the rate of pay in assessing the attractiveness of that occupation or job? What aspects of an occupation or job would you be unwilling to sacrifice, no matter how much it pays?

2. Have you ever held a job that paid only the minimum wage? How dependent were you on that wage for your living expenses? Under what circumstances would it be possible to live on that wage for an extended period of time?

3. How much of your decision to attend college or university can be attributed to your family background? In what ways did your family support or discourage your decision to continue your education? To what extent were the possibilities of improving your employment potential involved in your decision?

4. What sort of social networks do you belong to? How useful might they be in helping you find a job? Have you ever made use of a social network in order to find employment? How effective was it?

Notes

1. *Wages* are remuneration paid according to the number of hours worked; a *salary* is remuneration fixed for a long term, usually a year, that does not directly reflect the number of hours worked. Remuneration may also include benefits such as health insurance and employer contributions to a pension fund. These are not taken into account here.

2. Max Weber, *The Protestant Ethic and the Spirit of Capitalism*, trans. Stephen Kalberg (Los Angeles: Roxbury, 2002), 22–3.

3. See U.S. Department of Labor, "Minimum Wage Laws in the States," http://www.dol.gov/esa/minwage/america.htm (accessed February 12, 2007).

4. Donald Deere, Kevin M. Murphy, and Finis Welch, "Sense and Nonsense on the Minimum Wage," *Regulation: The Cato Review of Business and Government*, http://www.cato.org/pubs/regulation/reg18n1c.html (accessed February 12, 2007).

5. Stephen Meyer, *The Five Dollar Day: Labor Management and Social Control in the Ford Motor Company, 1908–1921* (Albany: State University of New York Press, 1981).

6. David Card and Alan B. Krueger, *Myth and Measurement: The New Economics of the Minimum Wage* (Princeton, NJ: Princeton University Press, 1995).

7. Rebecca M. Blank, *It Takes a Nation: A New Agenda for Fighting Poverty* (Princeton, NJ: Princeton University Press, 1997), 115.

8. Jared Bernstein and John Schmitt, *Making Work Pay* (Washington, DC: Economic Policy Institute, 1998). Cited in Robert Cherry, *Who Gets the Good Jobs? Combating Race and Gender Disparities* (New Brunswick, NJ: Rutgers University Press, 2001), 236.

9. Ibid.

10. Gary Becker, *Human Capital* (Chicago: University of Chicago Press, 1980).

11. U.S. Census Bureau, *The 2010 Statistical Abstract*, "Table 592: Civilian Labor Force and Participation Rates by Educational Attainment, Sex, Race, and Hispanic Origin, 2000 to 2009," http://www.census.gov/compendia/statab/2011/tables/11s0592.pdf (accessed September 20, 2010).

12. U.S. Census Bureau, *The 2010 Statistical Abstract*, "Table 691: Money Income of Households: Distribution by Income Level and Selected Characteristics 2008," http://www.census.gov/compendia/statab/2011/tables/11s0691.pdf (accessed September 20, 2010).

13. U.S. Census Bureau, *The 2010 Statistical Abstract*, "Table 225: Educational Attainment by Race and Hispanic Origin, 1970 to 2008," http://www.census.gov/compendia/statab/2011/tables/11s0226.pdf (accessed September 20, 2010).

14. Lawrence Mishel, Jared Bernstein, and John Schmitt, *The State of Working America, 1998–1999* (Ithaca, NY: Cornell University Press, 1999). Cited in Philip Moss and Chris Tilly, *Stories Employers Tell: Race, Skill, and Hiring in America* (New York: Russell Sage Foundation, 2001), 46.

15. Kenneth I. Spenner, "Deciphering Prometheus: Temporal Change in the Skill Level of Work," *American Sociological Review* 48, no. 6 (December 1983): 824–37.

16. Therese L. Baker and William Vélez, "Access to and Opportunity in Post-Secondary Education in the United States: A Review," *Sociology of Education* 69 (1996): 82–101.

17. Ibid.

18. M. A. Fox, B. A. Connolly, and T. D. Snyder, *Youth Indicators 2005: Trends in the Well-Being of American Youth* (Washington, DC: U.S. Department of Education, 2005). Cited in Lawrence Mishel, Jared Bernstein, and Heidi Schierholz, *The State of Working America 2008/2009* (Ithaca: Cornell University Press, 2009).

19. Pierre Bourdieu, *Distinction: A Social Critique of Judgment of Taste* (Cambridge, MA: Harvard University Press, 1984).

20. Randall Collins, *The Credential Society: An Historical Sociology of Education and Stratification* (New York: Academic Press, 1979), 182–204.

21. Ronald Dore, *The Diploma Disease: Education, Qualification, and Development* (Berkeley: University of California Press, 1976).

22. Ikuo Amano, *Education and Examination in Modern Japan*, trans. William K. Cummings and Fumiko Cummings (Tokyo: Tokyo University Press, 1990).

23. Arne Kalleberg, *The Mismatched Worker* (New York: Norton, 2007), 75.

24. Ivan Illich, *Deschooling Society* (New York: Harper & Row, 1971).

25. Mark Granovetter, *Getting a Job: A Study of Contacts and Careers,* 2nd ed. (Chicago: University of Chicago Press, 1995).

26. According to Richard N. Bolles, author of the widely read career guide *What Color Is Your Parachute?* (Berkeley: Ten Speed, 2002), Internet employment services provide the least effective means of finding a job, worse even than mailing out resumes to random potential employers. Organizational Development Institute, "The Effectiveness of Various Methods for Finding a Job," http://members.aol.com/ODInst/FindJob.htm (accessed June 12, 2006).

27. Roberto M. Fernandez and Nancy Weinberg, "Sifting and Sorting: Personal Contacts and Hiring in a Retail Bank," *American Sociological Review* 62 (December 1997): 883–902.

28. Harry J. Holzer, *What Employers Want: Job Prospects for Less-Educated Workers* (New York: Russell Sage Foundation, 1996), 51–4.

29. Nan Lin, Walter M. Ensel, and John C. Vaughn, "Social Resources and the Strength of Ties: Structural Factors in Occupational Status Attainment," *American Sociological Review* 46, no. 4 (August 1981): 393–405.

30. Granovetter, *Getting a Job,* 85–9.

31. Daniel Nelson, *Managers and Workers: Origins of the New Factory System in the United States 1880–1920* (Madison: University of Wisconsin Press, 1975), 79–82.

32. James E. Rosenbaum, *Beyond College for All: Career Patterns for the Forgotten Half* (New York: Russell Sage Foundation, 2001), 247.

33. Holzer, *What Employers Want,* 51.

8

Workplace Culture and Socialization

The workplace is not just a place for accomplishing job-related tasks and earning a living in the process. It is also a repository of values, attitudes, norms, and accepted procedures. In short, it has a culture—or, more likely, a dominant culture along with a multiplicity of subcultures. For individual workers, there are two sources of the workplace culture that shape the way they go about their work: the kind of work they do and the organization in which they do it. Some occupations do not carry much in the way of cultural baggage, but others may foster subcultures that exert significant influences on the way people do their work and interact with others. The same holds for the organizations in which the work is done. Organizations may have dominant, "official" cultures, but individual components of these organizations also are likely to contain distinctive subcultures. As will be noted in this chapter, these subcultures have variable effects, sometimes promoting personal identification with a work organization and at other times creating an alternative, even oppositional, source of identity.

The Significance of Workplace Cultures

"Culture" is one of the bedrock concepts in the social sciences. Many definitions of culture have been offered, and although they differ in what they emphasize, most include two broad elements of culture: the material and the nonmaterial. For society as a whole, material culture encompasses all the accoutrements of life—everything from cooking utensils to orbiting satellites, Barbie dolls to MRI machines. For a given occupation, the material culture comprises the things that are worked with and worked on. A machinist works with lathe in order to shape metal into a useful product, while a probation officer may consult a computerized listing of employment opportunities while trying to shape an ex-felon into a useful member of society.

The kinds of equipment and materials used at work may powerfully influence workplace culture, but they do not operate independently of the nonmaterial elements of workplace culture: beliefs, values, attitudes, norms, and accepted procedures. Because they are nonmaterial, these elements are intimately connected to the uniquely human ability to create, transmit, understand, manipulate, and respond to complex symbols. In the workplace, these symbols range from highly detailed written procedures to subtle gestures that may convey a lot of information to those who understand them. Symbols encompass anything that can be used to convey the values, beliefs, and norms of a culture: ceremonies, jokes, stories, rituals, myths, pranks, argot, dress, insignia, and so on.

Organizational cultures have been a topic of considerable interest in recent years as some influential writers have stressed how an organization's culture can contribute to its success or failure.[1] These descriptions and analyses of the cultures of various firms have emphasized the importance of clearly articulated goals and collectively held values, along with the ceremonies and rituals that express them, the "heroes" that exemplify them, and the modes of communication that convey them.[2]

Workplaces usually share in a society's overarching culture, but they also have cultures of their own. As with society as a whole, the organizations for which people work—be they business firms, churches, or charitable institutions—have a formal structure of some kind, along with both an "official" culture set by management and several subcultures tied to particular occupations or segments of the organization. Official cultures are likely to be manifested in clearly articulated organizational values, specific rules, and even dress codes. They might even feature regular renditions of the company song, as occurs in some Japanese firms.[3] Subcultures have their own values, rules, and sometimes even language. As we shall see, the relationship between the two may be complementary, but it also may be a source and reflection of conflict between different segments of an organization.

Some cultural elements emerge spontaneously and over time become embedded in the organizational culture through informal means. Others are deliberately propagated. One such example is McDonald's Hamburger University in Oak Brook, Illinois.[4] Every year, 3,500 owners and managers of McDonald's franchises from throughout the world put in 2 weeks at the "university," attending labs and classes while learning the techniques of fast-food preparation and other aspects of the business. No less important, the program also aims at creating managers and owners "with ketchup in their blood"—men and women who are devoted to their work, their restaurants, and the McDonald's way of doing things. This corporate culture is instilled through frequent invocations of the achievements and philosophy of Ray Kroc, the man who led McDonald's rise to becoming the world's premier fast-food operation. The "university" also organizes team-based contests that test the participants' knowledge of the firm's history and achievements. Socialization into the McDonald's culture continues when owners and managers return to their home bases. Ceremonies honor especially successful franchisees, and meetings of regional associations stress the continued implementation of McDonald's core values of "quality, service, convenience, and value."[5]

Organizational cultures become especially evident when two firms merge. Each has its own set of values and ways of doing things, which in many cases can be the source of considerable conflict. When Daimler-Benz acquired Chrysler in 1998, for example, employees of the combined firm had to contend with the differences of American and German national cultures. Even more important were their distinctive organizational cultures. In the months following the creation of DaimlerChrysler, marked differences emerged over substantive issues such as decision-making processes and how much decision-making authority should be given to mid-level employees. Opposing cultural orientations were also evident in trivial matters such as smoking in private offices and drinking wine with lunch. Even the size of business cards became a bone of contention.[6]

Socialization Into a Culture

Socialization is the process through which individuals become part of a human society through the assimilation of the society's dominant culture, and perhaps one or more significant subcultures. Through socialization, individuals acquire a working knowledge of their society's values and norms. In addition, they gain a sense of where they fit in by learning about the roles they are expected to occupy and how to relate to others while occupying those roles. In short, socialization is the essential process through which we become human. An unsocialized individual would be a kind of alien, adrift in a land where everything is a source of bewilderment. The activities of its inhabitants would be incomprehensible and their language unintelligible, while nothing in life would be predictable. Fortunately, except for a few isolated cases, all humans have undergone a process of socialization that has provided, and continues to provide—metaphorically speaking—the tools, maps, and codebooks that make it possible to survive and prosper amid other humans.

Socialization is a crucial part of working life because nobody chooses an occupation or takes on a job knowing everything he or she needs to know about doing the work. However, some people undergo "anticipatory socialization" by being exposed to a particular line of work through their families and social networks. This is particularly common for people who make a career of police work, which is disproportionately filled by men and women who grew up in families containing significant numbers of police officers.[7] A similar situation occurs in military families, which are major suppliers of future officers. But these are the exceptions. A large number of workers, perhaps the majority, have not consciously prepared for the work they do. They simply took a job after a brief search, or, as we have seen, they fell into one because their social network made it available to them. Many occupations, even high-level ones such as college professor and journalist, are staffed to a significant extent by people who just drifted into them.[8]

Settling into a job is not necessarily a permanent situation, as occupational careers are characterized by significant fluidity. According to the U.S. Bureau of Labor Statistics, in 2005, more than 3 percent of employees left their jobs each month, most of them taking a job with another employer.[9] The Bureau of Labor Statistics also determined that at the beginning of 2004, wage and salary workers had put in a median of only 4 years with their current employer. As might be expected, older workers stay at the same job for a longer period than younger ones do. Among workers 45 years of age and older, about half had been with their current employer for 10 years or more. In contrast, only about one-quarter of workers between the ages of 35 and 44 had a tenure of this length.[10] There are no current statistics on the number of jobs held by the average American worker during his or her working life, but a survey of American workers that commenced in 1979 found that between the ages of 18 and 38, men had held an average of 10.2 jobs and women had held 9.9 jobs.[11]

The significant amount of job hopping experienced by most workers means that work-related socialization will occur on numerous occasions. Many things learned in the past will be relevant to a present job, but there are likely to be a number of things that need to be unlearned, too. At the same time, socialization for an occupation or specific job is not likely to be an unambiguous process because cultures and subcultures are not always models of consistency. For example, American culture celebrates democratic egalitarianism, yet it places a great value on winning, success, and "getting ahead," none of which are particularly supportive of an egalitarian social order. Ambiguities and contradictions also may appear at the level of the individual organization, as when a business firm's avowed devotion to customer service exists uneasily alongside a commitment to maximizing short-run profits. Nor are cultures static. They can mutate as a result of technological and economic changes, the importation of elements of other cultures, the ascendancy of one group and the decline of another, or simply through the human desire for occasional novelty. These vagaries of culture mean that individuals are continually being socialized to some extent. Finally, although socialization is a fundamental process in our development as members of occupations, organizations, and society as a whole, there will always be an element of conflict in the process. Socialization creates roles and identities that are not always accepted by the individual being socialized. And that is as it should be; otherwise, we would all be little more than programmable robots.[12]

Socialization as an Ongoing Process

Socialization conclusively ends only when a person dies or ceases to be sentient. Some periods of socialization are more intense than others, but the cumulative effects of day-to-day socialization can be just as important as brief periods of concentrated socialization, as occurs in a military boot camp. Although it is an ongoing process throughout the life span, socialization may occur in distinct phases. For a person preparing for a particular occupation, these phases may be demarcated by shifting emphases over the course of a training program.

The uneven process of occupational socialization and individuals' shifting responses to it are well illustrated by a classic study of what happens to medical students as they go through the process of becoming doctors.[13] As the researchers discovered, many aspiring doctors entered medical school with a strong orientation to helping people. They also assumed that in the course of their studies, they would learn much of what they needed to know in order to be successful doctors. But during the first year of medical school, they had no contact with patients, and much of their coursework seemed highly academic and removed from the actual practice of medicine. In response, the students began to take a pragmatic—some might say cynical—approach to their education, letting go of the idea that they would learn everything there is to know and concentrating on what they thought would appear on the exams. This erosion of idealism was reinforced by a student subculture that supported this pragmatic approach to getting through medical school.

By their third year, the students began to be involved with actual patients by interviewing them about their medical histories and performing physical examinations. This made their education less academic, but it didn't restore their earlier idealism because it also was apparent that their patients were to be treated as "cases" rather than as individual men and women. The student subculture persisted, although some of the old idealism resurfaced when the students were detached from the group settings that reinforced the influence of the student subculture.

As their education neared its end, idealism reemerged, but in the form of "professional idealism." In the place of a rather vague sense of wanting to help people, students assumed an attitude of practical idealism as they embarked on the choice of a medical specialty that would allow them to truly master one area of medicine and as they considered the kinds of practices that would allow them to devote an adequate amount of time to each patient. At the same time, however, subsequent studies of medical education have shown that the socialization process tends to promote emotional detachment from patients.[14] Aspiring doctors do not lose their initial desire to help sick people, but this has been tempered by the realization that the time they can spend with patients is limited and that too close a relationship with them can get in the way of effective treatment.

Socialization and Identity

By the time they finished their training, the former medical students had taken on a distinctive occupational role, that of "doctor." In this, they were not unique; the work a person does is often a key element of his or her individual identity. In the words of Erving Goffman, "A self virtually awaits the individual entering a position. . . . He will find a 'me' ready made for him."[15] There is certainly a large element of truth to this; the occupations we hold and the jobs we do can substantially affect how we see ourselves and how we are perceived by others. To a significant extent, occupational roles carry certain expectations about individuals that are independent of their personal characteristics. As is frequently noted in the armed forces, "you salute the stripes, not the person." These "ready-made" qualities of occupational roles are the product of formal and informal socialization processes that affect both the individuals occupying these roles and the people with whom they interact. For future practitioners, occupational socialization entails learning how to assume an identity that is congruent with an occupation and the work done in this capacity. For clients and customers, prior socialization has provided fairly clear expectations about how people in particular occupational roles should act and how one should interact with them.

One source of occupational identity is a distinctive physical appearance. Sometimes, this is achieved through an alteration of the body, either temporary or permanent. The ordination ceremony that marks a man's entry into the Roman Catholic priesthood includes a moment when a lock of hair is snipped from the head—a remnant of times past, when monks had a distinctive hairstyle that marked their separation from the laity. More drastic is the absence of a little finger that marks members of the organized crime gangs in Japan known as *yakuza*.

One important marker of an occupational identity is a distinctive uniform. All of us have learned to take notice of different kinds of uniforms and the special occupational roles they denote. Some of these indicate a subservient occupational status, such as the outfits worn by domestic servants. Other uniforms, such as the ones worn by letter carriers, are indicative of a particular occupation but not one that is really special. In contrast, some uniforms, notably those worn by police officers, are meant to convey authority. The same can be said of the indications of rank displayed on the uniforms of military officers, the elaborate vestments worn by the clergy of many religions, and the faintly ludicrous cap-and-gown outfits worn by college professors at important ceremonial functions. Other sartorial occupational markers are the white outfits worn by doctors and nurses, which connote strict attention to cleanliness and hygiene; the pocket protectors (affectionately referred to as "nerd packs") favored by some engineers and computer programmers; and the ensemble of tools dangling from the belts of construction workers. Even an ordinary jacket and tie can be construed as a kind of uniform that confers on the wearer the appearance of fairly high-level status—identifying him or her as a "suit," someone set apart from rank-and-file workers. At the upper reaches of the occupational order, a conservative suit from a high-end clothier is essential apparel for aspiring attorneys interviewing with prestigious law firms.[16] Finally, consider the use of the terms *blue collar* and *white collar* to denote manual and nonmanual occupations.

Occupational identities also can be created and reinforced through distinctive vocabularies. Occupation-specific words and phrases serve an objective function by giving names to essential objects and processes, but their use also distinguishes a member of an occupation from the public at large, whose ignorance of the specialized vocabulary marks them as outsiders. What, for example, are a "whistle punk," "widow maker," "hogger," and "cat skinner"?[17]

Occupational roles and statuses also may be conveyed by physical surroundings. Many new employees quickly learn that certain areas of a building are reserved for higher-ups, corner offices being prime examples in many organizations. The vertical location of an office can also reflect location in the organizational hierarchy—the higher the floor, the higher the rank. At the General Motors Building in Detroit, offices on the 14th floor were synonymous with the upper reaches of the firm's hierarchy. The entrance to that floor was patrolled by a security guard, and lower-ranking employees had to have special permission in order to gain access to this executive sanctum.[18]

In a building's interior, furnishings and other accoutrements often serve a socializing function by providing unmistakable indicators of organizational positions. Before it came down in price, wall-to-wall carpeting was reserved for the offices of top executives. Stories have been told of the outer edges of a wall-to-wall carpet being cut away because the office was occupied by an employee deemed unworthy of this indicator of high organizational status. In some organizations, simply having carpeting on the floor can convey high status and authority. The old expression "to be called on the carpet" indicated that a worker had been summoned into the office of a higher-up, most likely in regard to some transgression.

Occupational and Organizational Heroes

In the nonmaterial realm, socialization into a particular occupational culture can be fostered by invoking the lives and deeds of people who have embodied the ideals of a particular occupation or organization. One prominent example comes from the history of nursing. Prior to the middle of the 19th century, the occupational standing of nurses was quite low. Nursing was practiced by ill-educated women from the lower strata of society who worked in dirty and chaotic hospital settings or served as little more than domestic servants in the homes of the sick. During the Crimean War, an English woman of aristocratic background named Florence Nightingale (1820–1910) took it upon herself to transform the horrible conditions of military hospitals. Through the force of her personality, she made sure that medical supplies and hot meals for hospital patients were always available. She also stressed paying attention to hospital hygiene. Nightingale recruited young women from "respectable" backgrounds to serve as hospital nurses and took the lead in establishing schools to train them. Through all these efforts, she greatly elevated the public image of nursing and established herself as someone to be emulated by other nurses all over the world.[19]

A roster of occupational heroes might include Edward R. Murrow for journalists, Albert Einstein for scientists, Thomas Edison for inventors, and Jane Addams for social workers. During the 19th century, Samuel Smiles's *The Lives of the Engineers* inspired many young men to try to emulate engineers such as the road builder John Metcalf, the bridge designer Thomas Telford, the railway pioneer George Stephenson, and the inventor James Watt and his entrepreneurial partner Matthew Boulton.[20] It also can be noted that over the centuries, *The Lives of the Saints* and other hagiographies have inspired many men and women to pursue religious vocations.

The elevation to hero status of a representative of a particular occupation usually occurs within that occupation, but some heroes have been manufactured by political authorities to suit their own purposes. The most notorious example comes from the Soviet Union in the 1930s, where a coal miner named Aleksey Stakhanov was lauded as a "model Soviet worker" after he greatly exceeded the daily quota for coal extraction. His feats were widely publicized in the hope that he would serve as an inspiration for other "hero workers," whose toils were to lay the foundation of Soviet industrialization. In fact, Stakhanov's great feats were either fictional or drew heavily on the contributions of other miners with the connivance of local officials. It hardly mattered. Reality was whatever the Soviet leadership decreed, and "Stakhanovism" became a national movement intended to inspire workers to greater productive heights.

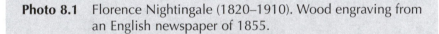

Photo 8.1   Florence Nightingale (1820–1910). Wood engraving from an English newspaper of 1855.

SOURCE: The Granger Collection, New York.

Socialization in Different Occupational Realms

Although all workers undergo some degree of occupational socialization, its extent and intensity vary considerably from occupation to occupation and from organization to organization. As a general rule, the more professional the occupation, the deeper and longer will be the process of socialization. This is due in part to the longer training periods required of physicians, attorneys, professors, nurses, and the like. A lengthy period of formal training is necessary to develop specific skills, but it also creates environments that are well suited to both formal and informal socialization for future occupational roles. For example, while in law school, a student learns how to understand and apply the law, but he or she also learns to *be* an attorney. To be an attorney means more than having the technical competencies necessary to practice law. It also entails the internalization of appropriate values, behaviors, attitudes, and demeanor. These are acquired, often subconsciously, by observing and interacting with practicing attorneys—perhaps in the course of an internship—as well as through more formal means, such as being exposed to an established code of ethics. Attorneys also have their occupational roles reinforced through interaction with clients, who define them as legal professionals and treat them accordingly.

Workers lower down on the occupational scale have fewer opportunities for socialization through long-term training programs, but other characteristics of their jobs may create a firm basis for intense socialization. One of the most important of these is danger. When a job puts a worker in potentially hazardous situations, the attitudes and actions of coworkers may literally become matters of life and death. This produces an extreme need for what Emile Durkheim called "mechanical solidarity," a commonality of values and behaviors, along with an adherence to traditional ways of doing things.[21]

Mechanical solidarity is of great importance for certain kinds of work because it makes for predictability and a measure of security in inherently uncertain and dangerous circumstances. Mechanical solidarity also solidifies the belief that workmates will support one another when a situation turns nasty. Work relationships based on a significant degree of mechanical solidarity amid potentially dangerous situations can be found among miners, police officers, and "high-steel" construction workers. Their circumstances are similar to those found in army units, where a sense of mutual support and the fear of letting down one's fellow combatants have been crucial motivations for acting courageously when one's life is on the line.[22] In turn, strong interpersonal ties are essential for the effective operation of small groups working under dangerous circumstances, and disaster can ensue when these ties are broken or attenuated.[23]

Socialization is likely to be at its most intensive and extensive when workers experience some degree of isolation from the outside world. Sometimes, this situation is deliberately manufactured, as in the case of monasteries and convents, or police and military academies. These locales for intense socialization can be viewed as "total institutions," places that are closed off from the outside world so they can control most aspects of a person's life.[24] Here, a sense of isolation is reinforced by systematic efforts to strip recruits of their individuality through such measures as requiring them to wear institutional clothing and to submit to regulation haircuts.

A degree of social isolation can also be the result of a value system that divides the social realm into "us" and "them." Once again, this is a situation that dangerous working environments foster. In this case, the source of perceived danger is outsiders, especially the ones who fall into certain categories. Rookie police officers, for example, are socialized in police academies and on the beat with senior officers to take on an attitude of generalized wariness. More specifically, they are directly and indirectly taught to be especially distrustful of certain groups, such as minorities, lawyers, judges, and the media.[25]

Adding to the distinctive job environment of soldiers and police officers is the likelihood that, at least sometimes, their work schedules will depart from "normal" working hours. They of course are not unique in this situation; workers in other occupations, such as musicians and railroad crews, also experience a fair degree of social isolation because of their "unsocial" work schedules. This means that their primary source of social interaction will be with fellow workers, and, once again, socialization into a particular line of work will be intensified as a result.

Just as some occupations separate workers from other people temporally, other occupations do so spatially. Although many occupations can be found just about everywhere, some are limited to specific locales. Miners have to work where there is ore or coal, deep-sea commercial fishermen live and work near harbors when they are not on the high seas, and loggers have to be in the vicinity of forests. Although they are rare today, during earlier phases of industrialization, many regions had company towns that housed large concentrations of textile mill hands, steel workers, and other employees whose lives were played out in these towns. Past and present, the conjunction of working life and residential life has often created a distinctive identity and, not coincidentally, a high degree of worker militancy in some industries. Some of the most intense labor actions in the United States have occurred in mining communities and company towns such as Pullman, Illinois (named after the passenger car manufacturer of the same name), and Homestead, Pennsylvania (a community of steel workers).[26]

Paradoxically, occupational socialization also can be intense under the opposite circumstances, when workers lack deep roots in the communities in which they live. In these situations, the organization in which people work may be their primary source of social relationships. This is especially evident in most branches of the military, where frequent moves from one post to another are commonplace. It also is worth noting that employees of IBM, a firm known for its strong and pervasive corporate culture, sardonically joke that the company's initials stand for "I've been moved."

Photo 8.2 Coal miners

SOURCE: ©Photodisc Collection/Getty Images.

Rites of Passage

Socialization is usually a long and drawn-out process, but there may be times when the transition to a new status occurs abruptly through a ceremony known as a "rite of passage." These are common in many cultures and include ceremonies that signify becoming an adult, getting married, or making the transition from life to death. Examples of rites of passage that mark the movement from childhood to formal adulthood include confirmation ceremonies practiced in many Christian religions, as well as bar and bat mitzvah ceremonies in Judaism. Modern societies are somewhat lacking in secular rites of passage marking the transition to adulthood. Graduating from high school may be one, but for many young people, a more significant rite of passage seems to be getting a driver's license.

Rites of passage have been analyzed as having three general phases: separation, transition, and incorporation.[27] The separation from others may be dramatic, perhaps requiring several days and nights alone in the wilderness. In modern societies, the separation phase is less stark; an example might be an aspiring doctor leaving her hometown to enroll in pre-med courses at a distant college or university. For medical students, the next phases of separation—internship and then residency—are even more intense, as long hours and moving to a new community can be a source of considerable isolation.

The transition phase of many rites of passage has been characterized as "an ambiguous, unstructured state of inbetweenness."[28] In this phase, initiates have lost some of their previous identity but have yet to take on a new one completely. In the occupational realm, it is a time of further learning and assimilating the subculture of the occupation, as well as a time for convincing established members that one is worthy of admission into it. This period may include a combination of further study and assuming a portion of an occupational role, as when a graduate student works as a teaching assistant or a professional in training takes on an internship.

The final stage, incorporation, is the most dramatic because it is usually marked by a rite or ceremony. The ceremony usually has a formal structure that may have remained unchanged for decades or even centuries. It may entail some degree of discomfort or even physical pain for the initiate. In some traditional societies, the passage to formal adulthood might have included knocking out a tooth or receiving distinctive tattoos. In contrast, the last phase of earning a PhD degree entails no physical pain but may still evince considerable discomfort: submitting to an oral exam based on the student's dissertation.

Pain, humiliation, or both can also be found in informal rites of passage administered by colleagues and workmates. One common informal rite of passage is hazing, such as that which occurs among certain coal miners. As noted earlier, underground coal mining is a dangerous occupation, and a high level of trust and respect for one's workmates helps mitigate some of the fears that are an inescapable part of the job. The personal qualities that make for trust and respect cannot be assumed, however; they have to be demonstrated in the course of daily work. Novice miners also have the opportunity to show that they have what it takes when they are subjected to initiation rites.[29] The practices in some mines would strike an outsider as nothing short of revolting. One of these is giving less-than-flattering names to new miners. In one mine, novice miners had to bear names like "plunger lip," "lard ass," and "maggot mouth." As with the more benign names given to novitiates in convents and monasteries, the assumption of a new name conveyed the message that their outside identities counted for little now that they were engaged in underground mining. Rookie miners also had to undergo the ritual of "making a miner," which entailed being vigorously swatted with a board by veteran miners. On occasion, novice miners who were adjudged guilty of real or imaginary transgressions were subjected to the degrading practice of having grease smeared on their genitals and serving as unwilling participants in "pretty pecker" contests. Odd or even disgusting though these ceremonies may seem to outsiders, they effectively transmitted the importance of solidarity with the work group and deference to its collective will.

Although rites of passage focus on the novitiates, these ceremonies also serve an important function for longstanding members of a society or organization. In addition to marking the induction of new members, they reaffirm existing values and social roles for everyone present. One example is the commencement ceremony that celebrates the awarding of an academic degree. To the students, it marks their graduation from school, along with a literal commencement—starting a new chapter in life as they stand at the threshold of taking on a new set of roles. For faculty and administrators, these ceremonies serve a different purpose because they do not mark the beginning of a new phase of life for them. Rather, they serve as a rite of renewal, an affirmation that their efforts have not been in vain and that, if nothing else, their students have successfully completed a course of study and are presumably better prepared to take on the world.

Organizations and Subcultures

Complex organizations are assemblages of separate units such as departments and divisions. Members of these different units not only have different tasks and skills, but they also are likely to have different visions of what is necessary for the success of the organization as a whole. Sales personnel may consider the key to success to be abundant spending on media advertisements, while members of the accounting department may give pride of place to careful control of expenses, advertising budgets not excepted.

One structurally-based source of subculture formation, and of conflicts between subcultures, is the longstanding bifurcation of many organizations into "staff" and "line" functions. This distinction initially emerged in military services. "Line" soldiers and their officers did the actual fighting; they were literally on the front line of battle. "Staff" positions provided behind-the-lines support, performing such functions as intelligence, maintenance and repair, provisioning, and so on.

Over the years, new technologies and other developments have stimulated the expansion of military staff positions to the point where they considerably outnumber the soldiers engaged in actual combat—in military parlance, an increase in the "tail-to-teeth" ratio. Nonmilitary organizations also have undergone a substantial increase in staff positions and a relative decline in line positions. A large manufacturing enterprise may still need a fair number of production workers, supervisors, engineers, and other line positions, but it will also have legions of employees working in personnel, legal, public relations, and maintenance departments.

Early organizational theory stressed that staff positions were to be excluded from the upper reaches of an organization's hierarchy and that staff members were subordinate to the appropriate line units.[30] Actual practice departed from theory, however, as shown by studies of the actual workings of organizations that revealed how staff members were able to accrue considerable power within the organization as a whole.[31]

The wielding of authority by staff members has not gone uncontested, and staff-line conflicts can be found in many organizations. But not all conflict centers on the allocation of authority; a clash of subcultures may also be at work. Conflicts may stem from differences in age or education, as well as fundamental disagreements over goals, values, and priorities. An example of a conflict caused by divergent staff and line subcultures can be seen in one urban welfare agency where caseworkers (line) found themselves at loggerheads with accounting office personnel (staff) over how much money was to be awarded to individual welfare recipients. For the caseworkers, the goal of their agency was providing funds to the needy, while the accountants believed that protecting taxpayers' funds had to be the agency's highest priority.[32] This situation embodied the old adage "Where you stand depends on where you sit." Both staff and line personnel believed that they had the best interests of their organization at heart, but their perceptions were strongly affected by the subcultures of their respective positions.

In many organizations, the distinction between staff and line has faded away. The provision of expertise was formerly thought to be primarily a staff function, but given the centrality of technology and technological change in many organizations, line officials now have to be directly involved with technical decisions. Even so, subcultures based on occupation and departmental affiliation can still generate a considerable amount of conflict. One dramatic, and ultimately tragic, case of subcultures working at cross purposes was revealed in 1986 when the Space Shuttle *Challenger* blew up shortly after launch, killing everyone on board. The proximate cause was the failure of an O-ring seal at a joint of one of the solid rocket boosters. This occurred because unusually cold temperatures had stiffened the O-rings and reduced their ability to provide a good seal. A flame emerged from the joint, igniting the fuel tank of the liquid rocket booster. At a deeper level, the catastrophe reflected the divergent subcultures of NASA's launch managers and engineers. The launch managers were carriers of a subculture that prized getting launches off according to schedule. The engineers, in contrast, were imbued with a spirit of caution and a propensity to take full account of every potential problem prior to launch.[33] Because the launch managers had the final authority over whether to launch or not, their subculture prevailed, and catastrophe ensued.

As with culture in general, subcultures can emerge from a variety of circumstances. Formal divisions, such as those separating staff and line, are one source, but even things such as spatial arrangements can be significant. Workers performing a particular task are more likely to form a subculture when they occupy the same space than when they are scattered throughout different locales. Workplace subcultures may also coalesce around distinctions found in the outside world, such as ethnicity, age, and religious affiliation. Hours of work also can be the source of a subculture. Employees on the night shift, in addition to being more isolated from people who work from 9 to 5, often expect a more relaxed style of supervision. As one study of janitors at a university indicated, a considerable amount of unhappiness can occur when workers are shifted to day work and its association with a more intense mode of supervision.[34]

Supportive Workplace Subcultures

Although separate from the "official" culture, a subculture imparted through informal, colleague-based socialization may be congruent with the formal goals and procedures of an organization. Informal socialization may even be essential to the effective operation of an organization because many jobs present workers with so many complexities and novel circumstances that no reasonable amount of formal training can provide adequate preparation. Through socialization, new employees learn the procedures to be performed and the reasons for doing them, along with the ones to be ignored and even violated if that is what it takes to get a job done.

Some occupationally-based subcultures mesh quite well with the dominant organizational culture because their goals and values parallel those of management. Two examples of supportive subcultures are the ones associated with accountancy and engineering. Accountants see themselves as "designers of order."[35] As such, they define their role as keeping their organizations on a rational footing by carefully tracking revenues and costs, profits and losses. This attitude may at times put them at odds with members of management who seek more operational elbow room, but on the whole, an accounting subculture permeates many organizations and is reinforced by the frequent ascent of managers with financial backgrounds to the highest managerial levels. Even when it is honored in the breach, as when an elaborate cost-benefit analysis is used to justify a pet project of an upper-echelon manager that ends up losing a sizable amount of money for the firm, the values of the accountancy subculture are affirmed.

As with accountancy, the occupational values of engineering center on rationality and objectivity. These values have had considerable influence over the structures and operations of many firms. Engineers have a long history of involvement in management, dating back to earlier times when they were likely to own the firms in which they served as both engineers and managers.[36] More recently, large numbers of engineers have traversed career paths that began with an engineering position and eventually proceeded to a managerial one. According to one survey of several industrial nations, 15 to 30 percent of engineers have management as their major responsibility, and much larger percentages are regularly involved with some aspect of management such as personnel selection or budgeting.[37] It has even been argued that a 40-year-old engineer still doing engineering instead of managing has to be deemed a career failure.[38] This is certainly an overstatement, but it seems evident that many people go into engineering with the intention of eventually becoming managers.[39]

Even if they do not join the ranks of management, engineers are in synch with managers and their culture because both are oriented to the financial success of their organizations. One aspect of this is an emphasis on keeping costs under control. As one old definition has it, an engineer is "someone who can design something that can be produced for a quarter that any fool can design to be made for 50 cents." More broadly, both engineers and managers are oriented to profitability. For engineers, technical virtuosity is important, but it is not an end in itself. What matters is a perspective that combines technical competence with a belief in the importance of making a profit.[40] Thus, engineering resembles accounting in its overall support of a managerial culture that emphasizes control, financial success, and a supposedly "objective" approach to getting things done.

Deviant Subcultures

To have a worker-based subculture that meshes with the official one is what all managers and administrators hope for. But in many instances, the subculture transmitted through interaction with workmates does not jibe with official organizational goals and procedures. It may even be in direct opposition to it, in which case it acts as a *counterculture*. As we will see in greater detail in Chapter 11, workers at a Western Electric plant, immortalized in a classic sociological study, engaged in a variety of practices that markedly departed from company expectations. Instead of working to the fullest extent of their capabilities, employees established informal output norms well below the capabilities of many workers. New employees quickly learned about these practices, and if they failed to adhere to them, a fair amount of verbal and physical abuse brought them back into line.

This example is hardly unique. The study of work and occupations has furnished us with many examples of occupational and organizational countercultures. In some cases, participants in an organizational counterculture have engaged in criminal activity, as when teams of longshoremen participated in well-organized schemes to pilfer some of the cargo they were unloading.[41] Many other cases of on-the-job theft, cheating, and general deviance could be cited, although some subcultures define what is and is not permissible theft. For example, these subcultures may allow and even encourage the pilferage of items from an employer, but stealing from a fellow worker is not to be tolerated.

A counterculture's values, norms, and behaviors often are maintained by restricting work groups to kin or neighbors (who are likely to have undergone anticipatory socialization) and scrupulously rejecting "outsiders."[42] The group's subculture may even be manifested by norms that limit competition within the group. Although deviant acts are committed by individuals, their ill-gotten gains are distributed through the group and its leadership.

By definition, countercultures are deviant to some degree, but their deviance need not be criminal or destructive. Quite the opposite, some countercultures can be an important source of vitality and innovation within an organization. One example is the famous Skunk Works that operated inside the Lockheed Aircraft Company.[43] Originally set up by Clarence "Kelly" Johnson (1910–1990) and a few other engineers in the 1940s, the Skunk Works insulated itself from Lockheed's top management and proudly rejected many of the firm's formal structures and procedures. In the place of Lockheed's conventional bureaucratic mode of operation, the members of the Skunk Works relied on individual creativity, strong leadership, close teamwork, and a willingness to accept risks in the course of designing and building prototypes of the P-80 jet fighter, the U-2 spy plane, and the record-setting SR-71 reconnaissance plane.

Socialization, Careers, and Strain

Socialization into a particular occupation is likely to be most thoroughgoing when individuals see their work as not just a way to bring home some money but as a career. What makes a career different from "just a job" is that it is deeply imbedded in a person's identity. To be a member of the clergy, a judge, or a commissioned officer in the military is to make a commitment that extends throughout one's working life. It is likely to entail a fair amount of sacrifice and an attenuation of other aspects of life from which an identity can be fashioned.

A key characteristic of a career is that it usually proceeds in a series of discernable stages, each of which may contain its own socialization episodes and experiences. The presence of distinct career stages provides an organized framework for life and work. Career military officers, for example, are given a series of assignments appropriate to their rank, and their performance in these assignments will go a long way toward determining if they get promoted to the next highest rank. It is here, however, that an individual's career can collide with the hierarchical nature of most organizations. Career progression in many occupations and organizations requires moving upward in a pyramidal structure that offers a diminishing number of positions at each successive career stage. Again, the military services provide the clearest example. Graduates of officer training programs begin at the lowest level of commissioned officer, second lieutenant in the case of the U.S. Army. The majority are promoted to first lieutenant and then captain within a few years, and most attain the rank of major by their 10th year of service. Ascending to the rank of lieutenant colonel is more difficult, and after attaining it, officers face the eventual prospect of "up or out." A few become generals, but for everyone else, a military career is effectively over by the mid-40s to early 50s, and socialization into civilian life begins.

Although it can be at the center of a person's life, with a few exceptions (a cloistered monk, for example), deep involvement in an organizational or occupational career does not obliterate all other social roles. Moreover, a single occupation may contain a multiplicity of roles that may be difficult to reconcile. Formal socialization procedures are likely to emphasize some occupational roles to the exclusion of others, but they do not put an end to individual role strains. In nursing, for example, most students enter training programs with a strong motivation to help sick people. This is not always reinforced in nursing school, where the development of "professional" technical and administrative capabilities makes up the core of the formal curriculum and permeates the values of the faculty.[44] But throughout their occupational lives, other socialization experiences will bring them back to the "helping role," underscoring the sometimes conflicting roles imbedded in a nursing career. As noted earlier, socialization ends only when life itself ends.

Previous chapters devoted a fair amount of space to the organizational structures and process, both past and present. There is another form of work organization, however, that governs the way some individuals go about their work. This is a mode of organization that purportedly rests on the superior skills and ethical standards of its practitioners, who are collectively labeled as "professionals." But this term is subject to a confusing array of definitions, interpretations, and evaluations. Making sociological sense of professions, professionals, and professionalization will, therefore, be the task of the next chapter.

FOR DISCUSSION

1. What have been the key determinants of the workplace environment for the work you do or hope to do in the future? How have they been transmitted? Have they ever conflicted with one another?

2. Many groups put new members through initiation rites of some sort. Have you ever undergone an initiation rite? How did it affect you? How do you think it affected other members of the group?

3. Who are your heroes, occupational and otherwise? Do you ever consciously look to them as models for some aspects of your life and work?

4. Did you ever have a job where the workers used a unique set of words and phrases? Was this specialized vocabulary a response to purely technical requirements, or was it used to indicate membership in a particular subculture?

Notes

1. Tom J. Peters and Robert H. Waterman Jr., *In Search of Excellence: Lessons From America's Best-Run Companies* (New York: Harper & Row, 1982).

2. Terrence E. Deal and Allan A. Kennedy, *Corporate Cultures: The Rites and Rituals of Corporate Life* (Reading, MA: Addison-Wesley, 1982).

3. Ronald Dore, *British Factory—Japanese Factory: The Origins of National Diversity in Industrial Relations* (London: Allen & Unwin, 1973), 52–3.

4. Robin Leidner, *Fast Food, Fast Talk: Service Work and the Routinization of Everyday Life* (Berkeley: University of California Press, 1993), 54–60.

5. Deal and Kennedy, *Corporate Cultures*, 193–4.

6. Bill Vlasic and Bradley A. Stertz, *Taken for a Ride: How Daimler-Benz Drove Off With Chrysler* (New York: HarperCollins, 2000), 302–3. In 2007, Daimler-Benz sold most of its Chrysler holdings to a private equity fund, absorbing a loss of several billion dollars in the process.

7. John van Maanen, "Observations on the Making of Policemen," *Human Organization* 32, no. 4 (Winter 1973): 410.

8. Ronald M. Pavalko, *Sociology of Occupations and Professions*, 2nd ed. (Itasca, IL: F. E. Peacock, 1988), 58.

9. U.S. Department of Labor, Bureau of Labor Statistics, "Job Openings and Labor Turnover Survey," http://stats.bls.gov/jlt/home.htm#overview (accessed February 1, 2006).

10. U.S. Department of Labor, Bureau of Labor Statistics, "Employee Tenure in 2004," ftp://ftp.bls.gov/pub/news.release/tenure.txt (accessed February 1, 2006).

11. U.S. Department of Labor, Bureau of Labor Statistics, "Number of Jobs Held, Labor Market Activity, and Earnings Growth Among Younger Baby Boomers: Recent Results From a National Longitudinal Survey," http://www.bls.gov/news.release/pdf/nlsoy.pdf (accessed February 1, 2006).

12. Dennis H. Wrong, "The Oversocialized Conception of Man in Modern Sociology," *American Sociological Review* 26, no. 2 (April 1961): 183–93.

13. Howard S. Becker and Blanche Geer, "The Fate of Idealism in Medical School," *American Sociological Review* 23, no. 1 (February 1958): 50–6.

14. William C. Cockerham, *Medical Sociology*, 10th ed. (Upper Saddle River, NJ: Pearson Prentice Hall, 2007), 199.

15. Erving Goffman, *Encounters* (Indianapolis, IN: Bobbs-Merrill, 1961), 87–8.

16. Robert Grandfield, "Making It by Faking It: Working-Class Students in an Elite Academic Environment," *Journal of Contemporary Ethnography* 20, no. 3 (October 1991): 340.

17. They are, respectively, a worker at a logging operation who signals the imminent falling of a tree, tree branches that can fall on loggers, a locomotive engineer, and a heavy-equipment operator. See Martin Meissner, "The Language of Work," in *Handbook of Work, Organization, and Society*, ed. Robert Dubin (Chicago: Rand McNally, 1976), 264–5.

18. J. Patrick Wright, *On a Clear Day You Can See General Motors: John Z. Delorean's Look Inside the Automotive Giant* (New York: Avon, 1979), 19–37.

19. Elvi Whittaker and Virginia Olesen, "The Faces of Florence Nightingale: Functions of the Heroine Legend in an Occupational Subculture," *Human Organization* 23, no. 2 (Summer 1964): 123–30.

20. Samuel Smiles, *The Lives of the Engineers*, 4 vols. (London: John Murray, 1861–1865).

21. Emile Durkheim, *The Division of Labor in Society*, trans. George Simpson (Glencoe, IL: Free Press, 1947).

22. S. L. A. Marshall, *Men Against Fire: The Problem of Battle Command* (Norman: University of Oklahoma Press, 2000).

23. Bruce Allen Watson, *When Soldiers Quit: Studies in Military Disintegration* (Westport, CT: Praeger, 1997), 158–60.

24. Erving Goffman, *Asylums: Essays on the Social Situations of Mental Patients and Other Inmates* (Chicago: Aldine, 1961).

25. Richard Harris, *The Police Academy: An Inside View* (New York: Wiley, 1973).

26. See, for example, Paul Krause, *The Battle for Homestead, 1880–1892: Politics, Culture, and Steel* (Pittsburgh: University of Pittsburgh Press, 1992).

27. Harrison M. Trice, *Occupational Subcultures in the Workplace* (Ithaca, NY: ILR Press, 1993), 118.

28. Ibid., 119.

29. Charles Vaught and David L. Smith, "Incorporation and Mechanical Solidarity in an Underground Coal Mine," *Work and Occupations* 7, no. 2 (May 1980): 159–87.

30. W. Richard Scott, *Organizations: Rational, Natural, and Open Systems*, 2nd ed. (Englewood Cliffs, NJ: Prentice Hall, 1987), 38.

31. Melville Dalton, "Conflicts Between Staff and Line Managerial Officers," *American Journal of Sociology* 15 (June 1950): 342–51.

32. Peter M. Blau and W. Richard Scott, *Formal Organizations: A Comparative Approach* (San Francisco: Chandler, 1962), 173–4.

33. Diane Vaughan, *The Challenger Launch Decision: Risky Technology, Culture, and Deviance at NASA* (Chicago: University of Chicago Press, 1996).

34. Jane C. Hood, "From Night to Day: Timing and the Management of Custodial Work," *Journal of Contemporary Ethnography* 17 (1988): 96–116.

35. Trice, *Occupational Subcultures*, 48.

36. Daniel H. Calhoun, *The American Civil Engineer: Origins and Conflict* (Cambridge: MIT Press, 1960), 77.

37. Wouter van den Berghe, *Engineering Manpower: A Comparative Study of the Employment of Graduate Engineers in the Western World* (Paris: UNESCO, 1986), 142, 171.

38. Everett C. Hughes, *Men and Their Work* (Glencoe, IL: Free Press, 1958), 137.

39. Robert Perucci and Joel Gerstl, *Profession Without Community: Engineers in American Society* (New York: Random House, 1969), 140.

40. Robert Zussman, *Mechanics of the Middle Class: Work and Politics Among American Engineers* (Berkeley: University of California Press, 1985), 121.

41. William W. Pilcher, *The Portland Longshoremen* (New York: Holt, 1972), 100–1.

42. Gerald Mars, *Cheats at Work: An Anthropology of Workplace Crime* (Boston: Allen & Unwin, 1982), 89–107.

43. Ben R. Rich and Leo Janos, *Skunk Works: A Personal Memoir of My Years at Lockheed* (Boston: Little, Brown, 1994).

44. Fred Davis, Virginia L. Olesen, and Elvi Waik Whittaker, "Problems and Issues in Collegiate Nursing Education," in *The Nursing Profession: Five Sociological Essays,* ed. Fred Davis (New York: Wiley, 1966), 138–75.

9

Professions and Professionalization

What do you think of when you hear someone say, "She's a real pro!"? Most likely, you'll assume she is a highly competent worker, someone who gets things done correctly because she knows what she's doing. But on other occasions, the term *professional* may have less exalted connotations in that it simply refers to someone who gets paid for what he or she is doing. The implied contrast is with an amateur, which literally means someone who engages in an activity for the sheer love of it, free from the taint of monetary gain. At the same time, however, the term *amateur* also may contrast with *professional* when it connotes a lack of competence, as in "that was a pretty amateurish job." Understandable though they might be in everyday speech when the context is evident, these conceptions of professions and professionals do not accurately convey what it is that makes the professions distinct from other occupations. In the pages that follow, we will go beyond these common perceptions of what it means to be a professional by considering how professions differ from other kinds of occupations, how they have achieved their special status, and the ways in which this special status is being challenged by other forces in the economy and society.

The Checklist Approach to the Professions

Everybody seems to know that certain kinds of workers, notably doctors and lawyers, belong to a special occupational category that bears the label "professional." Many decades ago, sociologists began to develop theories about what made the professions distinct from other occupational forms.[1] In effect, their efforts resembled the work of zoologists, who gained a better understanding of particular species of animals by noting and describing their key anatomical features. This mode of analysis has come to be labeled the "trait" or "attributes" approach because it singled out the characteristics of professions that seemed to be absent or less developed in other kinds of occupations. These attributes constituted a kind of checklist that could be used to determine if an occupation was a profession, an ordinary occupation, or perhaps something in between, a "semiprofession" or a "paraprofession," as they came to be called.

Checklists of this sort have been produced by a number of sociologists and other scholars.[2] None of them are exactly the same, but they reflect a general agreement on the key features of a profession. In the first place, professional practice is based on specialized knowledge. This is a major criterion used in the compilations of government statistics on professionals, which list a wide variety of occupations—everything from athletes to speech therapists—under the category "professional."[3] Sociological approaches to the professions are less inclusive on this count. Although many occupations require specialized knowledge of some sort, more is involved than accumulated job-specific information and experience-based rules of thumb. Professionals, as Herbert Simon has noted, cannot be satisfied with knowledge that is "intuitive, informal, and cookbooky."[4] Not only is a professional's knowledge deeper and more sophisticated than that of an ordinary worker, it is supposed to be grounded in well-established theories and conceptual schemes that give intellectual coherence to specific facts and procedures.

Although the possession of specialized knowledge is one of the prime characteristics of professionals, it is important that this knowledge not be too specialized. A professional with only a general knowledge of how to do the work is not much better than a layperson, but when the knowledge base is too narrow, it can be acquired by individuals in the course of a short, sharply focused training period. Under these circumstances, the knowledge used resembles that of a technician rather than that of a professional.[5] Consequently, striking an effective balance between general and specialized knowledge, along with tying the latter to the former, constitutes an important part of professional training.

Acquiring the knowledge essential to professional practice takes time, effort, and formal instruction, hence the second key feature of a profession, a university-based training program that prepares individuals to be competent practitioners. A century ago, a fair number of doctors, dentists, lawyers, architects, and engineers learned their trade through an apprenticeship of some sort, but the amount of knowledge that needs to be assimilated today cannot be learned at the knee of a master practitioner; intensive, extensive, and systematic instruction is now essential. In most cases, this means an education in a university setting. Universities, as many students of the professions have noted, have been key institutions in the historical development of the professions, although their exact relationship to individual professions has varied from country to country.[6] In addition to providing sites for professional training, universities are essential to the development and maintenance of professions because they lend legitimacy to certain kinds of knowledge, while through their admissions policies and practices, they determine who is allowed to pursue a professional career.

In recent years, there has been a significant escalation in the educational requirements of many occupations. In the not-too-distant past, many occupations such as nursing or pharmacy could be entered after a period of specialized training that did not necessarily entail the attainment of a college or university degree. Today, a college degree is usually required as a starting point, followed by several years of postgraduate training, which may include an internship in addition to regular classes.

Third, the work of a professional is deemed to be of great value, both to society as a whole and to the individual who makes use of professional services. For example, every society needs attorneys and judges to serve as intermediaries between the legal system and the citizenry through their interpretation and administration of the law. A legal system staffed by professionals makes it possible to settle disputes without resorting to violence, whereas a society lacking in attorneys and judges could easily dissolve into an anarchical "war of all against all." At the level of the individual, someone whose dog has bitten a neighbor needs to have his or her interests defended in the event of a lawsuit, while the person who was bitten wants to be fairly compensated for his or her injuries. Resolving this conflict is a job best done by expert professionals well schooled in tort law; lawyers are fond of noting that "anyone who tries to represent himself in a court of law has a fool for a client."

Fourth, the distinctive roles and specialized skills of professionals confer considerable power. It is, therefore, of great importance that this power not be abused or used for the wrong purposes. Professionals must put aside their own interests and give primacy to the needs of their clients and society as a whole. Unlike commercial relationships, where *caveat emptor* ("let the buyer beware") is the predominant attitude, the relationship between a professional and his or her client is supposed to be guided by the precept of *credat emptor* ("let the buyer trust").[7] The elevated ethical standards of professionals are embodied in a code of ethics (the most well-known example being the Hippocratic Oath taken by physicians), which defines the key values of the profession and provides general guidance for its practitioners. Violation of these codes, as well as other behaviors that go against professional norms, can result in expulsion from the profession, as when a lawyer is disbarred for unethical conduct.

Fifth, the ethical standards of professionals also apply to interactions with other members of the profession. Professionals are seen to be participating in a common endeavor, such as the collective efforts of nurses to care for patients and alleviate their suffering. Competition for clients is frowned upon, and even public criticism of a fellow professional is something to be avoided unless it serves some higher good. Relationships among professionals are supposed to be cooperative, and even when they are competitive, as with trial lawyers pleading a case, their actions are supposed to be governed by commonly accepted standards of professional practice.

Finally, professionals are distinguished from other occupational groups by their ability to function with a high degree of autonomy and self-governance. It is assumed that the extensive knowledge and high ethical standards of professionals insulate them from outside interference. A professional's actions are based on his or her evaluation of a situation and not on orders from a higher authority. Although state governments have statutory control over the licensing of professionals, in most cases, licensing boards are made up of members of the profession who define qualifications, establish standards of practice, and wield disciplinary power.[8] At the other end of the hierarchical scale, a professional's clients are expected to do what the professional tells them to do, even if it goes against their personal preferences. Common expressions such as "doctor's orders" and "you're the doctor" attest to the authority of professionals to control some aspects of their clients' behavior. Autonomy also extends to the determination of who is entitled to be accepted into the ranks of a particular profession. University-based professional schools serve as entry points for would-be professionals. As with governmental licensing boards, these institutions are dominated by established members of the profession. A profession, therefore, demonstrates its independence by effectively controlling who enters it and subsequently performs the tasks entrusted to that profession.

The Professional Continuum

It may be apparent that the above list of the attributes of a profession, along with most of the examples used to illustrate them, draws heavily from the established professions of medicine and law. Things get a bit more complicated when other occupations are taken into consideration. Engineers, teachers, librarians, and social workers—to name only a few—also have claims to professional status because their occupations exhibit some of the characteristics of the more established professions, or because all these characteristics are present but in attenuated form. For this reason, they are sometimes referred to as *semiprofessions*.[9] Another term in common usage is *paraprofessional*, which, as will be described below, refers to occupations that have some of the attributes of a profession but primarily serve as auxiliaries to the established professions.

The use of the terms *professional, semiprofessional,* and *paraprofessional* may convey the idea that these are absolute categories with firm boundaries separating them. Although members of the most high-status, well-paid professions would prefer to have it this way, these different categories might better be seen as occupying a multidimensional continuum where the boundaries separating one category from another often are indistinct. Are accountants best described as "professionals" or "semiprofessionals"? Are laboratory technicians "semiprofessionals" or "paraprofessionals"? Social workers, to take another example, occupy an uncertain territory as far as professional status is concerned. They often have a university degree (i.e., Master of Social Work) that is earned after getting a bachelor's degree, but much of their training is of a practical nature and isn't grounded in abstruse theory. Nor is autonomy much in evidence, because most social workers are not free to practice as they see fit but are enmeshed in a net of rules and procedures, many of which have been imposed by outsiders such as politicians and other government officials.

While the occupations often labeled as semiprofessions do not always make the grade when measured against the checklist presented above, more may be involved here than a failure to meet these criteria. It may have been noticed that, with the exception of engineer, all the occupations just noted have large numbers of female practitioners, a pattern that holds for many occupations with ambiguous professional status.[10] This makes it particularly hard to be recognized as a professional when "women's work" is often assumed to be of less value than the work done by men. Moreover, the kinds of virtues associated with women—compassion, self-sacrifice, and nurturance—are not the sorts of things associated with autonomous actions and the exercise of authority. For these reasons, female-dominated occupations face an uphill battle in achieving recognition as full-scale professions.

Another impediment to the efforts of many occupations to achieve professional status is the social position of their clientele. In general, the prestige of any occupation is influenced by the kinds of people being served, which is one reason why stockbrokers are ranked higher on the status ladder than insurance agents. Many occupations often labeled as semiprofessions involve working with clients who occupy the lower levels of the class and status pyramid, such as the poor people served by social workers or the children taught by elementary school teachers. The social position of the clientele being served also rubs off on established professions. Corporate lawyers, to take a notable example, enjoy considerably higher income and status than attorneys who prepare wills or divorce papers for middle-class clients.

Lying well below the established professions on the income and status scale are the occupations collectively known as paraprofessions. Dental hygienists, paralegals, and teachers' aides can be counted among the ranks of paraprofessionals. Their prime task is to the assist professionals and, in particular, to do the sort of "dirty work" that the latter try to avoid whenever possible. In some instances, the work really is dirty, as in the case of hospital orderlies, but for the most part, the work of paraprofessionals consists of routine activities that are nonetheless essential to the effective operation of a profession, such as the preparation of standardized legal documents by paralegals. Another example comes from higher education. Most university professors don't get much enjoyment out of grading student exams, so this work is delegated to graduate student teaching assistants, where it supposedly contributes to their learning how to be professors.

The case of paraprofessionals brings us to another aspect of the professions. To slip into postmodernist terminology, an occupation's attainment of professional status can be seen as resulting from a kind of discourse, through which practitioners have been able to convince government officials and the public (or at least significant segments of it) that they occupy a special occupational niche that has the requisite characteristics of a profession, whether or not it actually does. This discourse also includes efforts by members of an occupation to convince themselves that they have what it takes to hold the title of professional. As Kathryn Lively's study of paralegals has shown, there is a significant disconnect between the sociological definition of a profession and how paralegals see themselves and the work they do.[11] For many of the paralegals interviewed, being a professional was closely tied to their overall comportment, keeping their personal lives separate from their work at the office, and controlling their emotions when they were abused by lawyers and their clients. For these paraprofessionals, subordination had been redefined as a manifestation of professionalism.

Attaining Professional Status

During the 1950s and 1960s, sociologists called attention to the common processes through which certain occupations achieved professional status.[12] As they saw it, the process began with the creation of a full-time, distinctive occupation, as when surgery ceased to be a sideline occupation performed by barbers. At about this time, the occupation may be given a title that delineates the profession's exclusive domain; for example, "ophthalmology" came to be used to signify the domain of medical doctors uniquely qualified to treat disorders of the eye. A profession was also solidified through the formation of a national association and, most important, the establishment of specialized educational institutions for the training of future practitioners. Professional associations were prominent in another part of the process, the development and adoption of codes of ethics to govern the behavior of the members of the profession. Finally, professionals and their supportive associations engaged in political mobilization in order to gain popular and legal support for giving the profession its distinctive niche.

It may be evident in all but the last category that this process substantially replicates the checklist approach in its delineation of a set of characteristics that have to be attained if an occupation is to join the elite club known as "the professions." By the 1970s, however, sociologists and other scholars were becoming increasingly skeptical about both the validity of the checklist approach and conventional descriptions of the process of professionalization.[13] These critics pointed out that many professions have not emerged in accordance with these schemas and that earlier students of the professions had failed to take into account how particular historical circumstances affected the emergence of individual professions. Even more important, prior descriptions of professions and the process of professionalization failed to give sufficient attention to the last element in the process of professionalization, the political processes through which occupations and their members gained the prestige, autonomy, and other advantages conferred by the attainment of professional status.

Professionalization as a Means of Control

Mention of professionalization as a political process reminds us that there is a strong power dimension to the exercise of every profession. Trying to determine whether an occupation should be called a profession by referencing education, ethical standards, and inherent value to society is a valid exercise, but too much emphasis on these traits can obscure the most salient aspect of a profession, the ability of its practitioners to control the most important aspects of the work they do. This ability to exercise professional control over a particular line of work comes down to the ability to determine (1) who is allowed to do the work, (2) how they are prepared to do the work, and (3) who gets to evaluate their performance.

In a full-fledged profession, the authority to determine who is allowed to do certain kinds of work resides exclusively within the profession itself. The exercise of this authority is particularly evident in the field of medicine. Physicians, backed with the full force of civil and criminal law, exercise a monopoly on the most important components of medical care. This monopoly has not gone unchallenged, as other medical practitioners such as midwives, chiropractors, and nurse-practitioners have sought the legal right to treat some medical conditions and to perform certain procedures. This has resulted in occasional "turf battles" that center on challenges to physicians' monopolization of particular elements of medical practice, as when chiropractors have pressed for the legal right to prescribe drugs. These are almost always losing battles, but on a few occasions, "outside" practitioners have been incorporated into the dominant profession, as happened when osteopaths adopted the dominant (i.e., allopathic) medical paradigm.

As noted, maintaining professional exclusivity often depends on the ability to enlist the powers of the state to enact and enforce laws that restrict the performance of certain work activities to only one occupational group, whose special status is recognized by the licensure of its members. Professions, of course, are not the only occupational groups that have been able to restrict competition through the issuance of licenses.[14] Licensing requirements can be found in a variety of occupational groups, everything from barbers and beauticians to private detectives and collection agents. As with the justification for the monopolization of certain activities by particular professions, licensing requirements are defended on the grounds that they protect the general public by preventing unqualified workers from doing damage to people and property through their incompetence. There is certainly merit to licensure requirements; most of us gain some comfort from the knowledge that the people updating the wiring in our home have state certification that attests to their ability to do the job properly. But at the same time, it has to be recognized that, in the words of Robert A. Rothman, "licensing is probably the most important victory in the evaluation of a profession because it grants the profession exclusive jurisdiction supported by the authority of the state."[15] This "exclusive jurisdiction" restricts competition by limiting the number of individuals who can legally do certain kinds of work. The result is likely to be higher prices for the buyers of the service and higher incomes for the people who provide it.

Licensing of both professionals and nonprofessionals is an effective way to restrict entrance into an occupation and maintain control over a particular type of work. But professionals have an additional weapon to help them maintain their borders and guard their territory: a prescribed means of entering the profession. This process centers on a particular mode of training that can take place only in institutions overseen by members of the profession. In times past, an aspiring young person could become a lawyer or doctor through self-study and perhaps an apprenticeship. Today, attendance at an institution accredited by the profession is virtually mandatory.

The control of entry into a profession by the profession itself puts the role of education in a different light. It is undeniable that advanced training is essential for doing effective work, but at the same time, it also has to be recognized that educational requirements can be an effective means of restricting and controlling entry into a profession. Until fairly recently, the number of physicians was effectively held in check by the ability of the medical profession to limit the number of medical schools through its control of accreditation processes. Attorneys have been less successful in this endeavor, as nonaccredited law schools have offered an alternate route into the profession. But this situation also reflects an internal division within the law profession; the most prestigious and heavily remunerated positions are largely staffed by graduates of university-affiliated law schools, while the lower tier has been disproportionately occupied by graduates of lesser institutions.[16] The legal profession also has been able to regulate the size of its population through its oversight of the bar exam, the passage of which is essential for a state-approved law practice.

As with licensing, strict educational requirements and the control of entry into the institutions that provide a professional education are justified in terms of protecting the public, but they also have some negative consquences. Professional education is costly, and the prospect of running up tens of thousands of dollars in debt is likely to deter many men and women, particularly ethnic minorities and members of the working class, from embarking on a professional career. Those who are willing to take on considerable debt may decide to pursue the more lucrative specializations within their profession in order to eventually extricate themselves from a substantial financial hole.

The third key element of professional control over an occupation is the ability of a profession to police itself. Professionals are occasionally convicted of some transgression, which, if severe enough, may result in civil or even criminal penalties. But powerful sanctions can also be applied by fellow members of the profession, all the way to being expelled from the profession. As a practical matter, the powers of the state and the powers of a profession are often jointly exercised. A state government may revoke a physician's license to practice medicine, but since the licensing board is likely to be exclusively composed of other physicians, the decision is largely in the hands of the members of the profession.

In summing up what makes a profession different from other kinds of occupations, Richard Hall has stated that

> the key to understanding the nature of the professions is the power they have in relation to other occupations, the organizations in which they are employed, clients and the state. From this perspective the essence of the professions is their development and maintenance of power.[17]

George Bernard Shaw put it more pithily when he characterized a profession as "a conspiracy against the laity." It may be apparent, then, that today's professions have many of the attributes of the preindustrial guilds described in Chapter 2.[18] Members of a profession have specialized knowledge and skills that allow them to do things that are valued by the society as a whole. They have high standards, both technical and ethical, that are supposed to obviate the need for supervision from the outside. Knowledge, skills, and ethical values are acquired through a lengthy process of training largely overseen by accomplished practitioners.

These are the positive features of both guilds and professions. At the same time, however, it is important to consider how these institutions and practices serve to limit competition and insulate their members from external sources of control. As with the guilds of old, today's established professions have been able to restrict entry and demarcate territory that is closed off to members of other occupations. And like the guilds, professions have been largely self-governing entities. The ability of the guilds to limit competition was backed up by the state through its issuance of charters that allowed individual guilds to monopolize specific trades and industries. As we have just seen, a similar function is performed by the modern state through the issuance of licenses that restrict certain kinds of work to members of a particular profession.

Professionals in Organizations

Although the foregoing section may have conveyed the idea that members of the various professions have been able to control most aspects of their working lives, set against this is a basic fact of occupational life: most of today's professionals work within organizational settings that at least have the potential to set limits to professional autonomy. This is not a new development. Some professionals, notably college professors and members of the clergy, have almost always been the employees of an organization of some sort. On the other hand, until well into the 20th century, lawyers and doctors typically worked as solo practitioners or belonged to partnerships with only a few members. New lawyers or doctors would commence professional life by "hanging out a shingle" outside a small office to notify the world that they were now in the business of practicing law or medicine. Today, the self-employment of professionals has by no means vanished, but many professionals work in organizations of some sort. To note two important examples, 38 percent of physicians are not full or part owners of the practices in which they work,[19] and large numbers of attorneys work in law firms with dozens if not hundreds of practitioners or are directly employed by large organizations. Outside the classic professions of medicine and law, virtually every other profession has emerged in conjunction with the rise and growth of large-scale organizations.[20]

Since autonomy is a major attribute of a true profession, being the employee of an organization has the potential to subject a professional to its rules and regulations and to put professional employees in a subordinate position within an organization's hierarchical structure. Under such circumstances, professionals might be unable to participate in key processes and decisions, such as making budgetary allocations. Some observers even have

Photo 9.1   Engineers working amid massive stacks of blueprints. Blueprints stacked in the foreground were only a third of 5,328 necessary for an F-86E. Engineers spent 801,286 man hours to research and design the first model.

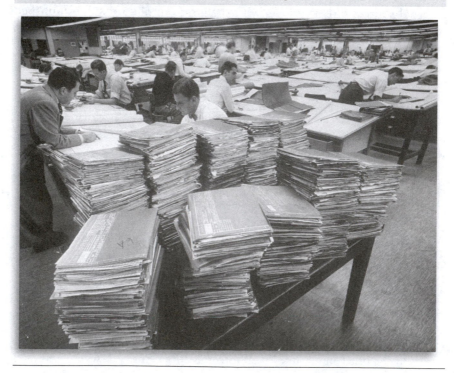

SOURCE: ©J R EYERMAN, Time & Life Pictures Collection/Getty Images.

argued that the incorporation of professionals into organizations, especially profit-seeking firms within a capitalist economy, has amounted to the "protelarianization" of professionals.[21]

These alleged threats to professional autonomy should not be exaggerated; most professionals continue to exercise a great deal of authority and discretion as they go about their work. With rare exceptions, hospital administrators do not tell doctors what medications to prescribe, and deans do not interfere with professors' grading policies. It is also important not to overstate the freedom of solo practitioners. In times past, independent professionals often were engaged in a constant struggle to attract and retain clients. As a result, many doctors and lawyers were inclined to do the sort of things their clients wanted them to do, even if it went against their professional judgment. In general, being a solo practitioner confers no guarantee of autonomous action. In the final analysis, the ability of professionals to control the market for their services is the most important determinant of professional autonomy and is much more important than being either self-employed or the employee of some organization.[22]

Engineers are an interesting case of an occupation that embodies many elements of a true profession but, at the same time, is firmly embedded in an organizational matrix. Engineers undergo lengthy periods of training that impart plenty of both specialized and theoretical knowledge, and they have considerable leeway in going about their work. At the same time, however, they usually are not engaged in choosing the projects their firms undertake, allocating resources, or making future plans.[23] Even so, engineers do take on these responsibilities when they become managers and executives. This, in fact, is a common career path. Research, development, design, and testing—the core activities of engineering—are for the most part the work of younger engineers. The majority of engineering careers culminate in managerial positions of some sort, and many individuals go into engineering with precisely this goal in mind.[24] Others go into management because the authority conferred by a managerial position allows more effective exercise of their technical capabilities.[25] But whatever the motivations of individual engineers might be, engineering exemplifies a profession with close ties to large-scale organizations and the people who manage them.[26]

Today's Challenges to the Professions

The ability of professions to distinguish themselves from other occupations, especially in regard to autonomy and self-regulation, has been a fairly recent historical development that reached its apogee in the middle of the 20th century. At that time, some observers of contemporary society believed that the professions had become one of the most important social forces in the modern world. The sociologist Talcott Parsons left little doubt about the significance of "the professional complex," which he characterized as

the most important single component in the structure of modern societies. It has displaced first the "state" . . . and more recently, the "capi-
talistic" organization of the economy. The massive emergence of the
professional complex . . . is the most crucial structural development in
twentieth-century society.[27]

This assessment of the professions had the ring of credibility when
Parsons wrote these words, but it is less likely to hold true today. If the professions are viewed as the culmination of a long process that took place
under particular historical circumstances,[28] it is also possible that the process
can run in the other direction as established professions lose at least some of
their special status in the occupational hierarchy.

The issue of deprofessionalization has been a contentious one. For some
observers, reports of the death of the professions have been greatly exaggerated, while others have noted the presence of many external and internal
threats to the established professions. In order to come to some tentative
conclusions, it is useful to consider threats to the professions on two levels:
(1) those that affect a profession as a whole and (2) those that affect the
working lives of individual practitioners. These, of course, are interrelated; a
degraded working environment for individual practitioners may reflect the
decline of a profession as a whole, while the recruitment of individuals of
lesser quality and/or diminished educational programs will undermine the
profession as a whole.

There are not many examples of an entire line of work losing prestige,
power, and other key attributes of a profession, but it has happened. Perhaps
the most notable example comes from the prototype profession: the clergy.
Religious practitioners certainly merit inclusion among the established professions: the word *professional* stems from the "professing" of religious vows
that occurred when one became a priest or nun.[29] As with the professions that
emerged at a later date, the high status of the clergy rested on a close association with medieval universities, even though the majority of the students at
these institutions studied law or medicine rather than theology. But in those
days, the practice of law and medicine was viewed as an elevated craft; the
highest knowledge was found in the religious sphere. As a group, the clergy
gained power, wealth, and prestige through their possession of widely held,
transcendent truths. Their office also included the ability to forgive sins, as
well as the power to bring on eternal damnation through excommunication.
Further reinforcing the power and authority of the medieval clergy was its
separation from the larger society. Joining the priesthood required years of
preparation and a willingness to renounce ordinary social ties, especially those
based on marriage and family. Free from the claims of family members and
other outsiders, the Church amassed a great amount of wealth and power.

Although individual religious practitioners may still enjoy considerable
authority and prestige today, the status of the clergy as a profession is less
solid than it was in the past. This decline is due in part to the erosion of the

clergy's intellectual hegemony, as rival sources of belief, both religious and secular, have competed with one another. In addition, many religious bodies have been either unable or unwilling to hold down the number of practitioners. This is especially evident within Protestant Christianity, where a surplus of ordained ministers has resulted in low salaries for all but a few high-profile pastors of large congregations. The Catholic Church has had the opposite problem, as it has met with serious difficulties in recruiting men to be priests. But the priesthood may be suffering an even greater loss of professional status as sexual abuse scandals, although involving only a small number of priests, have undercut the moral authority of the clergy as a whole.

The erosion of intellectual and moral hegemony that has befallen religious practitioners has occurred in other professions. As we have seen, expert knowledge is a key source of professional status; consequently, the diffusion of that knowledge to the wider public will diminish professional authority to some degree. This seems to be happening today. The clientele of today's professions is, on average, better educated and less likely to be awed by pretensions of superior learning. The lay public also has much easier access to essential knowledge and the tools for applying that knowledge; for example, computer software is readily available for such tasks as drafting a will or filling in an income tax form. In the medical realm, thousands of Internet sites help people diagnose their ills and learn about alternative treatments. In sum, a better-educated public with easy access to information has resulted in a "narrowing of the competence gap" between professionals and their clients.[30]

As we have seen in Chapter 5, one of the most important influences on work is technological change, and the professions have not been immune from its effects. Although the various professions have tried to control it, use it for their own purposes, or remain insulated from it, technological change has affected the structure and activities of the professions, and in ways that have not always been supportive of their interests. Just as individuals are now able to use new information-processing technologies in order to gain and apply knowledge that was once monopolized by professionals, organizations also can make use of new technologies that have the potential to take the place of professional expertise. In medicine, for example, computerized diagnostic systems can detect a large number of ailments, in some cases doing a better job than human diagnosticians. In higher education, to note another example, universities are making increasing use of distance learning programs that employ computer networks and advanced audiovisual technologies to diffuse professorial wisdom to a large audience.

On the positive side, some new technologies have made important contributions to the success of professional work, and in many cases, they have reinforced the status and authority of professionals. Medicine is a particularly striking example. As late as the 1930s, doctors had only limited ability to deal with many of their patients' medical problems; all too often, about all they could do was try to lend a little comfort while promoting the illusion that something useful was being done.[31] Things are dramatically different today, as antibiotics, sophisticated surgical procedures, and CT scans have greatly increased the ability of doctors to effectively diagnose and cure their patients. At the same time, however, new medical technologies have changed certain aspects of a physician's role. Improved diagnostic technologies, going back to the stethoscope in the 19th century and the spygmanometer (the instrument used for measuring blood pressure) in the early 20th century, have made medicine more impersonal and have caused doctors to fixate on particular organs and systems instead of diagnosing and treating the patient as a whole.[32] As a result, technology-intensive medical practices have had contradictory effects on the role and status of physicians. On one hand, the reliance on "objective" data has bolstered their authority, but on the other hand, it has contributed to patients' complaints that their doctors don't spend much time listening to them and that, in general, they seem to have little interest in them as patients, much less as individuals.

One of the most important changes in the status and role of professionals has occurred because their relationships with fellow professionals have become more overtly competitive. In the past, vying for clients through advertising was considered "unprofessional," and in fact, it was legally prohibited in most states. Also of importance in maintaining professional status was the avoidance of publicly revealing fee schedules, such as how much it cost to draft a will. This made it difficult for potential clients to "shop around" in order to find the most reasonable fee. But in 1977, the U.S. Supreme Court in *Bates v. State of Arizona* outlawed the practice of not publicly disclosing fees for legal services,[33] and since this decision, many lawyers and other professionals have advertised their fees and services, sometimes quite aggressively. The advertising done by personal-injury lawyers on daytime TV doesn't do much to enhance the status of the legal profession, and advertising in general has made professional practice a more competitive business and strengthened the hand of users of professional services. The established professions have a long history of containing and controlling competitive pressures, but many professionals today find it much more difficult to work in splendid isolation from market forces.

Resource Control and Professional Autonomy: The Case of Medicine

In times past, occupations such as law and medicine were sometimes labeled "free professions" because they were, for the most part, self-regulating. As we have seen, autonomy is still an important characteristic of a true profession, but maintaining self-regulation has become more difficult due to the increased involvement of government and private organizations in professional activities. Nowhere has this been more evident than in the field of medicine. The oversight of physicians by nonprofessionals is an inevitable consequence of medical economics; federal, state, and local governments pick up the tab for nearly half of medical expenditures,[34] while much of the rest is covered by private insurers. These agencies have a strong interest in holding down medical costs, and most medical practitioners have to accept payments that adhere to the fee schedules they have set.[35]

Increased government support of medical care also has affected the medical profession in less direct ways. Medical schools rely heavily on grants from the federal government, which in turn has used its power of the purse to impel medical schools to increase the number of medical students in order to provide care for underserved communities and to create more opportunities for women and minorities.[36] This has helped increase diversity among the ranks of physicians, but it also has produced a more competitive environment within the medical profession by expanding the number of practitioners.

The federal government also has attempted to stem skyrocketing medical costs by encouraging the production of more primary care physicians and trying to slow the growth of the number of specialists by increasing Medicare payments for the former and reducing them for the latter. This policy has been reinforced by private health maintenance organizations and other managed care organizations, which have attempted to limit access to expensive specialized care by bestowing "gatekeeping" functions on primary care physicians.[37] Although this practice has worked to the advantage of the latter, it also has driven a wedge within the profession by pitting primary care physicians against specialists.[38]

In general, it can be argued that the relationship between the government and physicians has been inverted in recent years. In the past, governments, through their licensing practices, conferred on doctors the legal right to control medical practice. Today, government is still the final source of licensing authority, but its heavy involvement in the financing of healthcare and its efforts to rein in costs have resulted in a relationship with doctors that borders on the adversarial. Meanwhile, nongovernmental organizations such as private insurers, health maintenance organizations, preferred provider organizations, and for-profit hospitals have their own interests, which also can put them at odds with the medical profession. How these conflicts will be resolved remains to be seen, but in any event, it is unlikely that doctors will be able to exercise the degree of control over medicine that they wielded in the 1950s and 1960s.

Diversity and Professional Status

Although this chapter has analyzed the characteristics of professions in terms of their essential qualities and their relationships with other elements of society, the social origins of the individuals occupying professional positions certainly have not been irrelevant to the status of the professions. To put it more concretely, at least until quite recently, the great majority of doctors, lawyers, and other well-recognized professionals have been white men of northern European background.[39] Professions also have been disproportionately staffed by individuals born into upper-class and upper-middle-class families, many of them headed by members of the professions. Class origins have an important influence on the decision to become a lawyer and make it through law school,[40] while a substantial percentage of practicing physicians are sons and daughters of doctors. This close identification of the professions with dominant social groups has been a significant source of professional status and authority.

This situation has changed to some extent in recent years, but taken as a whole, the professions still do not reflect the racial, ethnic, and gender composition of the United States as a whole. In regard to gender diversity, the legal profession has seen the greatest influx of women; 32.4 percent of lawyers were women in 2009.[41] This statistic would likely have been a source of considerable consternation to Supreme Court Justice Joseph Bradley, who, in an opinion that concurred with the Court's 1872 ruling that women could be barred from the practice of law, asserted that "the natural and proper timidity and delicacy which belongs to the female sex evidently unfits it for many of the occupations of civil life."[42] The share of women at the highest level of medical practice has increased to almost the same degree, with women now composing 32.2 percent of physicians.[43] It should be noted, however, that women are disproportionately represented in certain segments of the profession, such as pediatrics, psychiatry, and public health, which, not coincidentally, bring in the lowest incomes.

Photo 9.2 Nursing has been a classic female-dominated occupation.

SOURCE: ©image100/CORBIS.

Although women now have a growing presence in the well-established professions of medicine and law, the majority of women professionals can be found in occupations that have emerged in conjunction with the rise of large organizations. As we have just seen, a professional position within an organization often sets limits on the ability of professionals to control at least some aspects of their work. Accordingly, female-dominated professional employees such as librarians, elementary school teachers, and social workers may have a great amount of expertise gained through both formal training and experience, but their place in an organizational hierarchy often puts them in a subordinate position.

In another female-dominated occupational realm, nurses may find that their status as professionals is devalued because they are subject both to hospital administrators and to physicians. In the late 1960s, the relationship of doctors and nurses could even be described as a "caste-like system" that prevented nurses from intruding into what the doctors considered their exclusive realm, such as providing patients with information relating to their condition or treatment.[44] This hierarchical relationship is the source of what has been called "the doctor-nurse game." A nurse who participates in this "game" is able to control some aspects of patient care but only by making recommendations to doctors that make it seem as though the physicians themselves had taken the initiative, thereby maintaining their superior status. Today's nurses, however, seem less inclined to be treated as subordinates who are required to play this game. In recent years, their claims to professional status have been bolstered by higher levels of training, the shortage of nurses, and a cultural shift in the direction of greater assertiveness on the part of women. At the same time, gender-based subordination is less easily maintained when the ranks of both women physicians and male nurses have been steadily growing.[45]

While women have gained greater representation in many professions, the same cannot be said of most racial and ethnic minorities. Some professions, notably medicine and engineering, have experienced a large influx of immigrants of various races and ethnicities, but native-born Latinos and African Americans have made smaller inroads into professional occupations. To take two paradigmatic professions, African Americans accounted for 4.7 percent of lawyers and 5.7 percent of physicians in 2009. For Latinos, the percentages were 2.8 and 6.3, respectively.[46] As with women, larger numbers of African Americans and Latinos will likely occupy greater numbers of professional positions in the years to come, but it would be a sad irony if they were to do so while the established professions have been losing some of the authority, autonomy, and status that up to now have set them apart from other occupations.

Although a fair number of women and minority group members have successfully entered professional ranks, their relative underrepresentation reflects the continued importance of ascribed characteristics for the occupational structure and the workers who inhabit it. The issues that surround racial, gender, and ethnic diversity will be explored in Chapter 13, but before that, we will turn our attention to a fundamental aspect of working life: the allocation of wages, salaries, and benefits. Professionals generally enjoy higher rates of remuneration than other workers do; in the next chapter, we will consider why this is so, while more generally taking into account the structures and processes that determine why some members of the workforce are well rewarded while others are barely able to scrape by on what they earn.

FOR DISCUSSION

1. A key characteristic of professions is that their practitioners enjoy high levels of trust on the part of their clients. How is trust established? Is it merited?

2. Professions have been analyzed as organized efforts to dampen competition and circumvent the market. Is this necessarily a bad thing? Who benefits from these efforts when they are successful?

3. How might you characterize personal interactions between professionals and their clients? How have the socializing experiences of professionals and their clients shaped these interactional patterns?

4. Is the division between the professions and other kinds of occupations obsolete? If so, is it because the established professions have lost some of their key attributes, or is it because so many occupations now have the characteristics that were once largely confined to these established professions?

Notes

1. T. J. Marshall, "The Recent History of Professionalization in Relation to Social Theory and Social Policy," in *Class, Citizenship, and Social Development* (1939; repr., Garden City, NY: Anchor, 1965), 158–79; Talcott Parsons, "The Professions and the Social Structure," in *Essays in Sociological Theory* (1939; repr., New York: Free Press, 1954), 34–49.

2. One representative example is Ernest Greenwood, "Attributes of a Profession," *Social Work* 2 (July 1957): 45–55. For a more critical presentation of the attribute model, see Ronald M. Pavalko, *Sociology of Occupations and Professions* (Itasca, IL: F. E. Peacock, 1988), 17–50.

3. U.S. Census Bureau, *The 2011 Statistical Abstract*, "Table 615: Employed Citizens by Sex, Race, and Hispanic Origin, 2009," http://www.census.gov/compendia/statab/2011/tables/11s0615.pdf (accessed February 14, 2011).

4. Herbert Simon, *The Sciences of the Artificial* (Cambridge: MIT Press, 1972), 55. Quoted in Charles Derber, William A. Schwartz, and Yale Magass, *Power in the Highest Degree: Professionals and the Rise of the New Mandarin Order* (New York: Oxford University Press, 1990), 53.

5. On the ambiguous occupational position of technicians, see Stephen E. Barley and Julian E. Orr, eds., *Between Craft and Science: Technical Work in U.S. Settings* (Ithaca, NY: Cornell University Press, 1997).

6. Andrew Abbott, *The System of Professions: An Essay on the Division of Expert Labor* (Chicago: University of Chicago Press, 1988), 195–211.

7. Everett C. Hughes, "Professions," in *The Professions in America*, ed. Kenneth S. Lynn and the editors of *Daedalus* (Boston: Beacon, 1967), 3.

8. Robert A. Rothman, *Working: Sociological Perspectives* (Englewood Cliffs, NJ: Prentice Hall, 1987), 71.

9. Amatai Etzioni, ed., *The Semiprofessions and Their Organization* (New York: Free Press, 1969).

10. George Ritzer and David Walczak, *Working: Conflict and Change*, 3rd ed. (Englewood Cliffs, NJ: Prentice Hall, 1986), 237–9.

11. Kathryn J. Lively, "Occupational Claims to Professionalism: The Case of Paralegals," *Symbolic Interactionism* 24, no. 3 (2001): 343–66.

12. Theodore Caplow, *The Sociology of Work* (Minneapolis: University of Minnesota Press, 1954), 139–40; Harold L. Wilensky, "The Professionalization of Everyone?" *American Journal of Sociology* 70 (1964): 137–58.

13. For a particularly trenchant example, see Julius A. Roth, "Professionalism: The Sociologist's Decoy," *Sociology of Work and Occupations* 1, no. 1 (February 1974): 6–23.

14. Everett Cherrington Hughes, *Men and Their Work* (Glencoe, IL: Free Press, 1958), 78–87.

15. Rothman, *Working: Sociological Perspectives*, 70.

16. Elliot Krause, *Death of the Guilds: Professions, States, and the Advance of Capitalism, 1930 to the Present* (New Haven, CT: Yale University Press, 1996), 49–54. For a history of ethnic stratification in the practice of law, see Jerold S. Auerbach, *Unequal Justice: Lawyers and Social Change in Modern America* (New York: Oxford University Press, 1976).

17. Richard H. Hall, *Dimensions of Work* (Beverly Hills, CA: Sage, 1986), 45–6.

18. This is a key theme of Krause, *Death of the Guilds*.

19. Center for Studying Health System Change, "Physician Survey Summary File," www.hschange.org/CONTENT/170/170.pdf (accessed February 28, 2007), 34.

20. Kenneth J. Lipartito and Paul J. Miranti, "Professions and Organizations in Twentieth-Century America," *Social Science Quarterly* 79, no. 2 (June 1998): 301–20.

21. Charles Derber, *Professionals as Workers: Mental Labor in Advanced Capitalism* (Boston: G. K. Hall, 1982). For a refutation of this thesis, see Raymond Murphy, "Proletarianization or Bureaucratization: The Fall of the Professional?" in *The Formation of Professions: Knowledge, State, and Strategy*, ed. Rolf Torstendahl and Michael Burrage (London: Sage, 1990).

22. Eliot Freidson, *Professional Powers: A Study of the Institutionalization of Formal Knowledge* (Chicago: University of Chicago Press, 1986), 124–5.

23. Robert Zussman, *Mechanics of the Middle Class: Work and Politics Among American Engineers* (Berkeley: University of California Press, 1985).

24. Robert Perucci and Joel Gerstl, *Profession Without Community: Engineers in American Society* (New York: Random House, 1969), 140.

25. R. Richard Ritti, *The Engineer in the Industrial Corporation* (New York: Columbia University Press, 1971), 25.

26. John Rae and Rudi Volti, *The Engineer in History*, 2nd ed. (New York: Peter Lang, 2001), 169–71, 199–216.

27. Talcott Parsons, "Professions," in *International Encyclopedia of the Social Sciences*, ed. David L. Sills (New York: Macmillan, 1968), 545.

28. Magali Sarfatti Larson, *The Rise of Professionalism: A Sociological Analysis* (Berkeley: University of California Press, 1977).

29. Freidson, *Professional Powers*, 21.

30. Robert Rothman, "Deprofessionalization: The Case of Law in America," *Work and Occupations* 11 (1984): 183–206.

31. Lewis Thomas, *The Youngest Science: Notes of a Medicine-Watcher* (New York: Viking, 1983).

32. Hughes Evans, "Losing Touch: The Controversy Over the Introduction of Blood Pressure Instruments Into Medicine," *Technology and Culture* 34, no. 4 (October 1993): 784–807; Stanley Joel Reiser, *Medicine and the Reign of Technology* (Cambridge, UK: Cambridge University Press, 1978).

33. Hall, *Dimensions of Work,* 53.

34. David M. Cutler, *Health Care and the Public Sector* (Cambridge, MA: National Bureau of Economic Research, 2002), http://papers.nber.org/papers/w8802.pdf (accessed May 9, 2006), 9.

35. Frederic W. Hafferty and Donald W. Light, "Professional Dynamics and the Changing Nature of Medical Work," *Journal of Health and Social Behavior* 35 (1995): 136–7, 141–3.

36. Krause, *Death of the Guilds,* 45–6.

37. Kevin T. Leicht and Mary L. Fennell, *Professional Work: A Sociological Approach* (Malden, MA: Blackwell, 2001), 146.

38. Hafferty and Light, "Professional Dynamics," 136.

39. Steven Brint, *In an Age of Experts: The Changing Role of Professionals in Politics and Public Life* (Princeton, NJ: Princeton University Press, 1994), 67.

40. Howard S. Erlanger, "The Allocation of Status Within Professions: The Case of the Legal Profession," *Social Forces* 58 (March 1980): 882–903.

41. U.S. Census Bureau, "Table 615: Employed Citizens."

42. *Bradwell v. Illinois,* http://usinfo.org/docs/democracy/62.htm (accessed February 28, 2007).

43. U.S. Census Bureau, "Table 615: Employed Citizens."

44. Fred E. Katz, "Nurses," in *The Semiprofessions and Their Organization,* ed. Amatai Etzioni (New York: Free Press, 1969), 54–81.

45. William C. Cockerham, *Medical Sociology,* 10th ed. (Upper Saddle River, NJ: Pearson Prentice Hall, 2007), 260–3.

46. U.S. Census Bureau, "Table 615: Employed Citizens."

10

Who Gets What?

Work serves a number of purposes, not all of them monetary. Many things go into making a job worth having, such as prestige, independence, and authority; socializing with fellow workers; and the opportunity for personal growth. But the mention of these benefits should not obscure an inescapable reality of work: were it not for the daily wage or monthly salary it provides, many people would choose to do something else with their time. This chapter will consider the connection between work and income, particularly why some people are well rewarded for the work they do while others earn barely enough to get by from day to day. The size of a wage or salary is also important when occupations are ranked in terms of prestige, but it is not the only determinant. A number of attributes determine the relative prestige of occupations, and these will be taken up toward the end of this chapter.

The Determination of Wages and Salaries: Market Economics Once Again

It might be thought that the size of workers' paychecks is directly tied to their contributions to the firms that employ them. Yet, from the outset, it has to be recognized that variations in pay cannot be explained solely on the basis of the skills and abilities of individual workers. Formal education, race, gender, and age also are important determinants of wages and salaries. Then there is the puzzling fact that within the ranks of workers with similar or even identical characteristics, some workers may get substantially more or less than others for no apparent reason.[1] In the awarding of pay, as with most other aspects of life, quite a lot of variability cannot easily be explained through the invocation of economic and sociological reasoning.

Our inability to fully explain wage and salary differentials does not mean that the determination of worker compensation is a totally random process. The motivations of employers and their employees usually have a powerful overlay of economic self-interest, and as a starting point, we need to consider how the workings of the labor market affect wages and salaries. Chapter 7 noted how the rate of remuneration influences the number of hours an employee is willing to work at a given job and the number of hours an employer is willing to offer. The same supply-and-demand analysis can be used to explain a sizable amount of the variations in pay found among workers. That these differences exist is obvious; a movie star might make more in a week than a sanitation worker does in a year of difficult, odiferous work. At first glance, this seems to reflect a strange set of priorities. After all, what is more essential, entertainment or the safe disposal of waste? We could go for a long time without seeing a movie, but life would become pretty miserable if all the drains backed up for prolonged periods of time. We might, therefore, assume that the high level of demand for the safe disposal of sewage should result in high rates of remuneration for anyone willing to do the inherently unpleasant task of keeping the sewers clear. Such is not the case, of course, for a simple reason: this kind of work does not require uncommon talent and/or skills acquired through years of training. Anybody with sufficient physical strength and endurance can do the job, which means there is a large potential supply of sanitation workers. And when the supply of labor or any other commodity is easily expanded, the price paid for that commodity (in this case, unskilled labor) will be low unless the demand for it increases.

While an oversupply of workers and potential workers will drive down their remuneration, the same will happen when there is only a limited demand for a particular kind of work. Certain occupations have only a small market for their services—think of madrigal singers, professional lacrosse players, and goat herders—and this is likely to be reflected in low levels of remuneration for the few who are employed in these lines of work. There are some kinds of work that are not in great demand, but this is offset by an even more restricted supply of capable workers. Not many steam locomotives are in service today, but few people have the skills necessary to operate them. Consequently, it may be possible to earn a decent living operating steam locomotives used for tourist trains and other special attractions.

Following from this line of reasoning, the best-paid occupations are likely to be those where the work is much in demand but only a few people have the skills necessary to do it. This is a situation that may arise for many reasons. One of these is demographic change, as happened in the years following World War II. The postwar baby boom substantially increased demand for a variety of occupations, such as obstetric nurses, pediatricians, and primary school teachers. Because people with the necessary skills could not be produced overnight, workers in these fields had a lot of bargaining power, which was reflected in the salaries they received.

Technological change can also affect the supply–demand balance, with favorable results for certain kinds of workers and unfavorable consequences for others. According to some observers, the wages of unskilled manufacturing workers have fallen or remained stagnant in recent years as automated processes have become an integral part of industrial production. In sharp contrast, the development and rapid spread of personal computers have created numerous high-paying jobs for people with the requisite skills, such as computer scientists, engineers, programmers, and systems analysts. Whether or not technological change has been a prime reason for widening pay gaps remains controversial, however, and the topic will be taken up later in this chapter. In any event, the monetary gains made by the latter group are likely to be temporary as growing numbers of people acquire the necessary skills and increase the supply of qualified workers, thereby undercutting their aggregate bargaining power.

Useful though it may be, explaining wage and salary differences by invoking market-based economics takes us only so far. For one thing, "demand" has to be recognized as a social creation. Some kinds of jobs have been imbued with great value because their practitioners have convinced significant numbers of people that this is so. Atheists, agnostics, and other skeptics might put members of the clergy in this category. Academics have boosted their job prospects by successfully arguing that a college education is essential for future financial success. Medical care providers of all sorts have benefited from the "medicalization" of many human failings, everything from alcoholism to compulsive gambling.[2] Whether or not this process has been good for individuals and society can be endlessly debated, but it certainly has boosted demand for a variety of medical practitioners.

While trying to increase demand for their services, professionals and semi-professionals also have attempted to maintain their incomes at high levels by addressing the supply side of the equation. As noted in Chapter 9, holding down the number of practitioners is largely done by limiting access to credentialing institutions. To take two examples, the lawful practice of medicine is restricted to men and women who have attended an accredited medical school, while most full-time, tenured positions at colleges and universities are occupied by holders of PhD degrees. There is nothing inherently unreasonable about this; consumers of professional services expect that practitioners will be competent and adequately trained. At the same time, it is also true that the restriction of admissions to medical schools and graduate programs limits the supply of physicians and college professors, thereby reducing competition and protecting the incomes of established members of the profession.

The Widening Income Gap

The income differential that separates professional practitioners from most other workers is only one aspect of a larger phenomenon: the large and growing income gap that separates a relatively small number of income earners from the rest of the working population. This situation can be demonstrated by dividing households into quintiles (i.e., the bottom 20 percent, the next 20 percent, and so on) and noting the share of income that goes to each quintile. An analysis of this sort shows substantial inequality in the distribution of income in the United States. In 2009, only 3.4 percent of the nation's income went to the bottom quintile of American households. Families in the second, third, and fourth quintiles received 8.6, 14.6, and 23.2 percent, respectively, while those in the top quintile took in 50.3 percent of the nation's income.[3] Translated into dollars, this means that in 2009, the mean household income for the bottom quintile was $11,552, while the equivalent figures for the second, third, and fourth quintiles were $29,257, $49,534, and $78,694, respectively. The mean household income for the top quintile came in at $170,844.[4]

The gap between the incomes of the top quintile and those of everyone else has grown with few interruptions over the past three decades. In 1975, the top 20 percent of American households accounted for 43.6 percent of the nation's income. By 1985, the figure was 45.6 percent, and in 2009, as just noted, it had climbed to 50.3 percent.[5] During this period, the share of household income going to all but the top quintile declined or stayed the same, while the portion accrued by the top 5 percent of families increased almost without interruption from 16.5 percent in 1975 to 21.7 percent in 2009.[6]

These figures give a general idea regarding the distribution of income and wealth over the past 3½ decades. The stated numbers do not provide a completely accurate picture because they may be affected by sampling errors and the difficulty of putting a monetary value on some things that are not counted as income on official statistics, such as food stamps for the poor and lavish "business" trips for those at the other end of the scale. Charting the distribution of income also is complicated by the changing size and composition of households. For example, the increased number of households headed by single mothers has contributed to the decreased share of total income received by the lowest quintiles. Nonetheless, the trend is clear: income inequality in the United States has increased in recent years and shows no signs of abating (see Figure 10.1).

Along with a wage or salary, employee compensation often includes a package of benefits, primarily health insurance and a pension plan. The issue of health insurance is an important topic, one that deserves more space than can be devoted to it here. In virtually all economically developed nations except the United States, providing healthcare to everyone is a government responsibility, although employers usually are a prime source of funding. In the United States, the federal government covers men and women over the age of 65 through its Medicare program, and a joint federal–state program known as Medicaid provides healthcare insurance to the poorest segment of the population. For everybody else, the prime providers of health insurance are their employers—if they offer it. In reality, a significant portion of workers, including many with full-time jobs, lack this coverage, and they constitute a sizable share of the approximately 50 million Americans without health insurance. And even individuals with insurance have met with some unpleasant surprises as insurers have tried to limit coverage in the face of relentlessly rising healthcare costs.

Figure 10.1   Income Distribution in the United States, 1967–2001

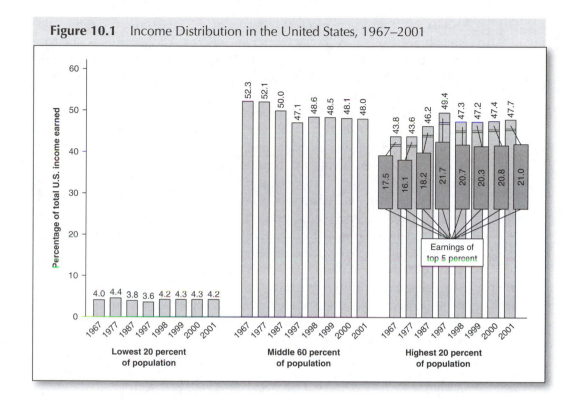

Employers also have been squeezed by rising healthcare costs. The large-scale adoption of HMOs (health maintenance organizations) and PPOs (preferred provider organizations) brought some temporary financial relief in the 1990s, but the United States still devotes a larger portion of its gross national income to healthcare (more than 17) than any other country does. Paradoxically, however, these costs are not matched by higher levels of health. Quite the opposite: the United States ranks 24th in life expectancy and 36th in rates of infant mortality.[7]

Some of the shortcomings of the American healthcare system were addressed when President Obama signed into law the Patient Protection and Affordable Care Act in 2010. The legislation contains a lengthy set of provisions and runs to about 1,000 pages, so only the briefest summary can be presented here.[8] The first phase allows men and women under the age of 26 to remain on their parents' policies and does away with the lifetime expenditure limits found on some policies. It also establishes a high-risk insurance pool for individuals who have had difficulty obtaining insurance and provides payments for a number of preventative procedures. Bigger changes come in 2014, with more individuals covered by Medicaid along with the establishment of regulated insurance exchanges expected to increase competition among insurers. The most controversial element prevents insurance companies from denying coverage while, at the same time, requiring individuals to buy a policy if they are not already covered. Mandatory purchase of health insurance is an essential part of the package; otherwise, many individuals would not buy insurance until they got sick. The legislation also funds a number of state-based programs to allow experimentation and innovation aimed at improving services and reducing costs. This latter point is significant. Although the legislation encompasses potentially cost-saving features, such as picking up the bill for some preventative procedures, it does not directly engage the seemingly inexorable rise in medical costs, which are likely to get only worse as the population ages.

The current pension system also should be a cause for concern. The provision of employee pensions increased substantially after 1974 when the Employment Retirement Income Security Act set minimum standards for employer-based pension plans and established the Pension Benefit Guaranty Corporation as a backstop in the event that an employer cannot meet its pension obligations. With the establishment of employer-sponsored pension plans, large numbers of employees have been freed from a future of subsisting on Social Security payments and whatever money they had been able to put aside during their working years.

For some commentators, this has represented substantial change in the distribution of wealth and income, a kind of backdoor entry into socialism.[9] As things have turned out, the revolution has been incomplete at best. In the first place, it is a strange kind of socialism that does little to close the aforementioned earnings gap. Unionized workers, who tend to have higher wages and salaries than nonunionized workers do, also are more likely to have pension plans—so this benefit has actually increased the income differential between them and nonunionized employees. Only when government-administered Social Security benefits are taken into account do pensions serve to reduce income inequality.[10]

Of greater importance to individuals, however, is whether their pensions will deliver what they promise. Until fairly recently, pensions were, for the most part, "defined benefit" plans. That is, they promised a certain sum would be paid out to retirees on a regular basis. Today, about 20 percent of private-sector employees have defined benefit plans. All other pensions are of the "defined contribution" variety, which directly tie future benefits to the money contributed by individual employees. These funds are often, but not always, supplemented by employer contributions. In either case, these plans usually are inferior to defined benefit plans in what they pay to retirees. But even defined benefit plans may be sharply reduced when a firm declares bankruptcy and leaves pensioners with far less money than they had expected. Some retirees with defined contribution plans have encountered a dramatic reduction of their pensions or even lost them altogether because the funds were invested in the stock of crooked employers, such as Enron and WorldCom. In both of these prominent cases, $1 billion in pension funds permanently disappeared.[11] Even the pension funds of financially healthy firms can be underfunded by hundreds of millions of dollars because management appropriated a portion of these funds when they were deemed excessive. As with provisions for healthcare, future retirees may find they will get a lot less than what they thought they had coming to them.

Why Has Income Inequality Increased?

There is no way to put a positive spin on the possible loss or precipitous reduction of pension and healthcare benefits for substantial numbers of workers. Many observers also find the widening income gap to be problematic, but some have seen it in a favorable light. It can be argued, after all, that unequal incomes reflect the greater contributions of high-income earners and that reduced income differentials might diminish the motivation to move up in the world.[12] There is certainly an element of truth to these assertions, but in regard to the first point, the ability to earn a high income reflects more than individual effort and talent. As we have seen in Chapter 7, membership in a social network considerably enhances the prospect of getting a good job, and such membership usually is based on the family one was born into or the neighborhood in which one lives. Having a college education also greatly enhances earning power, but as we also have seen, educational opportunities have a lot to do with the economic status of one's family.

In regard to the second point, that unequal rewards are effective sources of individual motivation, only the most idealistic would claim that personal ambition and the willingness to undergo long periods of training are not affected by the opportunity to earn more money in the future. But how wide an income gap is necessary to ensure adequate levels of motivation? There is no easy answer to this question, but it is worth noting that the income gap was much narrower from 1945 to 1975, yet worker productivity and the economy as a whole grew more rapidly than it did in the years that followed. It also can be noted that in all branches of the U.S. military, the income differences that separate the lowest-level enlisted man or woman from top commanding officers are far less than in civilian industries, where CEOs and other high-level managers enjoy incomes several hundred times greater than the earnings of ordinary workers.

It may be, of course, that what really matters to workers at all levels is the absolute size of their paychecks, not how they compare with their bosses or with other workers. But even here, the record of the past three decades has not given much reason for cheer, especially for employees with only high school diplomas or less. For the past three decades, these workers have experienced essentially flat or even declining real earnings (i.e., earnings that reflect increases in the cost of living). The incomes of workers with at least some college have moved generally upward, but most of the gains have gone to the most highly educated group, those with college and postgraduate degrees. And even if all workers had experienced some degree of wage growth, it is not certain that absolute increases in one's material standard of living compensate for the sense of falling behind other people whose incomes are advancing much more rapidly.

The existence of a large income gap that shows no signs of abating is indisputable. More difficult is explaining what has caused it. A major economic and social shift is likely to have multiple causes, and such has been the case with changes in the distribution of wages and salaries. A consensus on the exact contribution of each of these remains elusive, but there is general agreement regarding the sources of income inequality, delineated in the following sections.

Unemployment and Income

One of the strongest influences on wages, especially for workers at the bottom end of the scale, is the overall rate of employment. When the unemployment rate is low, the relative shortage of workers causes employers to increase wages for open positions. And even if workers are reluctant to move to a new job, the possibility of doing so gives them more bargaining power with their employers. Conversely, a high rate of unemployment limits workers' options and sharply reduces their ability to demand higher wages. This situation is particularly pronounced for low-income workers. According to one study, each percentage point increase in the unemployment rate lowers the income of families in the bottom quintile by 1.8 percent, in the middle quintile by 1.4 percent, and in the top quintile by 1.0 percent.[13] Conversely, when unemployment is low, the incomes of low-wage workers increase by a higher percentage than they do for other workers, but these increases are applied to a lower base, so the actual monetary gains will be modest.

Periods of large-scale unemployment have been recurring episodes in American economic history. The most severe was the Great Depression of the 1930s. Shorter and less intense periods of unemployment accompanied several economic recessions in the postwar era. Nothing in recent decades, however, has done as much damage as the Great Recession that began at the end of 2007 and the beginning of 2008. On Labor Day 2010, the ranks of the unemployed stood at 14.9 million people, or 9.6 percent of the labor force.[14] An additional 8.9 million were employed part time because they could not find a full-time job. To make matters even worse, three-quarters of the jobs created in that year were in low-paying areas such as food preparation and retail sales.[15]

Not only were millions of workers rendered jobless during the Great Recession, but large numbers of them remained unemployed for a long time; 42 percent were without a job for more than 6 months.[16] Extended periods of unemployment, especially at the beginning of a working life, have consequences that will be felt for many years. One study of workers who found a job after having been laid off during the 1981–1982 recession noted that, on average, they suffered an earnings loss of 30 percent when compared with workers who had remained employed and that even after the passage of 15 to 20 years, they still had not closed the gap.[17] For new entrants to the labor market, the effects of a recession may be even worse. According to one widely quoted study, white men who graduated during that same recession earned 6 to 8 percent less for each percentage point increase in the unemployment rate when compared with employees who had graduated in more prosperous times. Their situation improved by about a quarter of a percentage point in each following year, but 15 years after their graduation, their earnings were still 2.5 percent less when compared with workers who had graduated amidst better economic circumstances.[18]

Income Distribution in a Changing Economy

Another source of persistent income disparities has been structural change in the U.S. economy. In Chapter 3, we saw how the service sector has overwhelmed the primary and secondary sectors as a source of employment and now provides jobs for nearly 80 percent of the workforce. This has been a positive development for some service industry workers; physicians, bond traders, and attorneys earn handsome incomes for the work they do. But the service sector also includes vast numbers of janitors, fast-food workers, and retail clerks whose wages often are not much above the poverty level, if even that.[19] In contrast, the manufacturing sector does not exhibit as great an income spread, and on average, workers in this sector have enjoyed higher wages and salaries than have workers in the service sector. For these reasons, many economists and sociologists have pointed to the rise of the service sector and the parallel decline of manufacturing as important sources of increasing economic inequality.[20]

Computerization and Income Inequality

Technological advance has proceeded in parallel with some fundamental changes to today's economy and the kinds of work it supports. As we have seen in Chapter 5, technology has been assailed, not always fairly, as a source of unemployment. Technological change also has been implicated as a cause of widening income inequalities. Its effects can be seen in the widespread adoption of the most significant work-related artifact of recent decades, the computer. As with technological change in general, the use of computers has benefited some groups of workers and put others at a disadvantage, but its effects have been more indirect and subtle than is often appreciated.

More productive workers generally earn more than less productive ones, so it may be expected that employees whose work entails the use of computers will earn higher wages and salaries. One statistical analysis of wage trends did find a positive association between wages and the extent of computer usage, both within industries and across them.[21] Another study found that the frequency of computer use at work was highly correlated with workers' educational attainments, which in turn are important determinants of income.[22] But the real impact of computers on the distribution of wages and salaries may not be as much a consequence of what workers can do with computers as it is a consequence of what computers cannot do by themselves. As Frank Levy and Richard J. Murnane have emphasized, computers can take over routine tasks that employ set procedures, but human workers are still needed for dealing with problems that cannot be solved through the application of these procedures. Equally important, computers are poor substitutes for skilled employees when it comes to engaging in what Levy and Murnane call "complex communication," the ability to organize, interpret, and convey information in ways that are most useful and relevant to the recipients of that information.[23]

Looking at the other side of the coin, the widespread diffusion of computers in the workplace has diminished the need for employees who are capable of performing only routine manual or simple cognitive tasks. As a result, occupations and individual jobs that require little more than these capabilities have grown at a slower rate than the ones that require higher-order cognitive and communication skills.[24] Consequently, workers in the first category have had little leverage as far as wages, salaries, and benefits are concerned, while employees in the second category are in a much more advantageous bargaining position. In sum, it is not the possession of computer skills that has boosted the incomes of better-educated workers; their ability to do what computers are incapable of doing has been of greater significance.

Globalization, Employment, and Income

For many observers of the economic scene, the most important cause of current income disparities has been globalization, the collection of cultural, economic, and demographic changes described in Chapter 6. More specifically, it is often noted that jobs have been lost and wages driven down by "offshoring," the relocation of productive activities to low-wage countries overseas. Although offshoring has been most evident in the manufacturing sector, a growing number of service industry jobs have moved abroad in recent years. Radiologists in India interpret CT scans, accountants in the Philippines audit the accounts of American firms, engineers in China design circuits for the next generation of microchips, and engineers in Poland produce plans and blueprints for the construction of massive industrial complexes.[25]

According to critics of economic globalization, sending work abroad has had overwhelmingly negative effects on domestic labor. Since many poor countries have large reservoirs of skilled and unskilled labor, they can manufacture goods and provide services more cheaply than can be done in the United States and other advanced industrial nations, bringing a substantial loss of jobs in their wake. Even if jobs are not lost, it is argued, competition with foreign workers will inevitably drive down domestic wages and salaries.[26]

Are these fears justified? Although economic globalization is often blamed for job losses and falling incomes, its effects may not be as severe as its critics claim. In the first place, the number of unskilled but well-paying jobs lost to foreign competition has not been large up to now. Job losses caused by off-shore competition have been well publicized, but at least until the onset of the Great Recession, the number of jobs relocated abroad had been smaller than the number of new jobs being added to the economy as a whole.[27] Widespread unemployment caused by globalization is unlikely because tens of millions of jobs, both old and newly created, can be found in industries such as retail trade, healthcare, education, and law enforcement—jobs that are difficult or impossible to relocate abroad. Other types of work are more easily transferred to low-wage foreign countries, but the extent of relocation likely will be limited by communication difficulties, deficiencies of foreign workers, the loss of tacit knowledge acquired by home-grown employees, and the negative publicity that attends sending jobs abroad.

At the most general level, the effects of globalization are similar to those of technological change. As with technological change, globalization has directly created well-paying jobs in a number of industries and sectors, everything from action movies to soybean cultivation. It also has indirectly stimulated employment by increasing the spending power of consumers. For example, the globalization of the textile industry, which has been going on for decades, has brought significant reductions in the cost of fabrics and apparel. These reduced costs, in turn, have allowed consumers to spend more money on other goods and services, thereby creating new employment opportunities in the firms that supply them.

Globalization, however, also parallels technological change in that not everyone benefits from the process, and some suffer major losses. To return to the example of textiles, the economy as a whole has benefited from globalization, but this fact provides no comfort to American textile workers who have lost their jobs because their home-grown industry cannot compete with Asian or Latin American producers.

Unions and Workers' Incomes

Beginning in the 19th century and continuing through the 21st, labor unions have battled, with varying degrees of success, to improve the pay and working conditions of their members. Efforts to aggregate and mobilize groups of workers in the United States began with the formation of the Knights of

Labor in the years following the Civil War. At the turn of the 20th century, many skilled workers were organized into craft unions, which in turn were affiliated with the American Federation of Labor (AFL), founded in 1886. In the 1930s, a new form of unionization emerged, one that took in all the workers in a particular industry, skilled and unskilled alike. Under the banner of the Committee for Industrial Organization (CIO), several of its member unions won significant victories—most notably when the United Auto Workers Union (UAW) staged a sit-down strike at General Motors that forced GM's recognition of the union as the workers' bargaining agent in early 1937. The UAW then went on to successfully organize workers at Chrysler and Ford. Despite these successes, differences in organizing tactics led the AFL to expel the constituent unions of the CIO. The breach was healed in 1955 when the CIO (which now stood for Congress of Industrial Organizations) and the AFL reunited as the AFL-CIO.

In the year of the AFL-CIO merger, 37 percent of American workers belonged to unions,[28] but in the decades that followed, union membership declined substantially. By 2009, a mere 12.3 percent of all workers belonged to unions. Only 7.2 percent of workers in private industry were union members; in contrast, 37.4 percent of workers in all levels of government belonged to unions. Although the private sector employs five times as many workers as the public sector, there are now more unionized workers (7.9 million) in the latter than in the former (7.4 million).[29] The extent of union membership also differs considerably from industry to industry. Utilities and transportation have relatively high rates of union membership at 22.2 percent, followed by telecommunications (16 percent) and construction (14.5 percent). In manufacturing, a former bastion of union membership, only 10.9 percent of the workforce is unionized.[30] Bringing up the rear is financial services (1.8 percent), followed by agriculture and related industries (1.1 percent).[31]

Economists have long debated how much influence unions have exerted on the setting of wage rates. It seems evident that the power of a union, underscored by its ability to call for a strike, should make a union a more effective bargaining unit than a collection of unaffiliated workers. At the most general level, this is true; when background factors such as industry, occupation, region, education, and experience are comparable for union and nonunion workers, workers who belong to unions earn wages that are 14.1 percent higher than those of unaffiliated workers.[32] Unionized workers also receive 15 to 25 percent more in benefits such as health insurance.[33] Unionization also appears to have a positive effect on workplace training and development.[34]

Although the benefits of union membership extend to all members, some workers benefit more than others. The union wage premium for African Americans and Hispanics is 18.3 and 21.9 percent, respectively, whereas it is only 12.4 percent for whites. Women workers get the least relative benefit, a premium of 10.7 percent.[35] Union–nonunion wage differentials are especially pronounced for low-skilled workers,[36] and unions are particularly good at protecting the wages of the most vulnerable workers.[37] In some cases, unions also benefit nonunion workers through the "threat effect," which causes employers to set wages, salaries, and benefits at levels comparable to those found in unionized enterprises in an effort to forestall unionization.[38] This tactic has been particularly notable in the automobile industry, where Japanese, German, and Korean firms have set up most of their operations in the American South, a region where unions historically have been weak. Despite organizing efforts by the UAW, it has remained that way, in large measure because wages and benefits have remained closely tied to those received by union members in other parts of the country.

The ability of unions to deliver higher wages to their members and some nonunion workers is good news for them, but the gains that accrue for union workers have to come from somewhere. In the best of all worlds, the union premium would result from the higher productivity of unionized firms; instead of commanding a larger slice of a small pie, productivity gains would allow workers and management to share bigger slices of a larger pie. Unfortunately, such usually is not the case. As with all aspects of unionization, the relationship between unionization and productivity varies from firm to firm and industry to industry,[39] but on average, the effects of unionization on productivity are close to negligible.[40] It may be that firms with cooperative labor relations and effective approaches to human resource management boost productivity in unionized firms, but such combinations are rare.[41]

During the high tide of unionization in the 1950s and 1960s, many unions were able to obtain high wages, salaries, and benefits because their members were employed in large, oligopolistic industries. Under these circumstances, the cost of generous remuneration packages could be passed on to customers in the form of higher prices. But in today's globalized economy, competition from foreign firms has undermined the oligopolistic position once enjoyed by many domestic firms and has forced them to hold the line on prices by reducing their labor costs. In contrast, many of the services provided by federal, state, and local governments—such as education, infrastructure construction and maintenance, policing, firefighting, and public health—cannot be outsourced to a significant degree. Accordingly, the lack of competition in the public service sector helps explain why governments support significantly higher levels of unionization than firms in the private sector do.

In the absence of productivity improvements or oligopolistic markets, union premiums most likely will result in lower profits or lower employment as capital is substituted for labor. In regard to profitability, most studies point to lower profits for unionized firms.[42] Whether or not this is viewed as good or bad depends on one's beliefs regarding what constitutes a fair and proper apportionment of a firm's earnings between the owners of an enterprise and its employees. The tendency of unionization to slow the growth of employment in particular firms and industries[43] also raises issues regarding the fairness of one group making gains at the expense of another group.

Some firms have been willing, if only grudgingly, to accept unionization and the lower profits that sometimes come with it. On the other hand, many private-sector firms have engaged in aggressive efforts to undermine unions and diminish their influence. To do so, employers can legally prevent union organizers from contacting employees at the workplace, require workers to attend anti-union presentations, and make "forecasts" (threats are illegal) of plant closures and job losses.[44] Moreover, although it is illegal to fire employees for trying to organize a union, employers often are able to find other reasons to terminate would-be organizers and other union activists.

Unionization began in the 19th century as an effort to improve the wages and working conditions of rank-and-file workers. This effort achieved many successes during the first half of the 20th century, but today, unionization is at a low point, especially in the private sector. There have been a few victories, most notably the ability of the Service Workers' International Union to organize workers in the healthcare, private security, and public services industries. Yet, judged on the basis of how much their members earn, the most successful unions have worked on behalf of some of the best-paid members of the workforce: airline pilots, professional athletes, and upper-echelon public officials.[45] When the first leader of the AFL, Samuel Gompers (1850–1924), was asked what he wanted for the members of his union, he famously answered, "More." One can only wonder if these are the workers on whose behalf he would be speaking were he alive today.

Immigration and Income

As we saw in Chapter 6, large-scale immigration is not a recent phenomenon. The same can be said of the concerns that immigrant labor undermines the earning power of native-born workers. The presumed connection between immigration and low wages was an article of faith for early 20th-century union organizers, who were among the chief opponents of unchecked immigration. So great was their fear of cheap labor coming from abroad that the aforementioned Samuel Gompers, himself an immigrant, refused to support efforts to unionize Jewish immigrant garment workers in New York and Filipino farmworkers in California.[46]

Gompers and other early union leaders were wrong about the long-term effects of immigrant labor, but what about today? Although it is reasonable to expect that an increase in the supply of workers will drive down wages and salaries, at least in the short run, one recent study on the effects of immigration on remuneration came to the opposite conclusion.[47] Based on data spanning the years 1990 to 2004, the study found that in California, immigration *increased* the wages of native-born workers by an average of 1.8 percent each year. As with recent wage trends in general, the benefits were not distributed equally; as a result of immigration, the wages and salaries of high school graduates increased, on average, by 2.4 percent annually, and workers with some college experienced annual increases of 3.4 percent. High school dropouts, in contrast, lost 1.1 percent of their annual wages on average. What seemed to have happened was that while many immigrants took low-skilled jobs, significant numbers of native-born workers moved upward into jobs that required a better command of the English language and more familiarity with American culture. It is also likely that wages and salaries were boosted by increases in capital investments as employers slowly accommodated the influx of new workers.

In assessing the impact of immigration on wages and salaries, it is important to keep in mind that immigrants are a diverse population. In the crucial matter of educational preparation, although many immigrants are not well educated, others have university and postgraduate degrees that qualify them for high-level jobs in medicine, education, management, science, and engineering. At the other end of the scale, however, can be found large numbers of immigrant workers who have not finished high school. In 2007, 29.1 percent of adult immigrants had not completed high school, significantly more than the 6.1 percent of native-born men and women who lacked a high school diploma.[48]

Workers with poor educational credentials face bleak job prospects, no matter what their immigration status may be. But for many immigrant workers, even a poorly paying job in the United States or other developed country is a significant improvement over what could be found at home. These workers form the bulk of the labor force in certain sectors of the American economy. Some industries, such as vegetable and fruit cultivation in California and the Southwest, are heavily dependent on immigrant workers, many of them undocumented. The willingness of large numbers of immigrant workers to accept low rates of remuneration is, of course, what makes them appealing to employers, and for workers lacking legal immigration status, the threat of deportation produces a docility that can be easily exploited.

Employers are more likely to offer market-level wages and salaries to well-educated immigrant workers, many of whom intend to stay in the United States, where their skills are in greater demand than in their native countries. Although well-educated immigrants may have put some downward pressure on the salaries of engineers, nurses, and computer programmers, the chief victims of immigration have been low-skilled, U.S.-born workers whose already low wages have been further diminished by competition with unskilled immigrants.[49]

The debate over immigration and its effects is not likely to end soon. Although immigration may have increased wages and salaries overall, the complex effects of immigration make generalization hazardous. As with technological change and economic globalization, immigration has mixed economic and social consequences. While it is likely to be beneficial in the aggregate, large-scale immigration also has damaged particular groups of workers. Taking advantage of the benefits of immigration while mitigating the dislocations it engenders will be a major challenge in the years to come.

Photo 10.1   Migrant workers picking strawberries in the field

SOURCE: ©Glenn Frank/iStockphoto.

Occupational Prestige

Although the opportunity to earn a wage or salary is the primary reward for putting in time at work, some occupations offer an additional bonus: the prestige they confer on the men and women who hold them. Sociologically speaking, *prestige* should be distinguished from *status,* the latter meaning simply the position of a person or group in society without necessarily connoting a place in a hierarchical order. In this sense, widower, Rotarian, and sister-in-law all are examples of a particular status. Prestige, by contrast, implies a hierarchical arrangement. A high degree of prestige implies respect, admiration, and the ability to elicit some measure of deference. The prestige, or lack of it, of a particular occupation is an important component of individual identity because modern societies lack well-defined social divisions, such as religiously sanctioned castes or distinct lines separating nobles and commoners. Significantly, when two people meet for the first time, the first question likely to be asked is, "What do you do?" which is understood to mean "What kind of work do you do?"

Over the years, numerous surveys have been taken in order to assess the relative prestige of different occupations. Most of these assessments have shown a remarkable rate of stability over years, as well as little country-by-country variation in the ranking of occupations.[50] Moreover, the race, class, ethnicity, and gender of respondents have little effect on their assessment of occupational prestige.[51] However, a recent study using a more refined methodology found some changes over time, as prestige ratings moved upward for many occupations while a smaller number moved in the other direction. Perhaps most remarkably, the prestige of many low-end occupations has increased in recent years even though the wages they offer have stagnated or declined in real terms.[52]

The relative prestige of particular occupations is governed by a number of factors. The prestige of an occupation usually reflects the wages or salaries attached to it, but making a lot of money through drug trafficking obviously doesn't translate into much prestige, at least outside the circle of other drug bosses. Conversely, most ministers, priests, and rabbis earn modest incomes but enjoy high occupational prestige. This seemingly anomalous situation provides us with a key to understanding occupational rankings. In the first place, these rankings generally reflect how much educational preparation is required for a particular occupation. As we have seen in Chapter 9, the ratcheting up of educational requirements may have as much to do with elevating the prestige of an occupation as with improving the performance of its practitioners. Occupational prestige also has a lot to do with the perceived importance of a job and the kinds of responsibilities discharged by the people who do the work. A surgeon can save someone's life, and an attorney can save a client from a long prison term. To return to the case of members of the clergy, the special relation they have with God and the spiritual world gives them unique powers and responsibilities, at least in the eyes of believers.

In addition to being shaped by the qualities and qualifications of its practitioners, occupations also gain or lose prestige through the clients they serve. Selling insurance and working as a stockbroker—note the use of the term *broker* instead of *salesman*—have many similarities, yet the latter line of work enjoys higher prestige than the former, in large measure because stockbrokers serve a significantly more affluent clientele. Note, too, the different perceptions of elementary school teachers and graduate school professors; a higher intellectual level may be expected of the professors, but no less important is the fact they are teaching adults rather than children.

Finally, the prestige of an occupation is often closely tied to its work environment. A great deal of white-collar work does not differ fundamentally from blue-collar work in terms of skill, responsibilities, and pay, but most white-collar workers go about their tasks in air-conditioned offices rather than in factories where the work environment can be noisy, smelly, and dirty. A "clean hands" occupation is almost always more prestigious than an equivalent line of work that leaves its practitioners in need of a long shower at the end of the working day. To take one notable example, to be a good automobile mechanic requires intelligence, knowledge of a variety of complicated systems, strength, physical dexterity, and the ability to relate well to customers. Yet mechanics (many of whom have taken on the more prestigious-sounding title of "technician") have always suffered from a "grease monkey" image because working on cars is an inherently dirty business.[53]

It is not surprising that physicians and attorneys occupy the upper rungs of the prestige ladder while garbage collectors and parking lot attendants are found toward the bottom. In general, occupations with a successful claim to being professions cluster at the top, followed by administrative positions such as managers and elected officials. Clerical workers and skilled workers tend to occupy middling positions, while operatives such as assembly line workers and stock clerks are in a lower cluster. Service workers are the most heterogeneous in terms of occupational prestige. Physicians are near the top of the prestige scale, while police officers have rankings similar to those of lower-level administrative occupations, and maids and janitors rank close to the bottom.[54]

The income an occupation provides and whatever prestige it confers are the most obvious rewards for the work we do. But work can be a source of satisfaction for several other reasons. In the next chapter, we will take a closer look at life on the job, taking into consideration the circumstances that can make work a generally pleasurable experience.

FOR DISCUSSION

1. For most people, the opportunity to earn a higher wage or salary is an important source of motivation to work hard and improve one's skills. Are there any other sources of motivation? Which are the most important to you?

2. Are you or someone you know a member of a union? Was union membership compulsory? What have been the benefits and drawbacks of union membership as you see them?

3. Will a highly skewed pattern of income distribution, such as that which has become evident in the United States, cause problems in the future? Should governments intervene more forcefully to narrow the income gap? If not, why not? If so, how might this be done?

4. What jobs today seem to be the most vulnerable to technological change? Which are the least vulnerable? Have you given any thought to how technological change may affect your job or a job you hope to hold in the future?

5. Most Americans need only go back a few generations to find immigrants in their family tree. Where did your immediate ancestors come from? How did their status as immigrants affect the jobs they held and the work they did?

Notes

1. Leslie McCall, *Complex Inequality: Gender, Class, and Race in the New Economy* (New York: Routledge, 2001), 149.

2. Peter Conrad and Joseph W. Schneider, *Deviance and Medicalization: From Badness to Sickness* (St. Louis, MO: C. V. Mosby, 1980).

3. U.S. Census Bureau, "Table H-2 Share of Aggregate Income Received by Each Fifth and Top 5 Percent of Households, All Races: 1967 to 2009," http://www.census.gov/hhes/www/income/data/historical/household/H02AR_2009.xls (accessed September 12, 2011).

4. Ibid.

5. Ibid.

6. U.S. Census Bureau, "Table H-2: Share of Aggregate Income Received by Each Fifth and 5 Percent of Households: All Races, 1967 to 2009," http://www.census.gov/hhes/www/income/data/historical/inequality/H02AR_2009.xls (accessed October 28, 2010).

7. Erin McCormick and Reynolds Holding, "Too Young to Die," *San Francisco Chronicle*, October 3, 2004, http://www.sfgate.com/cgibin/article.cgi?f=/c/a/2004/10/03/MNINFANTMOMAP.DTL (accessed June 22, 2006); World Health Organization, "WHO Issues New Healthy Life Expectancy Ratings," http://www.who.int/inf-pr-2000/en/pr2000-life.html (accessed June 22, 2006).

8. For a brief introduction to the key elements of the legislation, see Henry J. Kaiser Family Foundation, "The Basics," http://healthreform.kff.org/the-basics.aspx (accessed October 29, 2010).

9. Peter F. Drucker, *Unseen Revolution: How Pension Fund Socialism Came to America* (New York: Harper & Row, 1976).

10. Mary Ellen Benedict and Kathryn Shaw, "The Impact of Pension Benefits on the Distribution of Earned Income," *Industrial and Labor Relations Review* 48, no. 4 (July 1995): 740–57.

11. Donald L. Barlett and James B. Steele, "The Broken Promise," *Time*, October 31, 2005.

12. The classic statement of this approach is Kingsley Davis and Wilbert E. Moore, "Some Principles of Stratification," *American Sociological Review* 10 (April 1945): 242–9.

13. Lawrence Mishel, Jared Bernstein, and Heidi Shierholz, *The State of Working America, 2008/2009* (Ithaca, NY: Cornell University Press, 2009), 48.

14. "The Unemployed," *Los Angeles Times*, September 6, 2010.

15. Ibid.

16. Ibid.

17. "Something's Not Working," *The Economist*, April 29, 2010, http://www.economist.com/node/16010303 (accessed October 29, 2010).

18. Lisa Kahn, "The Curse of the Class of 2009," *Wall Street Journal*, May 9, 2009, http://online.wsj.com/article/SB124181970915002009.html (accessed November 1, 2010).

19. For a personal account of working in various services at the minimum wage, see Barbara Ehrenreich, *Nickel and Dimed: On (Not) Getting By in America* (New York: Holt, 2001).

20. A large literature pool explores the connection between the absolute and relative loss of manufacturing jobs and greater income inequality. For one methodologically sophisticated example, see Albert Chevan and Randall Stokes, "Growth in Family Income Inequality, 1970–1990: Industrial Restructuring and Demographic Change," *Demography* 37, no. 3 (August 2000): 365–80.

21. Christopher H. Wheeler, "Evidence on Wage Inequality, Worker Education, and Technology," *Federal Reserve Bank of St. Louis Review* 87, no. 3 (May–June 2005): 375.

22. Lawrence Mishel, Jared Bernstein, and Sylvia Allegretto, *The State of Working America 2004/2005* (Ithaca: Cornell University Press, 2005), 211.

23. Frank Levy and Richard J. Murnane, *The New Division of Labor: How Computers Are Creating the Next Job Market* (Princeton, NJ: Princeton University Press, 2004).

24. Ibid., 47, 52.

25. Pete Engardio, Aaron Bernstein, and Manjeet Kripalani, "The New Global Job Shift," *Business Week Online,* February 3, 2003, http://www.businessesweek .com/magazine/content/03_05/b3818001.htm (accessed February 15, 2007).

26. George Borjas and Valerie Ramey, "The Relationship Between Wage Inequality and International Trade," in *The Changing Distribution of Income in an Open U.S. Economy,* eds. Jeffrey Bergstrand, T. F. Cosimano, J. W. Houck, and R. G. Sheehan (Amsterdam: North-Holland, 1994). Cited in Dani Rodrik, *Has Globalization Gone Too Far?* (Washington, DC: Institute for International Economics, 1997), 24.

27. Pamela Babcock, "America's Newest Export: White-Collar Jobs," *HR Magazine* 49, no. 4 (April 2004), http://www.shrm.org/hrmagazine/articles/0404/0404covstory .asp (accessed February 15, 2007).

28. Richard B. Freeman, *America Works: Critical Thoughts on the Exceptional U.S. Labor Market* (New York: Russell Sage Foundation, 2007), 77.

29. U. S. Department of Labor, Bureau of Labor Statistics, "Union Members Survey," January 22, 2010, http://www.bls.gov/news.release/union2.nr0.htm (accessed October 26, 2010).

30. Ibid.

31. Ibid.

32. Mishel, Bernstein, and Shierholz, *State of Working America,* 200. For an extended discussion of the "union premium," see David G. Blanchflower and Alex Bryson, "What Effect Do Unions Have on Wages Now?" in *What Do Unions Do? A Twenty-Year Perspective,* eds. James T. Bennett and Bruce E. Kaufman (New Brunswick, NJ: Transaction, 2007), 79–113.

33. John W. Budd, "The Effect of Unions on Non-Wage Composition: Monopoly Power, Collective Voice, and Facilitation," in Bennett and Kaufman, *What Do Unions Do?* 165, 166; Mishel, Bernstein, and Shierholz, *State of Working America,* 123, 202–3.

34. Anil Verma, "What Do Unions Do to the Workplace? Union Effects on Management and HRM Policies," in Bennett and Kaufman, *What Do Unions Do?* 287.

35. Mishel, Bernstein, and Shierholz, *State of Working America,* 200.

36. John Pencavel, "Unionism Viewed Internationally," in Bennett and Kaufmann, *What Do Unions Do?* 434.

37. Blanchflower and Bryson, "What Effect Do Unions Have?" 106.

38. Mishel, Bernstein, and Shierholz, *State of Working America,* 206–7.

39. Pencavel, "Unionism Viewed Internationally," 447.

40. Barry T. Hirsch, "What Do Unions Do for Economic Performance?" in Bennett and Kaufman, *What Do Unions Do?* 205.

41. Bruce E. Kaufman, "What Do Unions Do: Evaluation and Commentary," in Bennett and Kaufmann, *What Do Unions Do?* 544.

42. Ibid., 211–6.

43. Ibid., 217–8.

44. Freeman, *America Works,* 80.

45. Malcolm Gladwell, "Talent Grab: Why Do We Pay Our Stars So Much Money?" *New Yorker,* October 11, 2010.

46. Robert Cherry, *Who Gets the Good Jobs: Combating Race and Gender Disparities* (New Brunswick, NJ: Rutgers University Press, 2001), 117. It should be noted that in 2000, the AFL-CIO reversed course and began to emphasize the unionization of immigrant workers.

47. Giovanni Peri, "Rethinking the Effects of Immigration on Wages: New Data and Analysis from 1990 to 2004," *Immigration Policy in Focus* 5, no. 8 (October 2006): 1–7.

48. Mishel, Bernstein, and Shierholz, *State of Working America,* 188.

49. George J. Borjas, Richard B. Freeman, and Lawrence A. Katz, "How Much Do Immigration and Trade Affect Labor Market Outcomes?" in *Brookings Papers on Economic Activity,* eds. William C. Brainard and George L. Perry (Washington, DC: Brookings Institution, 1997); Cherry, *Who Gets the Good Jobs,* 124–6.

50. Donald Treiman, *Occupational Prestige in Comparative Perspective* (New York: Academic Press, 1977).

51. Ibid.

52. Keiko Nakao and Judith Treas, "Updating Occupational Prestige and Socioeconomic Scores: How the New Measures Measure Up," *Sociological Methodology,* 24 (1994): 1–72.

53. For a history of automobile mechanics in the United States, see Kevin L. Borg, *Auto Mechanics: Technology and Expertise in Twentieth Century America* (Baltimore: Johns Hopkins University Press, 2007).

54. Robert A. Rothman, *Working: Sociological Perspectives* (Englewood Cliffs, NJ: Prentice Hall, 1987), 215–7.

11

Life on the Job I

Work and Its Rewards

Landing a new job is usually a pleasant experience. After all, it is a good feeling to know you're wanted, even when all that is expected is the performance of routine duties in return for a modest wage or salary. The psychological boost that comes from being hired may persist for many years when the job serves as an important source of self-esteem and the workplace is a site for individual fulfillment. The workplace also can serve as a kind of school where new abilities and skills are developed, as well as a social club from which to draw friends and acquaintances. But in different circumstances, work can be an unending source of misery, suffused with danger, alienation, and stress. All in all, work can be a source of both satisfaction and dissatisfaction, but we will leave the latter for the following chapter. In this chapter, we will examine the evident benefits of having a job, beginning with simply being employed.

Employment and Unemployment

Work is not optional for most adults who are not young enough to be in school or old enough to be retired. Unless one is fortunate enough to be independently wealthy, the absence of gainful employment will lead to a financial squeeze within a short space of time. As noted in the previous chapter, unemployment is a major cause of poverty and income inequalities, and its effects can linger long after an unemployed man or woman has gone back to work.

Because it strongly affects both individuals and society as whole, the unemployment rate is a closely watched economic statistic. During the opening years of the present century, the official unemployment rate ranged from a low of 4 percent in 2000 to a high of 6 percent in 2003. Following the onset of the Great Recession at the end of 2007 and the beginning of 2008, the unemployment rate climbed sharply, reaching 9.6 percent toward the end of 2010.[1] These percentages, as with all other official tallies, provide only a rough measure of actual unemployment because a number of assumptions have to be made when reckoning the extent of joblessness. First, since it is a measure of the number of unemployed workers relative to the total labor force, the unemployment rate is affected by the size of the latter category. The labor force is officially defined as consisting of all noninstitutionalized men and women over the age of 16 who are either working for pay or unemployed and actively seeking work. "Actively seeking work" is defined as having answered a want ad or having registered with an employment agency within the past 4 weeks.[2] A number of factors can affect the size of the official labor force over time. One of these is the extent of incarceration. In 2008, federal and state prisons and local jails held 2,190,000 men and women, the great majority of whom were of working age.[3] The exclusion of these individuals, whose numbers have grown substantially in recent years, from the officially defined labor force will, therefore, reduce the official unemployment rate.[4]

As just noted, for an unemployed individual to be counted as a member of the labor force, he or she has to be actively looking for a job. But it is not uncommon for many jobless workers to despair of ever finding work while enduring a prolonged period of unemployment and to simply stop looking. Although their numbers may equal as much as 40 percent of the "officially" unemployed, these "discouraged workers" are not counted as members of the labor force.[5] This results in a paradoxical situation where the unemployment rate may actually rise during the early phase of an economic recovery because workers who had given up on finding a job perceive an improving situation and therefore reenter the job market. But until this happens, a large number of discouraged workers will lower the official unemployment rate even though there may be many people who want and need a job.

Official employment statistics do not take into account whether or not a worker has a full-time or part-time job. To be officially counted as being "employed" requires only that a worker put in a minimum of 15 hours a week on a job. An apparently robust employment picture may, therefore, obscure a fair degree of underemployment whereby workers who want full-time jobs have to settle for part-time work, a topic that will be taken up later in this chapter. In similar fashion, government statistics make no distinction between workers who were employed for the whole year and those who happened to have a job at the time they were surveyed but were unemployed at other times. The unemployment rate is a snapshot, and as such, it does not adequately capture the situation of many workers who experience prolonged periods of joblessness during a given year.

For the above reasons, it has been argued that the official unemployment rate provides an overly optimistic picture of employment and unemployment. On the other hand, a substantial number of men and women work in the "underground" or "shadow" economy, where they fall outside the statistical net. Some of the work done in this sector is clearly illegal in all or most parts of the country—for example, drug manufacture and dealing, prostitution, bookmaking, and bootlegging. A considerable amount of work also occurs in legitimate areas but is done "off the books." This segment includes such activities as repair work, gardening, and personal services done on a cash-only basis to avoid the payment and remission of sales taxes and to lower the taxable income of the person doing the work. It also happens that workers may be hired clandestinely so their employers can avoid making contributions to Social Security, Medicare, and other mandated programs, or because the business is violating health and safety codes. By its very nature, the extent of employment in the underground economy is difficult to determine, but according to one careful study, it accounted for an average of 12 percent of the gross national income in industrially developed economies and for much more in underdeveloped ones.[6] The inclusion of these workers in official statistics would, therefore, decrease the unemployment rate by a significant margin.

The Personal Consequences of Unemployment

Unemployment rates are cold statistics, but they signify a harsh reality for the individual men and women who experience prolonged joblessness. For many, the loss of a wage or salary during a period of extended unemployment can result in financial ruin. Making matters worse, the loss of a job usually results in the phasing out or outright loss of employer-sponsored health insurance. Terminated employees can maintain their policies for a fixed period of time by paying a monthly fee, but this will add considerably to the financial stress brought on by unemployment.

Unemployment takes more than a financial toll. Many psychological problems have been directly tied to joblessness. Getting through the working day may be a major source of stress for some people, but unemployment can be even more stressful. A large number of studies have found a well-defined link between unemployment and bad health. The most obvious consequence of unemployment is the loss of a wage or salary and the financial pressures that come with it. But lost income is not the whole story, as can be seen in the experiences of unemployed workers in western Europe, who were buffered from the financial pressures brought on by unemployment because they received generous payments from the state. Even so, surveys found them to be much less satisfied with their lives than people with jobs were.[7]

Joblessness can also be hazardous to a person's physical health. According to one recent study, workers between the ages of 51 and 61 who had lost their jobs had twice the likelihood of having a heart attack over the next 6 to 10 years when compared with employed workers.[8] Another study of workers who had lost their jobs during the recession of the 1980s found that in the year following a job loss, the death rates of high-seniority workers increased by 50 to 100 percent. Moreover, the consequences of unemployment persisted for a long time; this cohort exhibited a 10 to 15 percent higher death rate 20 years after the initial job loss.[9] The manner in which unemployment produced these negative health consequences is not entirely clear. The older members of the cohort tended to exercise less, smoke more, and put on weight. All these behaviors increase the risk of diabetes and heart disease.[10] It also seems highly likely that unemployment is accompanied by increased levels of stress, the consequences of which will be discussed in the next chapter. It is also worth noting that the study just summarized found that the *fear* of losing a job may be just as damaging to physical health as actual unemployment.

The financial, mental, and physical stresses brought on by unemployment can be hard on family members, too, as indicated by one study that found that unemployed men were nearly twice as likely to assault their wives as men with jobs were.[11] Wives are not the only victims; another study conducted by researchers at the University of Minnesota found a significant association between unemployment and higher rates of violence against children and other family members, in addition to spouses. These instances of domestic violence were found in 6.9 percent of households with an unemployed member but in only 2.8 percent of households free from unemployment.[12]

Given the many unfortunate consequences of unemployment, it is not surprising that job security is greatly valued by today's workers. Whether or

Photo 11.1   A Depression-era soup kitchen sponsored by the notorious Chicago gangster, Al Capone

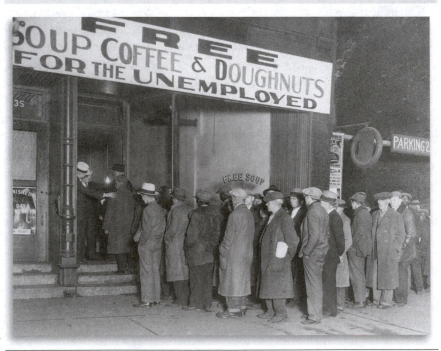

SOURCE: ©Bettmann/CORBIS.

not they have as much security today as workers in earlier decades did has been a matter of some debate. It is often assumed that globalization and rapid technological change have resulted in a less secure job environment, but as best can be determined from available information, there was not much change in overall job security from the mid-1970s to the mid- to late 1990s.[13] But job security became far more tenuous toward the end of the first decade of the 21st century, as the Great Recession was accompanied not just by high levels of unemployment but also by episodes of prolonged unemployment not seen since the 1930s.[14] According to one study, toward the middle of 2010, 70 percent of unemployed workers had been without a job for 7 months or more.[15]

Some categories of workers are more vulnerable to unemployment than others. Historically, less-educated manual workers have had the lowest levels of job security, while well-educated, white-collar workers have had the most. In the 1990s, this situation appeared to have changed, as attested by numerous television and newspaper stories featuring white-collar employees who had lost jobs they had occupied for many years. These stories often noted that white-collar workers had become as vulnerable to job losses as their blue-collar counterparts. Although the extent of job losses by college-educated, white-collar workers may have been exaggerated by the popular media, the unemployment rate for these workers in the 1990s was substantial, about as great as it had been during the much more severe economic recession of the early 1980s.[16] More recent statistics on the extent of white-collar unemployment convey a mixed message. At the end of 2008, white-collar unemployment stood at 4.6 percent, a substantial jump from the 3 percent rate of the prior year but far less than the 11.3 percent unemployment rate for blue-collar workers. But this advantage was offset by the fact that white-collar workers were overrepresented in the ranks of the long-term unemployed, workers who had been jobless for 6 months or more.[17]

Whether or not vulnerability to long-term unemployment will continue to affect substantial numbers of white-collar workers is difficult to say, but given the continuing and possibly accelerating advance of globalization and technological change, expectations of high levels of job stability and security will have to be accompanied by large doses of optimism. This does not mean that unemployment rates will necessarily settle at permanently higher plateaus, but it is likely that workers will change jobs more frequently and have less predictable careers, as noted in Chapter 8.

Varieties of Employment

Work is still closely tied to the lives of the majority of adults in the United States. In mid 2011, nearly 72.2 million American men 20 years of age and older who were not in military service or in prison were employed. For the equivalent cohort of women, the number was not much smaller at more than

62.8 million. Based on these figures, out of the total population of men and women 20 years old and over, 74.4 percent of men and 54.9 percent of women were reckoned to be in the labor force, and within this cohort, 67.6 percent of men and 54.9 percent of women actually had jobs.[18]

Some significant changes in employment and labor force participation emerge when the labor force is broken down according to gender and age groups over different time periods. Most notably, the labor force participation rate for women generally has moved upward in all age categories since 1970. The same has not been true for men, especially those aged 55 and older. In 1970, 83 percent of men between the ages of 55 and 64 were members of the labor force, but by 1999, that percentage had fallen to 67.9 percent. By 2008, it had climbed a bit to 70.4 percent. Employment also dipped and then rebounded for men 65 and older, from 26.8 percent in 1970 to 16.9 percent in 1999 and then up to 21.5 in 2008.[19]

Workers over the age of 65 have been able to remain in the workforce because mandatory retirement was outlawed in most industries in the 1980s. Some older workers relish the opportunity to go on working past the traditional age of retirement, but for many others, it is a matter of economic survival—even though Social Security payments have increased in most years due to federally mandated cost-of-living increases. But even with rising Social Security benefits, most retirees experience a loss of income when they leave their jobs, although a majority can look forward to receiving at least half what they had earned during their working years.[20] Less positively, many workers retire due to ill health or because their employers believe they are no longer as productive as younger workers and find ways of easing them out of their jobs. As with most other aspects of work, the propensity to retire is affected by one's occupation and the income and prestige associated with it. Men and women in the professions tend to work to a later age than manual workers, a reflection of better remuneration, differences in the physical difficulty of the work, the intrinsic value of the work to the worker, and the possibility of arranging flexible working schedules.

Many retirees work on a part-time basis, but in recent years, the Great Recession has greatly enlarged the number of traditional-age workers employed on a part-time basis. Part-time employment encompasses a large range of hours spent on the job, but a workweek of fewer than 35 hours is the threshold the U.S. Department of Labor uses to differentiate part-time from full-time employment. The number of part-time workers is sizable. In 2009, more than 37.6 million employees were part-timers, making up 27 percent of total employment.[21] Part-time work is appealing to some workers who want to spend more time with their families, while other workers choose part-time work because it allows them to continue with their education or spend more time on hobbies and other leisure activities. In recent years, however, many employees have not been part-timers by choice and would prefer a full-time job if only they could find one. According to the U.S. Bureau of Labor Statistics, at the end of 2008, 7.3 million employees had to settle for part-time work because their employers reduced their working hours or because a part-time job was all they could find.[22] Three years later, in another manifestation of the effects of the Great Recession, the ranks of involuntary part-time workers had swollen to 9.1 million.[23] As with many other aspects of work, age and gender differences are apparent in the distribution of part-time work. In 2009, 24.8 percent of women employees fell into this category, while 21.9 percent of male workers were part-timers.[24] In regard to age segmentation, despite composing only 14 percent of all employed workers, men and women under the age of 25 accounted for about a quarter of workers employed on a part-time basis due to economic exigencies.[25]

Engaging in part-time work results in a lower rate of remuneration, both absolutely and relative to the number of hours worked. Both male and female part-time workers earn less money per hour on average than full-time workers do, but male part-time workers take a larger hit than their female counterparts.[26] Part-time workers of both genders also are less likely to be covered by employer-sponsored pensions and health insurance.[27]

Although unemployment and involuntary part-time work have been a common if unhappy condition in recent years, some members of the labor force have been holding down more than one job. However, "moonlighting," as it is sometimes called, is not a common occurrence; in 2010, only 5.1 and 5.6 percent of men and women, respectively, worked at more than one job simultaneously.[28]

Another category of employees, who may be either full or part time, are temporary workers. The U.S. Department of Labor refers to them as "contingent workers" because their employment is not open-ended but is contingent on a contract or agreement between them and their employers that covers a limited period of time. The U.S. Bureau of Labor Statistics uses various methods to estimate the number of contingent workers, and depending on which estimate is used, in 2005, these workers accounted for between 1.8 and 4.1 percent of total employment.[29]

Contingent workers are most commonly found in the service sector, especially in healthcare, business services, and education, but construction also absorbs a significant number. Contingent workers have been prominent in the high-tech sector, where they work as software developers, systems programmers, technical writers, and in other jobs that require a high level of technical skill. Unlike many other segments of the contingent workforce, these "technical contractors" are usually well paid and have a great deal of on-the-job autonomy and flexibility.[30] More typical of the contingent workforce are the nearly 2.2 million workers who were employed by temporary help agencies in 2011 to do routine office work (i.e., "temps").[31] Although surveys indicate that more than one-third of temporary workers prefer their status to traditional work arrangements, their wages and working conditions leave a lot to be desired. In general, being a temporary worker comes with significant drawbacks, and for this reason, their workplace situations will be taken up in the next chapter.

Work Without Pay

To be an officially designated member of the labor force requires the receipt of a wage or salary for the work performed. This results in the exclusion of the large number of individuals who receive no remuneration for the work they do. The largest category of such workers comprises full-time homemakers, predominantly women, who are not paid for all the things they do at home. But housework is work, nonetheless, and attempts have been made to compute its monetary value. The attorney of the wife in a divorce case mounted one such effort.[32] In making a case for a generous financial settlement, the attorney argued that his client's occupation as homemaker included a variety of tasks—some of them well rewarded outside the home, such as child psychologist and interior decorator, along with others of lesser financial value, such as dishwasher and chauffeur. When summed up, these services were declared to be worth a bit more than $40,000 in 1986, which would be $80,365 in 2011.

Not only are homemakers ignored in official tallies of the labor force, but their efforts are not included in national income accounts. This results in a statistical anomaly when national income is reckoned. A man or woman could work all day cleaning the house, but this service would not be included in official tabulations of gross national income because no cash income has been earned. But if that same person did equivalent housecleaning tasks for someone else and received a payment of $50, that sum of money would be included in the nation's gross national income. More directly, homemakers are penalized by the rules governing Social Security benefits, which are tied to the money earned over the course of a person's working life. A full-time housewife receives survivor's benefits upon the death of her husband, but she has no direct claim on the Social Security system unless she worked for pay at some point in her life.

Another large contingent of unpaid workers consists of volunteers of every description. Volunteer work includes such activities as fundraising, coaching athletic teams and refereeing games, tutoring, preparing and serving food, and doing physical labor such as tree planting and building repair. Volunteer work is most commonly performed for religious organizations (accounting for 34 percent of all volunteers) and providers of educational and youth services (26.1 percent).[33] The amount of work done by volunteers is by no means trivial. In 2008 to 2009, 63.4 million people—or 26.4 percent of the U.S. population aged 16 or older—put in at least one stint as a volunteer over the course of a year.[34] Although a higher percentage of women than men engaged in voluntary activities (23.3 to 30.1 percent), the median amount of time spent in volunteer activities hardly differed, 52 hours for men and 50 hours for women.[35] Because volunteer activity by definition is unpaid work, it does not register in national income accounts. If it were included, it would have a substantial effect on economic statistics. When calculated at a rate of $17.55 per hour (based on national average remuneration for nonsupervisory production workers), the work performed by volunteers would have had a cash value of nearly $59 billion in 2004.[36]

Along with the economic contributions it makes, engaging in volunteer work also is advantageous for those who participate in it. Retirees in particular derive a number of benefits from engaging in volunteer work. According to a Cornell University study, volunteering provided routines, social connections, and social roles that resulted in older volunteers exhibiting greater psychological and physical well-being than other retirees.[37] Although the benefits of volunteering were most apparent among retirees at the upper levels of the education and income scale, volunteering also was associated with greater well-being for volunteers with low incomes and poor health.

The Workplace as School

Chapter 7 took a somewhat skeptical (some might say cynical) stance regarding the relevance of formal education to subsequent job performance. Implicit in such a view is an assumption that a great deal of work-related learning takes place while actually doing the work. This is a reasonable assumption; according to one estimate, as much as one-third to one-half of the development of job-related skills takes place after an individual leaves school.[38]

In some cases, job training has been deliberately and closely connected to employment. Some of the most thoroughgoing and successful examples of on-the-job training are the apprenticeship programs widely employed in Germany. Half of German high school students participate in these programs, which combine formal schooling with paid work. After completing an apprenticeship, student skills are certified through examinations administered by employers' representatives and the relevant labor unions. Apprentices who have successfully completed a program can look forward to starting wages that are considerably higher than those found in most other industrial nations. But the system also requires students to choose at an early age what could be a lifelong occupation, a rather daunting prospect for any young man or woman. This mode of training also has been criticized for its emphasis on specialized industrial skills, which may be of declining relevance in mature, service-oriented economies.

The German training system can be seen as a continuation of the apprenticeship arrangements described in Chapter 2. A common feature of preindustrial economies, apprenticeships went into eclipse in most parts of the world as enterprises became larger and more impersonal, and as labor markets became more fluid. When manufacturing was done primarily by artisans associated with particular craft guilds, training costs could be recouped during the long statutory period that bound apprentices to their masters. In contrast, in a modern economy, workers are free to leave an employer just about whenever they are so inclined. When they do, employers find themselves in the unpleasant situation of watching their investment in human capital walk out the door for good, perhaps to take a job with one of their competitors.

The likelihood of a company-trained worker jumping ship is reduced when both worker and employer expect a long-term relationship. This working arrangement has been especially evident in Japan, where, at least until recently, a substantial number of workers could expect to stay with the same firm for all their working lives.[39] The coupling of long job tenures with on-the-job training can be seen in the Japanese automobile industry, where in the mid-1980s, newly hired workers received 310 hours of training, a sharp contrast to the 48 hours received by workers in American plants. Even in the absence of lifetime employment, these practices have continued in Japanese-owned automobile plants in the United States, where workers receive an average of 280 hours of training.[40]

Although formal apprentice programs are rare in the United States and many other industrial countries, a great deal of job training, both formal and informal, still occurs in the workplace. Even when employer-sponsored training is lacking or altogether absent, workers often learn quite a lot through informal means.[41] A large part of this consists in learning by doing, which by its very nature entails making mistakes—but learning from one's mistakes can be the basis of some of life's most useful and enduring lessons. In addition, the work environment usually contains men and women who can serve as valuable sources of expertise regarding the technical features of a job. Their presence also can be invaluable when they serve as interpreters and exponents of an organization's subculture. And, finally, as Yogi Berra supposedly noted, "You can observe a lot by just looking."

As with most other aspects of working life, the benefits of on-the-job training are not equally shared. One study found that 35 percent of young college graduates were the beneficiaries of employer-sponsored training, while only 19 percent of high school graduates received it.[42] Ascribed characteristics also affect access to employer-sponsored training. As a group, white employees get more training than African American and Latino employees do, and mid-career employees get more training than younger and older workers do.[43] Gender also affects access to informal training. Mentorship, a relationship through which experienced staff members help lower-level employees develop their skills and abilities, tends to be confined to parties of the same sex. Cross-gender mentoring relationships are not unknown, but an unfortunate fact of organizational life is that a sexual relationship often is inferred when an upper-echelon male employee serves as mentor to a lower-level female employee.

Job Training and Employment Opportunities _____

Adherents of a human capital approach to work and remuneration often claim that education and training can go a long way in alleviating unemployment and advancing the fortunes of men and women who are already employed. In reality, this is a partial truth at best. Training programs not directly tied to an actual job have a mixed record of putting unemployed people to work. One study commissioned by the U.S. Department of Labor followed the experiences of 160,000 workers who had lost their jobs during the economically robust period stretching from mid-2003 to mid-2005. Unfortunately, their training didn't do much to augment their earning potential; when they eventually got a job, their wages were about the same as workers who had not received training, and this situation did not improve after 3 or 4 years. As the study concluded, "Overall, it appears possible that ultimate gains from participation are small or nonexistent."[44]

In part, the limited effectiveness of training programs can be attributed to the difficult situations faced by a significant portion of trainees. This has been particularly evident in recent years, when substantial changes in public assistance programs put a greater burden on training programs, particularly those designed to take adults off the welfare rolls by preparing them for permanent paid employment. On the whole, these programs have led to modest rises in average earnings for adult women and men. On the other hand, they haven't done much to improve the wages of workers who recently entered the labor force.[45]

The minimal results achieved by training programs that target the neediest members of the population do not prove that efforts to improve the skills of low-wage workers are of no value. With training programs, as with many other things in life, you get what you pay for, and most government-sponsored training programs have been low-budget operations. In contrast, public subsidies of university education, which primarily serve members of middle-class and upper-middle-class families, have been far more costly on a per-student basis. Second, as we have just seen, one of the most potent sources of learning is on-the-job training; in fact, the most successful training programs have been directly tied to a job of some sort. From this perspective, the most effective use of public funds for training would be to subsidize employer-based training programs, perhaps through the granting of tax deductions or credits. These subsidies would help private firms make investment decisions in better accord with reality. The existing tax code encourages investment in physical capital but is largely indifferent to investment in human capital. Government support of training programs conducted by individual firms would help rectify this imbalance.

Work and Social Interaction

Most kinds of work require sustained and sometimes intense interactions with other workers. Some of these can be unpleasant and a source of stress, but it often happens that the workplace serves as a prime site for socializing and forming bonds of friendship with fellow workers. In 21st-century industrial and postindustrial societies, extended families, neighborhoods, and public spaces no longer serve as the primary bases for social interaction, and the demands of working life may themselves undercut the ability to maintain and extend friendships away from the job.[46] Differences in work schedules also undermine social relationships because people who work at times other than the normal workday have fewer opportunities to interact with others. In at least partial compensation, many workplaces contain an ample number of potential friends, and collective work can be the basis for socializing while getting the job done.[47]

One example of the importance of on-the-job friendships comes from a study of two poultry processing plants.[48] Converting live chickens and turkeys into dressed meat is a thoroughly unpleasant activity that is not for the squeamish; blood, excrement, offal, and foul odors are an inescapable part of the work environment. The work is repetitious and fast-paced, as well as potentially dangerous. The pay is modest at best, and most of the work done rests far down the ladder of occupational prestige. Yet for all the inherent drawbacks of work in this industry, satisfaction with the job was surprisingly high in the plants that were the subjects of this study. When the workers in the processing plants were polled, 60 percent of them indicated that they were either "generally satisfied" or "completely satisfied" with their jobs. When asked to rank their job on a scale of 1 to 10, with 10 being an ideal job, 81 percent gave it a 5 or better. Clearly, something was offsetting poor pay, demanding work, and noisome working conditions. What made working life tolerable, even enjoyable, for many workers was the presence of an occupational community that provided opportunities for making friends and working with them. When workers were asked what they especially liked about their jobs, about 40 percent pointed to "people" or "coworker relations." When one worker was asked to name a particularly satisfying aspect of her job, she singled out "the people, I think, more than anything—that I work with. That really helps out. I mean, if you are working with somebody that you like. I just—I just like that kind of work." Equally important, a community made up of fellow workers helped individual workers shrug off the stigma of doing dirty, low-skilled, poorly remunerated work. The outside world may have offered little respect for the work they did, but compensating for this were friendships and relationships with people who shared a working environment and on-the-job experiences.

Not all work environments are equally conducive to the formation of on-the-job social relationships. In general, friendships are more likely to form when the work environment requires or encourages interaction and interdependence while keeping competition to a minimum.[49] In contrast, the possibility of forming friendships may be inhibited in work situations where workers are separated from one another by physical and spatial barriers. Social barriers in the form of rigid hierarchies also inhibit informal interactions and the opportunity to form friendships.

Photo 11.2 The workplace often is the site of informal social interactions that may help an organization achieve its goals.

SOURCE: ©CORBIS.

When unsociable hours or schedules limit their contacts with workers putting in normal hours, workers will naturally tend to find their primary opportunities for socialization among workers in similar situations. Workers in occupations as disparate as railroad engineers[50] and jazz musicians[51] have a strong tendency to form their friendships among people in the same line of work, which in turn contributes to the development of occupational subcultures.

Many occupations conducted outside normal working hours at least entail interactions with coworkers. Some jobs, however, are essentially solitary activities that prevent work from serving as a basis for socialization. One frequent complaint of stay-at-home mothers and fathers is the social isolation that comes from having limited opportunities to form friendships.[52] And even when they have a job that takes them away from home, many women encounter difficulties in forming friendships at their place of employment because their household responsibilities take up much of the time that could be used for socializing.[53]

At the other end of the scale, friendships can be particularly intense when workers depend on one another amid circumstances that entail physical dangers, such as warfare and subsurface mining. And more than being a side benefit of a particular line of work, the friendships that emerge in these circumstances may serve as powerful motivators for working amid difficult conditions, as studies of combat soldiers have indicated.[54]

Social Relationships and Job Performance

The crucial importance of friendships among soldiers is only an extreme example of the influence of social relationships on worker motivation and performance. The significance of these relationships was driven home more than 80 years ago when some administrators at Western Electric's Hawthorne assembly plant near Chicago began to study how workplace conditions affected worker output. At first, they confined themselves to altering physical variables, beginning with an effort to ascertain the importance of levels of workplace illumination on worker output. As it turned out, proper levels of illumination were not essential for a high rate of production; output actually went up as the experimenters' manipulation of the lighting caused the workplace to become quite dim. The reason for this was subsequently dubbed "the Hawthorne effect," the tendency of workers to improve their performance when they are being observed and their efforts are appreciated.[55]

Puzzled by the initial results, the firm's management then brought in researchers from Harvard University's Department of Industrial Research, and for a 5-year stretch beginning in 1927, a team of social scientists investigated manufacturing processes within the plant, in particular the assembly of electromechanical relays and the wiring of switchboards. The project encompassed many experiments and observations, too many to be summarized here.[56] Some of the research designs and methods used by the researchers came in for a great deal of subsequent criticism, but one key insight of what came to be called the Hawthorne Studies remains valid today: workplace friendships and other social ties can powerfully affect worker behavior. To take one notable example, when the researchers investigated the bank wiring room—the place where wiring connections were made on switchboards—they found that the workers informally set per-worker output at 6,600 connections per day.[57] Although several workers were capable of doing more, they ran the risk of being sanctioned as "rate busters," while those workers who failed to meet the group norm were branded as "chiselers." There also was a strong group sentiment that workers should never tell a supervisor anything that could cause a problem for a fellow worker. In sum, in order to grasp how the workplace really functioned, the researchers had to recognize the significance of the work groups in which the employees were enmeshed, and how these groups regulated the pace of work and interactions with supervisors. The Hawthorne Studies mark the beginning of what came to be labeled the "Human Relations approach" to organizational theory and research, and many of the findings, theories, and insights that followed informed and inspired innumerable studies of work, workplaces, and workers.

The Intrinsic Satisfactions of Work

As has been implicit in this chapter, satisfaction or dissatisfaction with a job is not solely driven by levels of remuneration. The need to earn a wage or salary may impel us to choose work over leisure, but it is not the only source of our motivation to spend a significant portion of our lives at the workplace. As the economist-sociologist Thorstein Veblen (1857–1929) noted more than a century ago, human behavior is also strongly influenced by what he called "the instinct of workmanship." For Veblen, working was instinctual because the absence of that instinct would result in the swift demise of the human race. But to be a source of personal gratification, work could not be a random process; work had to be a purposive activity that entailed "efficient use of the means at hand and adequate management of the resources available for the purposes of life itself."[58] Much of Veblen's discontent with early 20th-century American society lay in his conviction that capitalism promoted waste and inefficiency—along with the division of society between workers and a small, parasitic leisure class whose main activity was engaging in "conspicuous consumption," in Veblen's famous phrase.

Later generations of sociologists and psychologists who have concerned themselves with the meaning of work for the individual have been less concerned with efficiency and socioeconomic divisions. Following from the ideas of Abraham Maslow (1908–1970), much of their interest has centered on the psychological functions of work. In Maslow's schema, humans have a hierarchy of needs. When one set of needs is satisfied, people move on to needs of a higher order. At the base of the hierarchy of needs are the things and activities necessary for the survival of individuals and the species as a whole—food and sex, for example. When these are satisfied, human needs move, in ascending order, toward safety, affiliation with others, and the esteem that comes from the recognition and appreciation granted by other people. At the summit of the hierarchy of human needs is what Maslow labeled "self-actualization," the process of developing and using one's potential to the fullest extent.[59]

Maslow's approach to life and work has been quite influential in orienting the way we think about work and its effects on the human psyche. It has, however, not been without its critics. In general, it seems fair to state that individual motivations can be hard to discern, even for the actors themselves; all of us have, on occasion, wondered what caused us to do something we did. Second, questions also have been raised concerning the universality of Maslow's schema. "Self-actualization" seems most appropriate to cultures that put a high premium on individualism and personal growth. This was the culture of early Protestantism. As we saw in Chapter 1, with its linkage of a successful working life to spiritual salvation, the Protestant Ethic as described by Max Weber reflected an individualistic orientation toward both work and religious belief. In contrast, people in more collectively-oriented cultures might consider affiliation with other people to be more important than individual achievement and fulfillment. Third, it can be argued that Maslow's hierarchical ordering of needs detaches psychological states from their social context. To put it more concretely, how does one know when he or she has achieved a state of self-actualization? It may be a purely internal process, but in many cases, the recognition and respect conferred by one's reference group may be the surest indication that one has achieved his or her full potential. Finally, in regard to work's place in the life of an individual, is it essential that a job serve as the primary source of self-actualization? For some people, work might happily be done as a purely instrumental activity that pays the bills while they seek to realize their full potential as fly fishermen, softball players, or poodle breeders.[60]

This chapter had as its primary focus those elements of work that by and large serve as sources of satisfaction. It would be unrealistic, however, to expect workers to be satisfied with everything and at all times; difficulties inevitably arise even when circumstances promote the achievement of both organizational goals and a satisfied workforce. Some work environments, however, fail to provide even minimal levels of satisfaction for the men and women who work in them. Some jobs are truly miserable, and they can be that way for a variety of reasons. In the next chapter, we will look into the conditions that prevent work from being a satisfying, meaningful activity and, instead, render it an unpleasant exercise only undertaken for reasons of financial necessity. But putting the spotlight on bad work environments also provides some insights into what makes for good ones, so some good news will be mixed with the bad.

FOR DISCUSSION

1. Has anyone you know been unemployed for a long period of time? What were the consequences of unemployment for this person? Should federal and state governments do more to reduce the extent of unemployment? If so, what might they do?

2. Have you ever engaged in any kind of volunteer work? What motivated you to do it? What were the major benefits you got from the experience?

3. Has anyone in your family retired recently? What were their reasons for retiring? On the whole, have they found retirement preferable to the work they used to do? What was gained and what was lost as a result of retirement?

4. How well prepared were you for the work you have done in the past? Was there an adequate period of formal training? What sorts of things did you learn while doing the work? Did your coworkers help you learn what to do?

5. Is there really an "instinct of workmanship," as asserted by Thorstein Veblen? If so, is it really a natural instinct, or is it something instilled through socialization processes? Do today's work arrangements cultivate this instinct or suppress it?

Notes

1. For annual unemployment rates from 1948 to 2009, see the webpage posted by the U.S. Bureau of Labor Statistics, available at http://www.bls.gov/cps/prev_yrs.htm.

2. Arne L. Kalleberg, *The Mismatched Worker* (New York: Norton, 2007), 186.

3. Bureau of Justice Statistics, "Total Correctional Population," http://bjs.ojp.usdoj.gov/index.cfm?ty=tp&tid=11 (accessed November 8, 2010).

4. For a discussion of the effects of increased levels of incarceration on official employment rates for African Americans, see Bruce Western, *Punishment and Inequality in America* (New York: Russell Sage Foundation, 2006), 86–107.

5. David W. Livingstone, *The Education–Jobs Gap: Underemployment or Economic Democracy* (Boulder, CO: Westview, 1998), 66.

6. Friedrich Schneider and Dominik H. Enste, *The Shadow Economy: An International Survey* (Cambridge, UK: Cambridge University Press, 2002).

7. Andrew J. Oswald, "Happiness and Economic Performance," *Economic Journal* 107 (November 1997): 1822.

8. "Study: Longterm Unemployment Has Disastrous Effects on Health and Longevity," *Huffington Post*, November 5, 2010, http://www.huffingtonpost.com/2010/11/05/study-longterm-unemployme_n_779743.html (accessed December 9, 2010).

9. Michael Luo, "At Closing Plant, Ordeal Included Heart Attacks," *New York Times*, November 24, 2010, http://www.nytimes.com/2010/02/25/us/25stress.html (accessed November 8, 2010).

10. "Longterm Unemployment," *Huffington Post*.

11. Richard Gelles and C. P. Cornell, *Intimate Violence in Families*, 2nd ed. (Newbury Park, CA: Sage, 1990).

12. Ross Macmillan and Candace Kruttschnitt, "Patterns of Violence Against Women: Risk Factors and Consequences" (January 2005), http://www.ncjrs.gov/pdffiles1/nij/grants/208346.pdf (accessed November 8, 2010), 25.

13. David Neumark, *Changes in Job Stability and Job Security: A Collective Effort to Untangle, Reconcile, and Interpret the Evidence* (Cambridge, MA: National Bureau of Economic Research, 2000).

14. Although the unemployment rate, at 9.7 percent, was slightly higher in 1982, the average duration of unemployment was considerably shorter.

15. John J. Heldrich Center for Workforce Development, Rutgers University, "No End in Sight: The Agony of Prolonged Unemployment," http://www.heldrich.rutgers.edu/sites/default/files/content/Work_Trends_21_Press_Release.pdf (accessed December 2, 2010).

16. Jay Stewart, "Did Job Security Decline in the 1990s?" in *On the Job: Is Long-Term Employment a Thing of the Past?* ed. David Neumark (New York: Russell Sage Foundation, 2000), 293–4.

17. Michael Luo, "For Growing Ranks of the White-Collar Jobless, Support With a Touch of the Spur," *New York Times*, January 24, 2009, http://www.nytimes.com/2009/01/25/us/25support.html?pagewanted=1&_r=1 (accessed November 10, 2010).

18. United States Department of Labor, Bureau of Labor Statistics, "Table A-1: Employment Status of the Civilian Population by Sex and Age," "Table A:

Household Data by Sex and Age," http://www.bls.gov/news.release/empsit.t01htm (accessed September 12, 2011).

19. U.S. Census Bureau, *Statistical Abstract of the United States 2000*, "Table 644: Civilian Labor Force and Participation Rates With Projections: 1970 to 2008" (Washington, DC: Government Printing Office, 1999). Figures for 2008 from U.S. Census Bureau, *The 2010 Statistical Abstract*, "Table 575: Civilian Labor Force and Participation Rates With Projections: 1980 to 2016," http://www.census.gov/compendia/statab/2010/tables/10s0575.pdf (accessed November 8, 2010).

20. Lawrence Mishel, Jared Bernstein, and Sylvia Allegretto, *The State of Working America 2004/2005* (Ithaca, NY: Cornell University Press, 2005), 296–8.

21. U.S. Census Bureau, "Household Data, Annual Averages," http://www.bls.gov/cps/cpsaat19.pdf (accessed December 11, 2010). Once again, the effects of the Great Recession are evident, as the percentage of part-time workers in previous years was smaller and relatively stable.

22. U.S. Department of Labor, Bureau of Labor Statistics, "Involuntary Part-Time Work on the Rise" (December 2008), http://www.bls.gov/opub/ils/pdf/opbils71.pdf (accessed December 2, 2010).

23. Bureau of Labor Statistics, "Employment Situation Summary, Table A-8," http://www.bls.gov/news.release/empsit.nr0.htm (accessed September 12, 2011).

24. U.S. Department of Labor, Bureau of Labor Statistics, "Table 22: Persons at Work in Nonagricultural Industries by Age, Sex, Race, Hispanic or Latino Ethnicity, Marital Status, and Usual Full- or Part-Time Status," http://www.bls.gov/cps/cpsaat22.pdf (accessed December 9, 2010).

25. U.S. Department of Labor, Bureau of Labor Statistics, "Involuntary Part-Time Work on the Rise," http://www.bls.gov/opub/ils/pdf/opbils71.pdf (accessed December 9, 2010).

26. Lawrence Mishel, Jared Bernstein, and John Schmitt, *The State of Working America* (Armonk, NY: M. E. Sharpe, 1997), 259–60.

27. Ibid., 60–1.

28. HR.BLR.com, "Moonlighting," http://hr.blr.com/HR-topics/HR-Administration/Moonlighting-Policies/ (accessed December 11, 2010).

29. U.S. Department of Labor, Bureau of Labor Statistics, "Contingent and Alternative Employment Arrangements, February 2005," http://www.bls.gov/news.release/conemp.nr0.htm (accessed October 12, 2005).

30. Stephen R. Barley and Gideon Kunda, *Gurus, Hired Guns, and Warm Bodies: Itinerant Experts in a Knowledge Economy* (Princeton, NJ: Princeton University Press, 2004).

31. U.S. Department of Labor, Bureau of Labor Statistics, *The Employment Situation*, "Table B-1: Employees on Nonfarm Payrolls by Industry Sector and Selected Industry Detail" (April 2011), http://www.bls.gov/news.release/pdf/empsit.pdf (accessed May 7, 2011).

32. Michael H. Minton and Jean Libman, *What Is a Wife Worth?* (New York: Morrow, 1983), 178. Cited in Robert A. Rothman, *Working: Sociological Perspectives* (Englewood Cliffs, NJ: Prentice Hall, 1987), 185.

33. United States Department of Labor, Bureau of Labor Statistics, "Volunteering in the United States, 2009," http://www.bls.gov/news.release/volun.nr0.htm (accessed November 10, 2010).

34. Ibid.

35. Ibid.

36. Another source comes up with a figure of $272 billion for 2004 by using the same rate of remuneration but a larger number of volunteers and a much higher number of service hours performed. See "Value of Volunteer Time," http://www .independentsector.org/programs/research/volunteer_time.html (accessed October 14, 2005).

37. Cornell University News Service, "Senior Volunteering Indicates Well-Being," http://www.scienceblog.com/community/older/1999/B/199901111.html (accessed June 23, 2006).

38. James J. Heckman and Lance Lochner, "Rethinking Education and Training Policy: Understanding the Sources of Skill Formation in a Modern Economy," in *Securing the Future: Investing in Children From Birth to College,* eds. Sheldon Danziger and Jane Waldfogel (New York: Russell Sage Foundation, 2000), 49.

39. Rodney Clark, *The Japanese Company* (New Haven, CT: Yale University Press, 1979).

40. David I. Levine, *Working in the Twenty-First Century: Policies for Economic Growth Through Training, Opportunity, and Education* (Armonk, NY: M. E. Sharpe, 1998), 140.

41. For all its importance, informal on-the-job training has not received much systematic attention. One exception is Marc Sacks, *On-the-Job Learning in the Software Industry: Corporate Culture and the Acquisition of Knowledge* (Westport, CT: Quorum, 1994).

42. Levine, *Working in the Twenty-First Century,* 109. It must be recognized, however, that the extent of employee training is notoriously difficult to determine. See Sacks, *On-the-Job Learning,* 136–7.

43. David B. Bills, *The Sociology of Education and Work* (Malden, MA: Blackwell, 2004), 188.

44. Peter S. Goodman, "After Training, Still Scrambling for Employment," *New York Times,* July 18, 2010, http://www.nytimes.com/2010/07/19/business/19training. html?_r=1 (accessed November 10, 2010). The study, "Workforce Investment Act Non-Experimental Net Impact Evaluation," can be accessed at http://wdr.doleta.gov/ research/FullText_Documents/Workforce%20Investment%20Act%20Non-Experimental%20Net%20Impact%20Evaluation%20-%20Final%20Report.pdf.

45. Heckman and Lochner, "Rethinking Education and Training Policy," 72–5. In all fairness, it should be pointed out that these programs do seem to contribute to reduced criminal activity.

46. Theodore F. Cohen, "Men's Families, Men's Friends: A Structural Analysis of Constraints on Men's Social Ties," in *Men's Friendships,* ed. Peter M. Nardi (Newbury Park, CA: Sage, 1992), 126–9.

47. Beverley Fehr, *Friendship Processes* (Thousand Oaks, CA: Sage, 1996), 46–7.

48. Clifton D. Bryant and Kenneth B. Perkins, "Containing Work Disaffection: The Poultry Processing Worker," in *Varieties of Work,* eds. Phyllis L. Stewart and Muriel G. Cantor (Beverly Hills, CA: Sage, 1982), 199–212. Cited in Carol J. Auster, *The Sociology of Work: Concepts and Cases* (Thousand Oaks, CA: Sage, 1996), 240–50.

49. Gary A. Fine, "Friendships in the Work Place," in *Friendship and Social Interaction,* eds. Valerian J. Derlega and Barbara A. Winstead (New York: Springer-Verlag, 1986).

50. W. Fred Cottrell, *The Railroader* (Stanford, CA: Stanford University Press, 1940).

51. Howard S. Becker, *Outsiders: Studies in the Sociology of Deviance* (New York: Free Press, 1963), 79–119.

52. Graham Allan, *Friendship: Developing a Sociological Perspective* (Boulder, CO: Westview, 1989), 37.

53. Ibid.

54. Edward A. Shils and Morris Janowitz, "Cohesion and Disintegration in the Wehrmacht in World War II," *Public Opinion Quarterly* 12 (Summer 1948): 280–315.

55. W. Richard Scott, *Organizations: Rational, Natural, and Open Systems*, 2nd ed. (Englewood Cliffs, NJ: Prentice Hall, 1987), 57–8.

56. Much of the research is described in F. J. Roethlisberger and William J. Dickson, *Management and the Worker* (Cambridge, MA: Harvard University Press, 1939).

57. The research conducted in the switchboard wiring room is summarized in John Madge, *The Origins of Scientific Sociology* (New York: Free Press, 1962), 198–204.

58. Thorstein Veblen, "The Instinct of Workmanship," in *The Portable Veblen*, ed. Max Lerner (New York: Viking, 1948), 318. For an insightful ethnography of a modern exemplar of the instinct of workmanship, see Douglas Harper, *Working Knowledge: Skill and Community in a Small Shop* (Chicago: University of Chicago Press, 1987).

59. Abraham H. Maslow, *Motivation and Personality*, 2nd ed. (New York: Harper & Row, 1970).

60. For a discussion of how leisure pursuits can satisfy the instinct of workmanship when it cannot be achieved on the job, see H. F. Moorhouse, *Driving Ambitions: A Social Analysis of the American Hot Rod Enthusiasm* (Manchester, UK: Manchester University Press, 1991), 144–69.

Life on the Job II

The Perils and Pressures of Work

In the previous chapter, we saw how work can provide a number of benefits in addition to a wage or salary. Yet, as anyone who has put in time at work knows, even good jobs have their occasional unpleasant tasks and situations, and for many other kinds of work, the on-the-job problems can outweigh the rewards by a substantial margin. This chapter will survey some of the major woes engendered by work, along with the conditions that give rise to them. The story will not be of unrelenting gloom, however, as the chapter will note some efforts to improve life on the job and will conclude with a brief discussion of job satisfaction among workers today.

Work May Be Hazardous to Your Health

The workplace can be a danger zone that reflects and sometimes extends the perils of everyday life. People usually don't go to work worrying about being a crime victim, but it happens more often than might be thought. According to the National Institute for Occupational Safety and Health, from 1993 to 1999, an average of 1.7 million people were victims of violent crime at work or while on duty. Even worse, from 1992 to 2006, a yearly average of 800 men and women were murdered while at work.[1] As might be expected, police officers, corrections officers, and taxi drivers are the most likely to be murdered.[2] Many more workers have died from other causes while on the job; according to the U.S. Department of Labor, the number of workers who died in 2009 as a result of work-related injuries was 4,340, which comes out to 3.3 deaths per 100,000 workers.[3] Highway accidents involving truckers and other drivers were the leading cause of job-related deaths, followed by falls, homicides, and being struck by objects.[4] A few industries have much higher rates of accidental deaths than the overall average. In 2009, the category encompassing agriculture, forestry, fishing, and hunting had the dubious distinction of having the highest fatality rate, at 26.0 per 100,000 full-time equivalent workers. Next came mining, at 12.7 per 100,000. Other particularly dangerous sectors were transportation and warehousing (12.1 per 100,000) and construction (9.7 per 100,000).[5] The least dangerous sector encompassed educational and health services, with 0.7 worker fatalities per 100,000 employees.[6]

In regard to particular occupations, the highest fatality rates in 2009 were found among fishers and related fishing workers, at 200.0 fatalities per 100,000 full-time equivalent workers—more than 60 times the average for the workforce as a whole. Other occupations with much higher than average fatality rates were, in descending order, logging workers; aircraft pilots and flight engineers; farmers and ranchers; roofers; structural iron and steel workers; refuse and recyclable material collectors; industrial machinery installers, maintainers, and repairers; driver/sales workers and truck drivers; and construction workers.[7]

Less serious on-the-job injuries also pose a considerable threat to workers. In total, 4.14 million American workers suffered nonfatal injuries in 2009 while on the job, which translates to 3.9 injuries for every 100 full-time equivalent workers.[8] As with the figures for on-the-job fatalities, injury statistics differ markedly according to industry and occupation. In general, jobs in the manufacturing sector are more dangerous than those in the service sector, with 4.3 injuries per 100 full-time equivalent workers in the former and 3.4 in the latter. There is, however, a considerable spread within the service sector. Some services such as finance and insurance have only 0.8 injuries per 100 workers, a sharp contrast to the 11.1 to 100 ratio for workers employed in nursing and residential care facilities, which is considerably higher than the one for truck driving—4.6 to 100.[9]

Photo 12.1   Victims of the Triangle factory fire, a catastrophe that took the lives of 146 young women in 1911

SOURCE: ©Bettmann/CORBIS.

Statistics on workplace injury and death are troubling, but far worse is the situation in developing countries, where there may be little or no oversight of the workplace by governments or other agencies concerned with worker safety, such as insurance firms. In 2005, the International Labor Office reported that every year, 2.2 million people around the world die of work-related injuries and illnesses, the great majority of which are in the developing world. And, stunning as it is, this number may actually underreport the number of fatalities by a substantial margin.[10] One of the worst examples is China, where rapid industrialization and an impressive rate of economic growth have been accompanied by a high incidence of job-related deaths and injuries. According to government figures, 963,976 accidents occurred on Chinese worksites in 2003, and 136,340 workers were killed.[11] Appalling though these figures are, the actual number is likely to be much higher because local officials and the families of victims often are bribed in order to prevent them from reporting on-the-job fatalities.[12]

Stress at Work

In addition to causing physical injuries and even death, a job that poses physical hazards can also induce the psychological condition known as "stress."[13] But even a job that is not dangerous in a physical sense can be highly stressful. Some degree of job-related stress is not necessarily a bad thing. A challenging set of tasks may be stressful, but the stresses they induce also may promote a high level of performance.[14] But beyond a certain point, stress becomes an overwhelmingly negative aspect of working life that has been implicated in a number of physical and psychological ailments, such as depression, high blood pressure, and lower back pain, along with alcoholism and drug abuse. In addition to being a personal problem, stress also has been costly to employers; according to the American Institute of Stress, each year in the United States, $300 billion, or $7,500 per employee, is spent on stress-related compensation claims, reduced productivity, absenteeism, health insurance costs, direct medical expenses, and employee turnover.[15]

Work-related stress can be brought on by a great number of conditions: poor pay, tyrannical supervisors, petty regulations, unpleasant working conditions, the fear of job loss, uncooperative coworkers, difficult customers and clients, lack of recognition, and so on. A monotonous job can also be a source of stress. A particularly stressful type of job is one that is monotonous and uninteresting but still requires steady concentration, such as data entry and assembly line work.[16]

Having inadequate resources to do a job adequately is another source of stress. For many jobs, one of the most crucial resources is time, and time pressures are a leading cause of stress, as anyone who has faced a deadline can attest. Power and authority also are important resources that may be inadequate for the tasks at hand. One potentially stressful situation occurs when workers need to effect changes in people or things but lack the authority to do so, perhaps because their hierarchical position within the organization is not commensurate with what they are expected to accomplish. Finally, as will be explored in some depth in Chapter 14, workers' lives extend beyond the workplace, and trying to balance the competing demands of work and family can be profoundly stressful.

Stress is not randomly distributed. Certain occupations are more stressful than others, and stressful work situations are not always offset by higher wages or salaries. At the same time, having a good-paying position that is well up in the organizational hierarchy does not necessarily result in elevated stress levels. In fact, the opposite seems to be the case. Low-wage occupations that afford little control over the work environment are associated with elevated risks of hypertension, cardiovascular disease, and mental illness.[17] The health perils that may come with being at the lower end of a workplace hierarchy are underscored by a recent study of British government officials. Contrary to what might be assumed, one key indication of stress—the elevation of blood pressure during working hours—was found to be more pronounced among low-status workers than among high-status workers. Even more ominously, the lower-level workers had higher death rates than higher-level workers did, even when other variables such as age were taken into account.[18]

When the stress level is too high for too long, a worker becomes a candidate for what is popularly known as "burnout." This condition can be defined as a psychological and/or physical breakdown that renders a worker incapable of effectively doing his or her job. Burnout is the result of the interaction of individual psychological states on one hand and organizational structures and processes on the other. Vulnerability to burnout differs from individual to individual, but certain group characteristics seem to affect the propensity to suffer from this condition. For example, younger workers seem to be more vulnerable, perhaps because they lack the supportive social connections of older workers.[19] Also likely to experience stress-induced burnout are men and women with a "Type A personality," which is characterized by aggressiveness, a strong need for achievement, and an unrelenting sense of urgency. Although they may be quite productive, Type A men and women often have a low level of perceived control. This, in turn, can induce feelings of stress that may be accompanied by stress-induced physical and psychological ailments.[20]

A real or perceived lack of control is only one of the workplace conditions that may promote burnout. All the other conditions that produce stress can culminate in burnout. Although stress and burnout usually are characterized as individual psychological problems, they also have a clear social and organizational dimension. The way work is structured, especially in terms of the balance between responsibilities and access to adequate resources, will have a large influence on feelings of stress and proclivities toward burnout. In James O'Toole and Edward E. Lawler's summation, "Perhaps the strongest point to emerge from recent research is that employees who are able to control the demands of their work are much less likely to experience stress than those who are not."[21]

Jobs, Secure and Insecure

As noted in the previous chapter, unemployment, and even the fear of being laid off, can have serious consequences for physical and mental health. For many workers, therefore, a modicum of job security is one of the most important features a job can offer. Some occupations, notably teaching, offer the prospect of tenure in order to protect academic freedom. Tenure, however, is not ironclad; teachers and professors can lose their jobs as a result of serious breaches of established rules of behavior or because their institution has to reduce personnel for financial reasons. Other professions offer *de facto* tenure, as occurs when an attorney is made a partner in a law firm. Government workers and employees in some unionized industries and firms can be fired only after their employers have gone through formal procedures. Employers also are constrained by laws that prevent workers from being fired for trying to organize a union or for drawing public attention to malfeasance within the firm that employs them ("whistle-blowing"). Civil rights laws forbid dismissals on the basis of race, color, gender, creed, or national origin, while older workers cannot be fired simply because they are adjudged to be too old. But in general, the relationship between employers and employees in the United States is governed by the doctrine of "employment at will." This means that in most states, unless an individual's employment is governed by a specific agreement or discrimination of some sort can be invoked, an employee can be summarily fired for any reason or for no reason at all.[22]

Some of the most precarious employment positions are found within the ranks of contingent workers. One important segment of the contingent workforce is occupied by the men and women who work for firms that supply "temps," workers who are placed by specialized agencies to do short-term work in offices and other worksites. The supply of temporary workers is a big business; according to one reckoning, one of the world's largest employers is Manpower Inc., which in 2009 placed three million "associates" in permanent, temporary, and contract positions worldwide, and had 400,000 of these "associates" on assignment on any given day.[23]

Temporary workers are employed when firms find themselves with more work than their regular staff can handle, but many businesses make frequent use of these workers because they don't have to provide them with benefits such as health insurance. Given the advantage of lower labor costs, some employers have hired temporary workers for periods of time that stretch the meaning of the word "temporary" beyond recognition.

Temporary workers tend to be younger and are less likely to be high school or college graduates than members of the permanent workforce are.

About 40 percent of them are part-time workers.[24] Also noteworthy is that when compared with employees in traditional situations, temporary workers are more likely to be women, African Americans, and Latinos.

Many temporary workers are satisfied with working in this capacity; one study found that 40 percent of temporary workers are not interested in obtaining a permanent position.[25] The main advantage of doing temporary work is the flexibility it offers, but with it come a number of drawbacks. Temporary workers' median weekly income of $414 in 2005 put them well below the average for all workers; 80 percent of temporary workers had no health insurance coverage from their employers, and a similar percentage were not enrolled in employer-sponsored pension plans.[26] Temporary workers also have been subject to work-related problems that do not affect permanent workers. As their low median salary indicates, many temporary workers have not been able to get enough placements that provide an adequate income. Temporary workers are often given the most routine tasks, and paradoxically, they sometimes find themselves with the need to "look busy" because there may not be enough real work to do. The nature of their work also produces social isolation and a poor self-image, expressed in the phrase "just a temp."[27]

Sexual Harassment at Work

Many workers have complained about the unwanted sexual advances of coworkers. Actions of this sort are examples of *sexual harassment*. In extreme cases, sexual harassment may take the form of a quid pro quo whereby a sexual relationship is demanded in return for a work-related benefit such as a promotion. Although sexual harassment of male workers is not unknown, women are usually the primary victims. The tendency of men to be more sexually aggressive than women is only part of the reason for this behavior. Typical patterns of sexual harassment also reflect the hierarchical structure found in most work organizations, making women in low-status positions particularly vulnerable to harassment by men occupying higher rungs on the organizational ladder. Lower-status women employees may be viewed as fair game by men who feel that their rank invests them with special privileges, while the lack of power and influence characteristic of female employees may prevent them from responding assertively to harassing actions.[28]

Sexual harassment also entails being subject to a "hostile work environment," which encompasses behavior, remarks, or the display of objects that are offensive to coworkers and interfere with the performance of their work. Although individual workers are ultimately responsible for creating hostile work environments and perpetrating acts of sexual harassment, their employers may be held liable in a court of law for condoning or simply allowing them to occur in the workplace.

The concept of sexual harassment has only recently been defined as a legal issue, and there is still a fair degree of ambiguity about what constitutes an unwanted sexual advance or the creation of a hostile work environment, as well as the extent of an employer's responsibility for it. On the basis of past court rulings, for example, it is not clear whether an employee's posting of a pinup calendar in his cubicle is to be construed as an example of sexual harassment or as the exercise of an individual's right to freedom of expression. It is fair to assume that a substantial amount of litigation will occur before a body of case law can determine the exact legal parameters of sexual harassment.

Greedy Institutions

Dangerous working conditions and organizational structures that promote stress and sexual harassment are obvious workplace problems. More subtle is the threat posed by jobs that demand excessive degrees of personal involvement from the men and women who hold them. One such job, which was common until fairly recently, was that of domestic servant. For the men and women who worked as maids, butlers, cooks, gardeners, chauffeurs, and the like, the physical, social, and emotional boundaries of their lives were largely defined by their employer's household, a narrow world often further diminished by the requirement that they remain single. Living and working within one household and constantly under observation, servants were locked into a dependency relationship with their masters. At the same time, their close physical proximity to their employers gave them many opportunities to discover some of the most intimate details of their masters' lives. This situation made loyalty to their employers, or at least the willingness to exercise discretion, a paramount virtue for servants. Requiring servants to live on the premises and not marry did not guarantee unswerving loyalty, but it did reduce the opportunities for independent thought and action.

Very few households employ live-in servants today. According to the U.S. Census Bureau, in 1999, there were 831,000 "private household workers" who were employed as child-care workers, cleaners, and servants.[29] Although many families employ people to clean their houses, mow their lawns, and take care of their children, the terms of employment are usually limited to specific tasks and set hours of work and do not entail living on the premises. One of the reasons for the demise of live-in domestic servitude was that the master–servant relationship clashed with one of the key cultural trends of the modern era, the spread of egalitarian values. But perhaps of greater importance has been the expansion of alternative employment opportunities, especially for women. Servants in Europe and North America today are mostly immigrants, predominantly female, from Third World countries. Although some may start off as live-in maids and nannies, most do not remain in this position, preferring to have their own homes and put in regular working hours like other members of the workforce.[30]

The traditional relationship between a master and a servant was a personal one. Sometimes, however, an entire organization can place excessive demands on its employees. Lewis Coser dubbed these organizations "greedy institutions."[31] Early examples appeared centuries ago as kings and other political leaders sought to consolidate and extend their authority. These rulers needed competent administrators to oversee the collection of taxes, the maintenance of order, protection from enemies, and other crucial matters. Because many of these governmental activities presented tremendous opportunities for self-aggrandizement, both economic and political, it was of central importance that these tasks be done by individuals whose loyalty to the ruler was absolute. Competing loyalties to other power holders, guilds, ethnic groups, and even one's own family had to be eliminated, or at least attenuated. Rulers, therefore, were inclined to recruit and place their trust in individuals who lacked strong social ties with anyone or anything other than the rulers themselves.

Sexual relationships can be a particularly dangerous threat to political and organizational loyalties because they often produce a strong dyadic bond between partners. They also can lead to the formation of families that may become competing centers of loyalty. One response to this threat has been mandated celibacy, as is required of Catholic priests. The same demands for celibacy could also be found in some religious sects, such as the Shakers of 19th-century America, who forbade any sexual activities among their members. Paradoxically, however, other sects established at about the same time maintained organizational loyalty through the opposite strategy of encouraging promiscuity among the faithful. In the place of long-lasting monogamous relationships, sect members were urged to engage in temporary sexual liaisons and then move on to another partner. Because they were supposed to be short-lived, these relationships were less likely to create attachments that might undermine the individual's connection to the sect as a whole. Although they came at it from opposite ends, the religious organizations that required either celibacy or group promiscuity had the same goal: maintaining loyalty and organizational control over the members by weakening or eliminating competing social ties.

Greedy institutions are by no means confined to the past or to a few religious organizations. Businesses may act as greedy institutions when they require their employees to take on a public persona deemed appropriate by the firm. This can be seen in employees' performance of what has been called "emotion work," the required effort to create the kind of atmosphere that clients and customers have come to expect.[32] Sometimes, this entails nothing more than a perfunctory "have a nice day" at the conclusion of a purchase, but other workers may be expected to continuously exhibit an emotional façade in accordance with their occupational role. Flight attendants, for example, are expected to maintain a visage of cheerfulness, no matter what the situation or how churlish the passenger, while at the opposite pole, a collection agent may assume a hostile mien if that is what it takes to get someone to pay off a debt.

Alienated Labor

The submersion of the self into an involuntary, preordained organizational role is an example of a work-related malaise known as *alienation,* a state that has received a considerable amount of attention from psychologists and sociologists. The term "alienation" originally denoted having something taken away. A vestige of the older meaning endures when we use the term *inalienable rights*—that is, rights that endure and cannot be removed. When something is taken away, it is separated from us, and that is the core of the contemporary meaning of alienation. To be alienated from someone or something is to experience estrangement from or loss of a physical, psychological, or spiritual entity that had been of great value.

Alienation from one's work was an important theme for Karl Marx, especially in his early writings, which are often taken to have a more humanistic orientation than his later works centering on political economy. As Marx saw it, work was an essential human activity because, in addition to being the basis of physical survival, it was the vehicle through which individual men and women expressed their capabilities as participants in a social activity. Under capitalism, however, the workers' efforts are appropriated by their employers, and as a result, they find themselves estranged or alienated from the work they do, as well as from the products they produce. In Marx's words,

> What constitutes the alienation of labour? First, that the work is *external* to the worker, that it is not part of his nature; and that, consequently, he does not fulfill himself in his work but denies himself, has a feeling of misery rather than well-being, does not develop freely his mental and physical energies but is physically exhausted and mentally debased. The worker, therefore, feels himself at home only during his leisure time, whereas at work he feels homeless. His work is not voluntary, but imposed *forced labour.* It is not the satisfaction of a need, but only a *means* for satisfying other needs. . . . External labour, labour in which man alienates himself, is a labour of self-sacrifice, of mortification. Finally, the external character of work for the worker is shown by the fact that it is not his own work but work for someone else, that in work he does not belong to himself but to another person.[33]

Max Weber, whose seminal ideas about individuals and work have been featured in several places in this book, also was troubled by the alienating qualities of work, especially the modern trend of intensifying bureaucratization. Weber was acutely aware of the qualities of bureaucracies—hierarchical authority, specialized job tasks, rigidly circumscribed roles, and impersonality—that result in workers having little sense of the significance of their efforts for the achievement of their organization's goals.[34]

Marx's and Weber's ideas about alienated labor were pitched at a rather abstract level. In contrast, subsequent generations of scholars and organizational practitioners have expanded and refined the concept of worker alienation through empirical investigations of actual workplace situations. One important example is the research of Robert Blauner, who studied the work environments associated with four industrial processes: textile manufacture, chemical processing and oil refining, assembly line manufacture, and traditional printing (i.e., before computerized typesetting). In order to make the general concept of alienation more specific, Blauner adopted a schema first presented by Melvin Seeman, identifying four basic components of alienation: powerlessness, meaninglessness, isolation, and self-estrangement.[35] Some of these categories require little in the way of explanation. *Powerlessness* can be defined as the inability to control the conditions under which the work is done, and *meaninglessness* is a situation where workers feel that nothing of value inheres in the work they do. *Isolation* occurs when workers feel a sense of separation from their coworkers, society as a whole, or both. *Self-estrangement* is the sense that work is done only to earn money and that nothing of one's self is invested in the work he or she is doing. It also subsumes the condition of *normlessness,* the sense that no appropriate standards of behavior exist or that existing norms are invalid.

For Blauner, the key determinant of the extent of worker alienation was the technology involved. Printers enjoyed the least alienating work environment because they had ample opportunities to implement their skills and exercise control over the work they performed. In contrast, operatives in textile mills were not much more than machine tenders, with few opportunities for initiative or creativity. Assembly line workers were in an even worse situation because the unrelenting pace of the line rigidly dictated what they could do and the speed at which they could do it. Making matters worse was the extreme fragmentation of assembly line production, which made each worker a tiny cog in a giant machine. In contrast, workers in continuous process industries were in a relatively favorable situation. Their tasks were to carefully monitor production process and take decisive, knowledge-based actions when the inevitable problems cropped up.

It may be argued that Blauner's analysis makes technology an independent force and pays insufficient attention to the crucial aspect of Marx's perspective on worker alienation: power differentials between the workers and those who control them because they own their workplace or act as the owners' representatives. This critique can be taken a step further by arguing that workplace technologies have been developed and applied in order to reinforce and extend management's powers over the industrial workforce.[36]

Manifestations of Discontent

Feelings of on-the-job alienation may be associated with poor performance at work, but the relationship is considerably less clear-cut than might be thought.[37] Many studies have linked high levels of worker satisfaction with good on-the-job performance, beginning with the most basic requirements, such as showing up for work on a regular and punctual basis. Other studies have found positive correlations between satisfied workers and the productivity and profitability of the organizations they serve. But as with any correlation, a causal relationship cannot be simply assumed, and even if it is possible to do so, the direction of causality may not be at all clear. For example, in regard to worker satisfaction and productivity, it may be that being a member of a successful, productive organization is itself the source of satisfaction, and not the other way around. Then, too, a productive firm may be able to pay relatively high wages and salaries, which will likely contribute to worker satisfaction. To further complicate things, there may be a high level of worker satisfaction in a poorly performing organization, one in which the employees are quite satisfied with their jobs because they are able to spend half their work hours playing Internet poker. Their satisfaction is likely to be short-lived, however, because the organization employing them will probably go belly up before too long.

In many work situations, a fair degree of job dissatisfaction may even be irrelevant; a satisfied worker may be more inclined to go above and beyond the call of duty, but many jobs are structured in such a way that there is little opportunity for creativity and initiative. Under these circumstances, all employers expect is that their employees show up on time and do what is required of them. At the same time, however, even this minimal level of motivation cannot always be taken for granted, as dissatisfied employees demonstrate their discontent in numerous ways. One of these is absenteeism; workers may simply choose not to come to work, especially on Mondays and Fridays. According to one estimate, employees absent themselves on an average of 7 to 12 days a year, most of which is not due to illness.[38] Theft can be another response to workplace dissatisfaction. Although it is difficult to make a precise reckoning of losses stemming from employee pilferage, it surely amounts to several billion dollars annually. Depending on an employee's position in the organizational hierarchy, job-related theft can range from the petty appropriation of materials and tools to elaborate embezzlement schemes resulting in the loss of millions of dollars.[39] In an extreme manifestation of workplace dissatisfaction, workers may engage in sabotage, a word derived from the old practice of wrecking machinery by tossing a wooden shoe, or *sabot*, into the works. One shouldn't place too much credence in stories of auto workers deliberately dropping a handful of nuts and bolts into a car's bodywork before welding the panels together, but it is certainly true that, on occasion, workers have engaged in a kind of passive sabotage by not reporting obvious defects as incomplete cars make their way down the assembly line.

Responses to On-the-Job Alienation

Until recently, some firms compensated for the alienation caused by production technologies such as the assembly line by paying good wages, a policy that began with the $5 day at the Ford Motor Company in 1914. In the 1970s, a few firms directly confronted the problem by making a conscious effort to redesign production technologies in order to reduce or even eliminate the conditions that gave rise to worker alienation. One of these efforts, which received a considerable amount of attention at the time, centered on the Volvo assembly plants in the Swedish towns of Kalmar and Uddevalla.[40] The most innovative was the Kalmar factory, which went into operation in 1974. Instead of being designed to accommodate long assembly lines, the plant was laid out in a star-shaped configuration that contained 27 workstations. Workers did not stay in one place as a moving line brought the automobile assembly to them but were able to move along with the cars as automated guide vehicles transported them from station to station.

In another important departure from traditional assembly operations, workers were not confined to a single task. Instead, car assembly was performed by groups of 20 workers in individual sections of the plant. Workers in these teams could stick to one job or they could rotate from one job to another. In so doing, it was hoped, workers would gain a sense of greater control and involvement in a more meaningful activity than was the case when they endlessly performed the same operation. The new factories also were distinguished by an appealing working environment that kept noise to a minimum and situated workers near large windows that framed pleasant outdoor scenes.

These radically redesigned industrial workplaces were successful in that the quality of the assembled cars was up to standard and the pace of work was actually faster than on a traditional assembly line. But group production methods were not as efficient as traditional assembly lines, resulting in 10 percent higher manufacturing costs. Another disappointment was that absenteeism continued to be a problem.[41] In the face of a competitive market for cars and relentless cost pressures, Volvo closed both plants in 1993, although some of their features were transferred to Volvo's remaining factory.

Although Volvo's efforts to radically restructure traditional industrial operations did not endure, numerous other efforts have aimed to improve the quality of working life. These efforts are not entirely motivated by altruism. Industrial managers have come to realize that a better work environment in general, and empowered workers in particular, can improve productivity and product quality, which ultimately lead to higher profits and expanded market shares. In the American automobile industry, assembly line workers have gained a measure of control through the simple ability to stop the line when problems occur. For decades, management refused to entrust workers with this responsibility for fear they would misuse it by stopping the line for frivolous reasons. But as concerns about poor quality mounted, management became more inclined to empower line workers, who were in the best position to perceive assembly problems as they appeared.

Another successful innovation has been the introduction of quality circles in a number of industrial enterprises. Originating in Japan in the early 1960s, quality circles comprise groups of production workers who meet voluntarily to discuss on-the-job issues such as production methods and product quality. To their advocates, quality circles empower workers by giving them a firmer base for influencing production processes and working conditions. To their detractors, however, quality circles are little more than a way to co-opt workers and get them to accept management's values and policies.

Job Satisfaction and Dissatisfaction Today

In the 1970s, the media devoted a fair amount of attention to "the blue-collar blues," a condition marked by large numbers of working men and women being locked into unrewarding, alienating, dead-end jobs that were contributing to drug addiction, alcoholism, and general unhappiness, especially among younger workers. Interest in the topic receded in the years that followed, as neither management nor labor unions made improving the quality of working life a major priority. Interest in alleviating worker alienation waned as manufacturing employment remained stagnant; for many workers, holding on to a job in the face of a changing economy took precedence over attempts to humanize that job.[42]

Efforts to improve the quality of working life also have been met with indifference because workplace discontent is not rampant, at least if surveys of workers present an accurate picture of their evaluation of the work they do. When asked the general question of how they feel about their jobs, the majority of workers appear to be content; one representative Gallup poll found that 83 percent of respondents expressed satisfaction with their jobs.[43] Perhaps more significantly, another survey conducted in 2002 by University of Michigan researchers found that 54 percent of respondents indicated they were "very satisfied" with their jobs, while only 34 percent reported this level of satisfaction with their families and personal lives.[44]

Occupational psychologists and sociologists generally agree on the job characteristics that are particularly relevant to workplace satisfaction or the lack of it. Predictably, a high-paying job will be viewed as more satisfying than one that keeps a worker in poverty, although the correlation between job satisfaction and remuneration is not as great as might be expected.[45] The nature of the work being done has a lot to do with how the worker feels about it. In particular, job satisfaction is generally correlated with autonomy, the complexity and diversity of the tasks being performed, the ability to do a job in its entirety, the perceived significance of the work being done, and the regular receipt of feedback about job performance.[46] In other words, many of the conditions that produce job satisfaction are the direct opposite of the conditions implicated in workplace alienation.

At the same time, however, "objective conditions" take us only so far in understanding the causes of worker alienation. It is also necessary to take into account the values and attitudes—and, in particular, the expectations—workers bring to their jobs. Since the people who do research and write about work are, for the most part, academics and other well-educated members of the upper-middle class, their take on workplace alienation or satisfaction may reflect their own responses to particular jobs ("How would I feel if I were doing that kind of work?"). But the men and women actually doing the work may bring a different set of values and expectations to their jobs. For example, as noted above, workers who have suffered prolonged periods of unemployment will in all likelihood express a fair degree of satisfaction with any job that brings in an income.

That different categories of workers have different expectations also helps explain why younger workers tend to express more dissatisfaction with their jobs than older workers do.[47] People at the start of their working lives are likely to entertain higher expectations about jobs and careers than are older workers, who have become more realistic about—and resigned to—the jobs they hold and the work they do. The different expectations that groups of people bring to their jobs also help explain why women workers generally exhibit the same levels of job satisfaction as male workers, even though their jobs on the whole pay less, are less intrinsically interesting, and offer fewer opportunities for advancement. But, unlike the case of older workers compared with younger ones, this may not be a matter of having lower occupational aspirations than men; rather, the majority of women workers may be comparing their job situations with those of other women workers.[48] Evaluating one's job in comparison with those of others is, of course, not confined to women or to low-wage workers in general. Sports fans are all too familiar with pro athletes who make several million dollars a year demanding to renegotiate their contracts because a free agent with similar statistics has just signed for even more money.

The Elusive Search for Job Satisfaction

Although some workplaces can function tolerably well despite having a cadre of dissatisfied workers, more is at stake than maintaining acceptable levels of production. Too many working people spend too many hours on the job for their efforts to be dismissed as nothing more than showing up for work and doing as they are told in exchange for a paycheck. Even so, it has to be admitted that scholarly inquiries into the conditions that make for less alienating workplaces still have a way to go. Literally thousands of research projects have investigated the causes and consequences of worker satisfaction and dissatisfaction, but few hard-and-fast generalizations have emerged. As noted in one comprehensive textbook on industrial and organizational psychology, "Although we have half a century of research on [the causes and consequences of job satisfaction], there are as yet no compelling theories or conclusions."[49]

Such indeterminacy is an inevitable consequence of the slipperiness of the key variable; "satisfaction," like "happiness," is a personal, idiosyncratic, and subjective state. What any given person means when he or she claims to be satisfied or dissatisfied always requires some interpretation by others, and these interpretations will likely not be in perfect accord with the actual feelings of the first party. Systematic interviews or questionnaires may provide more insight into the psychological states of individual workers, but an unambiguous reckoning will likely remain elusive.

If expressed feelings of satisfaction and dissatisfaction can be hard to interpret, it is even more difficult to ascertain what it is about a job that induces these feelings. For one thing, there is a lot of variation in personal predilections toward feelings of satisfaction or the lack of it, no matter what the circumstances may be. In regard to the latter, all of us have at one time or another noted with exasperation that "Some people are never satisfied!" Second, much depends on the expectations that a person brings to a job. A recent graduate of a professional school may embark on his or her career with idealized notions of what the work will entail, only to find that a fair amount of time must be given over to routine activities that are neither pleasant nor challenging. Conversely, a worker who has landed a job after enduring a long period of unemployment may find at least a modicum of satisfaction in holding down that job even though it is tiring, highly routinized, and poorly paid. Further complicating matters is the likelihood that individual workers may not be fully aware of the sources of their satisfaction or dissatisfaction. An employee may express dissatisfaction with his or her wage or salary, but deeper and perhaps subconscious feelings of not being appreciated and respected by supervisors and coworkers may be more significant than the size of the paycheck. Human beings are complicated creatures, and our feelings about the jobs we hold and the work we do reflect all that complexity.

Previous chapters have noted the significance of gender, race, and class for virtually every aspect of work. But the coverage provided up to now has by no means exhausted the subject. As we shall see, jobs are no longer strictly allocated on the basis of ascribed characteristics, and overt prejudice and discrimination are far less common then they were in the past. Even so, only the naively optimistic would claim that a completely egalitarian order has been established in the world of work. The next chapter will address the continuing significance of ascribed characteristics, but it will also trace the advances made in recent years by women and minorities toward transforming the workplace.

FOR DISCUSSION

1. Have you or a member of your family ever held a job that produced a great deal of stress? What was it about the job that made it stressful? Could these stresses have been alleviated by redesigning the job or some elements of it?

2. In many workplaces, employees are treated as interchangeable parts who are there to do a job, no more and no less. At the other extreme are "greedy institutions" that demand the total incorporation of the individual into a work role. Although neither one may seem desirable to you, would you prefer an occupation or job that leans in the direction of greater or lesser involvement?

3. Is there an inherent conflict between workers and management (or labor and capital)? Can relations between the two be anything other than a zero-sum game? Under what circumstances will the two parties be able to work together to the advantage of both?

4. Many jobs are structured to produce maximum efficiency but at the cost of high levels of employee stress and other workplace problems. Is this a good trade-off for society as a whole? On a personal level, would you be inclined to patronize firms that charge more than their competitors but are known to provide better work environments for their employees?

5. Along with poor work environments, a number of circumstances in life can produce feelings of alienation. What are they? What do they have in common? In what ways, for example, does a sense of being alienated from one's culture correspond to feeling alienated from a job?

Notes

1. National Institute for Occupational Safety and Health, "Occupational Violence," http://www.cdc.gov/niosh/topics/violence/ (accessed December 12, 2010).

2. Ibid.

3. U.S. Department of Labor, Bureau of Labor Statistics, "National Census of Fatal Occupational Injuries in 2009 (Preliminary Results)," http://www.bls.gov/news.release/pdf/cfoi.pdf (accessed December 14, 2010), 1.

4. Ibid., 2.

5. Ibid., 3.

6. Ibid.

7. Ibid., 4.

8. U.S. Department of Labor, Bureau of Labor Statistics, "Workplace Injuries and Illnesses, 2009," http://www.bls.gov/news.release/archives/osh_10212010.pdf (accessed December 14, 2010), 6–17.

9. Ibid., Table 1.

10. International Labor Organization, "Global Workplace Deaths Vastly Under-Reported, Says ILO," September 18, 2005, http://www.ilo.org/global/about-the-ilo/

press-and-media-centre/press-releases/WCMS_005176/lang—en/index.htm (accessed May 5, 2011).

11. "China Reports 41,000 Workplace Deaths During the First Four Months of 2004," http://www.occupationalhazards.com.articles/11956 (accessed October 21, 2005).

12. BBC News World Edition, "Workplace Deaths Rise in China," http://www.news.bbc.co.uk/2/hi/asia-pacific/3206645.stm (accessed October 21, 2005).

13. *Stress,* as used to describe a psychological state, is a fairly recent term. Originally used to describe the physical forces acting on materials, it was imported into psychology by Hans Selye. See *The Stress of Life* (New York: McGraw-Hill, 1956).

14. Selye coined the term *eustress* to characterize stress that is beneficial, but the term is rarely used today.

15. Ken O'Malley, "Employee Stress: It's Costing You More than You Think" (December 1, 2010), http://www.injuryfree.com/4316/resource/prevention/employee-stress-it%E2%80%99s-costing-you-more-than-you-think/ (accessed February 16, 2011).

16. On the latter, see Charles R. Walker and Robert H. Guest, *The Man on the Assembly Line* (Cambridge, MA: Harvard University Press, 1952), 40.

17. Beth Schulman, *The Betrayal of Work: How Low-Wage Jobs Fail 30 Million Americans and Their Families* (New York: New Press, 2003), 98–100.

18. "The Whitehall Study," http://www.workhealth.org/projects/pwhitew.html (accessed November 1, 2005).

19. "Burnout," in *The Encyclopedia of Stress,* F. J. McGuigan (Boston: Allyn & Bacon, 1999).

20. John M. Ivancevich, Michael T. Matteson, and Cynthia Preston, "Occupational Stress, Type A Behavior, and Physical Well-Being," *Academy of Management Journal* 25, no. 2 (June 1982): 373–91.

21. James O'Toole and Edward Lawler III, *The New American Workplace* (New York: Palgrave Macmillan, 2006), 105.

22. Patrick J. Cihon and James O. Castagnera, *Labor and Employment Law,* 2nd ed. (Belmont, CA: Wadsworth, 1993), 4–5.

23. "About Manpower," http://www.manpower.com/about/about.cfm (accessed December 14, 2010).

24. U.S. Department of Labor, Bureau of Labor Statistics, "Contingent and Alternative Employment Arrangements, February 2005," http://www.bls.gov/news.release/conemp.nr0.htm (accessed October 12, 2005).

25. "Forty Percent of Temporary Workers Prefer Nonpermanent Employment Status, Cornell University Study Concludes," http://www.news.cornell.edu/releases/Oct97temp_study.dg.html (accessed June 27, 2006).

26. U.S. Department of Labor, "Contingent and Alternative Employment Arrangements."

27. Kevin Henson, *Just a Temp* (Philadelphia: Temple University Press, 1996).

28. James E. Gruber and Lars Bjorn, "Women's Responses to Sexual Harassment," *Social Science Quarterly* 67, no. 4 (December 1986): 814–26.

29. U.S. Census Bureau, *Statistical Abstract of the United States, 2000,* "Table 669: Employed Civilians by Occupation, Sex, Race, and Hispanic Origin" (Washington, DC: Government Printing Office, 2001).

30. Pierrette Hondagneu-Sotelo, *Doméstica: Immigrant Workers Cleaning and Caring in the Shadows of Affluence* (Berkeley: University of California Press, 2001).

31. Lewis Coser, *Greedy Institutions: Patterns of Undivided Commitment* (New York: Free Press, 1974).

32. Arlie Russell Hochschild, *The Managed Heart: The Commercialization of Human Feeling* (Berkeley: University of California Press, 1983).

33. Karl Marx, "Alienated Labour," in *Karl Marx: Early Writings*, trans. and ed. T. B. Bottomore (1844; repr., London: C. A. Watts, 1963), 124–5.

34. Ronald M. Pavalko, *Sociology of Work and Occupations*, 2nd ed. (Itasca, IL: F. E. Peacock, 1988), 202–3.

35. Robert Blauner, *Alienation and Freedom: The Factory Worker and His Industry* (Chicago: University of Chicago Press, 1964). Seeman's typology, which includes a fifth category, "normlessness," appears in "On the Meaning of Alienation," *American Sociological Review* 24, no. 6 (December 1959): 783–91.

36. David Noble, *America by Design: Science, Technology, and the Rise of Corporate Capitalism* (New York: Knopf, 1977).

37. Paul E. Spector, *Job Satisfaction: Application, Assessment, Causes, and Consequences* (Thousand Oaks, CA: Sage, 1997), 55–65.

38. Randy Hodson and Teresa H. Sullivan, *The Social Organization of Work*, 2nd ed. (Belmont, CA: Wadsworth, 1995), 110.

39. Stephen Rosoff, Henry Pontell, and Robert Tillman, *Profit Without Honor: White-Collar Crime and the Looting of America*, 4th ed. (Upper Saddle River, NJ: Pearson Prentice Hall, 2007), 337–73.

40. Jan Ake Granath, "Torslanda to Uddevalla via Kalmar: A Journey in Production Practice in Volvo," http://www.fm.chalmers.se/uploaded/publikationer/ArticleBrezil.pdf (accessed June 27, 2007).

41. James J. Flink, *The Automobile Age* (Cambridge: MIT Press, 1988), 348.

42. George Ritzer and David Walczak, *Working: Conflict and Change*, 3rd ed. (Englewood Cliffs, NJ: Prentice Hall, 1986), 371–2.

43. Spector, *Job Satisfaction*, 23.

44. O'Toole and Lawler, *New American Workplace*, 109.

45. Spector, *Job Satisfaction*, 42.

46. J. Richard Hackman and Greg R. Oldham, "Motivation Through the Design of Work: Test of a Theory," *Organizational Behavior and Human Performance* 16 (1976): 250–79. Cited in Carol J. Auster, *The Sociology of Work: Concepts and Cases* (Thousand Oaks, CA: Sage, 1996), 202–3.

47. Pavalko, *Sociology of Occupations and Professions*, 208.

48. Randy Hodson, "Gender Differences in Job Satisfaction: Why Aren't Women More Dissatisfied?" *Sociological Quarterly* 30, no. 3 (September 1989): 385–99.

49. Franklin J. Landy and Jeffrey M. Conte, *Work in the 21st Century: An Introduction to Industrial and Organizational Psychology*, 3rd ed. (Hoboken, NJ: Wiley, 2010), 411.

13 Diversity in the Workplace

When cartoonists depicted a "worker" in decades past, their illustrations usually featured a brawny, white male. Today, as we have seen, the typical worker is engaged in the provision of some kind of service that requires little in the way of physical strength. No less important, the workforce is more diverse than it was in the past. At the end of the first decade of the 21st century, women composed 46.8 percent of the American workforce, while 11.4 percent of all workers were African American, 14.5 percent were Latino, and 4.7 percent were Asian American.[1] To put it concisely, white males now constitute a minority of the American labor force. In this chapter, we will look at the various dimensions of workplace diversity, paying particular attention to the difficulties experienced by women and minorities while also noting efforts to create greater equality in the workplace and beyond.

Race, Ethnicity, and Hiring Practices

In Chapter 7, we saw how educational attainments, credentials, and social networks affect an individual's employment prospects. Yet ascribed characteristics such as race and ethnicity still influence hiring decisions. In the past, the linkage between hiring practices and the race or ethnicity of job seekers often was painfully evident. In the 19th century, newspaper want ads sometimes contained the phrase "Irish need not apply," and members of other ethnic groups were simply not considered for many positions. Well into the 20th century, African Americans were frequently excluded from jobs in the manufacturing sector, and when they were hired at all, the heaviest, dirtiest, and lowest-paying work was often reserved for them. Apprenticeships to prepare for skilled occupations were almost always limited to whites, and often just to whites of particular ethnic backgrounds.

Overt discrimination of this sort has been illegal since the 1960s, but many hiring barriers still exist. One important problem for many minority group members lies in their lack of incorporation into job-related social networks.

As we have seen, being connected to a social network considerably improves an individual's chances of landing a job. Consequently, the existence of networks that include some individuals while excluding others perpetuates existing patterns of discrimination and inequality. The problem is particularly acute for residents of America's inner cities, which are disproportionately populated by members of racial and ethnic minorities. Many of America's cities have experienced a "hollowing out" of their economic base as a large number of manufacturing firms have closed or departed for other locales. The loss of these enterprises has been accompanied by the disappearance of low-skill jobs that had offered decent wages and benefits. A large number of these jobs, particularly the best-paying ones, were not held by inner-city residents, but jobs paying even middling wages supported the families of many minority workers. The loss of these jobs has produced a ripple effect throughout their communities. With job losses has come an erosion of collective purchasing power, which has diminished the revenues of local businesses, such as retail shops, and service providers, such as barbers and beauticians. Lost revenues mean lost jobs, generating a downward economic spiral that leaves large urban areas in desperate straits, exacerbating criminal activities, drug addiction, and the whole catalogue of inner-city ills.[2]

There are many reasons for the departure of inner-city industrial enterprises. Some simply have gone out of business, victims of economic, cultural, and technological change. Others have gone abroad to places where labor is cheaper and environmental regulations are minimal. At the same time, however, a significant number of business relocations have taken place because the old neighborhood came to be viewed as "undesirable." The reasons for a place being so defined are many and varied, but it must be recognized that issues of race and ethnicity can figure prominently in this assessment.[3] Many inner cities have higher crime rates than those of outlying suburbs, although the media's propensity to focus on violent episodes can lead to exaggerated notions about their extent. But the risk of being victimized is a reality, and it often becomes a key component of a vicious circle resulting in diminished employment opportunities for inner-city residents; crime and the fear of it contribute to the flight of businesses, resulting in the loss of jobs and more poverty, which in turn fuels more criminal activity and more businesses departing for greener pastures.

It is possible, of course, for inner-city residents to find jobs in other parts of the city and its suburbs. But even if prospective employers are willing to hire them (and, after all, some employers left in order to get away from racial and ethnic minorities), difficulties still remain in getting to job sites, especially when they are not well served by public transportation and job seekers cannot afford to own, maintain, and operate a car. And to return to an earlier theme, people living in inner cities are further disadvantaged by being unable to tap into the informal social networks that, as we have just seen, often are of vital importance for learning about job opportunities.[4]

Differential access to networks is, of course, not the only source of unequal job opportunities. Prejudicial attitudes also prevent members of racial and ethnic minorities from getting jobs for which they are well qualified, although opinions differ as to how pervasive these attitudes are today. Still, it is evident that jobs and occupations are not distributed randomly through the population as a whole. At the most fundamental level, statistics on employment and unemployment clearly indicate unequal outcomes in regard to finding and holding a job. In the first quarter of 2011, for example, the unemployment rate for white men was 10.5 percent, while white women fared somewhat better at 8.3 percent. The corresponding figures for African American men and women were 18.9 and 13.2 percent. The unemployment rates for Latino men and women were 12.9 and 11.9 percent, while Asian American men and women fared best with unemployment rates of 6.6 and 7.3 percent.[5]

The exact contribution of discrimination to unequal outcomes in regard to hiring and job-retention decisions is difficult to ascertain. A few research studies have attempted to determine the extent of discriminatory behavior on the part of employers by sending to prospective employers black and white persons who were equally matched in terms of their references, employment backgrounds, and ability to present themselves. These studies found that discrimination against black applicants was not overwhelming, but neither was it insignificant. In one research project sponsored by the Urban Institute, pairs of matched white and black individuals applied for jobs in Chicago and Washington, DC. No difference was found in 79.9 percent of the cases; both applicants were either offered the job or rejected. But in 14.8 percent of the cases, the white applicant was offered the position while the black applicant was rejected. In the remaining 5.3 percent of the cases, the black applicant received a job offer.[6] In contradiction to these findings, however, were the results of a similar study conducted in Denver that found no difference in the job offers extended to white and black applicants. Both sets of studies have been criticized on methodological grounds. As might be expected, those convinced of the reality of racial discrimination criticized the methodology of the Denver study, while those taking the opposite position found flaws with the studies conducted in Chicago and Washington, DC.

Although few employers exhibit blatantly discriminatory behavior today, unintentional discrimination may result from the way job requirements have been stipulated. In particular, the use of educational qualifications in order to determine the suitability of an applicant for a position may have unfortunate consequences for some minority group members. Many jobs require a significant amount of educational preparation before competence can be assumed, but as Chapter 7 indicated, much of what is learned in school is of limited relevance to the performance of many, if not most, jobs. Seen from this perspective, educational requirements often qualify and disqualify job applicants on grounds that are largely extraneous to the demands of a particular job.

This situation is unfortunate for many reasons, but its contribution to hiring practices that work to the disadvantage of racial and ethnic minorities is particularly problematic. Although African Americans and Latinos have made substantial strides in educational attainment in recent years, they still lag behind whites. In 2008, 87.1 percent of whites 25 years and older had graduated from high school, and 29.8 percent possessed a college degree. For African Americans, the figures were 83.0 and 19.6 percent, respectively, and for Latinos, 62.3 and 13.3 percent, respectively. Asian Americans had the highest level of educational attainment: 88.7 percent had high school diplomas, and 52.6 were college graduates.[7] It should be apparent who is harmed the most when employers use educational credentials primarily as filtering or screening devices.

Credentialing aside, there remains the issue of how changing skill requirements have affected employers' hiring practices. The concept of "skill" encompasses a wide variety of on-the-job capabilities, but of particular relevance here is the distinction between "hard" skills and "soft" skills. The former have to do with technical capabilities, such as being able to effectively wield a hammer or use a spreadsheet program. "Soft" skills entail such things as motivation, demonstrating the ability to maintain good interpersonal relationships, and following orders without rancor. Skills of this sort have taken on greater prominence in recent decades, as service occupations have become the dominant source of employment. Unlike traditional industries such as mining or manufacturing, the majority of employees in service industries interact with members of the public, where well-developed social skills are essential for occupational success.

An emphasis on soft skills as an important criterion for hiring has been particularly problematic for many members of racial and ethnic minority groups. On one hand, marked differences in speech, dress, and demeanor may make a job applicant less attractive, especially when the job calls for intensive interactions with the general public or participating in work-related teams where the members come from different cultural backgrounds. On the other hand, whether or not an applicant has the necessary skills can largely be a matter of interpretation, one in which the biases of a manager or interviewer can easily come to the fore.[8] Either way, individuals outside the white, middle-class mainstream may face significant obstacles when trying to find work in many sectors of the service economy.

Employers have not been the only group engaged in discriminatory behavior. For much of their history, many labor unions engaged in exclusionary practices. In the late 19th century, efforts to integrate the workplace were met with strikes by white workers, and until the 1930s, union rules resulted in the exclusion of African Americans from manufacturing jobs in some northern cities.[9] Well into the 20th century, the United Mine Workers inveighed against the "yellow peril" supposedly posed by Chinese immigrant workers. The steelworkers union was less overtly racist, but it supported segregated job structures that excluded African Americans from skilled, high-paying jobs. Even the United Auto Workers Union, whose leader, Walter Reuther, was an active participant in the civil rights movement of the 1960s, staunchly defended established seniority systems that benefited white workers at the expense of African Americans and other minorities. In the summation of

Herbert Hill, a labor historian and former labor secretary for the National Association for the Advancement of Colored People,

> While not all white workers and their labor unions engaged in the same discriminatory practices at all times and places, racial subordination in many different forms became a major characteristic of the most important and enduring labor organizations.[10]

As a final point, even employers who are not personally prejudiced may engage in discriminatory practices because they feel that their predominantly white clientele will not accept minorities in certain occupational roles. Conversely, in some instances, a kind of reverse discrimination has occurred, and still occurs today, whereby employers are reluctant to hire white workers for jobs that are thought to be the domain of minorities, such as domestic service and migrant farm labor.[11]

Women in the Workforce

One of the most dramatic social and economic changes in recent decades has been the large influx of women into the labor force. In 1959, 83.4 percent of men but only 36.8 percent of women were employed or actively looking for work, a difference of 46.6 percentage points. Five decades later, that difference had shrunk to 12.4 percentage points, as women's participation in the labor force took off while men's declined slightly.[12]

Much of this increase has been due to large numbers of white women joining the workforce, as African American women already had high rates of labor force participation. In 1920, for example, 33 percent of married and 59 percent of unmarried black women were in the U.S. labor force, while for white women, the figures were 7 and 45 percent, respectively.[13] Not until the 1990s did white women's labor force participation catch up to that of black women.[14]

While women have joined the labor force in large numbers, the jobs they hold still differ substantially from those of male workers. As should be obvious to any observer of the working world, women are disproportionately represented among the ranks of secretaries, cashiers, and nurses. In some cases, the imbalance is overwhelming: more than 95 percent of dental hygienists, child-care workers, and receptionists are women. Conversely, less than 2 percent of women are employed as electricians, carpenters, or stonemasons. In general, women workers are concentrated in a relatively small number of occupations. Of the hundreds of occupations tallied by the Census Bureau, 10 of them accounted for one-third of women workers.[15] Remarkably, this tally of the most common women's occupations has hardly changed since 1940.[16]

One way to quantify the extent of gender-based occupational segregation is to calculate the percentage of men and women who would have to move into occupations where their sex is underrepresented in order to achieve complete equality. In 2000, 52.0 percent of the female labor force—more than 34 million women—would have had to move to male-dominated occupations in order to eliminate occupational segregation.[17] The division between "men's" jobs and "women's" jobs is even larger than these figures indicate because they do not take into account segregation within occupational groupings. For example, in the general occupational category of "managers and supervisors," women employees are disproportionately found in personnel departments, while men are substantially overrepresented in financial and legal departments.[18]

The causes of gender-based occupational segregation are still subject to considerable debate. According to one perspective, occupational segregation is grounded in biology; men's and women's jobs, to a significant degree, reflect innate skills, abilities, and preferences that result in women working as elementary school teachers and men as auto mechanics. In the not-too-distant past, one version of the biology-is-destiny ideology sharply restricted women's job opportunities; the primary roles for women were supposed to be those of wife, mother, and homemaker, and married women were legally excluded from a large number of occupations. School districts often refused to hire married women as teachers, and single women were terminated once they married. Similar patterns could be observed in many other occupations until these "marriage bars" began to be abolished in the 1950s, in part due to cultural shifts regarding the proper role of women but also because the supply of single women had dropped sharply due to the low birth rates of the 1930s.[19]

Although discrimination of this sort is now illegal, some employers continue to make employment decisions that work to the disadvantage of women employees and prospective women employees.[20] And even when there is no discrimination on the part of employers, many women are reluctant to pursue occupations where a hostile, male-dominated work environment may prevail. It can be argued that occupations with a high level of potential danger demand a high level of trust in one's coworkers, and that trust is more difficult to achieve when some of the workers are "different" (this argument, of course, could apply

Photo 13.1 Women wing riveters

SOURCE: From the Collections of The Henry Ford.

equally to workers of a race or ethnicity different from that of the dominant work group). But whatever the cause, the existence of an occupational culture that breeds hostility toward women workers constitutes a formidable obstacle to women seeking careers in many male-dominated occupations.

A different set of explanations for gender-based occupational segregation centers on the motivations and actions of women themselves. One approach stresses the greater degree of involvement of women in child care and other family matters. According to this perspective, women tend to self-select into jobs that allow them to balance work and family responsibilities, putting them out of the running for jobs that require large commitments of time and energy. Related to this explanation is a "human capital" approach, which hypothesizes that many women are unwilling to "invest" in the education and training that would qualify them for "male" jobs because their primary commitment is to their family and not their occupational careers. The human capital explanation also has been applied to the behavior of employers, who may be reluctant to hire and subsequently train women workers because they are thought to be less committed to their jobs.

Finally, a social-psychological explanation for gender-based job segregation stresses the different ways boys and girls are socialized. From infancy onward, boys and girls are treated differently, resulting in the acquisition of different skills and aspirations. To take one obvious example, boys are given toy trucks to play with while girls are given dolls. From this perspective, then, it is not surprising that men are inclined toward "male" occupations, such as engineering and truck driving, while women end up as nurses and child-care workers.

Trying to sort out the relative importance of these explanations for occupational segregation is a difficult enterprise. All of them contain at least a grain of truth, but some fit the evidence better than others do. In regard to inherent biologically based differences, we have seen that the sex-based division of labor found in gathering-and-hunting societies was strongly influenced by the demands that pregnancy and lactation placed on women. But hardly anyone earns a living as a gatherer or hunter in modern societies, and occupational trends in general have made physical attributes far less relevant than they were even a generation ago. With nearly 80 percent of all jobs in the service sector, the "masculine" virtues of physical strength and endurance are much less significant now than they were when a large segment of the adult population worked as miners, farmers, railroaders, lumberjacks, and factory hands.

As just noted, gender-based discrimination in job placement is now illegal, but it takes more than a small dash of optimism to assert that it no longer exists or that all male workers are completely accepting of female coworkers. Another explanation for gender-based occupational segregation, the hypothesized need for women to balance the requirements of work and family, raises a number of issues that will be explored in Chapter 14. For now, it simply can be noted that most "women's" jobs are not more easily accommodated to family responsibilities than "men's" jobs are and that single women are just as likely to be found in female-dominated occupations as women with families are.[21]

The "human capital" argument is more difficult to assess. It helps explain why women have been underrepresented in professions and the upper echelons of management, but as will be noted below, this situation is not simply the consequence of women's inability or unwillingness to invest in education and put in long hours on the job. Finally, explanations grounded in the different socialization experiences of males and females contain the assumption that no innate differences exist between the two sexes. Assessing the exact contributions of "nature" and "nurture" is always a controversial exercise, but at this point, there is no compelling reason to completely reject the idea that innate differences between women and men may affect their occupational choices. Moreover, an appeal to the predominant influence of socialization falters when it comes to explaining why women began to enter nontraditional occupations in substantial numbers in the 1970s despite having undergone their formative socialization processes in the 1950s.

Although occupational segregation is not likely to disappear soon, recent educational trends point to substantial changes in the years to come, especially in regard to professional occupations.[22] Of all professional and preprofessional educational programs, only engineering has not witnessed a sizable influx of women students. More educational preparation for women, of course, addresses only one aspect of occupational segregation, but it is likely that in the coming years, we will no longer automatically associate medicine and law with male practitioners.

Discrimination, Occupational Segregation, and Pay

Substantial differences in remuneration tied to race, ethnicity, and gender are striking features of the U.S. economy. Whereas the median white family income in 2008 was $65,000, for African American and Latino families, the figures were $39,879 and $40,466, respectively.[23] There are several reasons for these disparities. One of them is the previously noted historically higher rate of unemployment experienced by African Americans and Latinos. As we have seen, not only does unemployment depress income, but it also reduces the bargaining power of job seekers, which may be reflected in lower wage offers than the ones extended to workers who already have jobs but are looking for something better.

For many employed men and women, a major determinant of the size of their wages and salaries is seniority, and here, too, minorities have been less advantaged than white workers because in some industries, they are likely to have been hired more recently than white workers. The reason many minority workers find themselves in this situation is that, until the past few decades, they were largely excluded from certain occupations. Discrimination of this sort was freely practiced by many employers and labor unions, making entry into skilled trades difficult for minorities. As will be noted later, affirmative action programs have opened up many of these occupations, but these programs have not always been vigorously pursued and often have met with considerable hostility.

Gender-based pay differentials also are evident. In 2009, full-time women workers received an average of 80 cents for every dollar earned by male workers, and in years past, the gap was even wider—in 1979, the ratio was 62 cents to the dollar.[24] Some sources of pay inequalities are similar to the ones affecting racial and ethnic minorities, such as discrimination and exclusion from work-related networks. But others are of particular relevance for women workers, irrespective of their race or ethnicity.

One straightforward reason for the male–female earnings gap is that, on average, men work more hours per year. According to one calculation, this reason accounts for 14 percent of the difference in annual wages received by men and women.[25] Other, less direct contributors to employee productivity, such as education and on-the-job experience, also account for a portion of the pay gap. But these "objective" factors take us only so far, as discrimination cannot be ruled out as a source of male–female pay differentials. In the past, some discriminatory practices, such as limitations on the number of hours women could work or how much weight they could lift at work, had the benign intent of protecting women. These are now illegal, but certain physical standards such as height and weight requirements can have discriminatory effects. It is undeniable that some occupations, such as police officer, require particular physical abilities, but it has been argued that standards are sometimes set at a level that exceeds what is necessary for effective performance on the job.

Occupational segregation has been of particular importance for women's wages and salaries because when an occupation has a high proportion of women, it almost always has a level of remuneration lower than the earnings of workers in male-dominated occupations. Even occupations that once were male preserves pay more poorly when they become identified with women workers.[26] Gender-based occupational segregation diminishes women's wages and salaries in several ways. One of them is a consequence of supply-and-demand economics. When large numbers of women are confined to a small number of occupations, the supply of workers will be large relative to the demand for them, keeping wages and salaries low. Disparities in pay also may reflect the belief of some employers, the majority of whom are men, that by its very nature, the kind of work performed by women is of less value than the work done by men. This, of course, is a judgment with little grounding in objective reality. It can be argued, for example, that few tasks are more important than the care and education of young children, but categorizing these tasks as "women's work" has resulted in low pay for day-care workers. At the other end of the occupational spectrum, pediatrics, a medical specialty with fairly high numbers of female practitioners, is also one of the lowest paid.

Figure 13.1   Women's Earnings as a Percent of Men's, Full-time Wage and Salary Workers, 1979–2009 Annual Averages

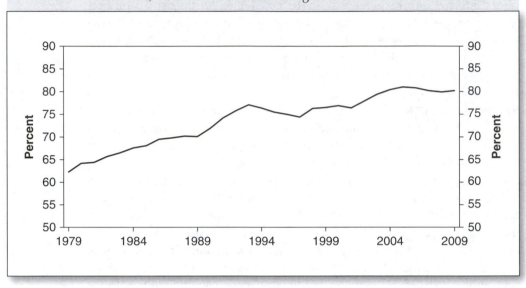

NOTE: Data relate to median usual weekly earnings of full-time wage and salary workers.

Although gender-based occupational segregation is still evident, it has declined somewhat in recent years, as women have moved into male-dominated occupations in significant numbers. The movement of women into "men's work" has occurred before—notably during World War II, when women substituted for men as bus drivers and manufacturing workers such as "Rosie the Riveter" were national icons. The conclusion of hostilities was accompanied by a return to the occupational *status quo ante* as veterans came home to reclaim the jobs they had left. As noted above, the situation is different now, as significant numbers of women have been moving into occupations and professions that were once exclusively male domains, presumably for the long haul. Some of these positions pay well, but at the top of the earnings pyramid, professions such as law and medicine constitute only a small percentage of the total workforce and by themselves do not dramatically alter the male–female wage and salary distribution.

Despite the sizeable inroads of women into "men's" occupations, sex-based occupational segregation continues to be a fact of working life. At the same time, however, the contribution of occupational segregation to the overall wage gap separating male and female workers is more complex than it may seem at first glance. Although workers in female-dominated occupations earn less on average than workers in occupations with a mix of men and women, workers in the most male-dominated occupations also earn less on average than do workers in gender-integrated occupations.[27] All in all, the division between "men's" jobs and "women's" jobs does contribute to the lower average earnings of women workers; according to one calculation, it accounts for about 20 percent of the male–female wage gap.[28]

While occupational segregation persists, the incomes of women workers also have been undermined by another longstanding difference between men and women workers: the continuity of their occupational careers. A person's working career generally parallels key stages of his or her life cycle. Beginning perhaps with a variety of jobs held as a teenager, a career track starts in earnest during the late teens or early 20s after formal education has been more or less completed, unless a post-university degree is pursued, postponing full-time work until the late 20s or early 30s. Then comes a period of "learning the ropes" for particular jobs and the organizations in which they are done, a process that may take several years before the attainment of real proficiency. All the while, a kind of sorting process has been taking place, whereby some people get ahead in terms of pay and position while others get left behind. In other words, employees arrive at the make-or-break phase of their careers. Yet this is precisely the time when many women take on the massive responsibilities of bearing and raising children. Male workers, of course, also may have significant family responsibilities, but in fact, few men leave their jobs to be stay-at-home fathers or even cut back on their workload in order to spend more time with their children. This, of course, may be an economically rational decision, given that men earn more on average than women do.

Motherhood doesn't necessarily mean the cessation of work; 62.0 percent of women with children under the age of 6 years and 58.3 percent of women with infants under the age of 1 year work at a paying job.[29] But as with housework, working mothers usually devote more time and energy to child care than their husbands do, a source of strain that will be explored in greater depth in the next chapter. As a result of the demands of parenthood, far more women have interrupted careers or careers with serious role conflicts, making career advancement more difficult than it is for most male workers, a situation reflected in long-term earnings.

We have seen that race and ethnicity are important sources of wage and salary differences. It might, therefore, be expected that the situation of women workers who also are members of minority groups is even worse when it comes to remuneration. In fact, the record is mixed. In aggregate, African American and Latino women earn less than white women do, but having a college degree or more reverses this situation, as African American women who are college graduates actually earn slightly more than white working women with the same credentials. This, in part, is due to the longer job careers of African American women, but it is also possible that they encounter less on-the-job prejudice than black male workers.[30]

In summing up gender differences in remuneration, we are confronted with a glass that is both half full and half empty. As we have seen, women workers on average earn less than men for a multitude of reasons. On the other hand, over the long term, the male–female earnings gap has narrowed, even though the general trend has been in the direction of greater overall income inequality for the workforce as a whole. But, here, an important qualification has to be made: although the male–female earnings gap has narrowed for workers lacking a college degree, this has been the result of a decline in men's wages and salaries, not an improvement in women's pay.[31] For college-educated women workers, the news has been mixed. Contrary to the general stagnation in wages from the mid-1970s onward, these workers have enjoyed increases in remuneration.[32] Even so, the male–female earnings gap increased for college-educated workers because, while women's wages and salaries rose, they did not rise as rapidly as men's earnings.[33] Unlike women workers who lack college degrees, college-educated women workers have enjoyed rising incomes, but their male counterparts have done even better.

Getting Ahead

One of the prime means for a worker to get a higher wage or salary is to be promoted. Promotion can be based on either seniority or merit. Both have their advantages and disadvantages, and both have the potential to affect male and female workers, as well as racial and ethnic minorities, in different ways. Seniority has the advantage of being the most unambiguous basis for promotion. The period of time a worker has been on the job determines his or her wage or salary, and it can also be the basis for other important features of the job, such as the shift to which one is assigned. Most workers would prefer not to work the swing shift (usually 3 P.M. to 11 P.M.) or the graveyard shift (11 P.M. to 7 A.M.), but they may have to accumulate a fair number of months or even years on the job before they are assigned to a shift with normal working hours. Seniority also can determine who has the opportunity to work extra hours for more pay.

The straightforward quality of seniority is one of the reasons it is often enshrined in labor contracts negotiated by unions and management. It eliminates or at least reduces the likelihood of prejudice, favoritism, or other discriminatory behavior on the part of management. At the same time, seniority-based promotion appeals to management because it has the potential to reduce turnover and foster loyalty within the workforce. On the other hand, using seniority as a basis for promotions and other benefits has the disadvantage of rewarding employees who simply show up for work on a more-or-less regular basis, not necessarily doing anything above and beyond the call of duty.

Promotion on the basis of merit appeals to workers' sense of fairness by recognizing their contributions to the success of their organization. For employers, promotion on the basis of merit is seen as an important tool for motivating employees to do more than the minimum. But merit-based promotion runs up against a formidable problem: how do you define "merit"? Most jobs have a number of discrete components; college professors, for example, may be expected to teach, advise students, conduct research, write books and journal articles, and participate in the governance of their institutions. These multiple occupational roles make it impossible to evaluate "merit" on the basis of a single criterion. But given the numerous aspects of a single job, how much weight should be assigned to each of them? This is a difficult task for those honestly attempting to assess the merit of individual employees, as well as for the employees themselves, who have to decide how to apportion finite amounts of time and energy to the multiple tasks expected of them.

Another difficulty in assessing individual merit lies in the collective nature of many jobs, which makes it hard to evaluate the contributions of each member. This is particularly apparent in team sports, such as football. A quarterback may be judged on how many passes he completes, but this statistic will be heavily influenced by the ability of the offensive line to protect him and of his receivers to elude defenders and hang on to the ball after it has been delivered. Most jobs do not require the precise teamwork necessary for success on the football field, but good workmates can make a mediocre employee look outstanding, while poor ones can make an outstanding employee look incompetent.

Promotion criteria based on either seniority or merit can pose special problems for minorities and women. Promotion on the basis of seniority would seem to eliminate prejudiced decisions, but because it rewards workers with a history of stable employment with one firm, it is likely to benefit white males more than women or members of minority groups, who tend to have shorter job tenures. Promotion on the basis of merit avoids this problem, but it, too, contains a number of pitfalls. Because defining merit is not a straightforward process, the assessment of job performance will always have a subjective element, and the process may reflect the prejudices and assumptions of the person doing the assessing. And as just noted, for employees under review, job success often depends on the skills, efforts, and, above all, the cooperation of coworkers. Due to lingering prejudices, women and minority group members may have more problems in securing the help and cooperation of fellow employees, resulting in poor evaluations of their job performance through little or no fault of their own.

The enduring significance of prejudice and discriminatory behavior, much of it unconscious, has been traced out by Rosabeth Moss Kanter in her influential book, *Men and Women of the Corporation*.[34] Based on extensive fieldwork at a single firm, Kanter's study revealed that the chances of moving to a higher position within the firm were affected by the race, ethnicity, and gender of the candidates up for promotion. Not all of this was the result of blatantly prejudicial attitudes. Rather, it often was a reflection of the uncertainties faced by managers and the insecurities these uncertainties engendered. In most enterprises, the chances for personal and organizational success are strongly influenced by a wide range of uncertainties—the course of technological change, the actions of clients and competitors, the vagaries of human attitudes and behavior, and changes in the surrounding society and culture. As one organizational analyst summarized the situation faced by managers, "Uncertainty appears as the fundamental problem for complex organizations, and coping with uncertainty [is] the essence of the administrative process."[35]

Most of these uncertainties cannot be resolved by individual managers; they are an inescapable part of the environment in which managers operate. Under these circumstances, managers try to gain a measure of control (or at least the illusion of it) by reducing those uncertainties over which they have some influence. The most important of these involve their subordinates. Most upper-level managers know that a great deal is riding on the actions of lower-level workers. At the same time, unlike many of the forces that affect an organization, the selection and promotion of underlings is one thing over which managers have considerable control. According to Kanter, many managers seek to reduce uncertainty by hiring and promoting workers who most closely resemble themselves.

The term Kanter uses to describe this process is *homosocial reproduction*. The first word of the term is derived from *homo,* meaning "the same," and "social," in the sense of social background. *Reproduction* here means the processes through which managers find and develop people to serve under them and perhaps take their places in the future. Through homosocial reproduction, the employees who are most likely to be favored are the ones most resembling their bosses in terms of race, ethnicity, gender, religion, and social class. Managers may also tend to look more favorably on subordinates who went to the same college as they did or belong to the same clubs. Much of this discrimination may be unconscious, but the result is the same: blocked opportunities for those with the "wrong" background, especially women and racial and ethnic minorities.

Legal Remedies for Discrimination and Occupational Segregation

Until the mid-1960s, any restraints on the hiring practices of employers were the responsibility of the individual states that had passed antidiscriminatory legislation. Involvement of the federal government began with the passage of the Civil Rights Act of 1964. In regard to hiring practices, Section 703 of Title VII declared it unlawful for an employer "to fail or refuse to hire or discharge any individual" on the basis of "such individual's race, color, religion, sex, or national origin." Similar provisions also applied to employment agencies, and they also enjoined labor unions from engaging in this sort of discrimination.[36] Inclusion of labor unions in the act was significant because, in many states, union membership was required for employment in certain industries and occupations, and as we have seen, labor unions sometimes engaged in discriminatory behavior.

The enactment and enforcement of antidiscrimination legislation have not transformed the workplace. As we have seen, substantial differences can be found in employment rates of different racial and ethnic groups, and many occupations continue to be segregated according to gender. One remedy that has been applied to counter these disparities is *affirmative action.* The underlying justification for affirmative action is that past discrimination has resulted in serious inequalities in American society and that continuing with the status quo will not remedy the situation. Instead, specific policies have to be enacted in order to right past wrongs and expand employment and educational opportunities for women and minorities.

It is hard to take issue with affirmative action when its goals are stated in such general terms. The difficulties come with the formulation and implementation of the specific policies intended to achieve these goals. According to one interpretation, affirmative action policies should be enacted in order to expand the ability of women and minorities to apply for the educational opportunities they will make good use of, as well as for the jobs they are capable of doing. As we have seen, many, if not most, jobs are filled through the use of personal networks. Since women and members of minority groups tend to have fewer personal connections to sources of potential jobs, legally mandated efforts to ensure that an applicant pool contains women, Latinos, Asian Americans, and African Americans may significantly improve their employment prospects.

A more stringent interpretation of affirmative action holds that simply widening access to jobs and educational opportunities will not adequately address the problems engendered by past discrimination. According to this perspective, realizing the intentions of affirmative action necessitates the imposition of quotas to guarantee the placement of minorities and women into jobs where they are statistically underrepresented. This is an extreme interpretation of affirmative action, and most programs specifically bar the use of quotas.

Another approach to affirmative action also holds that simply enlarging the applicant pool to include more women and minorities will not substantially change hiring practices. But instead of calling for quotas, this version of affirmative action favors educational and training programs aimed at developing skills that improve employment and promotion prospects for minorities and women or help minority students succeed in postsecondary education. In some cases, this may mean job-specific training, but in many cases, the primary need is to instill the kinds of skills that are essential for finding a decent job, such as filling out an application and making the best of a job interview, along with developing the aforementioned "soft skills" essential for landing many jobs in the service sector.

The circumstances that have produced the inequalities and iniquities of today's occupational structure have developed over the course of decades, if not centuries, and they will not likely be remedied in a short space of time. It also has to be recognized that efforts to improve the occupational prospects of women and minorities will sometimes be perceived as being in collision with the interests, rights, and perquisites of individuals who occupy favorable niches in the occupational structure. At the same time, modern societies have the great advantage of having escaped the zero-sum trap described in Chapter 3. Put less abstractly, this means that the gains of one group or individual will not necessarily produce matching losses for others. Rather, it is possible to play a positive-sum game, one in which a larger share of the population has the opportunity to develop and use its talents and skills and, in so doing, make greater contributions to the economy and society that end up benefiting everyone.

Comparable Worth Policies for the Workplace _____

While affirmative action has been implemented in a variety of workplaces, another initiative, the effort to pass "comparable worth" legislation, has failed to gain much traction. The idea underlying comparable worth is that gender-based occupational segregation should not result in unequal pay for women and men. Even though two jobs, one male dominated and the other female dominated, may entail different kinds of work, many of their essential features—such as the extent of training needed, job-related experience, mental and physical stress, and workplace responsibilities—can be compared through the use of standardized criteria. These features can even be assigned numerical values, and total scores can then be used in order to compare one job with another. Taken to the logical conclusion of the process, these scores could be multiplied by a dollar figure in order to determine a wage or salary.[37]

Remuneration according to comparable worth has been proposed regularly in state and national legislatures and has been implemented in a few instances for state and local government employees, but the chances of it being applied on a nationwide scale are slim. Although it may appear to be fairer than prevailing procedures, the initiation of a comparable worth program faces daunting economic and political obstacles. As a politically administered system, it stands in opposition to the setting of wages and salaries through the operation of market forces. Advocates of comparable worth programs counter that the importance of the market in the setting of wages and salaries is overrated; many organizations, both public and private, have wage and salary scales that are only loosely connected to the interaction of supply and demand. In regard to the top end of the scale, it would be hard to argue that the astronomical increase in the remuneration of top executives that has taken place in recent years reflects fundamental changes in the market for CEOs and other top executives. At the lower end of the scale, wages and salaries are often set by negotiations involving unions and, at the lowest end, by minimum-wage laws. In none of these cases is the market the sole or even the primary determinant of wage levels.

To be sure, selecting the elements of a job on which to base evaluations is a difficult and potentially contentious task, as just noted in the discussion of merit and its assessment. Can employees' skills and responsibilities be codified in such a way that numerical scores can be assigned to them? Should education and training be evaluated simply in terms of years of formal instruction, or should other aspects of education, such as the difficulty of an educational program, be taken into account? And how much weight should be given to each component relative to other components? These issues are not insoluble, but effectively addressing them requires a lot of negotiation involving different groups of employees and their bosses, and achieving consensus is certainly not easy. At this point, the difficulties of job evaluation and a decentralized, one-organization-at-a-time approach have blocked the large-scale adoption of comparable worth policies and programs.[38]

Above all, the design and implementation of an effective comparable worth policy would require a broad-based agreement that it is right and proper to equalize pay rates for employees with similar skills, responsibilities, years of training, and so on. A commitment of this sort would likely have to be preceded by a fair amount of prodding from employees who would likely benefit from a comparable worth policy, most of them women, while their efforts would surely meet with stiff resistance from other employees, most of them men. Most important, movement in this direction needs strong support from elected officials and other governmental actors. Although a few court cases have validated the use of comparable worth in determining remuneration, there has been little indication in recent years that broad-based political support will emerge anytime in the near future.

On several occasions, this chapter has noted the difficulties encountered by workers, women especially, as they try to meet their dual responsibilities as employees and members of a family. A combination of technological and organizational changes has made this situation a bit less difficult, but the inherent conflict between workplace and home is far from being resolved. In the next chapter, we will describe and analyze the struggle of many men and women to reconcile the demands of their jobs with the responsibilities and pleasures of being spouses and parents. Note will also be taken of government and private-sector programs aimed at alleviating some of these conflicts.

FOR DISCUSSION

1. Have you or anyone you know been a victim of discrimination in regard to hiring, pay, or advancement? How can you be sure that discrimination was operating and not some other factor, such as qualifications or on-the-job performance?

2. Why has the work done by women often been assumed to be of less importance than the work done by men? Is it due to the prevalence of men's ideas about the value of individual occupations, or have other forces been involved? Are these attitudes likely to change in the near future?

3. Would you prefer to work for an organization that promoted on the basis of seniority or merit? Why?

4. Affirmative action programs often have been criticized as constituting "reverse discrimination." Is this a fair characterization? Is the implementation of affirmative action necessarily a zero-sum game, or can it be beneficial to minorities and nonminorities alike?

5. The enactment of comparable worth policies has been proffered as a way to narrow gender-based wage and salary disparities. What is the likelihood of such policies being put into practice? What sorts of problems might arise in attempting to enact and implement comparable worth policies?

Notes

1. Statistics for women: U.S. Department of Labor, Women's Bureau, "Quick Stats on Women's Labor, 2009," http://www.dol.gov/wb/stats/main.htm (accessed December 20, 2010). For the other groups, percentages have been calculated from U.S. Census Bureau, *The 2011 Statistical Abstract*, "Table 585: Civilian Labor Force and Participation Rates With Projections 1980 to 2018," http://www.census.gov/compendia/statab/2011/tables/11s0585.pdf (accessed May 10, 2011).

2. William Julius Wilson, *When Work Disappears* (New York: Knopf, 1996).

3. Philip Moss and Charles Tilly, *Stories Employers Tell: Race, Skill, and Hiring in America* (New York: Russell Sage Foundation, 2001), 156–208.

4. Deirdre A. Royster, *Race and the Invisible Hand: How White Networks Exclude Black Men From Blue-Collar Jobs* (Berkeley: University of California Press, 2003); William J. Wilson, *The Truly Disadvantaged: The Inner City, the Underclass, and Public Policy* (Chicago: University of Chicago Press, 1987).

5. U.S. Bureau of Labor Statistics, "Table E-16: Unemployment Rates by Age, Sex, Race, and Hispanic or Latino Ethnicity," http://www.bls.gov/web/empsit/cpseed16.pdf (accessed May 10, 2011).

6. James Heckman and Peter Siegelman, "The Urban Institute Audit Studies: Their Methods and Findings," in *Clear and Convincing Evidence*, eds. Michael Fix and Raymond Struyk (Washington, DC: Urban Institute, 1992), Table 5.1.

7. U.S. Census Bureau, *The 2010 Statistical Abstract*, "Table 224: Educational Attainment by Race and Hispanic Origin: 1970 to 2008," http://www.census.gov/compendia/statab/2010/tables/10s0224.pdf (accessed December 20, 2010).

8. Moss and Tilly, *Stories Employers Tell*, 254.

9. Robert Cherry, *Who Gets the Good Jobs? Combating Race and Gender Disparities* (New Brunswick, NJ: Rutgers University Press, 2001), 68.

10. Herbert Hill, "The Problem of Race in American Labor History," *Reviews in American History* 24, no. 2 (June 1996): 195.

11. On the racial typing of domestic workers, see Judith Rollins, *Between Women: Domestics and Their Employers* (Philadelphia: Temple University Press, 1985).

12. Phyllis Moen and Patricia Roehling, *The Career Mystique: Cracks in the American Dream* (Lanham, MD: Rowman & Littlefield, 2005), 13–4. The 2010 figures are from U.S. Department of Labor, Bureau of Labor Statistics, "Table A-1: Employment Status of the Civilian Population by Sex and Age," http://www.bls.gov/news.release/empsit.t01.htm (accessed December 21, 2010).

13. Barbara Reskin and Irene Padavik, *Women and Men at Work* (Thousand Oaks, CA: Sage, 1994), 22–3.

14. Ibid., 146.

15. Institute for Women's Policy Research, "The Gender Wage Gap by Occupation" (April 2010), http://www.Iwpr.org/pdf/c350a.pdf (accessed December 21, 2010), 2.

16. Reskin and Padavik, *Women and Men at Work*, 53–4. Although nearly 20 years have elapsed, the list of the top 10 women's jobs that appears in this source and the previous reference are quite similar. The 2010 list added "accountants and auditors" and eliminated "bookkeeper, accounting clerk," "waitress," and "salaried sales supervisor, proprietor." Although some of the occupational titles have changed, a fair amount of overlap is evident.

17. David Cotter, Joan Hermson, and Reeve Vanneman, "Gender and Inequality at Work," in *Working in America: Continuity, Conflict, and Change,* 3rd ed., ed. Amy Wharton (New York: McGraw-Hill, 2006), 191.

18. Richard Swedberg, *Principles of Economic Sociology* (Princeton, NJ: Princeton University Press, 2003), 277.

19. Cherry, *Who Gets the Good Jobs?*, 95–7.

20. In fiscal year 2008, the U.S. Equal Employment Opportunity Commission received 28,372 charges of sex-based discrimination. During that period, the commission resolved 24,018 sex discrimination charges. Allegations of sex-based discrimination were not upheld in the majority of these cases, but some were affirmed, resulting in $109.3 million in monetary benefits for aggrieved parties, not including monetary benefits obtained through litigation. U.S. Equal Opportunity Commission, "Sex-Based Charges, FY 1997-2008," http://archive.eeoc.gov/stats/sex.html (accessed May 10, 2011).

21. Barbara Reskin and Heidi Hartman, *Women's Work, Men's Work: Occupational Segregation on the Job* (Washington, DC: National Academy Press, 1986), 71–2.

22. 22. In 2008–9, women composed 48.8 percent of medical school graduates: Association of American Medical Colleges, "Women in Academic Medicine: Statistics and Benchmarking Report" https://www.aamc.org/download/53502/data/wimstatisticsreport2009.pdf. In 2010, women received 45.9 percent of the law degrees awarded: "The Careerist: Women at Law Schools Decline," In 2010, 44 percent of the students enrolled in MBA programs were women: Jenna Goudreau and Ruchika Tulshyan, "Why More Women Are Heading To Business School," *Forbes,* April 16, 2010, http://www.forbes.com/2010/04/16/mba-women-business-school-forbes-woman-leadership-education.html. (Accessed December 21, 2010.)

23. U.S. Census Bureau, *The 2011 Statistical Abstract,* "Table 696: Money Income of Families; Median Income by Race and Hispanic Origin in Current and Constant (2008) Dollars: 1990 to 2008," http://www.census.gov/compendia/statab/2011/tables/11s0696.pdf (accessed May 10, 2011).

24. U.S. Department of Labor, Bureau of Labor Statistics, "Highlights of Women's Earnings in 2009" (June 2010), http://www.bls.gov/cps/cpswom2009.pdf (accessed December 21, 2010).

25. Reskin and Padavik, *Women and Men at Work*, 110–1.

26. Barbara F. Reskin and Patricia A. Roos, *Job Queues and Gender Queues: Explaining Women's Inroads Into Male Occupations* (Philadelphia: Temple University Press, 1990), 80–2.

27. Cotter et al., "Gender and Inequality at Work," 199.

28. Ibid., 201.

29. Moen and Roehling, *Career Mystique*, 14.

30. Andrew Hacker, *Money: Who Has How Much and Why* (New York: Simon & Schuster, 1997), 150–1.

31. Leslie McCall, *Complex Inequality: Gender, Class, and Race in the New Economy* (New York: Routledge, 2001), 123.

32. Ibid., 186.

33. It is important to keep in mind that these statements apply to the national labor force; there can be considerable deviations from general trends within regional labor markets. See McCall, *Complex Inequality*, 123, 126.

34. Rosabeth Moss Kanter, *Men and Women of the Corporation* (New York: Basic, 1977).

35. James D. Thompson, *Organizations in Action* (New York: McGraw-Hill, 1967), 159. Quoted in Kanter, *Men and Women*, 48.

36. The full text of the Act is available at http://www.eeoc.gov/laws/statutes/titlevii.cfm.

37. Hacker, *Money*, 219–21.

38. Margaret Hallock, "Pay Equity: Did It Work?" in *Squaring Up: Policy Strategies to Raise Women's Incomes in the United States,* ed. Mary C. King (Ann Arbor: University of Michigan Press, 2001).

14 Work Roles and Life Roles

Most adults who have not retired spend more of their waking hours working than doing anything else. In addition to absorbing a large amount of our time, work affects many other parts of our lives. Work can be a thoroughly positive experience, even an essential part of a satisfying life, but it can also be a source of considerable stress and unhappiness when it crowds out family life and other activities. Although the time spent working is not likely to substantially decline in the years to come, it is possible to diminish or even eliminate some of the conflicts between our working lives and the other roles and activities that make up the rest of our lives. To some extent, these accommodations will be based on individual decisions. Others, however, will require changes in the terms of employment, along with greater commitments by employers and governments to the support of working families.

The Separation of Work and Residence

Commuting is a way of life for most workers, whose working day starts well before they arrive at the workplace and doesn't end until they return home. For many people, work-related stress begins to set in as they get into their cars or board the buses, trains, or subways that take them to their jobs. In the evenings, the process is repeated, often adding to the stresses that have accumulated during the working day.

Although the intimate connection between working and commuting seems to be the normal state of affairs, it is in fact a recent phenomenon in historical terms. As we have seen, for most of human existence, workplaces and residences were one and the same. Gatherers and hunters lived in the midst of the territories that were the source of their sustenance, and when these were played out, they shifted their camps to take advantage of better opportunities for obtaining food. The invention of agriculture maintained the link between residence and workplace, with people living in towns and villages adjacent to the fields they cultivated.

Urbanization and industrialization at first did not change the close proximity of home and workplace. Cities were dense and compact, which allowed
most residents to walk to their place of employment. Commuting over relatively long distances was not possible until the second half of the 19th century, when the development of public transportation systems allowed people
to live considerable distances from their places of work. Initially, public
transit meant horse-drawn omnibuses and streetcars, along with steam-
powered railroads. During the 1880s, the speed and comfort of commuting
were greatly enhanced as cities around the world began to install electric
trolley lines, and toward the end of the century, large metropolises were
engaged in the monumental task of building extensive elevated railroad and
subway networks.

Railroads, trolleys, subways, and buses were the chief means of transportation for workers commuting from increasingly far-flung suburbs until the
1920s, when the private automobile became the vehicle of choice for growing
numbers of commuters. Encouraged by government policies such as subsidized loans for new homes in suburban developments and massive highway
construction programs, automobile-based commuting became a way of life
for the majority of American workers in the years following World War II, a
pattern replicated in many European countries a decade or two later.

Reliance on the automobile has allowed vast numbers of people to reside
in low-density communities far from their places of work, which may not be
desirable places to live. But suburban lifestyles also incur costs for individuals
and for society as a whole. Suburban residential developments sprawl over
large tracts of land, consuming space and energy, while automobile-based
commuting consumes more energy and is a major cause of air pollution.

Commuting allows working men and women to live in communities of
their choice, or at least in areas that provide affordable housing, but it also
absorbs a fair amount of time. According to the U.S. Census Bureau, the daily
commute absorbs 24.3 minutes of an average American's day, which comes
out to more than 100 hours a year. The residents of many big cities spend
considerably more time commuting either by car or public transit—38.3
minutes for New Yorkers, 33.2 minutes for Chicagoans, and 29.0 minutes for
residents of Los Angeles.[1] Many suburban residents exceed the national average by a considerable margin, spending 90 minutes or more getting to and
from work in extreme cases.[2]

Working Hours

The many hours spent commuting have contributed to a prevalent concern
over the use and management of time. One of the most commonly discussed
issues regarding work, both among academic researchers and in the popular
media, has centered on the amount of time we devote to our jobs. This concern is reflected in the everyday experiences of millions of men and women
who acutely feel the pressures of what has been called the "time bind," a

sense that the temporal demands of their jobs, homes, and families have increased to the point that they seem overwhelming.[3]

This apparent increase in the amount of time devoted to paid employment represents a reversal of a prior historical trend of gradual reductions in the time devoted to work. In the 1950s, some observers even worried that the productivity improvements wrought by labor-saving technologies were reducing the need for work to the point that, in the coming years, many people would have little or nothing to do. Idleness, not overwork, was seen as the emerging problem of the near future, and substantial adjustments were anticipated in order to accommodate the impending emergence of the "leisure society."

They needn't have worried. In the early years of the 21st century, American workers were anything but idle; it even seemed that they were putting in more hours at work than they had a couple of decades earlier. The plight of "the overworked American" came into focus with the publication of Juliet Schor's book of the same name.[4] According to Schor, although productivity grew after World War II with few interruptions, the average number of working hours actually increased from the early 1970s onward. According to Schor's calculations, far from having a dangerous surfeit of leisure time, American workers had only 17 free hours each week in 1988, a sharp drop from the 26 hours they had in 1973.[5] Americans had less time for leisure activities because working hours had increased to the point that workers in 1987 were doing the equivalent of an extra month's work each year when compared with workers in the late 1960s. When broken down according to gender, men were working an additional 98 hours per year, and women were averaging 305 extra hours per year.[6] These extra hours on the job resulted from longer working days, moonlighting (i.e., holding more than one job), having fewer days of vacation time, and taking fewer days of sick leave.

Although some workers may have been happy to extend their time on the job to earn more money or improve their career prospects, Schor attributed most of the expansion of work time to the motivations and actions of the organizations that employed these workers. Employers, of course, have always wanted to get as much work as possible out of their workers, but the circumstances of the past few decades have strengthened employers' desire to demand longer working hours while, at the same time, increasing their power to do so. In regard to the latter, employers were able to take advantage of the fact that many workers were willing to work long and hard because economic changes had widened the gap between well-paying jobs and ones that paid poorly. Workers were aware of this situation and knew there was little likelihood of getting a job that paid as well as the ones they currently held. Under these circumstances, they agreed to work extra hours for no extra pay.[7] At the same time, the increasing share of compensation taken by fringe benefits such as health insurance and pension plans motivated employers to increase the number of hours put in by their employees, because these benefits were awarded on a per-worker basis rather than a per-hour basis. It, therefore, made good business sense to have employees already on board to work more hours rather than hiring new workers and assuming greater benefit costs. This situation held even more strongly for salaried workers. Since they were not paid by the hour, it was to the advantage of their employers to get them to work more hours and avoid the need to take on new employees.

While employers were determined to extract more hours of work, many employees seemed to have accepted or even embraced a culture of overwork. In unionized firms and industries, workers' representatives appeared to have lost interest in reducing the time spent at work, in clear contrast to times past, when attaining an 8-hour day was a key goal of the labor movement. This lack of interest may have reflected economic realities. As we have seen, compensation for the majority of workers stagnated and even declined from the mid-1970s onward, making it necessary for many employees to put in more hours just to maintain existing standards of living. And not everyone has been content simply to maintain their present position. Although people today have levels of material consumption vastly greater than in times past (and much higher than found in most of the world today), satisfaction has remained elusive. What seems to matter is not one's present standard of living but the desire to attain the goods and services that are just out of reach. As critics of contemporary American society have noted, this acquisitive spirit has been continually fueled by the media, both through advertisements and the presentation of lifestyles that bear little resemblance to the everyday realities most people experience. Until the Great Recession and its accompanying sharp drop in consumer borrowing, the widespread availability of credit allowed consumers to acquire goods and services in excess of their earning power, and when reality intruded and the bills came due, there may have been no recourse other than to put in more hours or take on an additional job.

Schor's depiction of excessive work propelled by increasing employer demands and what she called "the insidious cycle of work-and-spend" struck a resonant chord with many harried men and women, but the data and analysis presented in *The Overworked American* have not gone unchallenged. Schor correctly noted that, on average, employees were working more hours over the course of a year when compared with workers in the 1950s and 1960s, but the length of the average workweek did not change much in the years that followed the publication of her book.[8] In fact, the Great Recession has resulted in a decline in the average number of hours worked, although not to a large degree. According to statistics compiled by the U.S. Census Bureau for the year 2009, the average workweek was 40.9 hours for men and 35.7 hours for women.[9]

Trying to discern the long-term trend in working hours is a difficult exercise. But to make sense of it all, it is necessary to take note of how the measurements are taken, what is measured, and whose work is measured. In regard to the first, research into the working hours of Americans has, for the most part, been based on two different sources of data. One is the Current Population Survey (CPS) conducted by the U.S. Census Bureau. This survey, which is administered on a weekly basis to a random sample of 60,000 Americans, asks a number of questions about individual activities, including the hours worked during the previous week. The other major source of information on time spent working is compiled from time diaries administered by the Survey Research Center of the University of Michigan and the University of Maryland. Unlike the CPS surveys, these diaries focus solely on how time is spent over a 24-hour period. According to the researchers who base their studies on this source, the data derived from the diaries are less vulnerable to defective memories, tendencies of respondents to give what they think are the "right" answers, and understandable confusion by respondents regarding the inclusion of time spent commuting, lunch and coffee breaks, and work done at home. CPS data also may be skewed upward by the stresses felt by people trying to balance work and family life, a topic that will be explored below. It is also possible that different segments of the working population will differ in their assessments of time spent at work—some underestimating the hours they work, others overestimating them. These differences may result from variations in the relative variability of work schedules, along with the intensity of the work they do, the need to meet rigid deadlines, and other sources of on-the-job stress.[10]

Although different measures have produced different results, some of these results converge when subjected to further examination. When Jerry Jacobs analyzed self-reports such as the ones contained in the CPS, along with time diary results, he found that much of the divergence was the result of random measurement errors. When these were taken into account, the two different sources of data about working hours were generally in agreement.[11] Jacobs also found that, contrary to what some researchers had hypothesized, the kinds of jobs people held did not affect their reported working hours, nor was there an exaggeration of working hours by employees who were experiencing high levels of conflict between the responsibilities of work and home. In similar fashion, demographic variables such as age, marital status, race, and ethnicity did not introduce any significant biases in reported working times. In sum, self-reports, which indicated an average workweek of 42.2 hours, provided a reasonably accurate indication of the average number of hours Americans, both men and women, spent at work each week in 1997.

Contradictory assessments of the time spent working also have resulted from a failure to distinguish changes in average *weekly* working hours from average *annual* working hours. Although there has been only a modest upward movement in the former, there is strong evidence that, until the Great Recession cut into the number of hours worked, the average American worker was putting in more hours at work over the course of a year when compared with workers in the 1960s and early 1970s. The explanation for this brings us to the second and third reasons for the misunderstandings and disagreements concerning the time spent at work. The problem lies with data that describe "the average American worker," as an individual who exists only in a statistical sense. To come to a more sophisticated understanding of work trends, it is necessary to tease out all the separate categories that have been rolled into a single score labeled "the average."

Almost every aspect of work has a gender component, and the work situations of men and women contain significant differences. As we have just seen, women on average put in fewer hours on the job than men do. But more important than this "snapshot" statistic is that the working hours of women have been steadily moving upward, in contrast to the relative stability of men's working hours. Of particular importance is the fact that women's labor force participation has become less episodic than in times past; that is, more women have been working year-round. The upward trend in the number of hours worked per year noted by Schor was mostly due to women employees putting in more hours annually because they worked more weeks per year, but not significantly more hours per week.[12]

While gender is an important source of differences in average working hours, it is not the only one. As with the distribution of income, recent years have seen a widening gap in the amount of time spent working by different segments of the labor force.[13] These differences, in turn, reflect some key social and occupational groupings. One of them is age. In both relative and absolute terms, the longest hours are put in by workers between the ages of 25 and 55. The age distribution of a population will, therefore, affect average working hours, and in fact, some of the increase in time spent at work that began in the 1970s can be attributed to the large cohort of baby boomers that were beginning to enter the full-time labor force.

The time people spend on the job also reflects the kind of work they do. Employees in the broad occupational categories of managers, salespeople, and professionals work longer hours, on average, than skilled blue-collar workers, operators, and laborers do.[14] As might be expected, longer working hours are associated with higher wages and salaries, but this is not primarily due to workers getting paid more because they work more hours. Rather, these greater rates of remuneration reflect the fact that the longest working days tend to be found in occupations that command relatively high salaries. Moreover, since wages and salaries are closely tied to educational accomplishments, well-educated workers may be expected to put in more hours at work than workers with less education do. This is exactly what the data show; nearly 40 percent of men with 4 or more years of college work 50 hours a week or more, while only 12 percent of men with less than a high school education do so. For women, the contrast is even sharper, as nearly 20 percent of college-educated women work 50 hours or more, while only 5 percent of women lacking a high school diploma work this many hours.[15]

Some of these differences can be attributed to the more demanding jobs held by well-educated workers, but they also reflect less secure employment situations encountered by workers with lower educational achievements. It is not usually by choice that less-educated workers work fewer hours than well-educated ones. The significant differences between the employment situations of these two groups are underscored by surveys that show a majority of high school dropouts expressing a desire to work more hours, while workers with undergraduate and graduate degrees would prefer to work fewer hours.[16]

Although generalizations about the "overworked American" have been overstated and sometimes fail to adequately take into account key social changes, such as the maturation of the baby-boomer generation and greater labor force participation by women, it is still evident that Americans put in considerably longer working hours than workers in other industrialized countries do. Although the Japanese have been thought to work the longest hours (and even have a term, *karoshi,* that denotes sudden death from overwork), according to some statistical reckonings, they now put in fewer annual hours on average than Americans do.[17] Employees in European countries spend considerably less time at work, and several countries even mandate workweeks of fewer than 40 hours. A particularly striking difference between the United States and Europe appears in the number of vacation days taken by workers. While American workers take an annual average of 14 days of vacation, Italians get 42 days off, and French and Germans are not far behind at 37 and 35, respectively. Even Japanese and Korean workers are able to take 25 days of vacation, although many end up taking fewer.[18]

Photo 14.1   Multitasking in the home office

SOURCE: ©CORBIS.

The above discussion has centered on data that can easily be quantified, such as the average number of working hours per week. But these units give us only a rough idea of the time devoted to work. For many men and women, time away from the workplace is not necessarily time away from work. Many employees and self-employed workers routinely take work home with them, and a significant portion of evenings and weekends may be devoted to work. This blurring of home and workplace has been reinforced by the rapid development of communication technologies in recent years. Many people now find themselves tethered to "electronic leashes" as cell phones, faxes, and e-mail keep them closely connected to their jobs. Even a vacation in a remote part of the world may be interrupted by an e-mail message that requires an immediate response. At the same time, however, being at a workplace is not necessarily the same thing as doing productive work. Anyone who has been employed knows that a fair amount of the working day may be taken up with socializing with coworkers, long coffee and lunch breaks, personal telephone calls, and other nonwork activities. It is not certain whether these activities have increased in frequency in recent years, but it can at least be hypothesized that the availability of the Internet and other computer-based diversions has diminished the time spent doing actual work. Employers certainly have recognized this possibility; according to a survey conducted by the American Management Association, more than 80 percent of firms have written policies that regulate Internet use while on the job. More than 75 percent monitor web surfing, and nearly two-thirds block sites that are deemed inappropriate.[19]

Paid Work and Housework

Although the time spent at work has not increased substantially in recent years, it is also true that, in the words of Barry Bluestone and Stephen Rose, "If individuals are not more overworked than before, families certainly are."[20] The large-scale entrance of women into the labor force in recent decades has rendered obsolete the traditional family arrangement of a working father and stay-at-home mother.[21] This change has brought financial and psychological benefits, but it also has been a significant source of work- and family-related stress.

It bears repeating here that "entrance into the labor force" is not synonymous with being a worker. Women have always worked, but for the majority, work meant employment in the home rather than earning a wage or salary. But with the spread of industry in the late 18th and 19th centuries, large numbers of girls and women began to be hired as operatives in textile mills, and even larger numbers were employed as domestic servants. Industrialization did not put an end to household-based manufacture. Although it was being crowded out by factory production, home-based manufacture continued to employ large numbers of women for the production of textiles and clothing.[22] The great majority of these workers were single—both widows and young, unmarried women.[23] Outside manufacturing, employers of domestic servants preferred to hire single women who did not have families that might distract them from their work. Married women did find wage employment, but it tended to be in the least industrialized sectors of the economy, notably farm labor and apparel production.[24] The pattern of women's employment changed toward the end of the 19th century with the expansion of clerical work, teaching, and shop assistant work, paralleled by a shift away from traditional sources of employment such as textiles and domestic service.[25] For many women, paid work was something to be done prior to getting married and perhaps during a later stage of marriage when child-care responsibilities had subsided. As noted earlier, this was not always by choice; many employers required that their female staff remain unmarried.

In both the United States and Europe, two world wars greatly expanded women's employment opportunities. At both times, the cessation of hostilities was accompanied by a drop in female labor force participation, but it lasted for only a short time in the years that immediately followed World War II, and by 1965, the percentage of women in the labor force was greater than it had been in 1945.[26] A variety of economic, demographic, and cultural changes resulted in increasing numbers of women joining the labor force. The continued expansion of the service sector, in both relative and absolute terms, absorbed large numbers of women who found jobs as nurses, teachers, administrators, secretaries, and retail clerks. By the late 1950s, the postwar baby boom had peaked, and family sizes trended downward, both a cause and effect of women's employment outside the home. Another important stimulus to women engaging in paid work was the rise of a consumer society, in which an ever-increasing number of goods were aggressively marketed, first through the medium of radio and print media and then through television's pervasive influence.

For many women, participation in the wage-earning labor force means, in effect, that they hold two jobs. In addition to putting in a full day of work at an office, shop, or factory, they also have to work what Arlie Hochschild has called "the second shift," serving as cooks, housekeepers, and child-care providers.[27] By the mid-1990s, women with full-time employment were estimated to be spending 19.4 hours per week on housework (for men, the figure was 10.4 hours).[28]

Studies of the number of hours taken up by women's domestic duties showed little variation for much of the 20th century.[29] In recent years, however, the situation has changed, with employed women spending about two-thirds as much time on housework and child care as do women without a paying job.[30] In general, it has been reckoned that each hour a woman spends doing paid work reduces the amount of housework she does by almost a half-hour.[31]

Although women continue to do the bulk of household chores, the ratio of housework done by men to that done by women has been moving in women's favor. In 1965, women did 6 times as much housework as men; 30 years later, they were doing only 1.8 times as much.[32] Some of this can be attributed to men doing more household chores, but most of the reduction comes from women doing less housework, as many women have abandoned the notion that a home should be so clean that "you could eat off the floor."[33]

Although men have been taking on more domestic tasks, a marked degree of gender-based segregation still exists in the allocation of household work. Women do most of the cooking, cleaning, laundry, and child care, while men are involved with home repairs, yardwork, and automobile maintenance. However it is allocated, housework still takes up a fair amount of time, even though most homes are equipped with a multitude of labor-saving devices. Not only are appliances such as stoves, refrigerators, electric irons, and vacuum cleaners virtually universal, innovations such as wash-and-wear fabrics, microwavable meals, and easily cleaned surfaces have substantially reduced the amount of time required for essential household tasks. But alongside labor-saving devices have come higher expectations. Family members assume they will always be furnished with clean clothes; underwear worn for more than one day and a slightly soiled shirt are simply unacceptable. Meals are supposed to be varied, appetizing, and of the highest nutritional standards; stews and other one-pot meals are not supposed to be regular fare in a modern household. Child care has become more than simply maintaining a safe environment; it is now deemed necessary to provide intellectual stimulation, enhance creativity, and nurture self-esteem if a child has any chance of success in an intensely competitive world. Finally, family and household responsibilities often require hours of driving every week. Note already has been taken of the time spent commuting to and from work; to this can be added many more hours spent behind the wheel in the course of shopping, running errands, and driving children to an endless variety of activities.

Photo 14.2 Conflicts over the allocation of domestic chores have a long history, as shown in the 1926 film *Just Another Blonde*.

SOURCE: The Granger Collection, New York.

Although they have lifted many of the burdens of housework, technological advances have tended to shift responsibilities from men to women. Prior to the widespread use of electric and gas stoves, women would expend a great deal of effort cooking on wood stoves, but men were expected to cut and haul wood and remove ashes at regular intervals. For the most part, men had the onerous chore of beating carpets at least once a year, a task made obsolete by the vacuum cleaner, which is used primarily by women. Indoor plumbing is an undoubted boon, but bathrooms need regular cleaning—once again, a task done primarily by women.[34]

Couples, Families, and Careers

In the majority of American families, both husband and wife hold down paying jobs. Moreover, for couples, the number of hours worked has trended upward in recent decades. In 1970, husband–wife couples averaged a total of 52.5 hours a week at work; 30 years later, the figure stood at 63.1 hours.[35] The number of couples putting in long hours at work also rose substantially, especially for husbands and wives without children. In 1970, 9.3 percent of these couples worked a combined hundred hours a week or more; by 2000, the percentage had climbed to 17.5. For couples with children, the rise was more modest, from 8.2 percent of couples to 12.2 percent over the same period.[36]

In most cases, dual-earner families enjoy higher incomes than would be the case if only one spouse worked, but more spending power is not the only benefit. We have already seen that the workplace is often an important source of friends, acquaintances, and opportunities for socializing. For many workers, women included, the hours spent at work are an important part of their lives and personal identities. For some, time spent on the job may even be preferable to time spent at home, given the demands of family life and the lack of appreciation for housework and child care.[37] This is likely to be one reason why women who work tend to be less depressed, have a better self-image, and in general are more satisfied than stay-at-home women.[38]

But along with benefits come stresses, especially for women. As we have just seen, although wives put in fewer hours on average at a paying job than their husbands do, they devote considerably more time to housework and child care. This is often a rational strategy from a financial standpoint. Since men earn more on average than women do, it makes economic sense for men to engage in more paid work and less unpaid work and for women to pursue the opposite strategy. Whatever the reason, many men seem to believe that the best way to meet their family responsibilities is not by doing more housework but by spending more time at work and increasing their earnings. According to one study, fathers with three or more children worked nearly an hour more each week than husbands with no children. In contrast, mothers with three or more children worked nearly 6 fewer hours than women with no children.[39]

Many careers entail putting in long hours at work, which is not easily reconciled with meeting family responsibilities, especially when both spouses are in similar circumstances. As we have seen, careers are characterized by a distinct series of hierarchical stages combined with expectations of high degrees of personal commitment. Both of these aspects are potential sources of stress for family relationships. Getting everything done can be particularly difficult during the phase of life when the demands of parenthood and career coincide. It is not surprising that survey respondents between the ages of 35 and 44 report feeling the greatest time pressures and stresses related to time management.[40]

Reconciling work and family can be further complicated when passing from one career stage to a higher one requires moving to a new locale.[41] A move of this sort can be upsetting because it means leaving a familiar place and its network of friends and acquaintances. Pulling up stakes is also likely to do some damage to the career of the "trailing spouse," because in most instances, a move results in the abandonment of the present position and then trying to find another one in new and unfamiliar surroundings. From an economic standpoint, this disruption is likely to benefit the family when the husband's job necessitates a geographical move. For many women, the situation is less clear-cut. Women are less likely to move for work-related reasons, which may hinder their opportunities for career advancement. At the same time, this may be a rational strategy in terms of family income because husbands in dual-career families usually earn more than their wives, and a move is likely to diminish their contribution when they are the trailing spouse.[42] Even so, the wife will likely pay the price in terms of her own career if she forgoes a job-related move.

Some couples elect to avoid the problems that come with family relocation by maintaining two separate residences.[43] This may be necessary because one spouse faces a lack of appropriate jobs in the new locale or because he or she has built up contacts and clients that cannot easily be found elsewhere. It may also happen that one spouse, usually the wife, has embarked on a career at a relatively late stage of life. Whatever the cause, the result is a long-distance marriage, one in which the commute between two residences may extend from one coast to the other. This is an inherently difficult situation, and it occurs only when there is as much commitment to the woman's career as there is to the man's. What matters in most cases is the inherent value of the career. The monetary rewards are likely to be slight, and for many couples, the expenses of maintaining two residences will overwhelm any income gains. At the same time, however, successful careers confer a number of psychic advantages that may, in turn, strengthen a marriage.

For some careers, it is essential that husband and wife remain together because the career of one requires not just the efforts of the occupant but of his or her spouse as well. In the not-too-distant past, these "two-person careers" were commonly found in business, government, and academia.[44] In a typical situation, the wife of an executive would be expected to take responsibility for the "social" aspect of the position by arranging dinner parties and other get-togethers. So important was this function that it was a common practice to conduct extensive interviews with the wives of candidates for an important position. This situation is less common today, now that many women have demanding careers of their own, and the notion of relying on a wife's unpaid labors can be properly construed as sexist exploitation belonging to another era. Today, there are a few examples of role reversals, with husbands working as unpaid auxiliaries serving the cause of their wives' careers, but these are clearly the exception.

_____ Reconciling Work Roles and Life Roles

Books, magazines, and other dispensers of advice often refer to the need to balance work, family, home, and all the other components of daily life. On the surface, this seems like reasonable advice, but everyday reality is not likely to match this ideal. "Balance" implies a point where everything rests in a state of equilibrium, but a more apt image is that of a dynamic, constantly changing situation in which work and its demands may be ascendant for a period of days, weeks, and even months and then give way to other roles and their requirements. Individuals have to make their own choices and decisions, but reconciling all life's roles and responsibilities should not be their task alone. Many of the difficulties that arise in the course of dealing with competing social roles can be alleviated through the development and implementation of appropriate policies in the public and private sectors.

As we have seen, a major source of stress in contemporary society comes from not having enough time to adequately fulfill the roles defined by work and family responsibilities. In the past, government policies were of central importance in reducing the length of the working day. But before government stepped in, the main source of pressure for fewer hours was a social movement led by labor unions during the late 19th and early 20th centuries. In addition to easing the working lives of individual employees, union leaders argued that an 8-hour day would create more job openings, reduce unemployment, and boost wages. On the other side, employers were beginning to realize that shorter working hours made good business sense because men and women on the brink of exhaustion were not likely to be productive workers.

During the first half of the 19th century, workers in some trades succeeded in reducing their work hours, and after the Civil War, agitation for an 8-hour day began in earnest. The working hours of women and children were frequently limited by state statutes, and federal workers got an 8-hour day with no reduction in pay in 1892. The 8-hour day became something close to a universal standard in the United States during the second decade of the 20th century, but it did not have the force of federal law behind it. This came with the passage of the Fair Labor Standards Act in 1938, which mandated an 8-hour day for most wage-earning workers and required time-and-a-half overtime pay when this standard was exceeded. In the years that followed, employers also began to offer paid vacations, and by 1940, half the U.S. workforce had this important benefit.[45] In the private sector, 78 percent of all employees and 90 percent of full-time employees received paid vacations in 2008. Workers in the public sector did not do as well; 60 percent of these employees and 68 percent of full-time employees received paid vacations, but these figures are skewed by the large number of teachers, whose working year typically spans 9 or 10 months. Employees in the private sector had a mean of 14 days paid vacation, and public-sector employees had 15, but there is a fair amount of variation around the mean because the number of vacation days received is often tied to the length of an employee's service.[46] The long-term reduction in the length of the working day has given workers more time for other things, but as we have seen, this trend has stalled out in recent decades, and if anything, the combined working hours of husbands and wives have moved upward. Moreover, although men have been assuming more of the responsibilities of maintaining home and family while women have been spending less time on housework, the amount of time spent on the most important domestic responsibility, the care of children, has hardly diminished. Working women spend less time with their children than stay-at-home mothers, but the difference is not large.[47] Consequently, caring for children while holding down a job is likely to be workers' major source of role conflict and attendant stress.

A small number of employers offer on-site child-care facilities—a practice that goes back at least to World War II, when retaining a large female workforce was a major concern for employers, but they were discontinued when the war ended and women workers were no longer deemed essential.[48] Only a few employers offer on-site child care today, but about half of employers do provide some kind of child-care assistance for their employees.[49] One common benefit is an employer-sponsored flexible spending account (FSA). An FSA allows a portion of a worker's wage or salary to be put into a special account for the payment of certain expenses, including child care. An FSA is advantageous to employees because the portion of income that goes into an FSA is not taxed, resulting in a kind of government subsidy for child-care expenses. The federal tax code also allows a portion of income spent on child care to be deducted from taxable income. Although helpful, the money saved through this deduction does not come close to offsetting the out-of-pocket expenses of child care.

Financial assistance of any sort is helpful, but it can never compensate for the fact that there are only so many minutes in the day. Many workers live lives of considerable stress because they do not have sufficient time to devote to both their jobs and their families. There is no way to expand a 24-hour day, but it is possible to make conflicting demands of work and family more manageable through the enactment of more flexible working schedules. For many family members, having more control over the time spent at work may even be preferable to shorter working hours that are rigidly scheduled.[50]

The fixed scheduling of essential activities contributes significantly to the harried lives of most working parents. The standard 9-to-5 working day does not mesh with regular school schedules, making it difficult for parents to be home with their children at the end of the school day or to be readily available in the event of the inevitable illnesses and emergencies. Even after-school child care, when available, may not meet the needs of parents who work at night or other atypical times. One partial solution is part-time work for one parent (usually the mother), but this may not be financially feasible, and it is likely to retard career advancement. Another possibility is shift work that allows one spouse to work nights in order to be with children during the daytime. Some firms operate on a 24-hour schedule, typically dividing the workday into three 8-hour shifts. Working on the "graveyard shift," typically from 11 P.M. to 7 A.M., may provide more time to be with children, but it is difficult to reconcile these hours with activities that are oriented to more conventional work schedules. Still, this is a popular strategy despite its drawbacks; one study found that nearly a third of dual-earner families with preschool-age children employed a split-shift strategy.[51] Another alternative schedule offered by some firms allows an employee to work 10 hours a day for 4 days, thereby freeing up a whole day to take care of household and family needs. Although both men and women can use flexible work schedules to better fulfill their home and parental roles, these arrangements seem to be particularly beneficial in helping fathers become more involved in parenting.[52]

Flexibility can be defined in a number of ways, and the implementation of flexible work schedules varies considerably. One study found a fair amount of apparent workplace flexibility in that 86 percent of the workers surveyed reported that they could change their working hours "as needed." However, only 40 percent could change them daily, and even fewer, 29 percent, could set their own hours.[53] Moreover, flexible work arrangements are not evenly distributed within the workforce as a whole. Scheduling flexibility is greatest for employees with workweeks that are both longer and shorter than average, but women at the high end have less flexibility and autonomy than equivalent male workers.[54]

When properly implemented, flexible work arrangements do more than just reduce some of the stresses of combining work and family. One study that used a number of variables to define flexibility found that the availability of flexible working hours was positively associated with higher job satisfaction, commitment to the employer, and a greater stated desire to remain with the current employer.[55] Improved employee morale, in turn, is reflected in greater business success, with firms benefiting from improved productivity, reduced costs of recruitment and training, and lower healthcare costs due to less employee stress.[56]

Important though they might be, having shortened or flexible workweeks does not meet the needs of many men and women who are facing critical episodes in parenthood, such as the birth or adoption of a child. Parents also may want to devote full-time attention to their children for an extended period of time. Many European governments address this need by replacing all or part of a worker's wage or salary for maternity or parental leave.[57] The member countries of the European Union must provide a minimum of 14 weeks paid maternity leave, although not necessarily at 100 percent the employee's wage or salary.[58] These programs are financed through employer and employee contributions, often supplemented with funds drawn from general tax revenues. They do not impose severe budgetary strains; even the most generous programs account for well under 1 percent of the country's gross domestic product.[59]

Parents in the United States get no direct financial support from the federal government, although some states cover maternity leaves as part of their disability insurance programs. If nothing else, expectant mothers and many parents can take time off from work without the fear of losing their jobs. In regard to the former, the 1978 Pregnancy Discrimination Act makes it illegal to fire or refuse to hire a woman on the basis of pregnancy or childbirth. Attending to parental obligations has been made a bit easier by the 1993 Family and Medical Leave Act, which gives employees the right to take up to 12 weeks of unpaid leave to care for a newborn, newly adopted, or foster child, as well as to provide care for a sick child or other family member. But this law applies only to firms with 50 or more employees and covers only employees who have worked at least 1,250 hours during the previous 12 months. Due to these exceptions, about 40 percent of workers are not covered.[60] One unintended consequence of this unequal coverage is that it discriminates against low-wage workers, who are more likely to be employed in small enterprises that are not required to offer unpaid maternity leaves.[61]

Since the Family and Medical Leave Act guarantees only an unpaid leave, many parents choose to remain on the job because they cannot afford to lose their regular income. It is, therefore, not surprising that nearly half the workers eligible for this benefit do not take advantage of it, and most of those who do rarely take all the weeks to which they are entitled.[62] Both mothers and fathers (including adoptive parents) qualify for a leave, but the majority of these leaves are taken by mothers.[63] This is a reflection of women's traditional role as the primary child-care provider, but it also reflects the reality that, since women are generally paid less than men, a leave taken by a woman employee will do less damage to the family's finances than if the leave is taken by the father. This situation also prevails in the European countries that provide paid leaves, as less than 10 percent of fathers take parental leave.[64]

Some American workers are fortunate enough to be covered by employers' programs that offer paid maternity and parental leaves. About 25 percent of employers pay their workers their full wage or salary while they are on leave, and another 25 percent make partial payments or offer full payment under certain circumstances.[65] These programs are most often found in organizations with large numbers of well-paid, skilled employees. In general, employees in managerial and professional positions enjoy more job flexibility and employer assistance with child care than workers in the lower ranks do. As one critic of current policies puts it, "The less you have, the less you get."[66]

Reconciling work roles and life roles will be a major challenge for working life in the years to come, but it will not be the only one. As previous chapters have indicated, throughout the modern era, work and occupations have had to adapt to many technological, economic, social, and cultural changes. The working world will not likely be any more stable in the years to come, although many aspects of work as we know it today will endure. The concluding chapter will review some of the key themes and issues presented in previous chapters, delineate the major influences on working life today and in the near future, and note how working lives could be improved through policy changes in the private and public sectors.

FOR DISCUSSION

1. Although the precise number of hours worked on average is a matter of some contention, it is indisputable that Americans put in more hours on the job than workers in most other countries do. Why is this so? Is this a national virtue or a vice?

2. Have you or any of your friends and family ever faced a conflict between the demands of career and those of family or a relationship? How was this conflict resolved?

3. Flexible schedules are greatly valued by many workers, but they may be difficult to implement. In which occupations is flexibility inherently difficult to achieve? How could these occupations be changed in order to provide greater flexibility?

4. Would it be beneficial for the United States to adopt policies similar to those in Europe regarding parental leave? Who would benefit the most? What would be the main sources of political opposition to the enactment of these policies?

Notes

1. "Americans Now Spend Over 100 Hours a Year Commuting," http://usgovinfo.about.com/od/censusandstatistics/a/commutetimes.htm (accessed September 13, 2011).

2. U.S. Census Bureau, "'Extreme' Commute Rankings," http://www.census.gov/newsroom/releases/pdf/2005-03-30_Commute_extremes.pdf (accessed September 13, 2011).

3. Arlie R. Hochschild, *The Time Bind: When Work Becomes Home and Home Becomes Work* (New York: Metropolitan, 1997).

4. Juliet B. Schor, *The Overworked American: The Unexpected Decline of Leisure* (New York: Basic, 1991).

5. Ibid., 22, 182, fn. 15.

6. Ibid., 29.

7. Ibid., 60–6.

8. John P. Robinson and Ann Bostrom, "The Overestimated Workweek? What Time Diaries Suggest," *Monthly Labor Review* (August 1994): 11–23; Philip L. Rones, Randy E. Ilg, and Jennifer M. Gardner, "Trends in Hours of Work Since the Mid-1970s," *Monthly Labor Review* (April 1997): 3–14.

9. Christin Hilgeman, "Usual Hours Worked in the Past 12 Months for Workers 16 to 64: 2008 and 2009" (U.S. Census Bureau, September 2010), http://www.census.gov/prod/2010pubs/acsbr09-4.pdf (accessed September 13, 2011).

10. John P. Robinson and Geoffrey Godbey, *Time for Life: The Surprising Ways Americans Use Their Time* (University Park: Pennsylvania State University Press, 1997).

11. Jerry A. Jacobs, "Measuring Time at Work: Are Self-Reports Accurate?" *Monthly Labor Review* 121, no. 12 (December 1998): 42–53.

12. Jerry A. Jacobs and Kathleen Gerson, *The Time Divide: Work, Family, and Gender Inequality* (Cambridge, MA: Harvard University Press, 2004), 23–5.

13. Jerry A. Jacobs and Kathleen Gerson, "Who Are the Overworked Americans?" *Review of Social Economy* 56, no. 4 (1997): 442–59.

14. Rones et al., "Trends in Hours of Work," 9.

15. Jacobs and Gerson, *Time Divide*, 35.

16. Ibid., 67.

17. Ibid., 127.

18. HRM Guide, "Overworked Americans Can't Use Up Their Vacations," http://hrmguide.net/usa/worklife/unused_vacation.htm (accessed March 3, 2006).

19. Chris Gaither and Dawn C. Chmielewski, "Basketball Through the Net May Cause Madness at Work," *Los Angeles Times,* March 15, 2006.

20. Barry Bluestone and Stephen Rose, "Overworked and Underemployed: Unraveling an Economic Enigma," *American Prospect* 8, no. 31 (March 1997): 58–64.

21. This arrangement was less common in African American families, where women had a higher rate of labor force participation. For a history of black women workers, see Jacqueline Jones, *Labor of Love, Labor of Sorrow: Black Women, Work, and the Family From Slavery to the Present* (New York: Basic, 1985).

22. Louise A. Tilly and Joan W. Scott, *Women, Work, and Family* (New York: Holt, Rinehart, & Winston, 1978), 104–5.

23. Ibid., 124.

24. Ibid., 124–5.

25. Ibid., 151–62.

26. See Francine D. Blau, "The Data on Women Workers Past, Present, and Future," in *Women Working: Theories and Facts in Perspective,* eds. Ann H. Stromberg and Shirley Harkess (Palo Alto, CA: Mayfield, 1978), 36, Table 1.

27. Arlie Russell Hochschild, *The Second Shift* (New York: Avon, 1989).

28. Suzanne Bianchi, Melissa A. Milkie, Liana C. Sayer, and John C. Robinson, "Is Anyone Doing the Housework? Trends in the Gender Division of Labor," *Social Forces* 79, no. 1 (September 2000): 209.

29. Joann Vanek, "Time Spent in Housework," *Scientific American* 231, no. 5 (November 1974): 116–20.

30. Schor, *Overworked American*, 103.

31. Ibid., 36.

32. Bianchi et al., "Is Anyone Doing the Housework?", 206.

33. Phyllis Moen and Patricia Roehling, *The Career Mystique: Cracks in the American Dream* (Lanham, MD: Rowman & Littlefield, 2005), 101.

34. Ruth Schwartz Cowan, *More Work for Mother: The Ironies of Household Technologies From the Open Hearth to the Microwave* (New York: Basic, 1983).

35. Arne L. Kalleberg, *The Mismatched Worker* (New York: Norton, 2007), 230.

36. Jacobs and Gerson, *Time Divide*, 50.

37. Hochschild, *Time Bind*.

38. See the numerous studies cited in Moen and Roehling, *Career Mystique*, 88.

39. Jacobs and Gerson, *Time Divide*, 49.

40. Robinson and Godbey, *Time for Life*, 236–7.

41. Anne B. Hendershott, *Moving for Work: The Sociology of Relocating in the 1990s* (Lanham, MD: University Press of America, 1995).

42. Linda K. Stroh, Jeanne M. Brett, and Anne H. Reilly, "All the Right Stuff: A Comparison of Female and Male Managers' Career Progression," *Journal of Applied Psychology* 77, no. 3 (1992): 257.

43. Naomi Gerstel and Harriet Gross, *Commuter Marriage: A Study of Work and Family* (New York: Guildford, 1984).

44. Hanna Papanak, "Men, Women, and Work: Reflections on the Two-Person Career," *American Journal of Sociology* 78 (1973): 852–72.

45. Benjamin Kline Hunnicutt, "Vacations," in *The Encyclopedia of Recreation and Leisure in America,* ed. Gary S. Cross (Woodbridge, CT: Scribner's, 2004), 398–9.

46. U.S. Bureau of Labor Statistics, "Vacations, Holidays, and Personal Leave: Access, Quantity, Costs, and Trends" (February 2009), http://www.bls.gov/opub/perspectives/issue2.pdf (accessed December 28, 2010).

47. Bianchi et al., "Is Anyone Doing the Housework?"

48. Barbara Reskin and Irene Padavic, *Women and Men at Work* (Thousand Oaks, CA: Sage, 1994), 156.

49. Ibid., 157.

50. Rudy Fenwick and Mark Tausig, "Scheduling Stress: Family and Health Outcomes of Shift Work and Schedule Control," *American Behavioral Scientist* 44, no. 7 (2001): 1179–98.

51. Harriet B. Presser, "Employment Schedules Among Dual-Earner Spouses and the Division of Household Labor by Gender," *American Sociological Review* 59 (June 1994): 348.

52. Kathleen Gerson, "A Few Good Men: Overcoming the Barriers to Involved Fatherhood," *American Prospect Online,* http://www.prospect.org/web/printfriendly-view.ww?id=5090 (accessed March 31, 2006).

53. Jacobs and Gerson, *Time Divide,* 106.

54. Ibid., 101–2.

55. James T. Bond, Cynthia Thompson, Ellen Galinsky, and David Prottas, *Highlights of the National Study of the Changing Workforce* (New York: Families and Work Institute, 2003), 33–7.

56. Corporate Voices for Working Families, *Business Impacts of Flexibility: An Imperative for Expansion,* http://www.corporatevoices.org (accessed March 28, 2006), 20–4.

57. Janet C. Gornick and Marcia K. Meyers, *Families That Work: Policies for Reconciling Parenthood and Employment* (New York: Russell Sage Foundation, 2003), 121–39.

58. Moen and Roehling, *Career Mystique,* 164–5.

59. Gornick and Meyers, *Families That Work,* 140.

60. Moen and Roehling, *Career Mystique,* 161, 221.

61. Gornick and Meyers, *Families That Work,* 118.

62. Moen and Roehling, *Career Mystique,* 161.

63. Ibid., 165–6.

64. Gornick and Meyers, *Families That Work,* 133.

65. Ibid., 118.

66. Thomas A. Kochan, *Restoring the American Dream: A Working Family's Agenda for America* (Cambridge: MIT Press, 2005), 25.

15 Conclusion

Work Today and Tomorrow

In the 1950s, many believed that modern societies were on the threshold of an unprecedented age of leisure. Several decades later, it has become apparent that those hopes and fears are nowhere close to being realized. The majority of men and women from their mid-20s to their 60s spend more of their waking hours working than doing anything else, and there is little indication that this situation will change anytime soon. No matter what our motivations for going to work may be, more is involved than earning a wage or salary. The time we put in at the workplace and what happens while we are there strongly influence the overall shape and trajectory of our daily lives. Moreover, while our lives are shaped by the jobs we hold and the work we do, these in turn are strongly influenced by all the forces that are continually reshaping society. Work is done by individuals, either singly or in groups, but it can never escape the pressures exerted by the larger society in which it is embedded.

In this, the concluding chapter, we will consider some of the key social, economic, and political forces that have been shaping work and will continue to do so in the years to come. In so doing, we will briefly review some of the major topics and issues that appeared in the earlier pages. Here, however, we will mix description with prescription by presenting some ways in which both the private and public sectors can improve life on and off the job for working men and women.

Technology, Work, and Occupations

In surveying the history of work, it is readily apparent that technological change has exerted a great influence, although it has not done so in a narrowly deterministic manner. Technology is a human creation, and as such, it has been shaped by culture, economics, politics, and gender relationships. But one needn't be a technological determinist to appreciate the effect of technological change on human societies. As pointed out on several occasions in this book, the kind of work most people do has changed dramatically in the past hundred years, as the service sector has displaced the agricultural and manufacturing sectors as the main source of jobs in the United States and other economically developed countries. In a relatively short space of time, we have gone from an economy where most adults (and many children as well) worked as farmers, miners, and factory operatives to one in which the majority of the workforce is employed in healthcare, education, government, sales, and other service industries. This has occurred because improvements in productivity, most of them the result of technological advance, have made it possible to meet a population's material needs through the efforts of a minority of the total labor force.

Manufacturing is still a crucial part of the economy, but much of it is now being done with little direct human intervention and effort, as computer-controlled processes and other advanced technologies have replaced a great deal of physical and even mental labor. Where large numbers of workers are still employed for industrial operations, in all likelihood, they are to be found in the factories of developing nations such as Mexico and China, where low wages encourage the use of labor-intensive modes of manufacturing. The importation of billions of dollars worth of goods from these countries is one of the most visible indications of a globalized economy. Globalization has benefited poor countries by creating wealth and jobs, while in the developed world, it has driven down the price of many commonly purchased items. Globalization has not been an unmitigated blessing, however. This is not the place to attempt an overall assessment of globalization, except to note that, as with technological advance, the benefits of globalization are not spread evenly. Globalization and technological advance are beneficial when considered in the aggregate, but they also can do considerable harm to particular individuals, occupations, industries, and geographical regions.

Making Globalization and Technological Change More Equitable

When globalization is discussed by individuals or in the media, it is often suffused with the vocabulary of competition. Politicians, journalists, academics, and members of the general public often claim that we have to boost our productivity, increase our research-and-development budgets, and reform our schools lest we end up on the losing side while participating in an intensely competitive global economy. But the language of sports and war can be misleading, sometimes dangerously so. The global economy is not a zero-sum game in which the winners vanquish the losers.[1] Instead, a nation's success in the global economy consists of making good use of productive resources, human and otherwise, in order to efficiently provide goods and services at a sustainable level. A successful economy also will preserve the physical environment and contribute to its renewal and revitalization.

Nobody loses when the individual nations of the world achieve these goals, unless of course some of them are so foolish as to devote a large share of their economic gains to military conquest.

Both globalization and technological innovation have the potential to substantially improve living standards, especially in the poor countries of the world. But this potential will not be realized unless these two powerful forces of change are coupled with appropriate policies to mitigate the inevitable damage they cause. As just noted, the benefits of globalization and technological change are spread over a wide area, while the pain they inflict is usually sharply focused. Neo-Luddite reactions and antiglobalization outbursts are, therefore, inevitable when particular segments of a society and its workforce are stuck with the all-too-evident costs of globalization and technological advance and nothing is done to offset their losses.[2]

There is no perfect strategy to completely compensate for the localized damage caused by globalization and technological change, but there are a number of ways to at least soften the blow. For many workers, retraining programs, especially when they are coupled with holding a real job, offer the possibility of replacing an obsolescent line of work with one more attuned to current needs. The costs can be directly borne by federal and state governments, or indirectly through the provision of tax deductions and credits for firms willing to employ and train displaced workers. Of course, some workers, especially those near retirement age, may not be willing or able to prepare for a career shift. The federal government has in the past provided financial compensation for workers who lost their jobs as a direct result of foreign trade, and some corporations have offered generous financial incentives to induce workers to take early retirement. More private and public programs of this sort may be needed in the future. At the very least, the loss of a job as a result of technological change, globalization, or anything else should not result in a loss of health insurance, an issue to which we will return shortly.

Work and Demographic Change

Almost without exception, the world's economically-developed countries exhibit low birth rates that in some cases fall below the level necessary for the maintenance of present population sizes. Moreover, as the birth rate has fallen, the median age of the population has been going up. Neither of these trends is necessarily a bad thing when projected well into the future, but there remains the immediate problem of replenishing workforces as the large baby-boom generation enters retirement age in large and growing numbers. A declining (or even negative) rate of population growth also spells trouble for government-administered pension programs, such as the Social Security system. These programs were established decades ago on the assumption that a large portion of the funds paid out to retirees would come from the paychecks of current workers. These plans work well when there is a favorable ratio of workers to retirees, but the ratio of retirees to active workers has been going in the wrong direction for a number of years and will get even worse in the future. Under these circumstances, an influx of workers from other lands may be essential for the maintenance of the economy as a whole, as well as for the financial security of the large cadre of baby-boom retirees.

Immigration, legal and otherwise, remains a topic of considerable controversy. Much of the debate on immigration centers on its cultural consequences, particularly with regard to the speed, extent, and desirability of assimilation into the cultures of the host countries. For host countries, the replenishment of the workforce by immigrant labor will require the provision of essential services such as education and healthcare for workers and their families. No less important is willingness on the part of the native-born citizenry to accept people from different cultures and to help them assimilate into a new culture. As a nation of immigrants, the United States has a long history of taking in people from other lands, although not without conflict. For many other countries, the lack of such a heritage will make things more difficult, but an influx of immigrants may be unavoidable if current living standards are to be sustained and retired workers are to receive the pensions to which they are entitled.

Ethnicity, Gender, and Work

Concerns about large influxes of immigrants are often exacerbated by the fact that the majority of current immigrants to the developed world are not of European origin. A hundred years ago, some American citizens of northern European ancestry decried what they saw as the corrosive influence of Poles, Italians, Hungarians, and eastern European Jews on American society and culture. Today, some of the grandchildren and great-grandchildren of these "undesirables" worry about the large-scale entry of Mexicans, Chinese, Guatemalans, and other Third World people. Although racism and xenophobia are far less evident than they were in the past, only the naively optimistic would argue that race and ethnicity have no significance in today's working world. As we have seen, for most of human history, ascribed characteristics such as race and ethnicity have been of paramount importance in determining the jobs people hold and the work they do. Race and ethnicity do not shape occupational destinies as they once did, but they are by no means irrelevant today.

The continued significance of ascribed statuses is evident when racial and ethnic differences are juxtaposed with the kinds of work people do. Sometimes, the connection is the result of prejudice and discriminatory behaviors that historically excluded certain categories of people from jobs they are capable of doing. More often, however, the connection is less direct. As we have seen, residential segregation based on race and ethnicity may result in a disjunction between where people live and where the jobs are. Residential segregation also limits the size and scope of social networks, which, as we also have seen, are of crucial importance for gaining entry to many jobs. Racial and ethnic divisions are also evident in de facto educational segregation and the generally lower quality of schools serving minority communities. Given the connections between education, occupation, and earnings, attendance at inferior schools can have consequences that last a lifetime.

As with race and ethnicity, gender continues to be a powerful influence on work, particularly in regard to occupational differentiation. Despite significant changes in gender roles in recent decades, much of the occupational structure continues to be divided into the separate realms of "men's work" and "women's work." This division is problematic in that it prevents individuals from pursuing careers that would have been beneficial to them and to society as a whole, and it continues to be one of the major sources of male–female income inequality. Although it has narrowed in recent years, the gender-based income gap is still evident today, and it is not likely to disappear anytime soon. Occupational segregation is almost as pronounced now as it was three decades ago, and political realities make it highly unlikely that the enactment of comparable-worth policies will render it irrelevant as far as pay is concerned.

On a more positive note, young women now exceed their male counterparts in school performance and educational attainments. Today, of all the men in their middle to late 20s, 26 percent have college degrees, a percentage that has hardly changed in nearly three decades. In contrast, 31 percent of the women in the same age cohort are college graduates, a sizable increase of 10 percentage points since 1980.[3] Women now compose 56 percent of college graduates, and they have become a large presence in most professional schools. Higher educational attainments will be reflected in the distribution of future jobs and occupations, but irrespective of the skills they bring to the workplace, many women workers continue to be penalized for bearing a disproportionate share of parenting and other home-based duties.

Women, Work, and Families

Although the differences in the allocation of child care and household chores between men and women are not as great as they were a generation ago, women on average still spend more time on household tasks than men do. This gap may continue to close slowly as the result of long-term social and cultural changes, but in the meantime, employer actions and government policies could go a long way toward helping workers, women and men alike, more effectively reconcile the demands of work and family.

As noted earlier, achieving a "balance" between work and other aspects of life may be an unattainable ideal. Life is too dynamic for one to expect a permanent and satisfactory equilibrium, but neither should it be necessary to choose between a wholehearted devotion to one's work and a satisfying life as a parent and spouse or partner. The simplest remedy would be to set limits on the number of hours worked weekly, as was done in France in 2000 in the vain hope that a mandated 35-hour workweek would reduce unemployment.

The many problems caused by this requirement were soon evident, and it was substantially modified in the years that followed. But even if neither workers nor employers are inclined to cut back on hours of work, the demands of work can be made less onerous. For many workers, the amount of time spent working is of less importance than the degree of flexibility in the scheduling of their work. Many jobs do not require adherence to a rigid 9-to-5 (and often overtime) workday. Flexible schedules, perhaps complemented by tele-work, would allow just as much work to be done while enhancing the ability of employees to meet their family and other obligations.

In addition to benefiting workers, employers in a number of industries now realize that building greater flexibility into jobs boosts the productivity of their employees. But not all employers have come to this realization, and even if they have, they may still find it difficult to offer flexible work sched-ules and parental leave programs when their competitors are not inclined to do so. Under these circumstances, a good case can be made for government actions creating a level playing field by mandating a period of paid parental leave for all employees and offsetting additional employer expenses through government subsidies. Many western European countries have been able to do this without incurring either significant losses of production or large gov-ernmental expenditures. In the United States today, many politicians claim to espouse "traditional values" and their adherence to policies that "support the family." As the experience of other countries has shown, government actions can help working men and women more effectively meet their parental responsibilities without being financially penalized for doing so. It remains to be seen whether federal and state legislators will couple their stated beliefs about the importance of the family with policies and programs that actually improve the lives of families headed by working men and women.

Closing the Income Gap

Two of life's most important resources are time and money. As we have just seen, many workers find themselves with too little time as they try to meet the responsibilities of work and family. Shortages of money are no less evi-dent. After narrowing during the first two decades of the post–World War II era, the income gap between the top quintile and everybody else began to widen. Since then, the majority of workers have seen only modest improve-ments in their earnings when inflation is taken into account, and much of that gain has been the result of working longer hours.

As we have seen, the reasons for substantial income inequalities are com-plex, and any attempt to single out one or two causes would be an exercise in oversimplification. Technological change and globalization often have been blamed for the large income gap, and while they surely have been con-tributors, the extent of their contribution remains a matter of considerable debate. Both technological change and globalization have put a squeeze on some segments of the manufacturing sector in the United States and other developed countries, resulting in the loss of a substantial number of jobs, many of which had provided decent wages and benefits for the men and women who worked in these industries. Widespread unemployment has not occurred in the wake of these losses, but many of the service-sector jobs that have taken up the slack offer lower rates of remuneration than were found in the manufacturing sector.

Although globalization often is targeted as the main source of job losses and reduced earnings for workers, there are limits to how far the process can go. In the private sector, the great majority of American workers are employed in businesses such as retailing, healthcare, construction, finance, and transportation, all of which have few overseas competitors. Another large portion of the workforce is employed in the various branches of federal, state, and local governments, which also are insulated from foreign competition to a large degree.[4]

Although assaying the precise effects of globalization and technological change on income distribution remains a difficult and controversial issue, one fact is indisputable: educational attainments have strongly influenced the wages and salaries earned by individual workers. As we have seen, the earnings of high school graduates have lagged well behind those of college graduates, and high school dropouts have fared even worse. As a result, the income gap between college graduates and all other workers has grown in recent years, and this trend will likely continue in the years to come.

Educational attainments have always been a major source of income differentials, but why they have taken on such a transcendent importance in recent years remains an open question. At this point, it can only be noted that, whatever the merits of using it as such, formal education is commonly employed as a screening device by prospective employers, and future job seekers will have to reconcile themselves with this fact. It also means that federal, state, and local governments need to develop programs that increase opportunities for postsecondary education, especially for the large segment of the population lacking a family history of college attendance.

Attendance at a college or university, however, is not for everyone. Many well-paying jobs require thoroughgoing training that is generally not offered in college settings. Unfortunately, vocational education often has received second-class status in the educational realm and often has been starved of resources due to the belief that college is the best educational option for most, if not all, students.[5] Providing more and better training opportunities for young men and women oriented to the skilled trades would help close the large income gap that separates college graduates from the rest of the workforce.

Other sources of income disparities between different segments of the working population are embedded deeply in the economy and society and will not yield easily to government programs and policies. But this does not mean that nothing can be done. Most notably, taken as a whole, the tax system is only moderately progressive and has tilted in favor of the wealthiest members of the population in recent years. Income differentials are an inescapable feature of capitalism, and few today advocate taxation policies that would massively redistribute incomes. At the same time, however, modest tax increases for the top quintile of income earners, and especially for the top 5 percent, would at least begin to reverse a system of taxation that has made a bad situation worse as far as income inequality is concerned.

Nowhere has the income differential between those at the top and everybody else been more evident than in a comparison of the income received by top executives and that of ordinary workers. At the beginning of the 21st century, CEOs of *Fortune* 100 firms had earnings 400 times larger than those of average workers in one of these firms. Even CEOs of midsized firms enjoyed earnings 34 times larger than those of their workers.[6] Rewards of this size are sometimes claimed to be necessary to attract and motivate top-level executive talent, but businesses a generation ago seem to have gotten by with much smaller differentials, as also is the case in every other developed country today. The argument for high levels of executive compensation is further undercut by the weak—and sometimes nonexistent—link between a firm's performance and the compensation paid to its top executives. Laws setting limits on executive compensation are not likely to be enacted and may not even be desirable, but it is reasonable to expect corporations to provide more detailed information regarding the sources and extent of managerial remuneration. More directly, stockholders and their representatives on corporate boards of directors need to exercise more oversight of executive remuneration. In the final analysis, excessive payments to high-level executives that bear no relationship to profits, market share, and stock performance are powerful indicators that boards of directors are not acting as responsible representatives of the firm's stockholders.

At the other extreme of the income scale, the lowest-paid workers have fared badly in recent years as minimum-wage provisions have failed to keep up with inflation. As we have seen, even full-time work at the minimum wage will put a worker well below the poverty line. Most minimum-wage workers do not live in poverty because they are not the primary sources of income for the households in which they reside, but there still remains a substantial minority of minimum-wage workers who are major sources of income for their families. For these workers, even a modest boost in the minimum wage would significantly improve the lives of them and their families. It also would be helpful to index the minimum wage in order to automatically offset increases in the cost of living, as has been done for many years with Social Security payments. As with making the taxation system more progressive, all that is required to at least bring the purchasing power of the minimum wage back to where it was in the 1960s and keep it there is to muster the political will to do so.

The Healthcare Morass

For large numbers of workers, including many who earn well above the minimum wage, a threat remains that can rapidly erode their financial foundations: the cost of healthcare. In the worst position are the estimated 47 million men, women, and children in the United States who are lacking health insurance. Many of these are full-time workers, and for them and workers with insufficient coverage, a serious medical problem can result in financial ruin; according to one study, half of all personal bankruptcy filings in 2004 were at least partly caused by medical expenditures.[7] Even workers who have employer-sponsored health insurance worry they will lose their coverage if they are terminated, and some hang on to jobs they dislike only for the insurance they provide.

Healthcare costs also are a significant concern for employers. As noted earlier, employment-based medical insurance is a historical accident, and no other developed country relies on employers for so large a share of medical insurance costs. But this is a burden that is increasingly difficult to shoulder, and many employers have coped with the steadily rising costs of health insurance by requiring their employees to pay a larger portion of premium costs, defining new hires as "independent contractors" who do not qualify for employee benefits, or doing away with insurance altogether. Employers who continue to offer adequate health insurance coverage may do so because they are bound by union contracts or through a desire to retain and reward high-quality workers. If so, they may be seriously handicapped when competing with overseas firms whose employees are covered by government-sponsored insurance plans.

Reforming the way healthcare costs are met has been a highly contentious issue involving a multiplicity of well-connected political interests. It also must be noted that attaining an ideal system that combines universal coverage, high-quality care, and low costs is impossible. If universal coverage is the goal, as is being argued here, the best that can be hoped for is a system that delivers decent care to everyone at a reasonable cost. This may seem a rather unambitious goal, but the United States is currently failing to meet even this modest standard. Whether or not the major reforms enacted in 2009 will effectively address the longstanding shortcomings of the American healthcare system remains to be seen.

The Fate of the Professions

The healthcare system is one of the largest employers of professional workers, but hardly the only one. Recent decades have seen a varied group of practitioners mount attempts to gain professional status for the work they do. As we have seen, being recognized as a member of a profession confers a number of benefits, not the least of which is a substantial degree of insulation from market forces. But just as many occupations are striving to take on the characteristics of a full-fledged profession, the long-established professions have come under pressure from a number of directions. A great amount of specialized knowledge, the possession of which has been the sine qua non of professionals, is readily available today, and a better-educated clientele is well positioned to take advantage of it. At the same time, financial concerns have threatened professional autonomy as the costs of healthcare, legal services, and higher education have exceeded the overall rate of inflation by large margins. In response, public agencies and private firms, insurance providers especially, have become increasingly involved in setting payments for professional services. This has not deterred other occupations from striving to attain professional status, but given the stresses to which the established professions have been subject, their quest may not come to a successful conclusion, at least as far as the pursuit of a large measure of autonomy is concerned.

Organizations for the 21st Century

As a field of study and as a practical activity, work is closely connected to organizational theories and practices. Any discussion of work today and in the near future will necessarily involve organizations and the ways they are changing. In the not-too-distant past, bureaucracies of various descriptions provided the organizational foundation for mass production, as everything from the manufacture of automobiles to the education of young people was driven by an effort to produce standardized goods as cheaply and efficiently as possible. That era is by no means over, but along with the consumption of standardized goods and services, a large demand also exists for individualized and customized methods of production. At the same time, rigid bureaucratic roles and hierarchies are being challenged by rapidly developing electronic technologies that give employees unprecedented abilities to retrieve and analyze information, as well as to directly communicate and collaborate with clients and fellow employees.

The dominance of the service sector as a source of employment has required the development of employee skills that were of less importance when a much larger portion of the labor force worked in mines, farms, and factories. Although some service occupations entail little in the way of social contact, the majority of the jobs in this sector require sustained and effective interaction with others. These social skills are stifled by organizational structures that lock employees into narrowly defined roles that prevent them from responding to the individual needs of clients, customers, and colleagues. Well-defined organizational roles and some degree of hierarchy are inescapable, but they are counterproductive when they turn workers into little more than preprogrammed robots.

For organizations of all sorts, one of the challenges of the years to come will be retaining the advantages of traditional bureaucratic modes of organization while at the same time devising organizational structures and processes appropriate to changing work environments. As they engage in new tasks and develop new capabilities, organizations have at their disposal communication and information technologies barely imaginable a generation ago. These technologies have the potential to improve production, productivity, and product quality, but they will realize this potential only when they are used by well-trained and motivated workers empowered to make full use of their capabilities.

Workers and Jobs for the Future

Making predictions can be a hazardous exercise, but some elements of the future trajectory of work and occupations can be charted with a fair amount of confidence. That demographic change will exert a considerable influence on the size and composition of the workforce in the years to come already has been noted. Neither the birth rate nor the death rate are likely to change dramatically, and knowing how many babies were born this year allows a reasonably accurate forecast of how many native-born 20-year-olds there will be two decades hence. The other key demographic variable, the rate of immigration, is much less predictable because it is strongly affected by government policies here, along with conditions in other parts of the world. Government actions, however, have not had much success in stemming the rate of illegal immigration into the United States up to this point. Stopping or at least slowing illegal immigration will continue to be difficult as long as the income gap between the rich and the poor countries of the world remains as vast as it is today and employers are willing and able to hire undocumented workers at low wages.

Demography tells us a lot about the sheer size of the future labor force, but it doesn't tell us much about the kinds of work people will do in the next decade or two. For the most part, the jobs people hold will be determined by what they are capable of doing and by what their employers want. Today's workers have, on average, more years of formal education than previous generations, although the time spent in school is not always an accurate reflection of how much has been learned. Of particular relevance to the capabilities of the future workforce is the mediocre quality of K–12 science and mathematics education. In the recent past, many jobs in science, engineering, and allied fields have been held by immigrants, a large number of whom had received advanced degrees from American universities. Immigration historically has been an important source of entrepreneurial and technological vitality, but there is cause for concern when about half of all the graduate students in science and engineering come from abroad. Although many will stay in the United States, increasing numbers of graduates will likely return to their native lands.

As far as the sources of employment are concerned, large firms provide paychecks for many workers; according to some reckonings, Wal-Mart is America's largest employer, with 1.4 million full- and part-time employees in 2010. But unlike the world's biggest retailer, the majority of large firms are situated in capital-intensive industries that use relatively little labor per unit of output. Consequently, small businesses (defined by the federal government as firms with fewer than 500 employees) are major sources of employment. These 17,000 firms account for about half of total employment, while 18 percent of American workers are employed by the approximately five million firms that have fewer than 20 employees.[8] As the working population has grown in size, firms with fewer than 500 employees have been even more important for the creation of new jobs. From 1992 to 2005, small businesses were the source of nearly two-thirds of net job gains (i.e., workers added minus workers lost).[9]

In regard to specific occupations, technological, economic, and cultural changes have given rise to many new occupations and employment opportunities, yet a substantial degree of continuity in the occupational structure can be assumed for the near future. Some new occupations can be expected to expand at a rapid rate, but dramatic percentage increases do not translate into large numbers of new jobs because they started from a small base. According to the U.S. Department of Labor, the two fastest-growing occupations between 2008 and 2018 will be biomedical engineers and network systems and data communication analysts, which are expected to grow by 72.0 and 53.4 percent, respectively. These are impressive rates of growth, but they translate into only 11,000 and 155,800 new jobs.[10] In contrast, jobs in many long-established occupations will undergo smaller percentage increases, but the net gains will be quite large because so many people already are in these occupations. For example, the number of retail salespersons is expected to grow by only 8.4 percent during this 10-year period, but this relatively modest percentage increase translates into 374,700 additional jobs.[11] In similar fashion, 191,500 more workers are anticipated to be employed as building cleaner workers, even though their ranks will increase by a mere 4.5 percent.[12]

In general, the greatest increase in the number of workers in the immediate years to come will be in occupations that have been around for a long time. From now to 2018, the largest job gains are expected to occur within the ranks of registered nurses (581,500); home health aides (460,900); customer service representatives (399,500); food preparation and serving workers (394,300); personal and home care aides (375,800); retail salespersons (374,700); office clerks (358,700); accountants and auditors (279,400); nursing aides, orderlies, and attendants (276,000); and postsecondary teachers (256,900).[13]

One striking fact emerges from a review of this list: only three of the occupations projected to add the greatest number of workers require a bachelor's degree or greater: registered nurses, postsecondary teachers, and accountants and auditors. For all the current concerns over increasing access to postsecondary education, a large portion of the labor force will not need a high level of education in order to qualify for the jobs that come available. At the same time, however, pursuing a college or university degree is a wise strategy for many individuals; the close correlation between years of education and job-related earnings is clearly evident today and will likely remain so in the future. Financial considerations aside, education makes for a more interesting and meaningful life, and it produces a more capable citizenry for society as a whole.

Formal education, of course, does not totally determine one's fate. In the future, as today, a successful working life will require ability, effort, preparation, and a measure of good luck. For society as a whole, the future of work will reflect broad social, cultural, and economic trends, and it will be heavily influenced by decisions made in the political arena. We have made the world we live in through our work, and that world will continue to shape the work we do.

Notes

1. Paul Krugman, *Peddling Prosperity: Sense and Nonsense in an Age of Diminished Expectations* (New York: Norton, 1994).

2. Martin Carnoy, *Sustaining the New Economy: Work, Family, and Community in the Information Age* (New York: Russell Sage Foundation, 2000).

3. David Finegold, "Is Education the Answer? Trends in the Supply and Demand for Skills in the U.S. Workforce," in *America at Work*, eds. Edward E. Lawler III and James O'Toole (New York: Palgrave Macmillan, 2006).

4. James O'Toole and Edward Lawler III, *The New American Workplace* (New York: Palgrave Macmillan, 2006), 22.

5. James E. Rosenbaum, *Beyond College for All: Career Paths for the Forgotten Half* (New York: Russell Sage Foundation, 2001).

6. O'Toole and Lawler, *New American Workplace*, 117.

7. National Coalition on Health Care, "Health Insurance Costs," http://www.nchc.org/facts/cost.shtml (accessed August 1, 2006).

8. Calculated from U.S. Small Business Administration, "Employer Firms and Employment by Size of Firm," http://www.sba.gov/advo/research/us_03_n6.pdf (accessed August 1, 2006).

9. Center for Innovative Entrepreneurship, "New Data Show the Importance of Small Firms for Employment Growth," http://www.vfinance.com/SIR/Special_Innovation_Reports_040606.pdf (accessed August 1, 2006).

10. Bureau of Labor Statistics, "Occupational Employment Projections to 2018" (December 22, 2010), http://www.bls.gov/opub/mlr/2009/11/art5full.pdf (accessed December 30, 2010), 91, 93.

11. Ibid., 93.

12. Ibid., 110.

13. Ibid., 93.

Glossary

achieved status   A position in society based on individual achievement; see also **ascribed status**

affirmative action   Policies enacted by governments and private organizations to increase opportunities for members of minority groups

alienation   A sense of detachment from life and work, characterized by feelings of normlessness, meaningnessless, and powerlessness

apprenticeship   A period of training for a future career in a skilled craft

artisan(al) work   The small-scale production of goods by skilled craftsmen using simple tools

ascribed status   A position in society based on attributes that a person has no control over, such as the family into which one was born; see also **achieved status**

assembly line   A manufacturing process in which a product is put together while being carried on a moving line to workers who remain in one place

automation   Manufacturing processes that run automatically and with little human intervention

baby-boom generation   The large cohort of today's adults who were born between 1946 and 1964

bureaucracy   An organizational structure based on impersonality, expertise, division of labor, hierarchy, written records, and definitive rules and procedures

capitalism   An economic system based on the private ownership of capital

caste system   A mode of social organization based on the rigid social segregation of individuals according to ascribed statuses

collective bargaining   A means of setting wages and working conditions in which a labor union represents the workers

comparable worth   A means of paying workers in different occupations on the basis of comparable attributes such as training, skills, and responsibilities

comparative advantage An important basis for international trade, which justifies the production of certain export goods even though the producers do not have an absolute advantage in the production of those goods

contingent employment Short-term employment based on a precisely defined set of responsibilities

counterculture A culture that stands in opposition to a dominant culture

credentialism The evaluation of workers and potential workers according to certain credentials, such as a university diploma

cultural capital The knowledge, values, tastes, speech patterns, and social skills often necessary for a successful career in many occupations

culture The assemblage of language, values, norms, arts, and artifacts that maintain the social order and help individuals make sense of the world in which they live

deskilling An effort by management to reduce the power of skilled workers by simplifying operations so they can be done by less-skilled workers

division of labor The allocation of specific work tasks according to either achieved or ascribed statuses

efficiency wage Remuneration at a level that results in the highest level of worker productivity

gathering and hunting A mode of life based on the gathering of edible plants and small animals along with the hunting of larger animals

globalization The processes through which individual businesses, political authority, and cultural patterns are diffused throughout the world

guild An organization of craftsmen intended to promote solidarity and limit competition

Hawthorne effect The phenomenon noted by researchers whereby the productivity of workers increased because the researchers were paying attention to the workers

homosocial reproduction The tendency of upper-echelon managers to hire and promote workers with similar social backgrounds

human capital The cognitive, physical, and social skills of individual workers

Industrial Revolution The epochal changes in production based on the use of new technologies, sources of energy, and organizational structures and processes

labor force The segment of the population that is either employed or actively seeking a job

labor union An organization representing workers during the process of collective bargaining

Luddism   The movement in early 19th-century England in which workers expressed their grievances through smashing machinery; also applied to anti-technology attitudes today

lump of labor fallacy   The notion that there is a fixed number of jobs and, thus, unemployed members of the labor force can find work only when employed workers lose their jobs or have their hours reduced

maquiladora   A labor-intensive industrial facility originally established in Latin America but also found in other low-wage countries

market economy   A production and distribution system in which economic decisions are based on supply and demand as reflected in the prices of goods and services

mass production   The production of standardized commodities, usually involving machinery, external sources of energy, and routinized procedures

matrix organization   An alternative to bureaucratic organization characterized by dual and sometimes conflicting sources of authority

minimum-wage laws   Rules promulgated by state and federal governments that determine the lowest wages that can be paid by employers to their employees

multinational corporations   Large for-profit organizations that conduct their activities in more than one country

NAFTA   A pact, initiated in 1994, to encourage trade between Canada, the United States, and Mexico through the elimination of tariffs and other barriers

nepotism   The practice of filling positions in an organization on the basis of familial relationships

network, social   A collection of interlinked social ties

opportunity cost   The losses incurred by forgoing one activity in order to do another one

postindustrial economy   An economy where the dominant productive enterprises are no longer in manufacturing but are involved in the provision of various knowledge-intensive services

profession   One of a number of occupations with certain attributes, characterized by efforts to preserve and enlarge the autonomy of its practitioners

Protestant Ethic   The value system thought to be characteristic of early Protestantism that emphasized hard work, accumulating savings, and taking a rational approach to business matters

rite of passage   A ceremony that marks the transition from one stage of life to another

Scientific Management   The managerial system developed by F. W. Taylor that emphasized a clear separation between workers and managers and made extensive use of time-and-motion studies

serfdom   An economic and social system in which agricultural workers are legally bound to the land owned by a dominant group

service sector   The largest part of a modern economy; based on the provision of services such as education, entertainment, and medical care

slavery   An economic and social structure in which some individuals are owned by others and are denied basic freedoms

socialization   The process through which children and adults learn the values, rules, and cultural elements of the groups, organizations, and societies in which they live

soft skills   The behaviors and interpersonal skills of particular importance in a service-oriented economy

staff and line   The division of an organization into personnel who do the actual work of the organization (line) and personnel who provide supportive services (staff)

subculture   Beliefs, values, material objects, and behavioral patterns, such as distinctive modes of speech, that serve to define particular groups within a larger culture

technology   The knowledge-based artifacts and processes used to shape and control the material world

technological determinism   The belief that technological change is the sole or most important determinant of particular social changes

technological unemployment   The loss of jobs due to the replacement of workers by labor-saving technologies

telework   Work performed away from conventional workplaces through the use of modern communication technologies

underground economy   Economic activities that are either illegal or hidden from government scrutiny

zero-sum economy   An economic system in which gains made by some individuals and groups are offset by the losses incurred by other individuals and groups

Credits

Chapter 1

Photo 1.1: Reprinted with permission of ©Peter Johnson/CORBIS.

Photo 1.2: Reprinted with permission of The Granger Collection/New York.

Chapter 2

Photo 2.1: Reprinted with permission of ©Leonard de Selva/CORBIS.

Photo 2.2: Reprinted with permission of The Granger Collection, New York.

Chapter 3

Photo 3.1: Reprinted with permission of The Granger Collection, New York.

Photo 3.2: Reprinted with permission of The Granger Collection, New York.

Photo 3.3: Reprinted with permission of ©Rykoff Collection/CORBIS.

Chapter 4

Photo 4.1: Reprinted with permission of ©Stefan Klein/iStockphoto.

Chapter 5

Photo 5.1: Reprinted with permission of ©Olivier Lantzendorffer/iStockphoto.

Chapter 6

Photo 6.1: Reprinted with permission of ©Bob Daemmrich/CORBIS.

Chapter 7

Photo 7.1: Reprinted with permission of ©CORBIS.

Chapter 8

Photo 8.1: Reprinted with permission of The Granger Collection, New York.

Photo 8.2: Reprinted with permission of ©Photodisc Collection/Getty Images.

Chapter 9

Photo 9.1: Reprinted with permission of ©J R EYERMAN, Time & Life Pictures Collection/ Getty Images.

Photo 9.2: Reprinted with permission of ©image100/CORBIS.

Chapter 10

Photo 10.1: Reprinted with permission of ©Glenn Frank/iStockphoto.

Chapter 11

Photo 11.1: Reprinted with permission of ©Bettmann/CORBIS.

Photo 11.2: Reprinted with permission of ©CORBIS.

Chapter 12

Photo 12.1: Reprinted with permission of ©Bettmann/CORBIS.

Chapter 13

Photo 13.1: Reprinted with permission from the Collections of The Henry Ford.

Chapter 14

Photo 14.1: Reprinted with permission of ©CORBIS.

Photo 14.2: Reprinted with permission of The Granger Collection, New York.

Index

Absenteeism, 217, 225, 226
Accountants, 87, 146, 147, 156, 182, 251 n. 16, 284, 285
Achieved status, 287, 20
Addams, Jane, 140
Adhocracy, 71–72
Affirmative action, 29, 241, 247–248, 287
African Americans, 247
  and education, 235, 236
  family incomes of, 240
  and professional occupations, 169
  as temporary workers, 220, 233
  and unions, 184, 236
  women's remuneration, 243
Agricultural production, 54–55
Agricultural Revolution, 6–8
Alienation, 223–224 and job performance, 225–226
Anticipatory socialization, 135, 148
Apprenticeship, 30, 32, 33, 34, 60, 154, 160, 203–204, 233, 287
Architects, 154
Aristotle, 27
Artisan work, 10–11, 12, 13, 26, 28, 30–31, 35, 39, 41, 43, 45, 53, 55, 203, 287
Ascribed characteristics, 3, 63, 287, 288
Ascribed statuses, xi, 20–21, 28, 56 63, 129, 276
  as a basis of work organization, 21–23
Asian Americans, 236, 247
Assembly line, xii, 51–53, 54, 69, 84, 85, 86, 93, n. 23, 190, 217, 226–227, 287
Attorneys, 138, 141, 154, 155, 157, 160, 162, 169, 181, 190
Automation, 80

Babylonia, 64
Barter, 42
Berra, Yogi, 204
Blauner, Robert, 224
Bluestone, Barry, 260
Boulton, Matthew, 140
Bradley, Joseph, 168
Bureaucracy, xii, 59–73
  alternatives to, 70–73, 287
  in the ancient world, 59–60, 64
  elements of, 61–65
  strengths and weaknesses of, 65–67
  and workers
Burnout, 217

Calvin, Jean, 14
Capitalism, xii, 10, 12, 13–15, 33, 41–43, 59, 73, 96, 209, 223, 280, 287
Careers, xiv, 136, 149–150, 199, 228, 239, 243, 263–264, 277
Caste, 28–29
Challenger Space Shuttle, 146
Child care, xvi, 221, 237, 239, 243, 261, 262, 263, 266–268, 277–278
Child labor, 129
China, 7, 9, 13, 20, 59, 63, 64, 102–104, 105, 182, 217, 274
Chiropractors, 159
Chrysler, 71, 135, 184
Civil Rights Act of 1964, 246
Clergy, 9, 15, 32, 138, 149, 164–169, 175, 189
Clerical workers, 190
Clock, xi, 13, 41
Collection agents, 159

Commuting, xvi, 88–89, 253–254

Company towns, 142

Comparable worth policies, 248–249, 277, 287

Comparative advantage, theory of, 101–102, 288

Computers, 73, 80, 83, 85–86, 90, 120, 174–175, 181–182

Container, shipping, 90–91, 101

Contingent workers, 201, 219

Countercultures, 148–149

Cultural capital, 124, 288

Daimler-Benz, 135

Deaths, work-related, 215–217

Demographic change, 109–110, 174–175, 182, 261, 275–276

Dentists, 154

Deprofessionalization, xiv, 164–166

De-skilling, 68

Division of labor, 20, 63–64, 68, 70, 72, 73, 84, 287
  gender-based, 3, 4, 8, 9, 46, 239

Doctors. *See* Physicians

Dual-career families, 263–264

Durkheim, Emile, 141

Education xiii, 121, 157, 185, 187, 201, 235, 236, 239, 241, 277, 283, 285
  and affirmative action, 247
  bureaucratic organization of, 66–67
  and comparable worth policies, 249
  as credentialing 124–125
  effects on caste, 29, 55, 146
  effects on job performance, 126
  as an element of professionalization, 158–165, 189, 240, 282
  and future jobs, 284–285
  medical, 137,
  public, 66–67
  and remuneration, 114, 122–123, 173, 175, 179, 182, 184, 258, 279, 285
  and socioeconomic status, 123–125, 277
  and volunteer work, 201, 203
  and women's earnings, 243–244
  See also Apprenticeship

Efficiency wage, 119

Egypt, 24, 64

Einstein, Albert, 140

Emotion work, 222

Employment Retirement Income Security Act, 178

Employment
  part-time, 200–201
  percentages of population employed, 199–200
  security of 198–199
  temporary, xv, 201, 219–220

Engels, Friedrich, 53–54, 96

Engineers, 71, 78, 81, 85, 138, 140, 145, 146, 147–148, 149, 154, 156, 163, 175, 182, 187, 284

Ethnicity, 21, 113, 122, 129–130, 146, 189, 233–237, 239, 240, 241, 243, 245–246, 276–277

European Union, 98, 267

Exports, 96, 105

Factory production, 11, 41–42, 44–47, 81, 226, 260

Fair Labor Standards Act, 118

Families, 11, 22, 23, 46, 107, 118, 120, 129, 135, 222, 227, 239–240, 260, 263–264, 267, 277–78
  and education 123–124, 205
  and professions, 168
  and income distribution, 176, 180, 240,

Family and Medical Leave Act, 268

Featherbedding, 80

Flexible spending accounts, 266

Flexible working schedules, 266–268

Flight attendants, 222–223

Ford Motor Co., 80, 84, 226

Ford, Henry, 51–52, 53, 84, 119

Foreign trade, 100–102

France, 15, 33, 54, 97 277

Foremen, 41, 44, 51, 71, 129

Friedman, Thomas, 97

Friendships, 205–208

Galbraith, John Kenneth, 64

General Motors, 53, 139, 184

Gathering and hunting societies, xi, 1–6, 7, 8, 9, 16, 20, 63, 239, 288

Germany, 10, 15, 33, 54, 62, 97
  job training in, 203

Globalization, xiii, xv, xvii, 56,
    95–109, 274–275, 288
    effects on jobs in the United
        States, 104–106
    and governments, 97–99,
    and multinational corporations, 99–100
    relationship to technological change,
        90–91,
Goffman, Erving, 138
Gompers, Samuel, 186
Granovetter, David, 127–129
Great Recession, the, 108, 190, 183, 195,
    199, 200, 201, 212, n. 21, 256, 257
Greedy institutions, 221–223
Guest workers, 108–109
Guilds, 29–34
    commonalties with modern professions, 34
    control of work by, 30–32
    and women, 30

Hall, Richard, 161
Hawthorne Studies, 208, 288
Health insurance, xiv, 130 n. 1, 176–178,
    184, 197, 201, 255, 275, 281
Heroes, occupational and organizational,
    139–140
Hill, Herbert, 236–237
Hispanics. See Latinos
Hochschild, Arlie, 261
Holmes, Oliver Wendell, Jr., 60
Home appliances, 262
Home health aides, 284
"Homosocial reproduction," 246
Horticulture, 6–7, 20
Hours of work, 254–260
    for couples, 263–264
Housework, xvi, 22, 202, 243, 260–263, 266
Human capital, 120–123,
    204–205, 239–240, 288
Hunting and gathering.
    See Gathering and hunting societies

IBM, 142
Immigrant workers, 108–109
Immigration, 106–110, 276
    effects on income distribution, 186–188
    and government policies, 107–110
    and high-tech industries, 109
    and population trends, 109–110

Income inequality 278–280
    as affected by computerization, 181–182
    as affected by globalization, 182–183
    and labor unions 183–186
Industrial Revolution, 39–41
    effects on wages and working
        conditions, 44–45
    and women, 45–47
    textile production in, 40
Injuries, work-related, 216–217
Intermodal transportation, 90–91

Janitors, 147, 181, 190
Java, 7
Job projections, 284–285
Job satisfaction, 88, 227–229, 267
Job security, 198–199, 219
    See also Unemployment
Job training, 203–205
Johnson, Clarence "Kelly," 149

Kanter, Rosabeth Moss, 245–46
Kroc, Ray, 134
!Kung san, 3–6, 42

Labor force, definition of, 199–200
Labor market, 113–119
Labor unions, 34, 88, 120, 183–186, 203,
    227, 236–237, 241, 244, 246, 248, 265
Latinos, 220, 243, 247
    and education, 235–236,
    family incomes of, 240
    professional occupations of, 169
    and unemployment, 240
Lawler, Richard, 218
Lawyers. See Attorneys
LeGoff, Jacques, 12
Leidner, Robin, 69–70
Lenin, Vladimir, 50
Levy, Frank, 73, 182
Linux, 72
Literacy, 15
Lively, Kathryn, 158
Lockheed Aircraft, 149
Luddism, 47, 289
Luther, Martin, 14, 15

Machine tools, 40, 80, 83, 85, 120
Malone, Thomas, W., 72

Manufacture, definition of, 39
Maquiladoras, 98–99, 289
Marx, Karl, 43, 48, 53, 96, 223
Maslow, Abraham, 209–210
Maternity leave, 267–268
Matrix organization, 71, 289
McDonald's, 69, 100, 134–35
Mechanical solidarity, 141
Mechanics, 189–190, 238
Medicare, 167, 176, 197
    See also Health insurance
Mentorship, 204
Merton, Robert, 68
Merit, promotion according to, 244–245
Meritocracy, 63
Metcalf, John, 140
Mexico, 98–99. 107–108, 273, 274, 289
    See also North American
        Free Trade Agreement
Midwives, 159
Miners, 140, 141, 144–145, 239, 274
Minimum wage laws, 118–120, 248, 289
Ministers, 165, 189
    See also Clergy
Mokyr, Joel, 89
Moonlighting, 201, 255
Multinational corporations
    (MNCs), 99–103, 105
Murders, work-related, 215
Murnane, Richard, 73, 182
Murrow, Edward R., 140
Musicians, 26, 80, 115, 142, 207

Networks, xiii, 59, 89, 126–130, 135,
    233–234, 241, 247, 276–277
    importance of weak ties in, 128–129
Night shift, 146–147
Nightingale, Florence, 139
North America Free Trade Agreement
    (NAFTA), 98–99, 107–108, 289
North Carolina, textile mills in, 104–105
Nurses, 138, 139–140, 141, 155, 159, 169,
    174, 187, 237, 239, 261, 284
Nursing, 150, 155, 216

O'Toole, James, 218–219
Occupational prestige, xv, 126, 188–189, 206
Occupational segregation, gender-based,
    xvi, 46, 237–243, 246–247, 277

Occupational titles, 63, 251 n. 16
"Offshoring," 192
"Onshoring," 105
Opportunity costs, 101
Osteopaths, 159
Otto, Nicolaus, 54

Paralegals, 158
Paraprofessions, 156–158
Parental leave policies. See Child care
Parsons, Talcott, 163
Part-time work, 120, 180, 196,
    200–201, 220, 266,
Patient Protection and Affordable
    Health Care Act, 177–178
Pensions, 178–179, 201, 220, 276
Physicians, 26, 141, 154, 155,
    159, 160–161, 166, 167–168,
    169, 175, 181, 190
Pilferage, 91, 148, 225
Police officers, 64, 135, 138,
    141, 142, 190, 215, 241
Postindustrial society, x, xii,
    54–55, 77–78, 206
Pregnancy Discrimination Act, 268
Priests, 8, 28, 164–165, 189, 222
    See also Clergy
Prison population, 196
Professions, 153–169, 281–282
    advertising by, 166
    associations, 158
    checklist approach to, 153–156
    codes of ethics, 141, 155, 158
    and diversity, 167–169
    and ethnicity, 169
    and licensing, 156, 159–160
    in organizations, 161–163
    and technological
        change, 165–166
    and universities, 154, 164
    and women, 167–168 and race
Professors, 138, 141, 157, 161, 163, 175,
    189, 219, 244
Promotions, 22, 89, 244–246
Protestantism, xi, 13–15, 165, 209, 289
    and the rise of capitalism, 13–15
Putting-out system, 10–11

Quality circles, 227

Rabbis, 189
  See also Clergy
Race, x, xi, 21, 25–26, 63, 122, 129–130,
    169, 173, 189, 219, 233–237, 239, 240,
    241, 243, 245–246, 257, 276–277
Railroad engineers, 207
Rationality, 61–64, 65, 68, 102, 115, 147
Retail sales, 180, 284
Retirement, 83, 178, 200, 275
Retraining, 83, 275
Ricardo, David, 101
Rites of passage, 143–145
Ritzer, George, 69
Rivoli, Pietra, 104
Rome, ancient, 9, 10, 24, 26, 59
Rose, Stephen, 260
Rothman, Robert A., 159
Russia, 25, 50, 109

Sabotage, 49, 225–226
Schor, Juliet, 255, 256, 258
Schumpeter, Joseph, 81
Scientific Management, 48–51, 69, 290
Second Industrial Revolution, 40, 54
Seeman, Melvin, 224
Semiprofessions, 156–158
Seniority, promotion according to, 197, 236,
    240, 244–245
Serfdom, 25, 33
Servants, 221–222
Service sector, 55–56, 70, 77–78, 96, 100,
    181, 185, 201, 216, 239, 247, 261, 274,
    279, 282, 290
  See also Tertiary sector
Sexual harassment, 220–221
"Shadow economy," 196–197
Shaw, George Bernard, 161
Shift work, 266–267
Simon, Herbert, 154
Sjoberg, Gideon, 12
Skills, 26, 32, 34, 56, 64, 67, 68, 69, 77,
    82–83, 85–87, 102, 115, 118, 119, 121,
    122, 124, 128, 141, 145, 150, 155, 161,
    173, 174–175, 182, 187, 195, 203–205,
    224, 236, 238, 239, 245, 247–248, 249,
    282, 288, 290
Skunk Works, 149
Slash-and-burn agriculture, 6–7
Slavery, 23–27

in the American South, 24, 25–26,
in the ancient world, 24–27, and
    technological innovation, 33–34
and worker motivation, 27
Small business, 284
Smiles, Samuel, 140
Smith, Adam, 33, 42, 63, 72
Social Security, 118, 178, 197, 200,
    202, 275–276, 280
Socialization, xiv, 32, 130, 135–139, 141–145,
    148–150, 240, 290
Staff and line, 145–146
Stakhanov, Aleksey, 140
Steam engine, 40
Stockbrokers, 157
Stress, 197–198, 205, 217–219, 221, 248,
    253, 257, 260, 263–264, 265, 266, 267

Taylor, Frederick W., xii, 48–51, 69, 290
Technological change and
    remuneration, 174–175
Technological determinism, 79
Technological fix, 79
Technology, xii, 39, 40, 51, 53–54,
    56, 64, 72, 73, 95, 97, 107, 109,
    166, 224, 273–274, 283, 290
  as a cause of unemployment,
    80–82, 181
  definition of, 78
  globalization and, 90–91
  as perceived during the
    Great Depression, 80
  and managerial authority, 83–86
  and worker skills, 86–87
Telecommuting. See Telework
Telegraph, 90
Telework, 87–89, 278, 290
Temporary workers,
    108, 201, 219–220
Tertiary sector, 55, 181, 274
  See also Service sector
Tests, standardized, 67
Thomas, W.I., 21
Time-and-motion studies, 49, 51, 290
Tools, stone, 2
Total institutions, 141
Trust, 23, 34, 73, 89, 128, 129, 144, 155,
    222, 238
Two-person careers, 264

Underground economy, 196–197
Underemployment, 196
Unemployment, xii, xv, 43, 54, 76–79,
    104–105, 180–181 211, n. 14, 228, 229,
    235, 240, 265, 277, 279
    calculating the rate of, 195–197
    caused by technological
        change, 80–82, 290
    effects of minimum wage policies, 118–120
    and family relations, 197–198
    and foreign trade, 98–99, 182–183
    health effects of, 197, 219
    job training as a cure for, 204–205
    white and blue collar compared, 199
Unions. See Labor unions
United Auto Workers Union, 184, 236

Vacations, 259
Veblen, Thorstein, 209
Vocational education, 279
    See also Skills
Volunteer work, 202–203
Volvo, 226

Waiters and waitresses, 118
Wal-Mart, 100, 105, 284
Warfare, 8–9, 13, 26, 207
Water wheel, 10, 40
Watt, James. 40
Weber, Max, 14–15, 61–62, 68, 116–117,
    209, 223–224
Western Electric plant, 148, 208
Whistle-blowing, 219

Wikipedia, 72
Windmill, 10
Women workers, 30, 88, 120, 136, 157, 184,
    200, 202–203, 207, 221–222, 237–244,
    in agriculture, 20–22
    earnings of 120–122, 240–244
    incomes, compared with
        men's incomes, 241
    in the Industrial Revolution xii, 45–47, 104
    job satisfaction of, 228
    labor force participation of,
        xvi, 233, 261–262
    part-time work done by, 201
    and the professions, 167–169
    and promotions, 240–246
    sexual harassment of, 220–221
    temporary employment of, 219–220
    unemployment rates of, 235, 237
    working hours of, 255–258, 263
    See also Affirmative action; Child care;
        Comparable worth policies; Division
        of labor, gender-based; Dual-career
        families; Housework; Maternity leave;
        Occupational segregation,
        gender-based
World Trade Organization, 98
Writing, 9

Yakuza, 138

Zero-sum economy,
    31, 48, 248, 274, 290
Zuboff, Shoshana, 86